LOCATING GLOBAL ORDER

LOCATING GLOBAL ORDER
American Power and Canadian Security after 9/11

Edited by Bruno Charbonneau and Wayne S. Cox

UBCPress · Vancouver · Toronto

© UBC Press 2010

All rights reserved. No part of this publication may be reproduced, stored in a retrieval system, or transmitted, in any form or by any means, without prior written permission of the publisher, or, in Canada, in the case of photocopying or other reprographic copying, a licence from Access Copyright (Canadian Copyright Licensing Agency), www.accesscopyright.ca.

20 19 18 17 16 15 14 13 12 11 10   5 4 3 2 1

Printed in Canada on FSC-certified ancient-forest-free paper (100% post-consumer recycled) that is processed chlorine- and acid-free.

Library and Archives Canada Cataloguing in Publication

    Locating global order : American power and Canadian security after 9/11 / edited by Bruno Charbonneau and Wayne S. Cox.

Includes bibliographical references and index.
ISBN 978-0-7748-1831-5 (bound); ISBN 978-0-7748-1832-2 (pbk.)

    1. Canada – Foreign relations – 21st century. 2. United States – Foreign relations – 21st century. 3. National security – Canada. 4. National security – United States. 5. Afghan War, 2001- – Participation, Canadian. 6. Canada – Social conditions – 21st century. 7. World politics – 21st century. 8. September 11 Terrorist Attacks, 2001 – Influence. I. Charbonneau, Bruno, 1976- II. Cox, Wayne S., 1962-

| FC242.L63 2010 | 971.07 | C2010-902165-7 |

e-book ISBNs: 978-0-7748-1833-9 (pdf); 978-0-7748-5966-0 (epub)

Canadä

UBC Press gratefully acknowledges the financial support for our publishing program of the Government of Canada (through the Canada Book Fund), the Canada Council for the Arts, and the British Columbia Arts Council.

Printed and bound in Canada by Friesens
Set in Futura Condensed and Warnock Pro by Artegraphica Design Co. Ltd.
Copy editor: Judy Phillips
Proofreader: Jillian Shoichet
Indexer: Patricia Buchanan

UBC Press
The University of British Columbia
2029 West Mall
Vancouver, BC V6T 1Z2
www.ubcpress.ca

Contents

Preface / ix

Introduction: Locating Global Order / 1
Bruno Charbonneau and Wayne S. Cox

Part 1: American Power and the Location of Global Order

1 Hegemony, Militarism, and Identity:
Locating the United States as the Global Power / 33
Dan O'Meara

2 The Neoconservative Challenge to Realist Thinking
in American Foreign Policy / 67
Alex Macleod

Part 2: Constructing Global Order at Home and Abroad – The Case of Canada's Mission in Afghanistan

3 Managing Life in Afghanistan:
Canadian Tales of Peace, Security, and Development / 87
Bruno Charbonneau and Geneviève Parent

4 Rethinking the Security Imaginary:
Canadian Security and the Case of Afghanistan / 107
Kim Richard Nossal

5 Constructions of Nation, Constructions of War:
Media Representations of Captain Nichola Goddard / 126
Claire Turenne Sjolander and Kathryn Trevenen

Part 3: Constructing Global Order at Home – Conceptualizations and Practices of National Security

6 Against National Security: From the Canadian War
on Queers to the "War on Terror" / 149
Gary Kinsman

7 Framing Post-9/11 Security: Tales of State Securitization
and of the Experiences of Muslim Communities / 167
Siobhan Byrne

8 Re-Conceptions of National Security in the Age of
Terrorism: Implications for Federal Policing in Canada / 183
T.S. (Todd) Hataley

9 Biosecurity in Canada and Beyond: Invasions,
Imperialisms, and Sovereignty / 200
Peter Stoett

Part 4: Constructing Global Order Abroad – Canada's Policies in Africa

10 Canada, Africa, and "New" Multilateralisms for Global
Governance: Before and After the Harper Regime in
Ottawa? / 219
Timothy M. Shaw

11 Mainstreaming Investment: Foreign and Security
Policy Implications of Canadian Extractive Industries
in Africa / 235
David Black and Malcolm Savage

12 Peace-Building between Canadian Values and Local Knowledge: Some Lessons from Timbuktu / 260
Jonathan Sears

Conclusion: Relocating Global Order / 276
Bruno Charbonneau and Wayne S. Cox

References / 292

List of Contributors / 332

Index / 338

Preface

BRUNO CHARBONNEAU AND WAYNE S. COX

This book began in the spring of 2007 when invitations were sent out to participate in a round-table discussion on Canadian security following 9/11. After the tragic events of 11 September 2001, claims about the rapidly changing nature of the international security environment and associated calls to wage war on "global terror," to promote democracy, and to liberate Afghan women were prominent and very often taken for granted. After the March 2003 American invasion of Iraq, such claims and calls became more and more the target of criticism and subjected to academic and political debates. In Canada, these debates took what seemed like an unprecedented turn when the Canadian government decided to send troops to war in Afghanistan in February 2006. The debates, but also the practical difficulties, surrounding the Canadian mission in Afghanistan were signs to us that it was more than time to discuss, reassess, and re-evaluate Canada's global policies and its role in the post-9/11 world order, notably in the context of arguments about American power, hegemony, and imperialism.

Hence, in March 2008, Bruno hosted a group session at Laurentian University (Sudbury, Ontario). The event brought together Canadian scholars of different disciplines (mostly political science but also from geography, sociology, and criminology), members of the Canadian Armed Forces, officials of the City of Greater Sudbury responsible for municipal security and emergency measures, and local members of the War Resisters and the

Against War and Occupation associations. The discussions focused on Canadian security, but broadly understood in order to include various issues and experiences: the war in Afghanistan, American power, practices of security within Canada, municipal aspects of security, gendered security, geographies of security, and the relationship between security and development. Although the focus on security never disappeared, what became more apparent as the discussions progressed was that all issues converged around the location and role of Canada within a global order largely defined by, but not limited to, American power. It seemed obvious that there was a need for a collected volume on Canada's role in the current global order, and despite individual examinations of different case studies and topics, many common threads tie them together. What became clearer in the following months as we edited, commented, and engaged with each chapter was that they all spoke of different experiences and location of political order, but that no single experience or location seemed to be greater than the other, or more important, and thus that they converged in a better and larger understanding of what is commonly referred to as global order. This is the final product of multiple perspectives and understandings of that order and the location of Canada and Canadians within it.

This book, of course, would not have been possible without the help and support of many people. First and foremost, we must acknowledge and be grateful for the financial support of Laurentian University – notably from the Research, Development and Creativity office and the dean of Social Sciences and Humanities – and of Queen's Centre for International Relations, which were crucial to the publication of our manuscript. We also want to thank all of our contributors, who fully engaged with our editorial comments and questions, always responded to our last-minute enquiries or demands, and thus fully contributed to make this collection better than the sum of its parts. Bruno is most grateful to his students and colleagues at Laurentian University who helped in one way or another, notably Daniel Mayer (a Laurentian University 2008 graduate, now studying law at McGill University), whose efforts and dedication made everything more manageable and efficient; Bob Segsworth of the Department of Political Science, whose unwavering support and friendship proved indispensable; and William Crumplin of the Department of Geography, whose organizational experience, help, and friendship were vital throughout. Wayne would like to thank Siobhan Byrne for her advice and support on our attempted trip to Sudbury, Kathleen Rühland for her editorial advice, and Bruno for his patience in dealing with a co-editor whose schedule and commitments over the past two years have been frustrating, to say the least. It should also be mentioned that the true friendship and support of John Sjolander over the years have been on the minds and in the hearts of many of the contributors to this book throughout the process. We also want to acknowledge the financial support of the Security and Defence Forum at the Department of National Defence, Laurentian University, and the Greater City of Sudbury for the round-table phase of this project. Last but not least, we want to thank Emily Andrew and her team at UBC Press, notably Ann Macklem, for their work, patience, support, and help throughout.

LOCATING GLOBAL ORDER

Introduction
Locating Global Order

BRUNO CHARBONNEAU AND WAYNE S. COX

For many Americans and others around the world, the events of 11 September 2001 radically transformed the ways in which they viewed international politics. The tragic events brought home a realization that defining the key global players, finding a consensus over "national security" threats and issues, and searching for the ends and means of security policies are far more complex problems than they are in a world system composed mostly of self-interested state actors. For many, the international security environment had shifted fundamentally. Threats such as al-Qaeda had become ubiquitous and vaguely identified as a global terrorist network. Linked to the threat of global terrorism was the perception that past failures and mismanagement of (in)security and (under)development in various areas of the globe had contributed to terrorism. These sites were largely identified as problems of "failed and fragile" states that represented challenges to international stability. Such states could exacerbate the terrorist problem, some argued, and thus translate into more terrorist attacks on Western interests and populations. The events of 9/11 accelerated the trend of the 1990s toward more rigorous military missions of nation-, state-, and/or peace-building (Baranyi 2008), and the decline of Western contributions to United Nations operations (Bellamy and Williams 2009) – two trends that culminated in the forceful US-led interventions in Afghanistan and Iraq. For many others, however, especially for those in the "ungoverned spaces" of marginalized people, 9/11 did not signify as much or translate to any dramatic change of global or local conditions. For many outside the United States and the developed West (and even for some inside it), the events of 9/11 were a symbolic marker of change rather than a tangible and radical transformation of the world itself. Certainly, the long-term structural and deep-rooted dynamics of contemporary political life had not changed overnight. Nevertheless, 9/11 provoked almost everywhere numerous academic and political debates about the present form of world order, as well as about the direction that this order should take in the future. For example, much was written on whether the United States should use its position as the sole global military superpower to establish an empire (or a neo-trusteeship international system) for the sake of order, stability, prosperity, and peace that can be shared by all (for example, Ferguson 2004; Ignatieff 2003).

Regardless of the specific form these debates took, the concept of political order itself was generally assumed to be organized as a hierarchy of power relations with actors such as the state and international institutions situated at the top, and individuals and social groups at the bottom. Within this mindset, a strong, powerful, and determined empire seemed like a reasonable solution, since it could *impose* order on those unreasonable, barbarian, and uncivilized people of the world who promote or tolerate the presence of terrorism. Even cosmopolitan views suggested that a benign worldwide state (of sort) could impose order, peace, and/or other ideals on all peoples. Put differently, whether it was the imperial state or the state writ large (world government) that was argued to be the solution to the post-9/11 era, the character and the location of the political were assumed to be known. Presumably, the location of contemporary political life was undisputable and thus marked the legitimate sites of political action. However, these simplistic and outdated views of politics, political life, and political order cannot, we suggest, capture fully the diffuse nature of relations within the post-9/11 world.

This book is designed to demonstrate and emphasize the increasing significance of uncertainties about the location of contemporary political life by engaging with the always double reciprocity between local and global practices. It interrogates the relationship between politics and location in order to problematize a range of powerful normative claims about where politics ought to be occurring, and about where contemporary global order is supposed to be found. Global order, we argue, is complex, multi-layered, and multi-faceted; often perceived to be highly centralized and hierarchical; always in the process of being imposed and reproduced; and always in the process of being contested, challenged, and negotiated. Global order is located in diverse spaces, including traditional and accepted sites of governance (various state bureaucracies, national and international institutions and organizations, and so on) and, crucially but often forgotten or invisible, in a multitude of sometimes overlapping new spaces, unseen connections, and/or taken-for-granted everyday routines. For many within a post-9/11 world, the practices of social relations that witness the real consequences of changing sociopolitical circumstances are as often rooted in the local as they are rooted in the global. Both these seen and unseen local-global connections are at the centre of the book's chapters. The case-study chapters in this book are not simply the stories of those who are dominated by a centralized world order, but are included as the unfolding of the construction and workings of local/global order itself. As such, the politics of global order is not just the use of power over the governed or over ungoverned spaces and peoples of the world but, rather, the interrelationship between the two. As Samuel Kim (1984, 54-55) put it: "We should not deny the power of the global dominance system with its self-repairing and self-regenerating capacity, but we must avoid exaggerating the power of the strong and underplaying the power of the weak in contemporary global politics. Great historical transformations are often wrought by those dismissed as marginal and powerless." On the streets of Canada and the United States, there are many who have been profoundly affected by changes in our collective understanding(s) of what security is or what ought to be done about it. With regard to the war in Afghanistan, for instance, what should be done (or not) and what we should think about it have become serious questions for all to consider (or not). But these same people affected by such changes and on which global order is in the process of being imposed are a very part of our collective understanding of what security is, who it ought to be for, what we ought to do about it, and so on. As such, they are a very part of the construction and legitimization of that order – of collective understandings of security, democracy, and the location of political life. Whether you are a Muslim woman from Ontario, a Republican from New York, Sunni from Baghdad, or Pashtun from Kandahar, you can be and often are affected by changes in world order and national security policies. Your individual and/or collective decisions to be supportive, indifferent, or even hostile toward the post-9/11 global security order are a very part of that order itself. To explore where such decisions and actions are taking place is to explore the new ways in which understandings of global order, security, and political community are produced or reproduced.

The core objective of this book is to open the debate and sustain discussion about the significance of the relationship between politics and location, notably in the specific Canadian context. Instead of taking the international system and the state for granted, we assume that the dynamics of the various relationships within local order *and* between local order(s) and global order are always contingent, negotiable, contested, and internationalized. In other words, neither the local nor the global is conceivable without the other. As editors, we would not presume to assign primacy to either. Furthermore, this book examines the relationship between politics and location as it is expressed in contemporary debates about security. Security is one of the key locations where lines are drawn and boundaries are established to discriminate between legitimate and illegitimate political space and practice. Of course, one book cannot possibly provide a comprehensive account of the multiple dimensions and interpretations of global order or how different people and collective actors respond to it, build it, or (re)produce it. Specifically then, this book examines the location of Canadian politics of security within a global order built on and around the pre-eminence of American power, especially since the end of the Cold War and after 9/11. One of the core assumptions of many chapters is that Canadian security, however defined, can be understood only as a part of larger global and American projects. The American state is central to an increasingly integrated and globalized order, but global order is not exclusive to the American state. In this regard, the Canadian state has been an integral component of American and Western forms of power and order well before 9/11 (see R.W. Cox 2005). Canada is the case study used here in an attempt to locate global order in both time and space. What are the sociological and sociopolitical processes, practices, and routines of global order? How are they maintained, reformed, and transformed over time? Where are the local and global? Where are the state and civil society? Whose or what order is the Canadian state promoting and for what purpose? In short, how do the Canadian state and its citizens participate, both at home and abroad, in the construction, maintenance, reform, and transformation of a global order that is centred on, but not exclusive to, the American state? Global order, we argue, is produced and located in complex and multiple global-local dynamics. That is, global and local practices are co-constitutive of global order, and we cannot simply assume the relationship between politics and location. Let us first elaborate more on the latter.

Locations of Knowledge: State, Global(ization), Security

R.B.J. Walker (1993) has argued that the contemporary political imagination is largely limited by the twin concerns with the conditions of the possibilities and necessities within, and with the conditions of possibilities and necessities outside, the sovereign state. These two discourses have worked historically "both individually and collectively, as a regulative idealization of what it means to act individually and collectively as modern subjects and modern subjectivities, under certain conditions and within certain limits" (R.B.J. Walker 2006, 65). Modern politics can thus be interpreted as the histories of crucial locations where lines are drawn between possibility and impossibility, universality and particularity, fragmentation and integration, normality and exceptionality, local and global. As one of the primary sites where such boundaries, borders, and limits are created, the distinction between domestic and international has served to reify the fallacy of the independent sovereign state-actor that seeks to survive and/or to promote its interests under conditions of international anarchy. This line articulates the limits and terms to legitimate political life, but it also identifies two distinctive places of political order: the local, where the state is conceived as central to political order, and the global, where the state manages its relations with other states avoiding or waging war in order to protect the local political order. Local political order is argued to be located exclusively within the physical borders of the sovereign state, to be clearly hierarchical, and to have its line of political illegitimacy marked by authoritarianism (or more recently, one could argue, by non-market-oriented and non-democratic regimes). Global political order is argued to be located outside the borders of the sovereign state, defined as anarchical, and with its line of illegitimacy found in imperialism (R.B.J. Walker 1993, 2006; for examples of the assumptions that Walker deconstructs in the international relations [IR] literature specifically, see Carr 1939/2001; Morgenthau 1973; Waltz 1979; Wendt 1999). Accordingly, post-9/11 political developments led many scholars, analysts, and others to make assertions about new modes of imperial or exceptional politics. Although they have been very helpful in understanding multiple aspects of the post-9/11 order, as R.B.J. Walker argues, the terms "international," "imperial," and "exceptional" are not completely persuasive on their own because an understanding of the dynamics of modern politics requires an acknowledgment that these broad concepts are mutually constitutive. For Walker, much of this literature on the international system is conceived "as a matter of fragmentation, of pluralism, of anarchy, of mere order, rather than as a matter of a very specific ordering of the relationship between fragmentation and integration, between pluralism and universalism." In this context, the sovereign state is an idiosyncrasy, "a mere *polis*," rather than a unique political ordering of the relationship between the particular and the universal, between the local and the global (R.B.J. Walker 2006, 65-67).

The theoretical and philosophical problem that Walker identifies is in fact an assumption about, and a practical representation of, the centrality of the state in political affairs and in most analysis and judgment about politics. The opposition made between a local political order and a global political order is essential to disciplines such as international relations, international law, and comparative politics. The state represents the coin where domestic and foreign, local and global are distinguished. This is a form of state-centrism. The traditional understanding of state-centrism is of a perspective (usually associated with the realist school of IR) that focuses on the state as the dominant actor of world politics, conceives of world politics as the relationships between unitary and independent states, associates the state with a specific and limited territory, and construes power as a possession or attribute of unitary state-actors. It can be, however, and it is usually much more. State-centrism is also a philosophical position and a set of assumptions about where politics happens and ought to be occurring. It carries implicit normative claims about the centrality of the state in establishing the location of all legitimate forms of politics, authority, control, and community. As John Agnew puts it:

> The dominant Westphalian model of state sovereignty in political geography and international relations theory, named after the Treaty of Westphalia of 1648, deficient as it has long been for understanding the realities of politics, is even more inadequate today, not only for ignoring the hierarchy of states and sources of control and authority other than states, but also because of its mistaken emphasis on the geographical expression of that control and authority (under the ambiguous sign of "sovereignty") as invariably and inevitably territorial. (Agnew 2009, 10)

In other words, politics is not necessarily territorialized, contained with national borders, or of the exclusive domain of the state. Agnew argues that the exercise of power and authority is not inherently territorial or state-based. Contrary to theorists of globalization who argue that globalization is eroding state power and authority (or sovereignty), Agnew argues that state sovereignty takes multi-faceted, diverse, and evolving spatial forms that have been made only more complex by the processes of what is called globalization (Agnew 2009). Taking into account non-state actors as they affect the state is insufficient because this still presumes the location of politics within the state.

The key point is that both an implicit and an explicit state-centrism translate into an undertheorized understanding of the meanings and effects of location on politics and of location on knowledge about politics. This has significant practical, policy, and theoretical consequences that underline the close connection between the production of knowledge and power. Conceptions of state and state security are intimately tied to conceptions of legitimate knowledge. Certainly, state-centric perspectives embody a particular set of assumptions about legitimate knowledge, not the least about where such legitimate knowledge comes from. In fact, knowledge itself is a function of its location, and it is modified as it circulates (Agnew 2007). Timothy Mitchell, for example, has argued that the elusiveness of the boundaries that separate the state from society should be explored as a clue to the nature of the state, and not as a need for sharper definitions. The appearance that the state is a separate thing from society is one of the important ways in which social and political order is maintained. That is, the state boundary does not mark the limit of political processes of regulation, but "is itself a product of these processes" (Mitchell 1991, 90). Mitchell does not argue that the state-society distinction should not be taken seriously. On the contrary, he argues, the state is largely an effect of "detailed processes of spatial organization, temporal arrangement, functional specification, and supervision and surveillance, which create the appearance of a world fundamentally divided into state and society. The essence of modern politics is not policies formed on one side of this division being applied to or shaped by the other, but the producing and reproducing of this line of difference" (95). Consequently, implicit claims about the location of world politics, political order, and security have important ontological effects.

Debates about security are significant expressions of how lines are drawn in modern political life. Indeed, it is constructive to reflect on the extent to which thinking about security generally, and Canadian security particularly, has come to depend on distinct categories of space, geography, and location. No matter how vague the concepts of state and security are, in fact partly because of the ambiguity, they work together to establish the legitimate location of security policy making. Security is a matter of the state (or of bureaucratic elites) for the protection of the state. As such, the state does not only claim its monopoly on the use of legitimate violence but its monopoly on the location and character of political activity. Security is premised on a sharp distinction between inside and outside (R.B.J. Walker 1993), which allows us to think of security in terms of securing the Canadian territorial state against the outside, but also to describe Canadian security in terms of North American, northern Atlantic, or Western alliances and cooperation to guard against "global" threats. This flexibility in defining and redefining the inside and the outside is the matter of modern politics, but it is obscured by state-centrism. By identifying the state as the exclusive location of modern politics, a normative judgment is made as to where political activity (relating to security or other) can occur and ought to occur, and where it cannot occur.

Terms such as "global security," "international stability," "global terrorism," and "global war on terror" have relocated the problem and politics of security. Since 9/11 in particular, but going back to at least the late 1980s, governments, their various security agencies, and most security experts and think tanks have periodically repeated that the globalization of threats requires the globalization of security – the global war on terror being only the quintessential example. Such statements have an explicit ideological role by offering a global-scale conception of problems and solutions and by depicting multiple experiences as universal. Hence, local preoccupations, problems, and solutions are conceived as of secondary importance. State, politics, and security are assumed to be located elsewhere, somewhere, in the "global" space. Such movements between national and global space of security mask the fragmentation and inequality on which traditional assumptions about location and politics are based and conceived. Such movements are reflected in knowledge practices that obscure the observable processes, routines, and practices of global order that are often found in a specific locale, in the day-to-day experiences of "ordinary" people, and in taken-as-given assumptions about the role and place of the local community in the world. This is not to argue that better and more coherent policies are not needed. They are, and badly so, but so are fundamental questions about the location and meaning of politics, democracy, and security.

What and Where Is Global Order?

The global order that leaders such as George W. Bush, Barack Obama, Stephen Harper, Tony Blair, Nicolas Sarkozy, and many traditions of academic and policy analysis usually present to the public is one defined implicitly (and sometimes explicitly) in self-interested terms. Global "order" is understood as ideally static. It is often synonymous with "international stability" and sometimes associated with ideas of progress, but it is always a specific arrangement of theoretically equal, but practically unequal, sovereign states. For the most part, peace and prosperity are best kept within this order if it is not disturbed or changed. In short, global order is a thing to accept, favour, protect, and idealize. In policy terms, such order means promoting the status quo because it presents the given order as the natural order, thus limiting political discourse and possibilities. Many scholars have exposed the knowledge practices found in IR theory that participate in giving credence to such an understanding of the world. Discussing "the *workings* of theoretical discourse on the anarchy problematique," Richard Ashley (1988, 228, emphasis in original) argues that it is "an arbitrary political construction that is always in the process of being imposed (229)." According to Ashley, the assumption about the anarchical nature of global order, however, must find the sovereign state as an essential, unquestioned, and indisputable ideological foundation of global order that implies an unproblematic hierarchical opposition between the local and global, despite that both the state and global order are "intrinsically contested, always ambiguous, never completed construct[s]" (231). So from this perspective, global order is something that must be *maintained*. The rhetoric of order and stability is invoked to legitimize and authorize the maintenance of existing conditions. The key objective of the policy makers and scholars who adopt this position is defensive and preventive. They work to defend and prevent against the breakdown of existing political processes and patterns, and they guard against disruption and rapid change. Marginal accommodations can be allowed, and sometimes are essential, but only to preserve the status quo. Global order is a world of states where war is inevitable, but where war must be avoided through the management of (in)stability.

Global order can also be understood as governance. Students and proponents of global governance embrace the view that global order can be *reformed*. Reformers seek a more efficient, coherent, and sometimes equitable management of world politics and the world economy. This second perspective does not seek to transform the states system. The legitimacy and authority of the Westphalian state model is not challenged but, rather, in need of reform in light of globalization, complex interdependence, and new technologies. Proposals are often limited to interstate social and political justice and economic well-being. Overall, reforms aim at greater international cooperation around the UN system and/or better international financial institutions. Crisis management capacity will be created or improved at the UN or through cooperation between UN and regional organizations such as the European Union in order to contain, prevent, and resolve conflicts, but it will not challenge the existence and necessity of the state as the space for the legitimate political community (see the practice of peace- and state-building). The 2008-09 economic crisis will bring institutional reforms, but it will likely not bring down global capitalism anytime soon. The most ardent proponents of global governance might call for some form of cosmopolitanism or world government, but such pleas embody the traditional spatial imagery in a state writ large (world government) and do not question the capitalist foundations of the world economy.

Better policies and management, and greater coherence and cooperation are certainly needed, but for others they are not sufficient. A third perspective challenges the legitimacy and viability of global order and presents alternative visions to *transform* the Westphalian framework. Global problems such as nuclear proliferation, climate change, ecological disasters, global economic and food crises, war and conflict, and so on underline how the current global order does not meet minimal requirements of human decency and survival. Strong critiques of the ways in which existing institutions reproduce structures of violence, death, and injustice are voiced and lead to social movements for fundamental transformations in the political, economic, and cultural contemporary structures. The essence and location of political life is questioned, and new spaces for political activity are generated. While it is far from clear on what grounds transformation is possible or even thinkable, proponents of transformation interrogate the fundamental assumptions about the meanings of being human and political community. They raise destabilizing questions and dispute the clichés about politics, democracy, community, order, security, globality, locality, and so on.[1]

In practice, these three perspectives of global order often overlap in local practices and reflect the daily dynamics of global order. In attempts and interactions to maintain, reform, and transform global order, we find the location of politics. The global-local nexus is complex and, more importantly, its lines are periodically redrawn. In this context of ever-contested and ever-changing conditions, the challenging questions about power and authority are located in the continuous interplay of the discourses that construe the lines and limits of political life, and of the individual and collective actions that put these boundaries into practice and/or create them through practice. The authorization of authority (the process by which one is given the authority to decide) is thus a crucial political moment about where and when to draw or to cross the line of political legitimacy. To distinguish between the local and the global is to make a claim about and for political authority, and about who decides the limitations of political life. Indeed, if we assume that, first, "it is a central feature of modern political life that neither the sovereign state nor the system of sovereign states can exist without the other" (R.B.J. Walker 2006, 68) and second, that local-global dynamics are contingent, contested, and never-ending projects, we must also presume that it often proves very difficult to tell a priori *when* and especially *where* the politics of authorization of authority will take place.

Arguably then, an examination of local practices should be as important to IR scholarship as an examination of the practices of the "major actors" (states, international institutions, and so on). This is so because the construction and reproduction of power relations is often taken-for-granted in a state-centred assessment of "the world as it is." In doing so, the statist analysis draws on the lines of political legitimacy, and that line does not allow for a serious examination of the local sources of legitimacy/dissidence to be considered. Global order is the sum total of a set of historically conditioned interrelationships within and between local communities, states, and the international system. The current global order is the end product of everything that has come before it, and its current configuration can change just as quickly and easily as changes have occurred to it in the past – if not sooner with the advent of globalization and its seeming ability to accelerate time and decompress space.

Our understanding of global order does not oppose the local to the global, does not find global order in a single actor, state, or institution, nor does it fix global order in time and space. It does not advocate, therefore, its maintenance, reform, or transformation. It does, however, problematize global order, meaning that it calls for historicizing the "processes of empowerment" and the "processes of marginalization"; how did we get here? Being in a constant state of flux, global order has to be located in a political *moment* and *place*. When and where its underlying hegemonic ideas and practices about the norms and rules of normal behaviour and relationships are accepted as legitimate and unquestionable, everyday practice is no longer a matter of politics and political order but only of rational technique, management, and problem-solving. When and where it is contested and faces the challenges of local order(s), actors, and their practices, we find politics – that is, attempts at maintaining, redefining, changing, or abolishing completely the norms and rules and the structures of power relations of the current global order. Global order is always negotiable, in the process of being en/forced, and thus, to appropriate Robert Cox's popular formulation about theory, we can also say that global order is always *"for* someone and *for* some purpose" (R.W. Cox 1981, 128, emphasis in original). Global order can only be partially defined, as it is always contested somewhere at some point in time, and thus always in the process of being (re)produced and imposed. Indeed, it is very often in the routine interaction of contestation to order and resistance to change that we observe the mechanisms, processes, and routines of order, power, and authority. We witness change, transformation, and/or reproduction when and where order is contested in one form or another. Nevertheless, as the events of 9/11 and their aftermath showed, both acquiescence and contestation can live together at the same time and in the same place. In fact, both can, and often do, feed off each other.

In the immediate aftermath of 9/11, for instance, the Bush administration used the terrorist attacks to call on all "real" American patriots to unite behind their government by quietly getting on with their day-to-day lives: by working, going to movies, spending time with their families, or by shopping. The delineation between those who accepted and those who did not accept this order was quite stark indeed. We were all told that you are either with "us," or you are with the "terrorists." Acts of contestation, both the reprehensible terrorist attacks and the open questioning of the policies of the American government by courageous Americans who were uncomfortable with the notion that they should hand their government a blank cheque in fighting the war on terror were helpful in strengthening this particular government and the ideologies it represented. Put another way, our starting point is that neither local order(s) nor global order can exist without the other: they are inextricably linked and ever evolving. We reject claims that there is a local political order that should be protected against an anarchic global political (dis)order. But how such lines and distinctions are established and enabled must also be studied. Instability and chaos may be out there, somewhere or elsewhere, but they can just as easily be in here too. In fact, the lines distinguishing local and global order are rarely where they are supposed to be.

This is not to argue that there are no conflict zones that can affect surrounding regions and beyond, nor that there are no threats to be found inside, but simply that the state-centric logic is the wrong starting point from which to think about conflict or order. Our starting point here is that global chaos and global order are, in large part, social constructions that have been assigned primacy to either the local or the global depending on a given scholar's theoretical defaults. We view this as problematic in the sense that the dominant lenses, in IR at least, assume that chaos and instability come from the outside (or from the Other inside), and as such, most security analyses since 9/11 have been fixated on externalizing and demonizing challenges to the status quo global order. This tendency makes it almost impossible to see both the local contributions to the construction of global order itself and, likewise, the effects that changes to global order have on local communities. So our starting point here is one that rejects the state-centric logic and its consequent inside/outside logic of most IR theorizing, and that believes global order is built out of both local and global conditions. Such a starting point has an enormous impact on our understanding of global politics because it means that global order is not necessarily located where we usually expect it to be. It is often in locally situated practices (wherever they are) that we find a significant place where necessary elements of state power and global order are produced and reproduced. These local orders can be distinguished according to the degree to which they accept and/or contest global order. As the chapters in this book demonstrate, it is often in global order that many local and national practices find political authority and legitimacy. But the reverse seems as true and as important: global order finds authority and legitimacy in local and national practices. The chapters that follow are designed specifically to display the extent to which such an understanding of how global order is constructed can influence research on security and foreign policy through the case of Canada and its role in global order.

Canada and Global Order

It seems almost intuitive that Canada's role within global order, especially in regard to issues of security, is inextricably linked to its relationship to the United States. This is mostly because of commonsense assumptions about shared interests and values that were construed and reinforced by joint experiences during the Second World War, increasing governmental cooperation and economic integration during the Cold War, and the perceived sole superpower status of the United States in the post-Cold War era, especially after 9/11. Although the United States is clearly a dominant state actor in world politics, the notions of its "actorness" and of its dominance are partially misleading. It is true that the American state has pre-eminent power and influence by comparison to other states in the international system, but the first notion oversimplifies the character of American power, which leads to the second notion that obscures how American power and influence are always in the process of being challenged and resisted. One would be hard-pressed to suggest that the insurgents in Iraq, the Taliban in Afghanistan, or other groups prone to the use of force do not present a challenge to American power. There are countless others within the United States itself, within other Western liberal societies, and around the world who use whatever means are available to identify, politicize, and coordinate social and political challenges to American power and influence. If the world were one of black and white (of "us" or the "terrorists"), these groups would have no choice but to be sided with the terrorists. Outside the apex of Western power and societies, there are many more who are increasingly uncomfortable with the seemingly uncontested nature of American power and influence in world politics, a fact exacerbated by the often racial, religious, and civilizational nature of the public discourse about the "enemy" in the aftermath of 9/11. For instance, although many Muslims do not associate themselves or even sympathize with populous Western definitions of jihad, fundamentalism, or the use of terrorism, many are extremely uneasy about the use of stereotypes and profiling in the rhetoric about the current war on terror. This nervousness is shared by other non-Muslim groups that find themselves on the outside of the Western "we." This, we argue, is highly problematic from the perspective of attempting to gain full insight into the social and political basis of power within global order. For the Canadian state at least, and for many Canadians, the role Canada plays within global order is clearly tied to its relationship with the United States, though it is not exclusive to this bilateral relationship. How individuals and groups within Canadian civil society experience the consequences of Canada-US security policies is a very part of the symbiotic relationships that make this order, and the power that sustains it. By virtue of Canada's historically conditioned social and political interrelationships with American state and society, and by virtue of Canada's geographic location, Canada's role within global order is at least partly defined by our integration within American society *and* their integration within our own.

However, the concept of the state-actor is based on a form of anthropomorphism that establishes and enables the Canadian state as an "actor" and the American state as a dominant "player" within global order. The actor status awarded to the state gives it individual characteristics, qualities, needs, interests, and so on. It is largely a theoretical construct, but one based on significant political and social practices that have important ontological effects. For example, the practices of "national security" rely on the territorialized understanding of power, authority, community, and security. The state represents the spaces in which identity and social mobilization are assumed to happen, and where the preferred identity is most often the nation group. Social practice and social identity being thus territorialized, national security is largely based on an imagined geography that can be deployed to authorize security practices that claim to protect the nation group. Put another way, the state-actor concept assumes, produces, and reproduces the common assumption of a symmetry between the space of authority, power, and politics (or sovereignty) and the space of collective identity. Physical, political, economic, and social spaces are understood to coincide naturally with state territory and state sovereignty (for instance Agnew 2009; Agnew and Corbridge 1995; Gregory 2004).

The increasing and globalized connections between Canadians and between Canadian and non-Canadian groups, actors, and various social forces are increasingly indicative of the uncertainties about the location of political life. The imagined geographies that underlie many of the assumptions of state-based national security policies are continuously challenged by the rising number of relationships and practices of sovereignty that transcend the territory of the state. In Canada, a key aspect of the imagined geography has been the notion of Canada as the site of a multicultural society. Multiculturalism reflects a partial truth about Canadian society, but it is also both a knowledge assertion claiming the existence and uniqueness of Canadian society (an exercise in nation-building) and an aspect of state policy. The ideal of multiculturalism serves the construction of a national identity, as it promotes universality of purpose over particularisms (regional, provincial, and other identities). As such, it has often been linked to the ideal and mythology of Canada as the benevolent internationalist power, Canada as the peacekeeper, and Canada as the good international citizen. Both narratives of multiculturalism and of internationalism work politically to produce and reinforce the spaces of security and the spaces of insecurity that justify the practices of national security. They serve many purposes and justify policy by bringing Canada's international "roles" into the day-to-day experiences of many groups and social forces. Hence, threats to the state can be construed as threats to the nation, where practices and practical representations of "national security" symbolize both the territorialized state authority and national identity. Many of the chapters in this book, however, attempt to bring these stories back into a discussion of Canada's role in global order, as these are stories that often rewrite or offer alternative views of Canadian foreign policy.

From a state-centric perspective, much has been written on the Canada-US relationship. For one, the economic relationship has long affected state policy, from the inception of the Canadian state itself in 1867 to the early-twentieth-century debates about reciprocity to resource and military production agreements during the Second World War, and so on, up to our current position within NAFTA. For the most part, analysts, politicians, and citizens on both sides of the border have viewed the ever-growing economic interrelationship as a mutually beneficial one. Although somewhat less well known than the economic and social interrelationships, there have been parallel military and security arrangements, especially during and since the Second World War. For the most part, this too has been accepted as mutually beneficial within civil societies on both sides of the border. From the early period of Canadian confederation in the late nineteenth century, Canadian security concerns were tied mostly to those of Great Britain. However, by the early twentieth century, and especially by the mid-twentieth century, the notion of continental defence had become a reality for both Canadians and Americans. The need for defence cooperation was partly driven by the shared values of these two societies, both having found themselves heavily involved in largely European conflicts during the world wars (although for different reasons), and both having defined these conflicts in terms of a military struggle to protect shared ways of life. It seemed obvious during and after these two wars that political regimes built on the ideas of national socialism, fascism, and later the totalitarian version of socialism, presented real threats to liberal democracies. This forced politicians and citizens alike, combined with the advent of the technical ability of military forces to project their presence with great speed across oceans and continents, to think of Canadian and American security in unified terms. Defence cooperation during the Second World War simply made *common* sense, and the onset of the Cold War and the realization that the United States would assume a leadership position in the reconstruction of the post-1945 global security order meant that Canada would be integral to that effort.

It is almost ironic then that perhaps the most important role the Canadian state has carved out for itself within the post-Second World War global order has been about differentiating the Canadian role in world politics from that of the United States. The Canada-as-peacekeeper image that was built out of successive (mostly Liberal) governments has been a pillar of Canadian defence and security policy since the late 1950s. Although it is true that the Canadian military was one of the most significant and reliable contributors to UN (and other) peacekeeping missions around the world, these were missions that never required the lion's share of Canadian military resources. Peacekeeping and faith in internationalism have always been popular among Canadians, so much so that in the current era of peace-enforcing and war-fighting missions, Liberal and Conservative governments have sought to paint all military and security missions in as much of an internationalist or peacekeeping light as possible. It is also true that the Canadian military has been well equipped to perform peacekeeping missions and has more expertise on how to successfully conduct these missions than perhaps any other state, but all through even the heyday of these peacekeeping roles, it was always but a fraction of Canadian military activities. During the Cold War, especially during the United States' Vietnam era, and even into the present, Canada-as-a-good-internationalist-state has been a means through which successive governments could claim to have found a niche for the effective use of military force, and it is a role that has placed the popular understanding of Canada as very different from that of the United States. Canadians could take pride in their identity and in belonging to a state that was well respected internationally as "selfless," making both state and community different from the "self-interested" American state. The internationalist mythology was also one that had great appeal to the various diasporas and ethnic minorities. In other words, Canadian internationalism was good for multiculturalism on the home front. The end of the Cold War brought an end to traditional peacekeeping, though the aspirations and myths of Canadian peacekeeping live on.

For the most part, however, Canadian defence and security policies since the end of the Second World War have been about defence integration within NATO and, more significantly, with the United States. From the early 1950s until the late 1980s, the majority of Canadian war-fighting military capabilities were positioned in Europe and under NATO command. These commitments involved a high degree of defence integration with NATO allies, the US military being the key player in this system. Meanwhile, the notion of continental defence in North America had become institutionalized since the Second World War, and this aspect of Canadian defence was further integrated with the creation of the Pinetree Line, DEW Line, and later NORAD systems of the 1950s. Integrated and shared naval responsibilities on both coasts complemented the air defence systems. By the early 1960s, the integrated command and control systems of the Canada-US defence system meant that, between NATO and NORAD, almost all Canadian national defence was integrated with that of the United States in some way. So effective was this defence integration (perhaps better described as a unified system) that during the Cuban Missile Crisis of 1962, almost all Canadian defence systems were on full-readiness and poised for a nuclear confrontation with the Soviet Union even before the Canadian government could meet and decide to place Canadian forces on alert, let alone decide to support the US government. Moreover, as these national defence systems became enmeshed into a single mega-system over the years, a common culture of militarism that held deep-rooted realist assumptions about the role of the state, military power, US hegemony, and the most effective role that the Canadian state should play within it, evolved within both the Canadian and American defence communities. This military subculture within both these civil societies shared an ideational worldview that increasingly thought of national security in continental geographic terms (see Charbonneau and Cox 2008).

The integration of continental and NATO defence systems did not end with the Cold War. The Canadian government continues to be one of the most important and reliable military allies of the United States. Part of this is driven by the very weapons systems that the Canadian military has acquired over time. During the early 1960s, Canadian fighter aircraft were designed to carry US nuclear missiles, and the BOMARC missile defence system in Canada was similarly designed to carry US nuclear warheads. Furthermore, Canadian destroyers and frigates are the only non-American naval ships designed to operate within US carrier and amphibious battle groups, and all Canadian warships are equipped with the same command and control communications systems of US vessels, meaning that Canadians are the only non-Americans regularly allowed to control US ships in combat. This has meant that at the level of operations and logistics, Canadian forces can operate seamlessly with American forces. During the first Gulf War, the NATO mission over Kosovo, Operation Apollo during the invasion of Afghanistan and the lead-up to the invasion of Iraq, and now in Afghanistan, the fully integrated nature of these systems has proven useful in multilateral missions.

The political implications of such a degree of defence and security integration have become more significant within the post-9/11 world order. The defence of North America itself has never been a highly controversial issue for most Canadians. With the possible exceptions of cruise missiles in the 1980s and the recent debate over missile defence, cooperation with the United States in continental defence has been widely accepted as natural. This was reinforced by the graphic nature of the 9/11 attacks. The same is not true when it comes to peace-enforcing, US-led alliance-building outside UN or other multilateral frameworks, or bilateral Canadian-American missions. Before Canada's NATO ground mission in Afghanistan, the Canadian naval role in the war on terror did not generate much debate so long as Canadians could be convinced that this mission was a direct response to 9/11. During Operation Apollo, Canadian naval deployments in the Gulf in support of the US-led mission in Afghanistan were generally deemed to be acceptable. However, as that mission also involved protection and support of American forces destined for Iraq, the political implications of support for such an operation became problematic. There was a realization among citizens and politicians alike that the close working relationship between Canadian and American military forces was not a non-political, natural endeavour (Charbonneau and Cox 2008).

The war in Afghanistan has brought the consequences of Canada-US defence cooperation into the public domain. Although both the Liberal and Conservative governments attempted to highlight the multilateral nature of the NATO effort there and further highlight the humanitarian aspects of the overall campaign, public support for the war has been tepid at best. This might be partly a result of Canadians having difficulty differentiating Canadian objectives in Afghanistan from American ones – some seeing an association between the wars in Afghanistan and Iraq (partly because of the Bush administration's insistence that the invasion of Iraq was a second front on the war on terror) – and of many Canadians not seeing the loss of Canadian soldiers as anything other than the consequences of a war-fighting mission. These associations are in stark contrast to the humanitarian-peacekeeping mythology of Canada, a mythology that is still used by Canadian governments through their insistence that the mission in Afghanistan is largely about humanitarianism. If the image of Canada-as-international-peacekeeper was indeed built out of a desire to portray Canada as a selfless international citizen, then fighting an unpopular war with the United States can hardly be sold using the same logic.

An emphasis on state-state relations, while important, can offer only a partial and often biased picture of a larger and complex story. More often than not, state-centric methodologies render invisible or irrelevant local practices where state-centric assumptions about authority, politics, and security are legitimized, challenged, or redefined. The commonsense view of Canada-US defence and security cooperation *is* a political construction, meaning on the one hand that successive Canadian governments over the past fifty years or so have played into the complexities of Canadian civil society and morphed the concepts of internationalism into those of Canadian multiculturalism, and on the other hand that it is a political production in that the state-sponsored worldview is resisted and challenged by various groups seeking to question or redefine the meanings of being Canadian, of Canadian democracy, of Canadian security, and so on. Critical social movements in Canada represent an amalgam of various groups, such as Muslim women's groups, retired soldiers, Jewish housewives, youth groups, anti-war protesters and war resisters, anti-poverty movements, ecological associations, feminist activists, anti-racism groups, gays and lesbians rights groups, and so on. These social movements, in all their variety and diversity, have been politicized in new ways, and they have created and opened new spaces for political activity. They have challenged and have worked directly or indirectly to define or redefine Canadian society, democracy, and security.[2] Among other things, it is these stories that this book attempts to integrate into a larger discussion of global order and the Canadian state. These groups, and the new alliances and interests between them, are the stories of both those who are affected by the new global security order on a day-to-day basis and of those who participate in the maintenance, reform, and/or transformation of global order.

Structure of the Book

The chapters that follow are divided into four sections. Each focuses on locating where and how the Canadian state and Canadian citizens promote or participate in the construction of global order. Obviously, given the nature of global order and local orders, each section is not intended to be a hermetically sealed unit. That is, it is only by taking into account all sections as a whole that we can locate global order and Canada's multiple roles in it. The book is also structured around case studies. A case-study approach comes with advantages and disadvantages. Case studies allow us to offer a wide range of themes and diversity. Each case can be explored in detail and offers important empirical material. Moreover, our case-study structure offers a variety of theoretical perspectives that focus on the local, the global, or on their connections, and it also offers numerous contending views about the need to maintain, reform, or transform global order. The case-study structure and the diversity in case studies should also sustain discussion rather than promote specific claims. The most important disadvantages, however, are the obvious absences. Some theoretical perspectives, some regions of the world (Asia in particular), some Canadian actors (provinces especially), and some issues are not presented or addressed. This is partly because of the nature of such a project as ours, partly because of hard choices we had to make as editors. We can offer only apologies but find comfort in knowing that our readers can find other texts by making good use of our list of references.

Part 1, *American Power and the Location of Global Order,* focuses primarily on the role of the United States within global order. Interpretations of this are diverse and contested, and we do not want to suggest that the two chapters of this section cover it all.[3] These chapters focus on the role of American security and militarism in structuring global order. In Chapter 1, "Hegemony, Militarism, and Identity: Locating the United States as the Global Power," Dan O'Meara discusses the historical evolution of the militarized notion of security within, and projecting outward from, the United States. He argues that, historically, militarized understandings of security have long been a key component of American political culture. This American militarism has been a key part of the establishment of American hegemony in the sense that it has permeated the ways in which the United States has understood itself and the ways in which it has used its power to structure global order. More importantly, O'Meara argues that an analysis of such militarism "involves unpacking the 'seats of power' and the roles of 'authoritative actors' ... implicated in constructing the webs of meaning underlying such politically charged notions as national security, national identity, and national interest." The militarized nature of American political culture "embodies a social project understood as an ongoing and highly politicized process of forging support for policies that entail the construction of a particular national identity and form of society, ones that foster some sets of interests over others, and that promote a particular form of global order." As such, global order and world politics cannot be disconnected from the American state itself, nor from the legitimacy and inspiration it derives from its long internal association with militarism and security. In many ways, O'Meara presents theoretical themes that can be found in many of the remaining chapters in this collection.

In Chapter 2, "The Neoconservative Challenge to Realist Thinking in American Foreign Policy," Alex Macleod follows with an examination of what the changes in emphasis on security and militarism in the post-9/11 world order have meant for the debates within the discipline of IR. Specifically, Macleod looks at the academic debates within realist theory to examine how they adapted to both the post-9/11 era and the neoconservative challenge. Macleod examines the neoconservative movement within IR theory with an eye to evaluating this movement's worldview – both in terms of its application as a matter of practice and as a theory of IR. This notion of Washington's neoconservatives as the practical representation of a particular worldview raises important questions about the relationship between theory and practice in IR, and forces us to consider just how realist or liberal their ideas are.

The remaining sections of this book present a series of case-related chapters divided into sections that use Canada and the changing nature of its security policies as the central case for an examination of the global-local relationship. The second section examines the specific case of the Canadian mission in Afghanistan in order to analyze the political dynamics of how and where Canada participates in the construction of world order, both locally and globally. The third section focuses on how local and national practices and discourses build and/or work with social assumptions and practices of political order and national security. Lastly, the fourth section discusses Canadian policies in Africa in order to analyze how global order is promoted and exported abroad. Given that Canada has found itself heavily involved in the NATO mission in Afghanistan, as well as its historically close security relationship with the United States and its legacy of internationalism, the war in Afghanistan, Canadian responses to 9/11, and the war on terror are common themes throughout this book.

Part 2, *Constructing Global Order at Home and Abroad – The Case of Canada's Mission in Afghanistan*, presents three chapters that examine significant theoretical and practical issues relating to the Canadian mission in Afghanistan. In Chapter 3, "Managing Life in Afghanistan: Canadian Tales of Peace, Security, and Development," Bruno Charbonneau and Geneviève Parent assess the war in Afghanistan in terms of both the role that Canada has played in the global order under US leadership and its consequences for those who experience this war first-hand – that is, the people of Afghanistan. They argue that Canada's peacekeeping role has always been part of a US-led world order but that it has also moved away from the traditional form of UN-mandated peacekeeping, with revealing effects. Although successive Canadian governments have continued to exploit the appeal of Canada's peacekeeper image, Canada has increasingly become an active player in more offensive military operations that are a major component of global order. Canada's traditional peacekeeping role, Charbonneau and Parent argue, has evolved into a much wider project encompassing attempts at democratization, economic development, and the rebuilding of "fragile states." However, given the particular consequences and the human toll in

Afghanistan, Canada's mission suggests that the mix of war-fighting and humanitarianism merged for the purposes of the management of Afghan life. In the name of international stability, Charbonneau and Parent argue, Canada's war in Afghanistan is an attempt to impose global order on Afghans.

In Chapter 4, "Rethinking the Security Imaginary: Canadian Security and the Case of Afghanistan," Kim Richard Nossal examines the shifts in Canada's foreign and security policies in terms of the debates about foreign policy within Canada. Nossal identifies the changes in Canadian foreign policy between 1993 and 2006 to suggest that the socialization process of hegemonic orders does not necessarily flow unidirectionally outward from the hegemon, as suggested by Dan O'Meara, and that in the case of Canada, political leaders were openly encouraging Canadians to rethink American assumptions about world politics and recast the Canadian role in world order based on uniquely Canadian values and assumptions. Nossal is quick to point out that much of this self-congratulatory constructing of Canada as a selfless rather than self-interested state actor was motivated by the domestic politics of the day, but he also emphasizes the differences within various Liberal governments. Regardless of these differences, however, the overall Canadian foreign and security policies were significantly at odds with the orthodox ways in which the United States conceptualized another country's role in world politics. Nossal then proceeds to an assessment of what this has meant for Canada's role within the NATO mission in Afghanistan in order to explain Canadians' tepid support for the war.

In Chapter 5, "Constructions of Nation, Constructions of War: Media Representations of Captain Nichola Goddard," Claire Turenne Sjolander and Kathryn Trevenen take a close look at a specific case. They examine the Canadian media representations of the combat death of Captain Nichola Goddard, killed in Afghanistan in May 2006. Their analysis of these media representations explores how manipulations of gender and the roles of women have been used to shape and limit the parameters of the public debate over Canada's mission in Afghanistan. Goddard was celebrated on the one hand as a gender-neutral soldier and on the other as a textbook peacekeeping soldier. Their analysis is based on more than 250 newspaper articles from major Canadian dailies in the period after Goddard's death. They argue that gender has been used to portray Canada's mission as a war-fighting mission that has underlying humanitarian objectives similar to the motivations of Canada's more traditional peacekeeping mythology. As such, Goddard has been celebrated as a war fighter in the traditionally masculine image, and as having a compassionate feminine quality that has traditionally been associated with peacekeeping. This representation, they argue, has been sold to an increasingly skeptical Canadian public and has informed the public debates about the war in Afghanistan.

Part 3, *Constructing Global Order at Home: Conceptualizations and Practices of National Security*, examines Canadian security as it is construed and practised at home. The four chapters look at both the efforts to rearticulate and implement security policy in Canada and the effects these efforts have had on various elements of Canadian society. In Chapter 6, "Against National Security: From the Canadian War on Queers to the 'War on Terror,'" Gary Kinsman examines the historical consequences of Canadian practices of national security, as both a social practice and an ideological one. Unlike many scholars who highlight the exceptionalism of the post-9/11 era, Kinsman underlines the continuities of Canadian national security campaigns since the early days of the Cold War. He argues that national security campaigns work to exclude and marginalize the members of Canadian society who are identified as different and thus as possible national security threats to the established order. Through an examination of Canada's war against queers during the early Cold War period, its assault on anti-poverty and anti-globalization groups and other subversives, and its involvement in the recent war on terror, Kinsman argues that Canadian national security campaigns are gendered and Otherizing ways in which the Canadian state defines politically legitimate Canadian identities. As an ideology, national security works to transform into threats identities and communities that challenge the established order, as defined by the Canadian state. And yet, Kinsman argues, the historical record suggests that there are practical strategies for marginalized and repressed groups that have been effective. He calls on these strategies as a way in which queers and other marginalized and/or subversives might be able to resist the dangers that currently exist for them in an era of legal exceptionalism brought on by the war on terror.

Following this, in Chapter 7, "Framing Post-9/11 Security: Tales of State Securitization and of the Experiences of Muslim Communities," Siobhan Byrne looks at the case of Muslim communities in Canada since 9/11 using a feminist framework. She argues that although security policy in Canada since the 9/11 attacks has been devised to increase security for most citizens, the ways and means through which these policies have been put in place have worked to actually increase the insecurity of many other groups and citizens, leaving them more vulnerable to racial profiling, stereotyping, and acts of intimidation. Byrne provides an analysis of changes in government policy and of media reports to establish how the war-on-terror script of identity construction has portrayed Muslim women as victims of tyrannical regimes and repressive social norms, and how this has been utilized in support of policies that further repress Muslims within Canada. She looks specifically at high-profile cases such as Project Thread and the Maher Arar case to display the extent to which the script of Muslim vilification has real impacts on the lives of Muslim Canadians. Byrne argues that these cases suggest the need to unpack our conceptual understanding of security in the post-9/11 era in order to see how security is both a concept and an operational idea that, if not effectively put into place, serves to systematize marginalization and repression. It is only through this unpacking, she argues, that we can begin to rearticulate security as both a concept and practice that can serve to increase peace and prosperity for all citizens.

In Chapter 8, "Re-Conceptions of National Security in the Age of Terrorism: Implications for Federal Policing in Canada," Todd Hataley begins by looking at the changing roles of federal policing since 9/11. Hataley suggests that while US domestic security policy has been coordinated through the creation of the Department of Homeland Security (for better or worse), the Canadian case is very different, and this comes with very different implications. Hataley suggests that multi-levels of policing in Canada have not been effectively coordinated in their efforts to identify and protect us from threats that emerge domestically, and that this is particularly troubling given that in a state such as Canada, 9/11 and other recent acts of terrorism suggest that the front lines of national security are increasingly found within sovereign states. Given the limited resources and the limited institutional framework for coordination among Canada's various police forces, Canadian federal police forces and security-related agencies are often dependent on smaller and local police forces to identify, and report on, possible domestic threats. However, many of these smaller forces do not have effective training in place to prepare their officers for such tasks, and if any possible activity is identified, the information and communications systems that will assist in developing appropriate responses to these activities are simply not available.

In Chapter 9, "Biosecurity in Canada and Beyond: Invasions, Imperialisms, and Sovereignty," Peter Stoett pushes the parameters of the difficulties associated with the local-global divide the furthest. He examines the inherently transnational nature of the global ecology through the concept of biosecurity. Stoett challenges the idea of externalizing environmental threats to

Canada by revealing that invasive species often find their way into Canada's ecology slowly and practically unnoticed, and that oftentimes these threats are more dangerous to Canadian economic and political well-being than are the traditional "foreign" threats found in security studies. As such, Stoett argues, there is a need to reconceptualize the concepts of security and threat beyond the local-global dichotomy, and Canada should develop appropriate multilateral frameworks through which it can play an effective role in devising policies that can deal with the problems of biodiversity, environmental protection, pollution control, and global warming. After providing a detailed assessment of key issue areas and problems associated with biosecurity, Stoett warns of the dire economic and political consequences of our continuance to define and develop security policies in traditional state, local and global narrow ways.

The final section, *Constructing Global Order Abroad: Canada's Policies in Africa,* is composed of three chapters that focus on Canadian foreign and security policy in Africa. They suggest clear linkages between distinctly Canadian values and traditions, and assumptions of global order and the way that Canada conducts itself internationally. In Chapter 10, "Canada, Africa, and 'New' Multilateralisms for Global Governance: Before and After the Harper Regime in Ottawa?" Timothy Shaw uses the case of Canada's interests in Africa to suggest that the past successes enjoyed by Canada as a respected player in multilateral forms of governance have been seriously eroded through the current government's emphasis on mostly military security missions that are primarily driven by a desire to preserve a close working relationship with the United States. Moreover, Canada's valued multilateral tradition is further eroded, or complicated, by the heterogeneous coalitions of state and non-state actors engaged in human development, rights, and security. His analysis of the diversity of global coalitions from the more successful (Kimberley Process, conflict diamonds) to the less successful (small arms and child soldiers) suggests that such global campaigns are really networking for human development, rights, and security. For Canada, such global coalitions represent both opportunity and increasing marginalization. The Kimberley and Ottawa processes showed that Canada can play a leadership role in the creation and management of successful multilateral global coalitions. This, he argues, has allowed Canada to be an effective player in dealing with issues of global security – a humanitarian role that many Canadians are most comfortable with. Although we may lament the impact today of American unilateralism on human security issues such as the International Criminal Court, Canada should already consider both the interests and impacts of emerging economies such as China and India, and the emergence of larger and more effective "new" multilateralisms for global governance. Shaw concludes that these issues will be of increased significance in a globalizing world order and, thus, he suggests that Canada should use its respected position and expertise to foster successful multilateral forums for global governance.

In keeping with many of the themes presented by Timothy Shaw, in Chapter 11, "Mainstreaming Investment: Foreign and Security Policy Implications of Canadian Extractive Industries in Africa," David Black and Malcolm Savage examine the specific case of Canadian extractive industries in Africa. They argue that there are significant social and political implications for human security in Africa that come from the activities of Canadian extractive industries. Many of these firms have been implicated either directly or indirectly in numerous conflicts throughout the African continent. The Canadian government and these firms are often in a position to promote change and greatly alter the security of individuals and parties directly involved in these conflicts. Black and Savage, however, highlight the inherent contradictions of Canadian policies toward Africa. On the one hand, Africa has traditionally been considered one of the key areas for Canadian humanitarian and developmental assistance. This has reinforced the idea of Canada as a nurturing and benevolent international citizen and has fit in well with the Canada-as-peacekeeper image that has remained a key pillar of how Canadians define themselves internationally. On the other hand, parts of the Canadian state have provided as much support as possible to promote the activities of Canadian extractive industries in Africa, and much of this activity has been either indirectly or directly linked to many of Africa's most serious humanitarian crises. This contradiction, Black and Savage argue, needs to be fully understood if we are to effectively examine the roles the Canadian state can play in establishing and supporting the idea of corporate social responsibility. They do so by assessing Canada's efforts thus far in this process and speculating on what this means for Canada's role in fostering human security in Africa.

In Chapter 12, "Peace-building between Canadian Values and Local Knowledge: Some Lessons from Timbuktu," Jonathan Sears examines the specialized role Canada can play in the management and longer-term resolution of conflict in Africa. Specifically, he looks at the peace process in Mali and the role Canada has played in this process. Sears suggests that the only effective and lasting peace is one in which participants in the conflict are brought into the conflict resolution stage and make a contribution to proposed solutions. This, Sears argues, can be done only with international participation in the case of Africa, given the limited resources and expertise that many fragile African states face. Local knowledge brought together with the expertise and humanitarianism developed in Canadian foreign policy provides Canada with an opportunity to become an effective player in building peace and stability in Africa. Sears argues that this is in Canada's national security interests. He then proceeds to a detailed case study of the process in Mali in the 1990s by highlighting the need for local inclusiveness and the roles multilateral institutions and states such as Canada can play.

Finally, in "Conclusion: Relocating Global Order," we develop further the overall claims of the book. The chapter suggests how the book's contributions open an interesting range of research agendas. We discuss the theoretical and methodological consequences of bringing forward the issue of the relationship between location and politics. The question of location, we argue, highlights the importance of a politics of knowledge, of representations of the intellectual, and of scholars' social and political responsibilities and how they involve difficult matters of judgment.

The sum total of the chapters is presented in such a manner that the reader of the entire collection can see the interrelationships between how security in the post-9/11 global order conditions both the state and the local, and how the local and state condition global order. The earlier chapters, with their emphasis on the international, fit more squarely into the traditional domain of IR, but the book evolves in such a way as to transition itself into the more narrow focus of Canadian foreign policy, and finally into the case material that is often described as comparative politics. These disciplinary divisions, we argue, are arbitrary, and this book serves as a set of case studies to demonstrate how an effective understanding of broad concepts such as security and global order requires a variety of perspectives from a variety of disciplines.

NOTES

1 These three perspectives on global order are inspired by Samuel Kim's (1984, 61-68) "Contending Images of World Order."
2 For instance, Ann Denholm Crosby (2003) studied the ways in which the group Voice of Women has worked, since the early days of the Cold War, to redefine the meaning of Canadian security. Decades before the Canadian government appropriated the term, Voice of Women promoted the idea of human security to replace the Cold War, state-centred, and machoist views of security. Crosby argues, however,

that the Canadian government interpretation of human security since the 1990s has little resemblance to what Voice of Women promoted for many years.
3 On the various interpretations see, for instance, Agnew (2005); Bacevich (2002); Calleo (1987); Carroll (2006); Chomsky (1999); Enloe (1990); Ferguson (2004); Gill (1990); Gowan (1999); Harvey (2003, 2007); Hossein-Zadeh (2006); Johnson (2000, 2004, 2006); Kagan (2004); Kennedy (1988); Keohane (1984); McCormick (1989); Nau (1990); Nye (1991); Robinson (1996); Slotkin (1973); T. Smith (2007).

PART 1

AMERICAN POWER AND THE LOCATION OF GLOBAL ORDER

1

Hegemony, Militarism, and Identity
Locating the United States as the Global Power

DAN O'MEARA

Like the miniskirt, academic fashions come and go.

Seemingly oblivious to theoretical and ideological fault lines, notions of American hegemonic decline were all the rage in the late 1970s and the 1980s (D. Bell 1976; Kennedy 1988; McCormick 1989; Modelski 1978; Rosencrance 1976; Wallerstein 1984). As scholars probed the likely trajectory of global politics "after [US] hegemony" (Calleo 1987; Keohane 1984), a major Hollywood film – *Rising Sun* – echoed predictions of an unprepared America being overwhelmed by a calculating Japanese behemoth (Kearns 1992; Prestowitz 1988; Tolchin and Tolchin 1992). However, this declinism was increasingly challenged as the 1990s progressed (Gill 1990; Nau 1990). Globalization, the dotcom boom, and Asian financial woes seemed to validate claims that American soft power guaranteed decades of US predominance (Nye 1991). The Y2K hysteria notwithstanding, in 2000 the "received opinion" of the Davos global elite held that "no one else could ever catch up" with the United States (Buruma 2008, 127).

George W. Bush's presidency changed all that. As the forty-third president left office, the United States was widely viewed in the terms that its second president described himself: "obnoxious, suspected and unpopular."[1] Its belligerent unilateralism, inability to stem Iraqi and Afghani insurgencies, exploding external debt, permanent trade deficits, recurring financial crises, dependence on Asian banks, and insatiable thirst for oil and cheap Chinese manufactured goods all suggest that soft power alone will not suffice: "This year in Davos, America's fall was on everybody's lips" (Buruma 2008, 126). A newly fashionable declinism focuses on the economic rise of China and India (Emmot 2008; Kagan 2008; Khanna 2008; Leonard 2008). Little in this latest literature on a "post-American world" (Zakaria 2008) explores the "paradox of unparalleled American [military] power and diminished American Hegemony" (McCormick 2005, 75). Such silence is unsurprising: most social science writings strikingly ignore the military's central role in US domestic and foreign politics (Boggs 2005, xxv-xxxvi).

Those texts that do examine contemporary American military power fall into two broad camps. The first reprises Russell Weigley's notion (1973) of an American way of war, one combining the sheer weight of numbers with technologically superior firepower in campaigns of attrition against a usually weaker enemy. Mostly published by American war colleges or associated think tanks, these authors grapple with how the United States might prevail in twenty-first-century armed conflicts.[2] Ranging from exultant triumphalism (Boot 2003; Cebrowski and Barnett 2003) to qualified pessimism (Gray 2005, 2006), they ignore all non-military practices that generate and sustain this American way of war. On the other hand, echoing yet another past debate, an array of critical texts probes the role of militarism and war in the "American empire."[3] However, as I have argued elsewhere, these notions of American empire and imperialism function more as epithets than useful analytical categories:

> "American empire" and "US imperialism" ... are concepts rather than ontological realities. Anchored in concrete but bygone historical conjunctures, forms of rule and resistance, cultural practices, and economic and state policies, such concepts reflect particular epistemological strategies whose contemporary validity can most charitably be described as questionable. Thus, whether conceived as "informal" or as decentred or "without an address," notions of American "empire" and US imperialism are, at best, little more than *weak historical analogies* which obfuscate more than they reveal. (O'Meara 2006, 28, emphasis in original)

This chapter explores the ways in which American military practices worked to fashion the post-1945 global hegemonic order. It highlights the role of warfare within long-standing continuities in US public culture, examines the place of militarism in evolving geographies of power, and locates key transition moments in the institutions of American militarism.

American Hegemony

Any discussion of hegemony in global politics must distinguish between three separate aspects. The first is the particular form of power wielded by the sets of social agents collectively known as the hegemon:

> Hegemony is the enrollment of others in the exercise of your power by convincing, cajoling and coercing them to believe *that they should want what you want.* Though never complete and often resisted, it represents the binding together of people, objects and institutions around cultural norms and standards that emanate over time and space *from seats of power (that have discrete locations) occupied by authoritative actors.* (Agnew 2005, 1-2, emphasis added)

Among the elements making up hegemonic power, the most significant is the capacity to envelop other agents within an animating myth that frames the hegemon's own particular interests as embodying universal ones (Gramsci 1971, 57-58). Accepting the hegemon's leadership as the least costly means of achieving global stability, other agents come to embrace this animating myth as the only possible way of seeing the world. This underscores, second, the historical conditions, struggles, and alliances giving rise to and reproducing these forms of power and the hegemon's preponderance. Third, hegemonic power induces other agents to collaborate in a global hegemonic order that regulates relations between them and consolidates the interests underpinning the hegemon's power.

Described against the backdrop of collapsing British hegemony, conventional narratives explain the international instability and conflict from 1920 to 1939 in terms of America's refusal to pick up Britain's fallen baton. This misconceives how hegemony is established. Although the United States was indeed the "main pole of attraction for the labor, capital and entrepreneurial resources of the world-economy" (Arrighi 1993, 176) after the First World War, it was not yet a credible global military power. With America's force projection capabilities dwarfed by Britain and France, neither its political class nor broader society had developed a consensus on a global role.

Six factors condensed to alter this. Subsequent changes to any one factor had spillover effects on each of the others and on the US capacity to exercise hegemonic power. First, by 1945, the "systemic chaos" (Arrighi 1993, 151) in the global order had assumed calamitous proportions: two catastrophic wars in thirty years, the collapse of European land empires and imminent disintegration of the colonial ones, the breakdown of the world market and financial system, and the tide of socialist and nationalist rebellion across Europe and the Third World. Leaders of the vanquished German and Japanese imperial projects and of the wilting European colonial ones all accepted the need for a new global order to reconstruct their economies and repulse the challenge to prevailing property relations.

There was, second, no alternative to American leadership. Their own economy in ruins, the Soviets and their force projection capabilities offered no threat to American dominance. Only its acquisition of nuclear weapons, and more particularly its development in the late 1950s of a ballistic missile capability, enabled Moscow to parody a competition for global power. Absent a countervailing power, the major states (except the USSR and China) acknowledged that embracing US-propagated norms and rules would be easier than pursuing autarky.

Third, the experience of the Second World War finally produced agreement among American elites over the need to exercise global leadership, the multilateral forms this should take, the threat they imagined they confronted, and the budgetary price leadership entailed. This new consensus was predicated both on transforming the employment-focused social alliance underlying President Roosevelt's New Deal into President Truman's "guns and butter" coalition organized around national security, *and* on revising long-standing notions of the role of the military in the American state.

This crucial latter point underscores the unique ways in which power is exercised in the United States. Until the 1940s, the federal government was relatively weak with respect to civil society:

> The functionally and geographically divided character of the U.S. government [historically] made American society particularly open to reliance on the market as both model and metaphor. In its seeming passivity relative to society, American government has usually served, except during special periods such as the New Deal in the 1930s, to make possible or give public blessing to private initiatives. The terms public and private have taken on meanings in the United States different from those they had in Europe in the eighteenth and nineteenth centuries. In particular, the scope of government action has been restricted to that of either constraining government itself or encouraging private enterprise, *except crucially in relation to "national security."* (Agnew 2005, 57-58, emphasis added)

Fourth, overwhelming American commercial, productive, technological, and financial preponderance enabled Washington to impose the Bretton Woods settlement on its Western allies, punish states that declined to conform, dictate the terms of the integration of emerging states into the global economic order, and oversee its later modifications as European and Japanese reconstruction tempered American primacy.

Fifth, as projected by Hollywood and television, an idealized image of the American way of life – oriented around sassy individualism and levels of consumption unparalleled elsewhere – offered an appealing animating myth of modernity, prosperity, and freedom to exhausted class-ridden western Europe and Japan. With their economies largely reconstructed on American terms, these societies absorbed ever-greater doses of American culture, particularly the cult of the consumer as the basis of social order.

Finally, this reconstruction of international capitalism was conditional on US force project preponderance (Leffler 1992, 15-19). NATO and the American nuclear umbrella provided the allies with multilateral forms of defence more extensive and cheaper than a return to *chacun pour soi*. The global network of US military bases injected significant investment into the host countries, while the presence over sixty years of thousands of American troops in western Europe and Asia had transformative economic and cultural effects on these societies. All of this combined to underwrite the American model of militarized Keynesianism, facilitate growing European economic cooperation, foster cultures of individual consumption, guarantee social control and elite stability in countries with powerful left-wing parties, and sanction states that strayed from the fold (Iran in 1953; Guatemala in 1954; Cuba, 1960; Brazil, 1964; Chile, 1973; and Portugal, 1976).

The vital military component of hegemony involves more than superior force projection capability. As the "'imperial' military educator" (Sokolsky 2002, 211), the hegemon propagates cultural practices that potential competitor states are obliged to emulate or counter (Arrighi 1993, 164). Socialized by the threat discourse of the hegemon's *security imaginary*, both allies and rivals adopt complementary forms of strategic culture.[4] Moreover, the hegemon's model of force design has one of three effects on the armed forces of major and middle powers: (1) they are effectively integrated in the hegemon's overall force structure and associated political economy (Britain and Canada); (2) they endeavour to retain some strategic independence while adopting a version of the hegemon's model (France); or (3) they seek to counter the hegemon's force design (Russia and China). Finally, norm diffusion is promoted through military exchange programs and the education of allied officers in American military academies. These foster an international "fraternity of the uniform whose purpose is to influence, both collectively and individually, allied policies in directions favorable to the United States" (Sokolsky 2002, 222).

Under US hegemony, the rights and powers of sovereign states have been considerably curtailed (Arrighi 1993, 182). The principal effect has been the successful, if uneven, projection onto much of the planet of a marketplace society hinged on a particular view of state-market relations, and on individual consumption (Agnew 2005). Here I advance the thesis that an essential underlying condition of such hegemony has been *the ways in which a uniquely American form of militarism constitutes an integral part of the evolving cultural and economic practices that propagated, fashioned, and sustained this global hegemonic order.* This chapter examines the evolution of American militarism as a constituent element in a range of cultural practices that I term "Americanism." By the latter I understand a set of so-called authentic values, norms, standards, and representational practices that sustain the public culture and proscribe the limits of what positions, attitudes, and policies can legitimately be adopted in political life.[5]

Americanism and Militarism

Americanism sprang from the fissiparous character of US society and polity. The War of Independence was hardly the act of a unified people. As the thirteen colonies each "traveled its own road to independence" (W.A. Williams 1961/1973, 109), the social composition of each underlay its particular vision of the republic. Dominant elites defined their specific interests and identities in local rather than national terms. Given this local basis of identities, of federal representation and politics, and of the ceaseless culture wars since 1789, Americanism is fruitfully understood as an ongoing discursive strategy to forge an always fragile national identity (D. Campbell 1998). To hold this fragmented and fractious republic together, a narrative of Americanism emerged as a Manichaean tale of good and evil, of them and us, of progress, truth, justice, and the American way. Americanism defines national identity, warrants some forms of action, and disqualifies others. Among its constituent elements are particular representations of warfare and an associated set of cultural practices.

I examine these latter elements through the concept of militarism. This term conventionally refers to two linked phenomena: the domination of public life by a bureaucratized military apparatus and the subsequent ideology promoting the glorification and aggressive use of military force as the principal means by which the political elite should realize its objectives (Bacevich 2005; Hossein-Zadeh 2006, 26; Johnson 2004, 23-24). We conventionally distinguish militaristic societies (pre-1945 Germany and Japan, post-1948 United States) from less militaristic (pre-1945 United States) and non-militaristic ones (Switzerland). However, I use the term in a broader sense, taking "militarism" to comprise the myriad ways in which the specific security imaginary, strategic culture, force design, and military routines and practices of *any* state articulate with broader public and political cultures in the construction of an official national identity – and hence in the definition of and modes of pursuing so-called national interest(s).

Analyzing militarism so defined involves unpacking the "seats of power" and the roles of "authoritative actors" (Agnew 2005, 2) implicated in constructing the webs of meaning underlying such politically charged notions as national security, national identity, and national interest. "Militarism" embodies a social project understood as an ongoing and highly politicized process of forging support for policies that entail the construction of a particular national identity and form of society, ones that foster some sets of interests over others and that promote a particular form of global order.

American Militarism and the Meaning of War

Understanding the role of warfare in American history requires holding in mind a paradox. On the one hand, war and armies have been the "engine of change in North America for the past five centuries" (Anderson and Cayton 2005, xiv). They are "as important as geography, immigration, the growth of business, the separation of powers, the inventiveness of its people, or anything else that contributes strongly to its unique identity among the nations of the Earth" (Perret 1989, 562). Having fought 12 major wars and close to 120 minor ones since 1775, "no nation on Earth has had as much experience of war as the United States ... America's wars have been like rungs on a ladder by which it rose to greatness" (558).

Although the United States is "a country made by war" (Perret 1989), suspicion of a standing military is deeply rooted in American society and has long been the bane of its generals (Upton 1905/1917, ix). Formalized in Washington's farewell address, this anti-militarism was best expressed by the principal author of the constitution and fourth president, James Madison:

> Of all the enemies of public liberty, war is, perhaps, the most to be dreaded because it comprises and develops the germ of every other. War is the parent of armies; from those proceed debts and taxes, and debts and taxes are the known instruments for bringing the many under the domination of the few. In war, too, the discretionary power of the Executive is extended; its influence in dealing out offices, honors, and emoluments is multiplied; and all the means of seducing the minds, are added to those of subduing the force, of the people ... No nation could preserve its freedom in the midst of continual warfare. (Madison 1795/1865, 491)

Millions of Americans remain wary of foreign military entanglements. Their political weight and ability to locate anti-militarism within core American values hobbled the United States in Vietnam. It put an end to conscription, significantly proscribes the range of politically feasible military policies, and is the main reason that, until Korea, all of America's wars were followed by wholesale reduction of its armed forces.

War and militarism are thus omnipresent in the public imagination, both as the engine of national greatness and as the main threat to the values proclaimed by the republic. Exploring how militarism constructs two key elements of Americanism – national identity and geographies of power – the chapter concludes with a discussion of the evolving institutions of American militarism.

Militarism and Identity

The United States was founded in and forged by war. A particular view of when and how it engages in war is anchored in three of its foundation myths. The first, *American exceptionalism,* is "a rags to riches story that focuses on the luck and pluck and not on the stealing and killing entailed in becoming a continental and then a global empire" (Costigliola and Paterson 2004, 12). Exceptionalism holds that "Americans do not fight, therefore, except to fulfill a solemn obligation to defend their own – or others' – liberty" (Anderson and Cayton 2005, xiii). This was always ambiguous, however. The revolution waged war on empire and tyranny even while the Founding Fathers agreed that they were writing "a constitution to form a great [American] empire" (W.A. Williams 1961/1973, 116). This tension created by warfare being ostensibly conducted against tyranny while deliberately extending American *imperium* and *dominium* has persisted ever since. Even America's most nakedly imperialist wars – the 1775 and 1812 invasions of Canada, Andrew Jackson's wars of annexation in the southeast, the seizure of half of Mexico in 1846-48, the 1898 grab of Spanish colonies – were all said to have freed the oppressed and expanded the realm of liberty (Anderson and Cayton 2005, 160-273, 317-60). George W. Bush repeated this refrain ad nauseum.

Many American historians see this ambiguous belief in war fought in the name of freedom in order to extend American dominium as the corollary to a second founding myth, *American universalism* (Anderson and Cayton 2005; Carroll 2006; W.A. Williams 1959/1984). This holds that "the ideal of America is the hope of mankind ... the light [that] shines in the darkness" (Bush 2002b). Rooted equally in seventeenth-century puritanism (Stephanson 1996, 3-27) and Locke's notion of natural man (W.A. Williams 1961/1973, 250), universalism complements a third foundation myth: America's *manifest destiny* to spread liberty, private property, and the pursuit of individual happiness (Fousek 2000, 5). In the words of President Woodrow Wilson, "Providence and ... divine destiny" have decreed that "we are chosen and prominently chosen to show the way to the nations of the world how they shall walk in the paths of liberty" (Wilson Center n.d.).

Yet, "the Force" of such universalism has a "Dark Side." Those who resist universalism and manifest destiny oppose both humanity and the logic of providence/history. They are necessarily, as George W. Bush frequently asserted, "the enemies of freedom." Contest the American definition of freedom as consisting of free markets, property rights, and the rule of law, query the right of the United States to impose its own rules on humanity, and you are no longer a Lockean natural man – thus absolving the United States of the obligation to treat you as such. In 1902, General Robert Hughes justified torturing Filipinos fighting American occupation on the grounds that "these people are not civilized." Senator Henry Cabot Lodge blamed American "cruelties" on "the war that was waged by the Filipinos themselves, a semi-civilized people, with all the characteristics of Asiatics, with the Asiatic indifference to life, with the Asiatic treachery and the Asiatic cruelty, all tinctured and increased by three hundred years of subjection to Spain" (quoted in Kramer 2008, 42-43). Yesterday Filipinos, today "Islamic fundamentalist terrorists" passing through the Phoenix program and Operation Condor; Abu Ghraib is very far from an exception.

These foundation myths themselves rest on a five-step rhetorical elision around difference. First, difference is transformed not just into Otherness but a form of *unbeing* ("these people are not civilized"). Second, such alienated Otherness is securitized as a threat to America and its so-called universal values. Third, since the United States is good, free, brave, and progressive, this menacing alienated Otherness morphs into the incarnation of evil. It threatens not just American interests but humanity, civilization, and progress. Evil cannot be rendered "good." It can only be rooted out, usually through military action, with the United States in the vanguard of "the Great Cosmic Battle between Good and Evil" (Rediehs 2002, 71). Fourth, such evil, threatening, and alienated Otherness is profoundly racialized. This has a dual aspect. On the one hand, the threatening Other is represented in exaggerated racist stereotypes. On the other hand, those "other" races that ally themselves with the United States are depicted as "good," "loyal," and "plucky." A fundamental trope of the American western (the good Indian versus the bad), this distinction between the faithful and the evil Other is today expressed in distinctions between peaceful Islamic "moderates" bravely resisting evil fundamentalist "fanatics."

Finally, the racialized Other can achieve redemption through embracing American superiority and leadership. Days after Pearl Harbor, the influential *Life* magazine instructed Americans on "how to Tell Japs from Chinese," contrasting the "lighter facial bones" of the former with "squat Mongoloid ... flat, blob nose ... Japs [who] show [the] humorless intensity of ruthless mystics."[6] A decade later, during the Korean War, these stereotypes were reversed. The Japanese (no longer "Japs") were now loyal allies in a mortal struggle against suddenly "bestial" and evil "Chinks" (no longer Chinese). Japanese culture became exotic and unthreatening difference, while Chinese culture was suddenly fundamentally suspect and threatening. While Hollywood filmed cross-racial love stories between Americans and alluring (and passive) Japanese women, the Chinese were depicted as ugly, conniving, devoid of humanity, and profoundly menacing.[7]

Americanism assumes that "other people cannot *really* solve their problems and improve their lives unless they go about it in the same way as the United States" (W.A. Williams 1959/1984, 13, emphasis in original). From Jefferson's campaigns against "Barbary Pirates" (Naylor 2006) to the invasion of Iraq, war against an alienated, threatening, racialized Other has been represented as being waged on behalf of universal values and human progress. Defending America's brutal war of occupation in the Philippines, President Theodore Roosevelt asserted in 1903 that "our armies do more than bring peace, do more than bring order. They bring freedom ... The warfare that has extended the boundaries of civilization at the expense of barbarism and savagery has been for centuries one of the most potent factors in the progress of humanity" (quoted in Kramer 2008, 43). A century later, George W. Bush insisted that

> the United States must defend liberty and justice *because these principles are right and true for all people everywhere* ... America must stand firmly for the nonnegotiable demands of human dignity; the rule of law; limits on the absolute power of the state; free speech; freedom of worship; equal justice; respect for women; religious and ethnic tolerance; and respect for private property ... The aim of this strategy is to help make the world not just safer but better. Our goals on the *path to progress* are clear: political and economic freedom, peaceful relations with other states, and respect for human dignity. (Bush 2002a, 1-3, emphasis added)

Americanism also embodies a particular narrative of American wars. Drawing on and supplementing Englehardt's analysis (1995, 16-65), I suggest that six tropes underpin this recurring "American war story."

The first is a tale of *victory and vindication*. Until Vietnam, the story of American arms tells of seamless success against aggressors. Battlefields defeats (the War of 1812, Kasserine Pass) become object lessons in an army of free citizens learning to vanquish professional soldiers. Vindicating exceptionalism, universalism, and manifest destiny, this narrative reflects the justice of America's cause; the superiority of its endeavour, know-how, and enterprise; and the courage, prowess, and ultimate magnanimity of its citizen-warriors.

A second trope recounts the *captivity* of white women (Englehardt 1995, 23-28). First appearing in 1682, over five hundred such accounts were published in the nineteenth century, and they became a staple of the twentieth-century western. Here masculinity and state power commingle in an imperative to protect the weak (white women, never Native Americans); to defend (colonized) territory, property, and (white) personal freedom; and to uphold male authority. Most crucially, captivity narratives "instantly turned the invader into the invaded and created the foundation myth for any act of retribution that might follow" (23).

Third, from Fennimore Cooper's Huron lurking in the forest to massacre Anglo-Americans marching in the open, the trope of the *ambush* of white settlers by cowardly, cruel, and hidden savages constantly reoccurs in the American war story. This provided

> extraordinary evidence of the enemy's treacherous behavior. While all ambushes involved deceit, none was more heinous than the "sneak attack," that surprise assault on a peaceful, unsuspecting people. Pearl Harbor stood at the end of a long line of sneak attacks that helped explain any success a

nonwhite enemy might have against American forces ... In their hearts, *they desired our total annihilation.* (Englehardt 1995, 39, emphasis in original)

The explosion that sank *The Maine;* Pearl Harbor; Filipino or Viet Cong guerrillas who "refused to stand and fight like men"; 9/11; and suicide bombers all exemplify the "cowardice" of those who ambush Americans. Cowardice is quintessentially "un-masculine": the discourse of cowardice exhorts the United States to "heroism," to "fight back with military force lest we became the [emasculated] cowards" (Egan 2002, 55).

Since the United States supposedly wages only defensive war, the ambush trope proves the inhumanity (the "unbeing") of a racialized Other, further legitimizing a ferocious military response in, fourth, a ritualized *spectacle of slaughter:*

This slaughter was meant to be seen. It gave Western/non-Western power relations – and the colonized world that followed from them – a sense of the foreordained. Only when it was reversed, as with the massacre of British general Charles Gordon's forces at Khartoum or George Armstrong Custer's at the Little Big Horn, was it denounced as a horror and an outrage to humanity. Otherwise the sight of such carnage and the production of such casualty figures were considered in the nature of things, visible evidence of a hierarchical order, racially (later, genetically) coded into humanity ...

All these murderous battles ... only reinforced the irrational quality of the Other. To oppose the foregone conclusion of such war seemed so lacking in sanity that a resistant enemy leader was often considered quite mad ... The enemy's incomprehensible infamy and deceit ... ingrained them in the [American] national memory as proof of the righteousness of subsequent acts of vengeance. (Englehardt 1995, 37-39)

A fifth trope depicts the *frontier* as a racialized and gendered zone of confrontation between civilization and barbarism, backwardness and progress, order and disorder. Here the hunter/warrior/vigilante tames the wilderness, pushes back the savages, secures such "liberated" space, dispenses rough frontier justice (McCarthy 2002, 128), and imposes the rule of law in strictly masculine terms. Often abandoned by a cowardly (international) community, despite his wish for a peaceful life, the hunter/warrior/vigilante is often obliged to act alone to wreak terrible and righteous vengeance on "evil doers" so as to establish law and order for an ungrateful community. His necessarily violent labours make possible the work of a second agent of civilization and progress: the settler/businessman who transforms the now-liberated domain into a flourishing and regulated part of the market economy (Slotkin 1992, 51-87).

The final trope running through the American war story is a *fetishism of weapons technology*. From the bowie knife, through the Colt 45, Springfield rifle, Winchester repeating rifle, Gatling gun, "precision" bombing, and the atom bomb to "smart" weapons and the revolution in military affairs, superior weapons technology is depicted as permitting often ambushed and allegedly outnumbered Americans to focus overwhelming firepower and obliterate their enemies.

Each of these tropes leads to "regeneration through violence" (Slotkin 1973, 1992). Embodying a singular un-Clausewitzean notion of war – one focused on killing and eradicating enemies rather than achieving political objectives[8] – they are discursively reproduced through a uniquely American relationship with the past: "As many have noted, our national memory is meager ... the fifties and even Vietnam seem as remote as the Peloponnesian war ... we don't respect our history as Europeans do ... Our talent is for living in the present ... the past itself is suspect: arthritic as well as old" (Sayre 1978, 5). From the Puritans seeking to inscribe the Kingdom of God in the New World, white Americans have constructed a peculiarly forgetful and wishful narrative of origins. Occluding the unpleasant, the seamy, and the violent, this "bowdlerized fairy tale" (Englehardt 1995, 20) forges a linear account of progress and chosen-ness. Expressed in the common American put-down "You're history, buddy," the past disappears into irrelevance. The present and future become a blank slate on which Americanism writes scripts of progress and inclusion. Such "social organization of forgetting" (Kinsman 2005b) discursively affirms and reproduces "authentic" red-blooded American values while simultaneously excluding as un-American the history and values of significant sectors of society, particularly those of black and Native Americans.

Colin Gray (2006, 42) argues that the "culturally ignorant" American way of war frequently induces "self-inflicted damage caused by a failure to understand the enemy of the day." I suggest that such self-inflicted damage grows less out of a failure to understand the Other than a prior inability to comprehend how Americanism imagines the United States *itself*. The Declaration of Independence trumpets the supposedly self-evident truths that "all men are created equal, that they are endowed by their Creator with certain unalienable Rights." Yet, the constitution enshrined slavery among these "rights," directing that slaves be counted as comprising three-fifths of a person. Of the four presidents carved as gargantuan icons into Mount Rushmore, Washington and Jefferson were large-scale slave owners. Lincoln did reluctantly free some of the slaves, all the while suspending habeas corpus, imprisoning politicians and newspaper editors, ignoring Supreme Court judgments, and arguing that black Americans be resettled in Africa. Theodore Roosevelt was an unabashed imperialist whose paeans to vigour, virility, warfare, and superior "Anglo-Saxon blood" would not have been out of place in 1930s Germany (Roosevelt 1923; Slotkin 1992, 29-62).

A society that treats its past this cavalierly is ill-equipped to assess the truth claims of those empowered to command its mythology. And when such truth claims – the "yellow peril," the "Communist threat," the domino theory, or "Iraq has weapons of mass destruction" – invoke national survival, peering through the rose-tinted spectacles of Americanism, the blind eyes of cultural ignorance and paranoia see only what they are instructed to see.

American Militarism and Evolving Geographies of Power

The foundation mythology represented America as pristine space. Before colonization, wrote an historian in 1834, "the whole territory was an unproductive waste ... Its only inhabitants were a few scattered tribes of feeble barbarians ... In the view of civilization the immense domain was a solitude" (quoted in Englehardt 1995, 21-22). Territorial expansion was triply implicated in the founding and growth of the republic. The 1756-63 Franco-British war for empire led directly to the American Revolution. With territorial expansion inscribed in the mercantilist ethos of northern nabobs (W.A. Williams 1961/1973, 77-148), it was likewise "imperative for Virginia's elite," grown prosperous, like other Southern gentry, from a plantation economy that rapidly depleted the soil, that "Virginia had to grow or die" (Anderson and Cayton 2005, 109). Finally, the promise of a vast, open "west" was *the* crucial safety valve in the acute eighteenth- and nineteenth-century class conflicts. Exemplified in Horace Greeley's exhortation "Go west, young man!" migration and the prospect of wealth in "virgin" territory were key ingredients in America's ideological glue. The frontier carried a double promise: that every red-blooded American might strike it rich and that he was free to move where he pleased ("she" would tag along as his faithful helpmeet).

From the outset, the values and economic practices of Americanism constructed an infinitely elastic sense of internal (sovereign) space. This represented the "external" space of the Other as wild and anarchic, obliging

Americans to tame and domesticate it. From the seventeenth century to the 1890 Battle of Wounded Knee, the seizure of Native American land was the *sine qua non* of American geography.

Expansion and expropriation were accompanied by securitization, by the demonization of the barbarous Other as existential threat to the American Self. As war became the principal means of enlarging the republic, "a special ferocity accompanied the push 'westward' and gave a particularly savage quality to warfare, even among Europeans in North America" (Englehardt 1995, 25; see also Anderson and Cayton 2005, 206-46). Americans learned to make war through mass slaughter. The Other was not simply to be defeated and his lands seized; his very mode of life was to be eradicated. "Universal" American values were mapped onto the lands west of the Appalachians via war, annexation, and cultural genocide.

Such elastic geography facilitated a profound distancing of warfare from (white) American society. As the frontier was pushed westward and then beyond the continent, the Other receded ever further from the daily consciousness of "ordinary" (white) Americans. With the exceptions of the War of 1812 and the Civil War, most American wars until the First World War resembled Frederick the Great's definition of a perfect war – one that occurs without the population being aware of it (Holsti 1990, 708). And as the wars in Iraq and Afghanistan show, most daily life in the United States proceeds under the illusion that no war is taking place.

Superior technology ever further removes American warfighters from bloody contact with the body of the Other. This characteristic fetish of high-tech war obfuscates the often indiscriminate slaughter inflicted by American arms. The performance of "Nintendo warfare" by precision-guided munitions, combined with the Pentagon newspeak of "collateral damage" and tight restrictions on which images may be disseminated by the "great hegemonizing power of media culture" (Boggs 2005, xiv), all further distance Americans from butchery committed in their name. The corollary to such distancing of war is the belief in the inviolability of American space and persons. Alone among the major powers, the United States has no folk memory of invasion and occupation (or, as in Britain, a national narrative of narrowly averting such threats). This helps explain the depths of rage, fear, and paranoia elicited by Pearl Harbor and the attacks of 9/11. That the United States should rain fire, death, and havoc on Native American villages, on German and Japanese cities, on Korean and Vietnamese hamlets, and on Iraq and Afghanistan seems part of the natural order. Yet, such things are not supposed to happen to history's "good guys" in their pristine American space. Only evil, cowardly, and barbarous people could commit such outrages against the home of the free and the land of the brave.

Americanism's elastic geography was famously summed up by Frederick Jackson Turner (1893/2003). His frontier thesis held that, by obliging settlers to adapt to new conditions, the frontier was *the* source of exceptionalism, vitality, and freedom. Generating a mercantilist "bonanza economy" (Slotkin 1992, 30), it was the foundation of America's wealth. Since the 1890 US Census declared the frontier "closed," American exceptionalism and wealth should be preserved through expansion overseas. Echoing Turner, a circle of Republican Party bluebloods advocated vigorous and martial imperialism as "an extension of centuries of frontier expansionism" (Adas 2005, 160). The most influential of these, Theodore Roosevelt was an early theorist of both naval power (1882) and the frontier tradition (1889-96/2004). As assistant naval secretary and later as president, Roosevelt oversaw the construction of a powerful navy as the engine of expansion. During his time in high office from 1897 to 1909, the United States annexed Hawaii and seized the Philippines, Cuba, Puerto Rico, Guam, and Wake Island; fought "a bloody colonial war of subjugation" in the Philippines (Stephanson 1996, 75); dispatched marines to Beijing to quell the Boxer Rebellion; and engineered Panamanian secession from Colombia to secure the construction of a canal under US extraterritorial sovereignty.

Yet, these policies provoked fierce domestic opposition. A range of social forces claimed that such imperialism was un-American. The solution was Secretary of State John Hay's 1899 "Open Door Notes." Originally intended to cajole the great powers into allowing American interests into the Chinese ports and territory under their control, Hay's notes sought "to open the world to American enterprise" (Bacevich 2002, 31). Promoting American expansion based not on the seizure of foreign lands but, rather, on motherhood values of equality, freedom, and fairness, the Open Door required only that the world accept that state sovereignty no longer entailed control over national economic space. Winning virtually unanimous support from former anti-imperialists, Hay's policy helped fashion a new domestic consensus just when industrialization and immigration were provoking sharp social and labour conflict. Entering the pantheon of Americanism, the Open Door has been the watchword in US foreign policy ever since. Globalization, and the reorganized topography of power it represents, is its ultimate product.

If war has been the principal instrument to enlarge elastic American space, the projection of force, the conquests, annexations, territorial expansion, and extension of American enterprise have all been predicated on an equally vital aspect of American geography – what Chalmers Johnson (2004, 151-85) terms the "empire of [military] bases." From the days of rival British and French forts in the Ohio valley, a growing network of bases was essential to pushing back the frontier and absorbing Native American and Mexican land. Providing the pegs around which the elastic frontiers of American space were stretched, military bases furnished – if I may mix my metaphors – the jumping-off points for further expansion. The annexation of Hawaii and conquest of Spanish territory in 1898 extended this triptych of bases, frontier, and American space beyond the continent. Then enjoying a "large degree of self-sufficiency" in all key raw materials (G.O. Smith 1926, 116), America's turn-of-the-nineteenth-century imperialism was driven by the need for external markets (W.A. Williams 1961/1973, 27-57).

This would soon change. The navy converted to oil in 1911, and the mechanization of the 1914-18 battlefields made oil the essential strategic commodity. American oil consumption doubled from 1911 to 1918 and quadrupled from 1919 to 1929 (Yergin 1992, 194-209). Although the United States was still the largest producer, Britain, France, and the Netherlands initially excluded American companies from vast new oil fields under their control. As "the face of America was changed by a vast invasion of automobiles," government circles were gripped by "a virtual obsession" with imminent oil depletion. A new sense of strategic vulnerability was reinforced by a growing dependence on rubber and other raw materials lying largely within the European colonial empires (Collings 1924).

Although new domestic oil fields soon ended fears of oil depletion, the collapse of the gold standard and the trade bilateralism and autarky of the 1930s provoked concern that the Open Door was insufficient to secure vital raw materials and essential markets (Yergin 1992, 269). Drawing on fashionable geopolitical theory, a new elite consensus emerged in the late 1930s over the need to prevent potentially hostile states (especially Japan) from dominating trade routes and controlling the oil fields, raw materials, infrastructure, and skilled manpower of European colonial powers (Leffler 1992, 9-15). A key 1940 Council on Foreign Relations study proposed the "enlargement of the United States' economic domain" and expansion of the armed forces to secure military supremacy "within the non-German world" (Shoup and Minter 1977, 128-30). The elastic was stretched accordingly in

September 1940 when, in return for fifty obsolete destroyers, the United States acquired eight western hemisphere bases from a desperate and bankrupt Britain. Within five years, America had military bases on every continent, enjoying "unrivalled military control of the world's landmasses, sea lanes and air spaces" (Boggs 2005, 4) – and of global energy sources and raw materials.

Fearing that "regimented economies" would become "the pattern of the next century," President Truman asserted in 1947 that free enterprise "could survive in America only if it becomes a world system ... the whole world should adopt the American system" (quoted in Fleming 1961, 436). As the United States imposed Western economic interdependence and the dismantling of colonial empires (Gardner 1993; Pollard 1985, 247-49), its global network of military bases fixed a new frontier between (now-Americanized) civilization and (Communist) barbarism. Securing the increasingly deterritorialized international economic space fashioned by US policies, they opened the door for its oil interests, corporations, and arms manufacturers to expand their markets and secure privileged global access to energy, raw materials, labour, and finance. NATO enlargement after 1990 continued this logic, one pushed further by the extension of the "empire of bases" post-9/11. The war against Iraq represents a conscious effort to remap the Middle East and extend the internal space of globalization.

At first glance, 9/11 seems to have provoked scant change in US overseas basing strategy. Pentagon data for September 2001 lists 6,425 US military "locations" in thirty-eight foreign countries (see Table 1.1). Fifteen key Cold War allies accounted for 473 of the 492 large, medium, and small US overseas military locations (including all of the large and medium ones), and for all but 27 of its 243 "other" overseas locations. Further, they made up 97.8 percent of the US$117.7 billion total plant replacement value (PRV) for all listed overseas locations.[9] Five years later, these fifteen Cold War basing countries still accounted for 505 of the 544 large, medium, and small overseas sites (and all the large and medium ones), for all but 38 of its 278 "other" overseas sites, and for 97.3 percent of PRV.

These Pentagon data omit known bases in Bosnia, Kosovo, Bulgaria, Afghanistan, Iraq, Kuwait, Saudi Arabia, Uzbekistan, Kyrgyzstan, Djibouti, and elsewhere.[10] Nonetheless, even the apparently minimal changes shown by these data point to significant post-9/11 modifications to American basing strategy. Although the number of declared military "locations" or "sites" declined by almost one-fifth between September 2001 and September 2006 (from 6,425 to 5,311), the number and percentage of such sites located in foreign countries rose slightly, from 735 (or 12.3 percent of the total) in thirty-eight countries to 820 (15.4 percent) in thirty-nine countries. Total plant replacement value of overseas military sites increased from US$117.7 billion to $126.3 billion, and US military personnel serving oversees jumped from 254,788 to 412,910 (United States, DOD 2002b, 2007b).

Although the Pentagon struggles with bureaucratic inertia (and associated sets of interests), two trends seem clear. The first is a "seismic shift in the center of gravity of American military capabilities from the western and eastern fringes of Eurasia to its central and southern reaches, and to adjacent areas of Africa and the Middle East" (Klare 2005). This reflects, second, a stress on facilities enabling rapid-force deployment and long-range force projection. The introduction of high-capacity C-17 transport aircraft during this period reduced reliance on European staging and refuelling bases, permitting the rationalization and reinforcement of strategic force projection capabilities. Several Cold War bases were closed. The army lost twenty-five overseas bases, while the number of large overseas air force bases rose from five to eight, the total number of navy sites almost tripled, and the Marine Corps acquired three new medium bases.

These changes embody a new binary geography of "disconnectedness" and "ideological reterritorialization"; the "Pentagon's new map" divides the globe into a "functioning core" and a "non-integrating gap," with the latter as the key site of US military intervention (Barnett 2004).[11] This literally maps "the true sources of mass violence and terrorism within the global community, so as to facilitate, at first, their containment through diplomatic and military means, but ultimately, their eradication through economic and social integration" (Barnett 2004). Like eighteenth- and nineteenth-century Native Americans, those Others whose cultural or economic practices do not accord with the "universal" values of Americanism are demonized as unbeings, securitized as a threat and source of contagion. The "empire of bases" delineates the new frontier between civilization and barbarism, "order" and "disorder" (T.L. Friedman 2003, ix-x). The Other's territory is targeted for potential military action until his Otherness can be obliterated through incorporation into marketplace society and the universal paradise of the individual consumer.

The Institutions of American Militarism and Politics in the American State

Having stressed continuities in American militarism, it is necessary to grasp the discontinuities and moments of qualitative change. This section sketches key transitions in the evolution of four interlinked elements of American

TABLE 1.1

Declared US military "sites" overseas

Country ranked by 2006 PRV[a] (2001 rank)		Number of US "locations"									PRV US$m
		Army		Navy		Air Force		Marine Corps		Other Total	
		Total L,M,S[b]	# of L/M	Total L,M,S	# of L/M	Total L,M,S	# of L/M	Total L,M,S	# of L/M		
1 Germany	September 2006	197	0/5	-	-	28	2/0	-	-	62 287	42,685.8
(2)	September 2001	220	1/3	-	-	32	1/1	-	-	73 325	37,670.9
2 Japan	September 2006	14	0/1	35	1/2	19	3/0	21	1/3	38 127	36,765.5
(1)	September 2001	14	0/1	11	4/2	21	2/0	2	1/0	25 73	40,268.5
3 South Korea	September 2006	60	0/3	5	-	11	1/1	1	-	28 105	13,814.5
(3)	September 2001	64	0/2	1	-	12	1/1	-	-	24 101	11,441.8
4 Italy	September 2006	12	-	21	0/1	16	0/1	-	-	40 89	6,312.6
(5)	September 2001	12	-	5	-	11	-	-	-	23 51	4,213.9
5 United Kingdom	September 2006	6	-	2	-	20	1/1	-	-	29 57	5,947.4
(4)	September 2001	1	-	2	-	21	1/1	-	-	31 55	4,942.6
6 Iceland	September 2006	-	-	8	1/0	-	-	-	-	3 11	2,700.5
(6)	September 2001	-	-	1	1/0	-	-	-	-	- 1	3,292.5
7 Diego Garcia	September 2006	-	-	1	1/0	-	-	-	-	- 1	2,541.2
(9)	September 2001	-	-	1	1/0	-	-	-	-	- 1	1,917.8
8 Greenland	September 2006	-	-	-	-	1	1/0	-	-	- 1	2,436.8
(7)	September 2001	-	-	-	-	1	1/0	-	-	- 1	2,418.3

#	Country	Date									
9	Marshall Islands	September 2006	-	-	-	1	1/0	-	-	1	2,436.8
	(10)	September 2001	1	1/0	-	-	-	-	-	1	1,911.3
10	Cuba-Guantanamo	September 2006	-	-	1	1/0	-	-	-	1	2,037.5
	(8)	September 2001	-	-	2	1/0	-	-	-	2	2,012.6
11	Spain	September 2006	-	-	1	0/1	-	-	-	5	1,962.3
	(11)	September 2001	-	-	2	0/1	-	-	-	6	1,598.6
12	Turkey	September 2006	-	-	-	-	8	0/1	11	19	1,421.5
	(12)	September 2001	-	-	-	-	9	0/1	10	19	1,265.3
13	Portugal	September 2006	-	-	-	-	9	0/1	12	21	1,168.1
	(13)	September 2001	-	-	-	-	8	0/1	13	21	990.8
14	Belgium	September 2006	7	-	-	-	2	-	9	18	646.1
	(15)	September 2001	8	-	-	-	2	-	10	20	568.0
15	Baharain	September 2006	-	-	5	-	-	-	3	8	502.6
	(20)	September 2001	-	-	1	-	-	-	-	1	245.5
16	Qatar	September 2006	-	-	-	-	1	-	-	1	384.7
	(no rank)	September 2001	-	-	-	-	-	-	-	-	
17	Netherlands	September 2006	5	-	-	-	-	-	5	10	378.4
	(14)	September 2001	7	-	-	-	1	-	5	13	691.4
18	Bahamas	September 2006	-	-	2	-	-	-	4	6	358.7
	(17)	September 2001	-	-	1	-	-	-	-	1	314.0
19	St. Helena	September 2006	-	-	-	-	1	-	-	1	347.9
	(18)	September 2001	-	-	-	-	1	-	-	1	304.1

▼ TABLE 1.1

		Number of US "locations"											
		Army		Navy		Air Force		Marine Corps					PRV
Country ranked by 2006 PRV[a] (2001 rank)		Total L,M,S[b]	# of L/M	Total L,M,S	# of L/M	Total L,M,S	# of L/M	Total L,M,S	# of L/M	Other	Total		US$m
20 Australia	September 2006	-	-	1	-	-	-	-	-	3	4		331.4
(16)	September 2001	-	-	1	-	-	-	-	-	3	4		343.2
21 Greece	September 2006	-	-	3	-	-	-	-	-	4	7		313.6
(22)	September 2001	-	-	1	-	-	-	-	-	-	1		203.2
22 Luxemburg	September 2006	2	-	-	-	-	-	-	-	1	3		269.0
(19)	September 2001	2	-	-	-	-	-	-	-	1	3		286.3
23 Ecuador	September 2006	-	-	-	-	-	-	-	-	1	1		181.9
(no rank)	September 2001	-	-	-	-	-	-	-	-	-	-		-
24 Singapore	September 2006	-	-	1	-	1	-	-	-	2	4		177.5
(21)	September 2001	-	-	1	-	1	-	-	-	-	2		244.0
25 Denmark	September 2006	-	-	-	-	1	-	-	-	1	2		109.6
(24)	September 2001	-	-	-	-	1	-	-	-	2	3		121.1
26 Antigua	September 2006	-	-	-	-	1	-	-	-	-	1		94.2
(26)	September 2001	-	-	-	-	1	-	-	-	-	1		101.2
27 Oman	September 2006	-	-	-	-	3	-	-	-	1	4		78.2
(27)	September 2001	-	-	-	-	3	-	-	-	-	3		49.7
28 Egypt	September 2006	-	-	1	-	-	-	-	-	1	2		49.4
(28)	September 2001	-	-	1	-	-	-	-	-	-	1		29.7

29	United Arab Emirates (33)	September 2006 September 2001	- -	1 -	- 1	- -	2 1	47.4 8.0
30	Netherlands Antilles (no rank)	September 2006 September 2001	- -	1 -	- -	- -	1 -	46.1 -
31	Kenya (no rank)	September 2006 September 2001	- -	1 -	- -	1 -	2 -	24.8 -
32	Columbia (31)	September 2006 September 2001	- -	- -	- -	6 4	6 4	20.1 13.8
33	Indonesia (32)	September 2006 September 2001	- -	1 -	- -	1 1	2 1	12.3 8.2
34	Peru (30)	September 2006 September 2001	- -	- -	- -	1 3	1 3	9.7 17.2
35	Norway (29)	September 2006 September 2001	- -	- 1	- -	3 6	3 7	6.8 26.4
36	Hong Kong (34)	September 2006 September 2001	- -	- -	- -	1 1	1 1	4.5 6.0
37	Aruba (no rank)	September 2006 September 2001	- -	- -	- -	1 -	1 -	1.6 -
38	Kuwait (no rank)	September 2006 September 2001	1 -	- -	- -	1 -	2 -	0.9 -
39	Canada (38)	September 2006 September 2001	- -	- -	- -	2 1	2 1	0.0 0.0

▼ TABLE 1.1

Country ranked by 2006 PRV[a] (2001 rank)		Number of US "locations"										PRV US$m
		Army		Navy		Air Force		Marine Corps		Other	Total	
		Total L,M,S[b]	# of L/M	Total L,M,S	# of L/M	Total L,M,S	# of L/M	Total L,M,S	# of L/M			
No rank - Honduras (23)	September 2006	-	-	-	-	-	-	-	-	-	-	-
	September 2001	1	-	-	-	-	-	-	-	-	1	122.4
No rank - New Zealand (37)	September 2006	-	-	-	-	-	-	-	-	-	-	-
	September 2001	-	-	1	-	-	-	-	-	-	1	n/a
No rank - France (25)	September 2006	-	-	-	-	-	-	-	-	-	-	-
	September 2001	-	-	-	-	1	-	-	-	-	1	110.4
No rank - Venezuela (35)	September 2006	-	-	-	-	-	-	-	-	-	-	-
	September 2001	-	-	-	-	-	-	-	-	2	2	5.7
No rank - Austria (36)	September 2006	-	-	-	-	-	-	-	-	-	-	-
	September 2001	-	-	-	-	-	-	-	-	1	1	0.4
Totals	September 2006	305	1/9	90	4/4	125	8/5	22	1/3	278	820	126,350.4
	September 2001	330	2/6	32	7/3	128	6/6	2	1/0	243	735	117,764.8

a PRV = plant replacement value
b L = large, M = medium, S = small
Source: Calculated from United States, DOD (2002a, 17–27; 2007a, 77–96).

militarism: threat discourse, strategic culture, force design, and civil-military relations.

For most of its history, the United States faced no external threat. Until the 1940s, the omnipresent fear of the Other focused on representations of domestic threat and contagion (Rogin 1988, 4-32). Despite the central role of warfare in expanding the republic's domain, America's armed forces developed no threat discourse capable of rallying popular support for high defence spending. Except during the Civil War, US strategic culture and force design rested on an insignificant standing army and negligible intelligence-gathering capabilities. So ingrained was the suspicion of standing armies that victory in each major war was followed by wholesale demobilization, reducing the army essentially to a frontier police. Moreover, with the exception of the failed war of 1812-15, America's nineteenth-century wars were waged against societies with an insignificant industrial base. When the United States finally involved itself in European wars in 1917 and 1941, its forces initially found themselves operating military technology dramatically inferior to those of foe and ally alike (Perret 1989, 322, 357).

In the final decades of the nineteenth century, widely circulated writings by two military strategists launched a debate over the need to modernize and enlarge America's armed forces. Major General Emery Upton (1905/1917, vii-xv) argued that excessive civilian control of the military left the country chronically unprepared for war. He proposed revising civil-military relations along Prussian lines: a strong standing army led by professional officers, with minimal civilian interference. However, the extreme unlikelihood of an attack on continental America made it virtually impossible to build support for expanding the army, and Upton's writings began to have a real impact only in the second decade of the twentieth century.

Immediately more significant was Captain Alfred Thayer Mahan's *The influence of sea power on history, 1660-1873* (1890/1957). This located the key to global power in a battle fleet's mastery of the sea and capacity to control maritime choke points. Mahan argued that the United States should acquire a modern navy to develop its commerce, control the Caribbean, and construct a canal across Central America. *Sea power* became "the canonical reference work for the growing naval world community, providing ample historical justification for the vigorous expansion of navies that was already under way" (Stephanson 1996, 84). It furnished the rationale for the 1890 Navy Act, which ended a tradition of passive coastal defence. Within fifteen years, the US Navy was the world's third largest. In the process, "another big business lobby had been created" (Perret 1989, 274-75), one whose interests depended on the maintenance of a big navy (275). The future was being born.

However, this change in force design was confined to the navy. As late as 1939, the army was only the world's nineteenth largest, with little independent offensive capability. Its army air corps had but eight hundred – largely obsolete – combat aircraft. A crash expansion program and vast industrial conversion initiative were launched in January 1939. Within fifteen months, the army had grown from 185,000 to 1.6 million men (Perret 1989, 354-60), and by May 1945 the renamed US Army Air Forces was the world's largest, with over 41,000 combat aircraft and 2.3 million men (USAF n.d.). American military expenditure skyrocketed from 17.5 percent of the federal budget in 1940 to 89.4 percent by 1945, or from just 1.6 percent to 37.1 percent of GDP. As the war shattered all other major economies, measured in constant 1940 dollars, American GDP jumped from US$101.4 billion to $173.5 billion from 1940 to 1945. Unemployment fell from 14.6 percent to just 1.9 percent of the labour force (Tassava n.d., Tables 1 and 3): "The Depression was over. The national defense program had ended it" (Perret 1989, 358).

The transformation of America's armed forces into the world's most technologically sophisticated moved scientific and technological innovation to the forefront of the economy and popular imagination. Full employment, deep labour shortages, and a no-strike pledge by the AFL (American Federation of Labor) and CIO (Congress of Industrial Organization) closed a ten-year cycle of social instability and labour unrest. Despite government efforts to restrict wage increases, "incomes rose for virtually all Americans – whites and blacks, men and women, skilled and unskilled" (Schumann 2003; see also Tassava n.d.). Predicated on massive military expenditure and ever-expanding defence commitments, planned and organized by the federal government, this new prosperity provided a key ideological foundation for the social alliance underpinning the Cold War military Keynesianism and the rapid expansion of American consumer demand that followed. It likewise cast in stone what President Eisenhower would later famously label as the military-industrial complex. Maintaining technology-driven military spending became the key to the profitability of a very significant proportion of American business. The knock-on effects went far beyond firms involved in supplying and equipping the armed forces: America's business class and society at large had become "addicted to military spending" (Hossein-Zadeh 2006, 15-16).

Businessmen and generals were determined that the end of hostilities should not end the bonanza. But such hopes seemed dashed as GDP shrank by 0.36 percent in 1946 (Tassava n.d., Table 7). Amid fears of a depression, the CIO launched "the greatest wage offensive in U.S. history with more than five million workers engaged in strikes across America" (REAP n.d.). To stave off the downturn, President Truman slashed military spending by almost 90 percent between 1945 and 1948 (Tassava n.d., Table 7), crippling key high-tech industries. Military aircraft had accounted for $45 billion of the $183 billion spent on war production (Tassava n.d.). However, the value of all airframes produced plummeted from $16.7 billion in 1944 to just $0.671 billion in 1947, or from 96,000 to just 1,800 military aircraft (Yergin 1977, 342). Demobilization devastated the soon-to-be-independent US Air Force. Within fifteen months, its combat-ready bomber groups were sliced from 218 to fewer than 10. The unsurprising result was a powerful lobby of aircraft manufacturers and generals demanding massive rearmament. The first-ever secretary of the air force, fervent advocate of strategic air power and ardent Cold War warrior W. Stuart Symington, was the president of a company making bomber gun turrets. He "understood better than most that the American aircraft industry would not survive without a fresh infusion of military orders" (Carroll 2006, 109).

The Second World War transformed civil-military relations. For four years, the military had driven national policy, moving from bit players to the lead actors in Washington bureaucratic politics. After the lean 1920s and 1930s, generals and admirals had grown accustomed to massive budgets and vast bureaucratic power and influence. Henceforth, the Pentagon would wield its now immense prestige and resources to retain its preponderant role. Pearl Harbor provided the rallying cry. That "sneak attack" seemed utterly to vindicate Emory Upton: in a world of nasty dictators, the good guys had been woefully unprepared to defend themselves because of a lack of vigilance and perfidious/idealistic politicians unwilling to finance a strong military. Now parodying Poe's raven, the military endless croaked "Nevermore,"[12] insisting that victory had not ended the threat. New enemies would have to be found, or fabricated.

The political balance within the US armed forces had also shifted. The air forces' bombing campaigns were depicted as having played *the* crucial role in defeating Germany and Japan. Emerging as the quintessentially American way of war, bombing embodied US technological superiority, delivered "shock and awe," and distanced the spectacle of slaughter to mere "collateral damage," allegedly reducing American casualties. Having vaporized Hiroshima and Nagasaki, the air force monopolized the world's most fearsome weapon and strenuously promoted air power as America's strategic priority. This produced "a bitter half-decade struggle" (Yergin 1977, 201) between air force and navy. Pulling out all stops to regain its position on the strategic cutting edge, the navy's projects to develop supercarriers and its own strategic bomber capability were sabotaged by the air force in a vicious "bureaucratic bloodletting" (203). Some historians see this bureaucratic war as a key catalyst of the Cold War (Carroll 2006, 102-60; Yergin 1977, 201-20, 336-65).

The bureaucratic power and standing of the military (and particularly the air force) within the American state was transformed, together with the political culture and budgetary logic of that state (Rothkopf 2005, 4-107). Military spending rose by 44.4 percent in 1949 (Tassava n.d., Table 7) – with over half (and 15 percent of the total budget) "related to aviation" (Yergin 1977, 343) – and more than tripled from 1950 to 1953 (Hossein-Zadeh 2006, 76). The military-industrial complex was off and running. Within fifty years, the once tiny Department of Defense had morphed into "the largest company in the world, with more than 3 million employees ... [and] an annual budget of a quarter of a trillion dollars" (Carter and Perry 1999, 191-92).

Seen in Washington as "a veritable revolution in international relations,"[13] the new global doctrine of national security broke with traditional, purely continental defence. The idea of national security "both described a new relationship between the United States and the rest of the world" (Yergin 1977, 195) and prescribed the policies to be followed. It postulated

> the interrelatedness of so many different political economic and military factors that developments halfway around the globe are seen to have automatic and direct impact on America's core interests. Virtually every development in the world is perceived to be potentially crucial. An adverse turn of events anywhere endangers the United States. Problems in foreign relations are viewed as urgent and immediate threats. *Thus, desirable foreign policy goals are translated into issues of national survival, and the range of threats becomes limitless.* (Yergin 1977, 195-96, emphasis added)

Establishing the primacy of national security required dissolving anti-military sentiment and overcoming war fatigue. When President Truman enquired whether the Republican Congress would approve his vastly increased military budget, Republican senator Arthur Vandenberg advised him to "scare the hell out of them" (Stone 2004, 326).

National security doctrine produced crucial modifications in the American security imaginary. The first was an exponential increase in "the paranoid style in American politics" (Hofstadter 1965). The military and the intelligence services now depicted any questioning of their budgets, bureaucratic fiefdoms, and political clout as threatening national survival. Soviet capabilities and intentions were consciously distorted and the Communist "threat" vastly inflated (Leffler 1992, 130-38; Yergin 1977, 336-65). Reds were said to be hiding under beds throughout the United States, a cancer eating away at the body politic, Armageddon poised to happen. Threat could never be expunged; it could only be deterred via a ruthless Otherization of even those Americans who challenged the paranoid definition of America and "its" values. "Un-Americanism" and "appeasement" became, and remain, the most deadly accusations in the American lexicon.

The new gospel of national security generated its own high priests, mandarins, and Inquisition: a new "expertocracry" claiming exclusive knowledge of mortal existential threats said to confront America – all requiring repressive powers, massive military preparedness, expanding budgets, and bureaucratic fiefdoms. Chief among these were functionaries of an array of new intelligence services established following the 1947 National Security Act: the CIA, the National Security Agency, and the Defense Intelligence Agency. This national security priesthood and mandarinate extended far beyond the military and the intelligence agencies. Beginning with the air force's transformation of Douglas Aircraft's research and development branch into the RAND Corporation, a vast web of think tanks, research centres, academics, journalists, and other "experts" joined the minor priesthood, all preaching the national security gospel, scrutinizing the purity of the faithful, and disciplining skeptics and unbelievers. As the American power elite abandoned "any real image of peace" (Mills 1956, 184), the academic discipline of International Relations emerged as an integral element of this military-intellectual complex (Robin 2001), one heavily subsidized by the high priests of the cult. The advent of "realist" international relations theory provided "scientific" rationalization for the rupture with traditional isolationism and suspicion of the military. With war now decreed to be inevitable, those who advocated peace became utopians/idealists/appeasers. Only ever-expanding preparation for war could preserve the republic.

The hitherto relatively weak federal government was transformed into a vast surveillance state, ceaselessly probing the furthest reaches of the planet, plumbing the most private household secrets (Staples 1997). National security (and a radically policed set of approved values enshrined in

Americanism) was now grafted onto the perennial squabbles for turf of localized US politics as the supreme "real American" value and ultimate ideological warrant to legitimize or discredit any actor, sanctify or silence any debate. To be labelled soft on national security was to be painted as un-American, and politically dead and unemployable.

The national security state brought American militarism full circle. Vindicating all of James Madison's warnings, it generalized the belligerent expansionism first exemplified in President Madison's war of 1812. Inscribed in the norms and practices of Americanism and US capitalism since 1775, militarism is more than the simple product of a postwar military-industrial complex, a permanent war economy, or a reaction to Vietnam. It will not depart with George W. Bush nor abate under President Barack Obama's ardent advocacy of Americanism.

Conclusion

Disputing the notion that "Americans in our own time have fallen prey to militarism" since Vietnam (Bacevich 2005, 2), I have advanced two principal arguments: that militarism has *always* lain at the heart of American identity and notions of space, and that understanding such militarism is essential to grasping the particular forms of US hegemonic power and the global order it has fashioned.

Huge upsurges in military spending after 1948 and during the 1980s were crucial to propping up aggregate demand in periods of economic downturn (Hossein-Zadeh 2006, 8-9) and in forging new social alliances that undermined and then destroyed the global left. This, in turn, facilitated globalization and the consequent vast increase in global inequality. Some have argued that, through its very success, US hegemony "has made itself increasingly redundant" (Agnew 2005, 32). As its relative economic and political position weakens, the United States increasingly turns to military might to impose its rules. Real US military spending is estimated to have exceeded US$700 billion or 48 percent of the world total in 2007 (CACNP 2008), being "more than the next 46 highest spending countries in the world combined" (Global Issues 2008).[14] Since the 1980s, the United States has maintained its expanding military presence through growing indebtedness. Even before the financial crisis, its projected 2007 budget deficit was $427 billion, while the deficit for the month of February 2008 *alone* reached a then record $175.56 billion (roughly equal to the budget supplement to finance the wars against Iraq and Afghanistan).[15] By March 2008, total external US debt stood at just under $13.8 trillion (United States, DOT 2008).

Although no other major state has yet challenged America's central position, "the declining hegemon" no longer has "the financial means necessary to solve [global] system-level problems that require system-level solutions" (Arrighi and Silver 1999, 278). Moreover, America's ability to finance its wars and expanding global military commitments depends on the willingness of China and Japan to purchase US Treasury securities.[16]

Since the Second World War, the United States has enjoyed a virtual monopoly in defining the parameters of international security discourse and practice. It largely imposed its post-9/11 global war on terror agenda on both friend and foe. However, the refusal of all but one of its principal allies to participate in the invasion and occupation of Iraq, and the reluctance of most NATO countries to commit their troops to combat in Afghanistan, suggest that America's ideological hegemony over "international security" is weaker than at any point since 1945.

Collectively referred to as "blowback" (Johnson 2000), localized forms of armed resistance to globalization and American dominance have exploded since 1989. Largely taking the form of terrorist attacks, these pose no serious challenge to global capitalism. However, they *do* highlight glaring structural problems in US militarism. American hegemony and the cult of individual consumption have transformed citizens into consumers. Significantly less likely to challenge relations of power and privilege than are citizens, consumers are equally less willing to die in the name of "their" state – particularly in distant countries that patently pose scant threat to their personal security and ability to consume. Manipulating a post-9/11 climate of fear, crying wolf over weapons of mass destruction in Iraq, and lying over alleged links between Iraq and al-Qaeda, the Bush administration was briefly able to rally a new national security coalition. In the medium-term, however, these tactics have sapped the domestic consensus and eroded the manpower necessary for the expanding military commitments. Its growing dependence on Asian bankers aside, America's ability to wage war is further limited by factors similar to those forcing Napoleon's retreat from Moscow: the refusal of the enemy (Vietnamese, Somali, or Iraqi) to "recognize" their own defeat, and the unwillingness of young American males to risk their lives in wars whose rationale escapes them.

Mired in wars in Iraq and Afghanistan, while simultaneously retooling to confront future strategic challenges, the US Army is deeply overstretched. Acute personnel shortages have led to significant modifications in deployment and recruitment practices (United States Army 2008). In 2006, 8,330 so-called moral waivers were granted to previously undesirable volunteers with criminal convictions or charges. Retention bonuses to encourage re-enlistment increased almost ninefold from 2003 to 2006 (Coll 2008, 21). Between 2003 and 2008, almost 43,000 troops were deployed to Iraq "after being deemed 'medically undeployable'" (Harper's Index 2008). The army increasingly relies on foreign nationals lured by the promise of a green card should they survive military service. This creeping mercenarization is reflected in the pervasive privatization of a vast array of logistical, intelligence, and actual warfighting activities (Singer 2005).

The American way of war seems chronically incapable of transcending a purely military mentality in order to develop the appropriate *political* strategies necessary to prevail in the kinds of blowback conflicts provoked by American hegemony:

> The military still does not understand that victory on the battlefield does not equate with political victory. American strategic culture has many impressive features, but lacks a meaningful dialectical relationship and better balance between political and military demands. Strategic culture and military thinking cannot defer to technology or a professional understanding based on RMA, now mutating into Network-Centric Warfare. (Lock-Pullan 2006, 394)

Such incapacity grows out of more than mere strategic culture and bureaucratic inertia favouring conventional forms of warfare. This chronic inability to grasp the political nettle of emerging contemporary forms of warfare is deeply rooted in a form of militarism that shaped the very notion of what "America" is, and what "Americanism" stands for.

NOTES

My thanks to George Archer, Bruno Charbonneau, Thomas Chevalier, Wayne Cox, Frédérick Guillaume Dufour, Pauline Gélinas, Jason Keays, and Tom Naylor for comments and suggestions on an earlier version. Errors of fact and interpretation are mine alone.

1 John Adams, quoted in Lepore (2008, 90).
2 See Boot (2003); Cebrowski and Barnett (2003); Echevarria (2004a, 2004b, 2005, 2006); Gray (2005, 2006); Jager (2007); Kaplan (2007); Lock-Pullan (2006); Mahnken (2003); Record (2006).
3 See Anderson and Cayton (2005); Bacevich (2005); Boggs (2002, 2005); Carroll (2006); Grondin (2007); Hossein-Zadeh (2006); Johnson (2004, 2006).
4 A security imaginary is "a structure of well-established meanings and social relations out of which representations of the world of international relations are created ... The

security imaginary of a state provides what might be called the cultural raw materials out of which representations of states, of relations among states and of the international system are created" (Weldes 1999, 10). A security imaginary thus provides a definition of Self in relation to a particular depiction of the external world. It specifies which "Others" inhabit that external world; represents the relationship of Other to Self; lays out the conditions, contexts, and cultural mechanisms under which the Other becomes represented as threat to Self; and specifies the broad parameters of how to "defend" Self against such a menacing Other. Analysis of the security imaginary of any state must grapple with the cultural representations and practices through which difference becomes securitized *and* institutionalized as threat.

5 Public culture is "the arena in which social and political conflict is played out and in which consensus is forged, manufactured, and maintained, or not. It is the place where all segments of the society either speak to each other or fail to speak to each other – where they must content if they wish to advance their own interests and values or to influence the direction of the larger society. It is a 'place' that exists in print, on the airways, and in the meeting hall" (Fousek 2000, ix) and, no doubt, also now in cyberspace. *Political* culture, on the other hand, refers to the narrower sets of values and practices associated with the predominant political institutions. Political culture is subordinate to, and largely shaped by, public culture.

6 *Life*, 22 December 1941. Reproduced on MIT Asian American Studies homepage, http://web.mit.edu.

7 Examples of the former include *The Teahouse of the August Moon* (1956), *Sayonara* (1957), and *The Geisha Boy* (1958). Examples of the latter include *The Manchurian Candidate* (1962); see Jackson and González (2006).

8 See Colin Gray's analysis (2005, 2006) of "the American way of war" as apolitical, a-strategic, a-historic, culturally ignorant, aggressive and offensive, technology dependent, and firepower-focused.

9 "Large" sites had a plant replacement value (PRV) of US$1.5 billion-plus in 2001 and $1.64 billion-plus in 2006; "medium" sites a PRV of $800 million to $1.5 billion in 2001 and $0.875-1.64 billion in 2006; and "small" sites a PRV of between $10 and $800 million in 2001 and $10 and $875 million in 2006. Including such vital installations as "unmanned navigational aids or strategic missile emplacements" (Johnson 2004, 154), "other" sites had a PRV of less than US$10 million.

10 These data also exclude newer categories of military sites linked to the so-called global war on terror. Consisting of "logistical facilities (an airstrip or port complex) plus weapons stockpiles," what are known as "forward operation sites" or "forward operating locations" house "a small permanent crew of US military technicians but no large combat units." Similarly, so-called "cooperative security locations" have no permanent US presence but are "maintained by military contractors and host-country personnel." These bare-bones facilities allow American forces to "hop in and out of them in times of crisis while avoiding the impression of establishing a permanent – and provocative – presence" (Volman 2006; see also Ral 2008). Among countries reported to have provided such facilities are Algeria, Ethiopia, Gabon, Ghana, Mali, Namibia, Senegal, Uganda, and Zambia. Chalmers Johnson (2004, 153-55) claims that the United States also has secret military sites in Israel.

11 See http://www.thomaspmbarnett.com/images.
12 Edgar Allen Poe, "The Raven," http://www.heise.de.
13 Joseph E. Johnson, chief of the State Department's Division of International Security Affairs, quoted in Yergin (1977, 195).
14 Although Department of Defense spending was just short of US$530 billion (United States, OMB 2008), this excludes wars in Iraq and Afghanistan; nuclear weapons storage, testing, research, and development; the Coast Guard; Homeland Security; weapons grants to allies; interest payments on borrowing to fund previous military spending; and veterans services and retirees payments.
15 "U.S. budget deficit hits record $176 billion," *National Post*, 12 March 2008, http://www.nationalpost.com.
16 Because of declining Japanese exposure, the share of such securities held by Japan, China, and Hong Kong fell from 51 percent to 44 from January 2007 to April 2008 (United States, DOT 2007).

2

The Neoconservative Challenge to Realist Thinking in American Foreign Policy

ALEX MACLEOD

A superficial glance at realist literature published since 11 September 2001 would lead us to conclude that most of the ongoing debates within post-Cold War realist theory have continued unabated. Yet, on closer inspection, one can see that things are not quite the same, and that realists made some changes, but only to the extent that their theory could remain the same. Of course, they had to contend with the problem of including a non-state actor within realism's highly state-centric ontology, but above all, they had to meet the challenge of one of the most important consequences of 9/11: the growing influence of neoconservatism on the foreign policy of the Bush administration, and its advocacy of a security policy in opposition to the realists' emphasis on caution and risk-avoidance.

This chapter begins by looking at how American realists have tried to integrate, and subsume, the consequences of 9/11 into their own conceptual framework. Secondly, it examines neoconservatism as an international relations (IR) theory and how realists have engaged the debate with neoconservatives since 11 September 2001. In the third and final section, it analyzes the neoconservative conception of US national security as embodied in what is now called the Bush doctrine and the subsequent realist response to this new vision of American security.

Realism after 9/11

Christopher Layne (2004, 103) undoubtedly spoke for most realists when he wrote: "Contrary to the conventional wisdom that September 11 'changed everything,' from a geopolitical perspective, the attacks launched by Osama bin Laden changed virtually nothing." Yet, some realists have been uncomfortable with the idea that such a devastating attack, led by a non-state actor against the most powerful state in the world, can be so easily accounted for. Before looking at how realists have tried to cope with this particular problem, it is useful to return briefly to the problems realists experienced in adapting their theories to the end of the Cold War – a moment in history considered by most commentators of international politics to have had a demonstrably more profound effect on the functioning of the international system than the events of 9/11.

For supporters of neorealism, the dominant form of realism during the 1980s, the end of the Cold War did not affect any of the general principles regulating international politics. According to Kenneth Waltz (1993; 2002), for example, all that had changed was the distribution of power between the great powers, the move from the relative stability of bipolarity to the uncertainties of unipolarity. Writing just after the fall of the Berlin Wall, John Mearsheimer (1990) predicted that the post-Cold War era meant nothing more than a trip "back to the future," that is, a return to a more brutal period that would miss the moderating influence of bipolarity. Christopher Layne (1993) noted that we were living under a "unipolar illusion" and that other great powers would rise to balance US power. He was forced to reassess this position a few years later, but without changing his main message that unipolarity could not last (Layne 2006b). This view was hotly disputed by some realists who consider that unipolarity is here to stay, and that the likelihood of the rise of any rivals to US power in the foreseeable future is remote (Brooks and Wohlforth 2002, 2005, 2008; Mastanduno 1999; Wohlforth 1999).

However, despite general resistance to change, especially among neorealists, academic realist theory responded (in part at least) to the new theories that developed after the Cold War, notably constructivism. The latter has been referred to as "an approach" (Hopf 1998, 196), "a method more than anything else" (Checkel 1998, 325), or just "a group of *related* approaches, rather than one completely coherent approach" (Rengger 2000, 80, emphasis in original). Nevertheless, constructivism has presented a serious challenge to realist ontology with, in particular, its emphasis on the importance of ideas, the role of identity in IR, and the need to problematize a state neorealists have construed as functionally identical. Critical constructivists also strongly criticize realism's empiricist epistemology and its positivism.

The most significant realist answer to the constructivist challenge was the emergence of neoclassical realism, which stresses the inclusion of domestic factors in any realist analysis, and which is slowly but surely establishing itself as the dominant version of realism.[1] Another important development in realism, which has affected classical realism and neorealism alike, was the introduction of the distinction between defensive and offensive realism. Supporters of the former insist that states seek above all to maximize their security through defensive policies, whereas adepts of the latter claim that states tend to look for security through maximizing their power and must, therefore, always be prepared to go on the offensive. One of the results of 9/11 was to further blur the fine line between the two.

Given these rather modest responses to the major event to shake IR theory since the Second World War, it should hardly seem surprising that realists also reacted defensively to the impact of 9/11. As several authors have pointed out, the central problem for realism is how to account for 9/11 without contradicting its basic concepts. William Brenner (2006, 508) warns fellow realists that they "should avoid the temptation to diminish the importance of September 11 in order to make the world conform to the expectations of theory." There seems little reason to share the optimism of Jack Snyder (2004, 56) when he claims that, despite certain "conceptual difficulties," "realism is alive, well, and creatively reassessing how its root principles relate to the post-9/11 world."

Although Snyder offers a positive evaluation of realism's handling of 9/11, he puts his finger on one of the most difficult problems for this approach: "How can realist theory account for the importance of powerful and violent individuals in a world of states?" (Snyder 2004, 55). His answer – that the central battles of the war on terror have been waged against two states (Afghanistan and Iraq) – is not very satisfactory. Another leading realist, Robert Jervis (2002, 40), has tried to grapple with the problem by noting that terrorism and 11 September seem to reflect "the declining relevance of states" and that a "world characterized by extensive terrorism is one in which states are not the most important actors." He puts forward two arguments to support this conclusion: (1) terrorist groups are transnational, united by religious and ideological beliefs; and (2) 9/11 demonstrated the importance of globalization not only because the hijackers depended on the efficient movement of information and money but because they were also seeking to stem the global flow of corrupting ideas (see Hataley's Chapter 8).

However, according to Jervis, these events also confirmed the continuing importance of the role of states. First, al-Qaeda owed much of its strength to its ties with the Afghan government, and it is the latter that the United States has held responsible for the attacks. Second, major elements of state power were targeted by the attackers. Third, the American response showed the centrality of states: public opinion looked to the government for protection, and 11 September certainly led to a larger and more powerful state apparatus. Lastly, states were the dominant actors of the international response, with the United States creating a coalition of states to fight the Taliban (Jervis 2002, 40-41).

Jervis' reflections on the role of the state in the events of 9/11 have undoubtedly some validity, but several questions remain. The first is the problem of integrating into a realist theoretical framework non-state groups that have expressed no clear aspiration to create a state. Brenner suggests realists should adopt a more nuanced view of states than the neorealist concept of undifferentiated like-units. He follows Gilpin and others by replacing the concept of the state by the broader one of conflict group (Brenner 2006, 519), but without offering any clear way of doing so. This does not really solve the issue because a nebulous formation such as al-Qaeda is by no means neatly covered by this concept. Brenner (2006, 525) raises another very important point when he remarks that no "plausible explanation for September 11 can exclude ideational variables." Of course, it is true that at least one attempt was made to include such variables in a realist framework: the much-maligned "clash of civilizations" proposed by Samuel Huntington. But few realists, if any, accepted its validity, let alone the idea of trying to incorporate it into their theory.

Realists and the Neoconservative Challenge

If its critics seem to be convinced that neoconservatism constitutes a fairly coherent set of ideas, its proponents seem uncertain and prefer to describe it as a "persuasion" (I. Kristol 2003), as an "intellectual disposition" (Wolfson 2004, 226), as "more a tendency than a movement" (Stelzer 2004a, 8), or simply as a "sensibility" (Muravchik 2004, 254). Despite these expressions of intellectual modesty, neoconservatism has become an identifiable body of thought, with its own internal divisions and debates, and is at least as united as realist and liberal theories.

Like realist and liberal approaches, neoconservatism offers an interpretation of US international behaviour and is engaged in the debates that have dominated mainstream IR theory in the United States since the end of the

Cold War. It is particularly present in those debates that focused on the United States' use of its overwhelming power to ensure international order in the post-Cold War world. At least one academic observer has even claimed that it "emerged as one of the millennium's defining and most controversial perspectives on security and international relations" (M.C. Williams 2007a, 93).

Neoconservatism as IR Theory

Although neoconservatism gained public prominence in the aftermath of 9/11, it has deep roots in American political thought. This is not the place to present the intellectual history of the neoconservative movement.[2] It will suffice to indicate that it finds its inspiration in several strands of American intellectual thought, notably that of American exceptionalism, Wilsonianism and liberal internationalism, realism, and traditional conservatism.

The notion of exceptionalism has always been part of the American view of the world and of American national identity. It conveys not only the idea that the foundation of the United States represents a new form of society and a model type of constitutional government but also that the American state has its own particular view of the world and the place it occupies in it. Above all, this country believes profoundly that it stands for universal values that all peoples, given the chance, spontaneously share. As the Canadian historian Margaret MacMillan pointed out, American exceptionalism has always had two sides:

> the one eager to set the world to right, the other to turn its back with contempt if its message should be ignored ... Faith in their own exceptionalism has sometimes led to some obtuseness on the part of Americans, a tendency to preach at other nations rather than to listen to them, a tendency as well to assume that American motives are pure where those of others are not. (MacMillan 2001, 14)

In the words of a leading neoconservative, "This enduring American view of their nation's exceptional place in history, their conviction that their interests and the world's interests are one may be welcomed, ridiculed or lamented. But it should not be doubted" (Kagan 2004, 88). We find this view expressed in the neoconservative conception of the United States' role in the world as that of "benevolent hegemony" (Kristol and Kagan 1996, 20), as a country with a "messianic impulse ... rooted in the nation's founding principles and [that impulse] is the hearty offspring of the marriage between

Americans' driving ambitions and their overpowering sense of righteousness" (Kagan 2006).

As embodied in President Woodrow Wilson's famous "Fourteen Points," his objective of "making the world safe for democracy," and the notion of collective security as a replacement for power politics, Wilsonianism is considered to be the starting point for modern liberal internationalism. In its modern form, liberal internationalism emphasizes the ideas of multilateralism, defence of human rights, liberal democratic values, and the democratic peace thesis, which postulates that democracies do not go to war against each other. As Tony Smith (2007, 77) argues, liberal internationalism has evolved tremendously over the years and has now entered what he calls the age of "liberal imperialism" as it "grew more and more comfortable backing up its claims to legitimacy with a call to arms not simply in self-defense but especially in order to promote liberal values and institutions over peoples who did not share them." This new form of liberal internationalism, which gave full support to the war in Kosovo, led many of its supporters to back the war in Iraq, at least initially. It easily converged with neoconservative thinking. In particular, neoconservatives adopted and adapted the democratic peace thesis to justify the idea of imposing democracy from above in order to create "zones of democratic peace" (Ish-Shalom 2006). Hence, neoconservatism is "Wilsonianism with a very big difference": neoconservatives "would make democracy possible by deposing dictatorial regimes that threaten American security and world order – using military force if all else fails; they would follow regime change with nation-building; and they would rely on varying 'coalitions of the willing,' rather than on the United Nations" (Stelzer 2004a, 9).

As we will see, a great gulf exists between traditional realists and neoconservatives on many fundamental questions, especially the idea of violating another state's sovereignty to effect regime change. But neoconservatives have retained the ontology of the nation state as the basic unit of the international system, and of hard power (military capabilities) as a measure of a state's power in international affairs. They tend to be dismissive of the value of soft power and, like most realists, mistrust international institutions.

Finally, although traditional conservatives tend to distance themselves from neoconservatives on questions of foreign policy, they share common views on the need to reform the welfare system, lean toward cultural conservatism, and distrust all domestic forms of social engineering. However, neoconservatives are not libertarians, do not eschew budget deficits, accept a much greater social role for the state than most traditional conservatives, and reject their realist stance in foreign policy (I. Kristol 2003).

Although neoconservatism has been part of the American political and intellectual landscape since the early 1970s, it was in decline to some extent by the early 1990s to the point where one of neoconservatism's critics claimed that it was surviving only "as cultural nostalgia rather than distinct politics" (Judis 1995, 129). Even one of its most prominent supporters, Norman Podhoretz, wistfully pronounced the movement dead in early 1996. In particular, he regretted the passing of neoconservative foreign policy:

> In foreign affairs, neoconservatism has not so much lost its distinctiveness within the larger conservative community as its own internal identity ...
>
> At the same time, I can name only a tiny handful who still support the kind of expansive Wilsonian interventionism that grew out of the anti-Communist passions of the neoconservatives at the height of the Cold War and that repeatedly trumped the prudential cautions of the realists among them. Today my impression is that the realists have the upper hand in the neoconservative community, or what is left of it. But whatever the precise balance of forces may be among these contending schools of thought in foreign policy, it has become impossible to define a neoconservative position on, say, Bosnia, or the question of NATO expansion, or how to deal with China. (Podhoretz 1996)

In fact, Podhoretz simply confirmed that the first, Cold War, generation of neoconservatives, guided above all by its general opposition to totalitarianism and by its implacable war against Communism, had lost its raison d'être. However, a new generation, which emphasized generalizing the fight for liberal democratic values under American leadership, began to emerge in the early 1990s. Thus, less than six months after Podhoretz pronounced his eulogy, two members of the new generation, William Kristol and Robert Kagan (both sons of leading first-generation neoconservatives), published an article that became one of the texts of reference for the revival of neoconservative foreign and security policy. Noting that in foreign policy, "conservatives are adrift," they called for a "neo-Reaganite foreign policy" to preserve American hegemony "as far into the future as possible" (Kristol and Kagan 1996, 27). Adopting such a policy had three major implications: (1) an increased defence budget; (2) greater citizen involvement (since it would be "foolish to imagine that the United States can lead the world effectively while the overwhelming majority of the world neither understands nor is involved, in any real way, with its international mission"); and (3) moral clarity, meaning that "American foreign policy should be informed with a clear moral purpose, based on the understanding that its moral goals and its fundamental national interests are almost always in harmony" (27). Fundamental to this neoconservative interpretation of Reaganism was the close link made between domestic and foreign policy: "The remoralization of America at home ultimately requires the remoralization of American foreign policy" (31). In another key neoconservative foreign policy document, they declared, four years later, the need for regime change as the most effective way of ensuring non-proliferation of nuclear weapons: "When it comes to dealing with tyrannical regimes, especially those with the power to do us or our allies harm, the United States should seek not coexistence but transformation" (Kristol and Kagan 2000, 20).

Both texts were written before 9/11. Although it made the Bush administration much more sensitive to neoconservative ideas, the basic tenets uniting neoconservatives over foreign and security policy remained remarkably unchanged after 9/11. According to Irving Kristol (2003), "There is no set of neoconservative beliefs concerning foreign policy, only a set of attitudes derived from historical experience." Four such attitudes can be identified. First, "patriotism is a natural and healthy sentiment and should be encouraged by both private and public institutions." Second, world government is "a terrible idea since it can lead to world tyranny." Third, "statesmen should, above all, have the ability to distinguish friends from enemies." Finally, and this is a major point, for a great power, the notion of national interest is not simply a "geographical term." It must go beyond the mere territorial so that the United States "will always feel obliged to defend, if possible, a democratic nation under attack from nondemocratic forces, external and internal" (I. Kristol 2003).[3] Another leading neoconservative, Joshua Muravchik, writing six years after 9/11 and more than four years after the beginning of the war in Iraq, noted that "some kind of common neoconservative mentality endured beyond the cold war" whose elements still make up the "neoconservative mindset." Namely:

- Moralism, which made neoconservatives despise dictators and their acts of aggression and recognize that "America had gone farther in the realization of liberal values than any other society in history." America was "a force for good in the world."

- Internationalism, and not just for moral reasons but also because "America's security could be affected by events far from home, [so] it was wiser to confront troubles early even if afar than to wait for them to ripen and grow nearer."
- Trust in the efficacy of military force, and doubt that "economic sanctions or UN intervention or diplomacy, per se, constituted meaningful alternatives for confronting evil or any determined adversary."
- Belief in democracy both at home and abroad. (Muravchik 2007, 21-22)

As recent history suggests, this moralistic and idealist view of American foreign policy has had significant practical consequences. There is no need to cover that ground again here. The story of the war in Iraq has been told time and time again. Yet, what even the most committed neoconservatives now see as a failure is interpreted more as a failure of execution than one of conception. William Kristol even goes so far as to claim that, despite being weakened by the Bush administration's poor performance, "neoconservatism is today stronger than ever, for it continues to provide the most plausible basic guidance for America's role in today's world" (W. Kristol 2004, 76). For Muravchik (2006), neoconservatism is not dead, for "it can be renovated and returned to prominence, because it remains unrivalled as a guiding principle for US foreign policy in the Middle East and beyond."

The Realist Debate with Neoconservatism

As we will see in the next section, realists were much more active vis-à-vis the Bush doctrine and the war in Iraq. However, as M.C. Williams (2007b, 216-17) argues, "Contemporary realism has by and large failed to come to terms with the neoconservative challenge at its most fundamental levels." Many realists would reject such a charge on the grounds that they are solely concerned with explaining the functioning of the international system and not with the cultural and ideological foundations of public policy that lie at the heart of the neoconservative project. That being said, neoconservatives have strongly criticized realism and have engaged in a form of debate with realists.

It sometimes proves difficult to know exactly where to locate this debate. Much of the confusion comes from the very indeterminate nature of realism itself. Beyond the now accepted distinctions between various forms of academic realism (classical realism, neoclassical realism, neorealism, defensive realism, offensive realism), the relevance of realism has also become very much a part of the internal debate within American conservatism. However, it is vitally important not to conflate the conservative implications of realist theory for international politics and conservatism as a general political philosophy.[4] Although it is true that realists of all stripes base their theory on what they claim to be the immutable features of the international system, it does not follow that all academic realists consider either that this system is just or that change *within* the system is neither possible nor desirable.

The situation is made no clearer by the fact that, in spite of the very real differences between neoconservatism and realism, many neoconservatives consider that "what so many disparage as 'neoconservatism' is a variant of realism" (Owens 2006). Charles Krauthammer (2004, 16) has even proposed a neoconservative version of realism, dubbed "democratic realism," which shares the general neoconservative belief in the virtues of democracy but not the will to intervene on all occasions: "We will support democracy everywhere, but we will commit blood and treasure only in places where there is a strategic necessity – meaning, places central to the larger war against the existential enemy, the enemy that poses a global mortal threat to freedom." Under these rules, Iraq qualifies but, as far as Krauthammer is concerned, Kosovo did not.

Despite such references to realism, neoconservatives disagree profoundly with most of its basic tenets, especially those associated with the *realpolitik* of Henry Kissinger, the *bête noire* of most neoconservatives. As we have already seen, neoconservatives do not share the realist conception of the national interest, which they consider far too limited and prosaic. A former neoconservative intellectual, Francis Fukuyama, captures very well the moral and cultural objections that neoconservatives harbour toward all realists:

> Realism can at times become relativistic and agnostic about regimes; realists by and large do not believe that liberal democracy is a potentially universal form of government or that human values underlying it are necessarily superior to those underlying nondemocratic societies. Indeed they tend to warn against crusading democratic idealism, which in their view can become dangerously destabilizing. (Fukuyama 2006, 37)

The Bush Doctrine

Today most observers would likely agree with Robert Litwak (2002-03, 58) that the events of 9/11 did not really change the structure of IR, but that "they did usher in a new age of American vulnerability." Debates have been about how to deal with this feeling of increased vulnerability. The Bush administration's answer was the publication, in September 2002, of the *National security strategy of the United States of America* (NSS), which was revised in March 2006.

In his address on the State of the Union in January 2002, President Bush had already sketched out the main points of what has become known as the Bush doctrine, which he further elaborated on in a speech made at West Point in June 2002. In particular, he declared that containment and deterrence were no longer sufficient doctrines for defending against terrorism, that US security "will require all Americans to be forward-looking and resolute, to be ready for preemptive action when necessary to defend our liberty and to defend our lives" (White House 2002). Just what was meant by "preemptive action" was spelled out in the NSS, which immediately became the centre of the debates over how far the United States should and could go to defend its security. A second issue that concerned many within and outside the country was the implicit declaration of war against so-called rogue states. The NSS was clear that the United States would act multilaterally if it could, but also that it would not "hesitate to act alone, if necessary, to exercise our right of self-defense by acting preemptively against ... terrorists, to prevent them from doing harm against our people and our country" (Bush 2002a, 6).

The NSS defined first the main threat to the United States and the international system: "The enemy is terrorism – premeditated, politically motivated violence perpetrated against innocents." Furthermore, in the NSS the United States declared that there was "no distinction between terrorists and those who knowingly harbor or provide aid to them" (Bush 2002a, 5). Preemption and prevention were now synonymous, but it was more than simply arguing for the right to first-strike against an imminent threat: "To forestall or prevent ... hostile acts by our adversaries, the United States will, if necessary, act preemptively ... in an age where the enemies of civilization openly and actively seek the world's most destructive technologies, the United States cannot remain idle while dangers gather" (15). As far as the NSS was concerned, this was nothing new, and the United States "has long maintained the option of preemptive actions to counter a sufficient threat to our national security" (15). Key among other preventive actions was to avert the acquisition of weapons of mass destruction by rogue states and their possible dissemination to terrorist groups. Rogue states were those states that "brutalize their people"; "display no regard for international law"; "are determined to acquire weapons of mass destruction ... to be used as threats or offensively to achieve the aggressive designs of these regimes"; "sponsor terrorism around the globe"; and "reject basic human values and hate the United States and everything for which it stands" (13). Although no state seems to fit this portrait exactly, the document named Iraq and North Korea, two of the original members of the infamous "axis of evil."

In many ways, the NSS deserves its description as "a quintessentially neoconservative document" bestowed on it by an iconic neoconservative, Max Boot (2004, 22). Although it made no explicit reference to regime change, the NSS affirmed the need to stand "firmly for the nonnegotiable demands of human dignity: the rule of law; limits on absolute power of the state; free speech; freedom of worship; equal justice and respect for women; religious and ethnic tolerance; and respect for private property" (Bush 2002a, 3). In a fervour of American universalism, the NSS stated that "the United States must defend liberty and justice because these principles are right and true for all people everywhere" (3). In the global war against terrorism, in "a war of ideas," the United States "will never forget that we are fighting ultimately for our democratic values and way of life" (6-7).

Assessing how much this document has actually impacted American security policy is no easy task. It may well be, as Trachtenberg (2007) argues, that the principle of preventive war has a long history in US foreign policy. However, as Litwak (2002-03, 60) points out, there "are strikingly few prior cases in which military force was either used or seriously contemplated for purposes of pre-emption." Unsurprisingly, neoconservatives welcomed the Bush doctrine. Thomas Donnelly (2003) hailed it as a policy "likely to shape U.S. policy for decades to come" that "reflects the realities of American power as well as the aspirations of American political principles." Despite some reservations about the administration's unilateral tendencies, Cold War historian John Lewis Gaddis understood it as a "plan for transforming the entire Muslim Middle East: for bringing it, once and for all, into the modern world." According to Gaddis, the NSS could be "the most important formulation of U.S. grand strategy in over half a century" (Gaddis 2002, 55-56). On the other hand, President Bush's then security adviser Condoleezza Rice (once considered a traditional realist) offered a much more modest reading of the NSS and of its pre-emption and prevention doctrine. According to Rice (2004, 82), the strategy has three pillars: (1) defending the peace "by opposing and preventing violence by terrorists and outlaw regimes"; (2) preserving peace "by fostering an era of good relations among the world's great powers"; and (3) extending the peace "by seeking to extend the benefits of freedom and prosperity across the globe." She played down the novelty of prevention and pre-emption by declaring:

> This approach must be treated with caution. The number of cases in which it might be justified will always be small. It does not give a green light – to the United States or any other nation – to act first without exhausting other means, including diplomacy. Pre-emptive action does not come at the beginning of a long chain of effort. The threat must be very grave. And the risks of waiting must far outweigh the risks of action. (Rice 2004, 83)

Realists were not convinced that this attempt to qualify the Bush doctrine changed the fundamental thrust of the NSS.

Realist Responses to the Bush Doctrine

The theoretical debate between realists and neoconservatives over the Bush doctrine and the war in Iraq focused on three key issues: the strategy of containment, the balance of power, and preventive war. In the end, on all three counts realists challenged neoconservative ethics.

On containment, to the neoconservatives who claimed that containing Saddam Hussein was not viable because of his "character and the record of his behavior" (Lieber 2003, 19), Mearsheimer and Walt (2003, 50) replied that, on the contrary, Saddam Hussein had always behaved as a rational actor and that "scrutiny of his past dealings with the world shows that Saddam, though cruel and calculating, is eminently deterrable." In other words, containment works, especially where nuclear weapons are involved, because, in the words of Kenneth Waltz, "it [containment] deters other countries from using their weapons in ways that would endanger manifestly vital interests of the United States or those it supports" (quoted in Kreisler 2003).

Thus, most realists found little need to revise a strategy that served so well their notion of security during the Cold War. The question of balancing is another issue, and one of the most debated topics within realism itself since the end of the Cold War (Ikenberry 2002; Paul, Wirtz, and Fortmann 2004; Vasquez and Elman 2003). At the heart of this debate is the question of how a state should ensure its security when it feels threatened by the power of another state or group of states. Does it join the threatening state or states (bandwagoning), or does it "balance" or counter the power of the threatening state by allying itself with other states and allies (balancing)? Most realists have historically argued in favour of balancing state behaviour.

For Mearsheimer (2005), one of the main distinctions between realists and neoconservatives lies in the neoconservative belief that "international politics operate according to 'bandwagoning' logic" and that fear of US power will cause other states to join the United States rather than challenge it. This bandwagoning logic inspired the domino theory that justified the war in Vietnam (though the logic was reversed, as a Communist victory would, it was argued, make states join the Communist camp). The same logic was adapted to the war in Iraq on the mistaken belief that the "Iranians, the North Koreans, the Palestinians and the Syrians, after seeing a stunning victory in Iraq, would all throw up their hands and dance to Uncle Sam's tune" (Mearsheimer 2005).

According to Richard Jervis, we should not be totally surprised by the actions of the Bush administration because "power is checked most effectively by counterbalancing power." For Jervis, there lies the "problem" of the post–Iraq invasion international situation. The United States has always claimed its objective to spread liberalism and democracy throughout the world, but "having so much power makes this aim a more realistic one." The new assertiveness of American hegemony was simply "an accident waiting to happen," which does not mean that it *had* to occur. It is "the combination of power, fear, and perceived opportunity" that led the Bush administration "to seek to reshape global politics." It believed that without US intervention, "the international environment will become more menacing to the United States and its values" and that "strong action can help increase global security and produce a better world" (Jervis 2003, 84). By arguing that the Bush administration overestimated US capacity to go it alone, Jervis implicitly supported the position of offensive realists such as Mearsheimer, who claimed that the pursuit of global hegemony is an illusion that can never be attained (Mearsheimer 2001, 40-42).

Many realists have advocated a return to what they conceive as America's historical grand strategy: a strategy of offshore balancing where the United States uses its power selectively to counter the direct threats to its vital interests (Layne 2006a; Schwartz and Layne 2002; Walt 2005). Others have concluded that although unipolarity prevents the forming of a conventional balance of power, a new form of balancing appears to be emerging. Unable to practice "hard" balancing against the United States (which would involve such measures as military buildups or alliances), major powers have resorted to "soft" balancing: "Actions that do not directly challenge U.S. military preponderance but that use non-military tools to delay, frustrate, and undermine aggressive unilateral U.S. military policies" through international institutions, diplomacy, and economic measures (Pape 2005, 10). Signs of soft balancing are observed, for example, in the ways in which several powers, including France, Germany, Russia, and China, reacted to the US decision to intervene in Iraq with or without UN Security Council approval, and in the Russian hard-line position on Kosovo's independence.

One issue on which all realists agree is their total opposition to the notion of preventive war. Not only does this idea set aside the more prudent and, in their eyes, more effective strategy of containment, it is also based on what they see as faulty reasoning and has thus little chance of achieving its objectives. For Walt, the NSS's argument that rogue states must be prevented from getting weapons of mass destruction because they could make them available to terrorists is implausible. It seems highly improbable that such regimes would hand over weapons of mass destruction obtained at great cost and high risk to uncontrollable terrorists, all the while knowing that exposure was possible and they would thus be susceptible to US retaliation (Walt 2005, 224). Most realists would also agree that putting preventive war at the centre of United States national security policy has seriously damaged the country's international image, by making it appear "eager to use force – at times and places of its own choosing – whether or not a genuine threat was actually present" (Walt 2005, 225).

For neoconservatives, the "fact" that the United States is a benevolent hegemon and a "force for good in the world" provides a sufficient basis for an ethical foreign policy. Neoconservatism represents a classic example of what Max Weber called the "ethics of conviction," which emphasizes the principle of "doing the right thing" whatever the cost. It is a strong element found in liberal approaches (especially after the Cold War) and more recently in the discourses of Tony Blair, George W. Bush, and many supporters of the idea of humanitarian intervention. Realists react strongly to the suggestion that because they reject this form of moralism, they are advocating policies based on pure *realpolitik*. Following in the footsteps of the founder of American realism, Hans Morgenthau (1967, 10), who wrote that realism "considers prudence – the weighing of the consequences of alternative political actions – to be the supreme virtue in politics," realists subscribe to an "ethics of responsibility." Such an ethical standpoint considers the consequences of actions rather than their motives. In the words of Richard Betts (2007, 142), if realists are guilty of a tragic cast of mind, "it is because they notice how often the enthusiasm of righteousness yields destruction instead of salvation."

Conclusion

Well after the events of 11 September and Iraq, realists have persisted in denying there was any reason to make profound theoretical adjustments to explain the new realities of world order. This is not surprising given that realists argue that "international politics is the same damn things over and over again: war, great power security and economic competitions, the rise and fall of great powers, and the formation and dissolution of alliances" (Layne 1994, 10). Such theoretical "stubbornness" leaves us with the impression of a theory on the defensive, one much more intent on showing where neoconservatives went wrong than questioning its own premises.

The post-9/11 debates between realism and neoconservatism remind us that IR theory has political consequences, especially American IR, which often offers explicit prescriptions for the conduct of US foreign policy. Each offers a very different view of the world and the ways in which the United States should conduct itself or contribute to global order. In a post-9/11 "realist world," the United States might have insisted on playing its leadership role. It might even have launched a war against the Taliban in Afghanistan to root out the immediate terrorist threat, but it would not have got involved in any long-term nation-building venture. Moreover, it is highly unlikely that it would have invaded Iraq without hard proof that it represented a direct threat to American security or interests. The strategy of containment would have likely been the preferable option. In short, a realist world would have been business as usual, with its emphasis on promoting stability through global and regional balances of power.

Instead, under neoconservative influence, the United States used its hegemonic position to promote and impose democratization and liberal values, and thus to create a "zone of democratic peace" (Donnelly 2000, 2). Zealous neoconservatives discussed the use of military force to accomplish such objectives in places such as Iran, but also the use of more "energetic" strategies in democratizing countries such as China and Saudi Arabia. Although geopolitical realities have made such a policy highly unlikely, a neoconservative world would be relatively turbulent, as the quest for establishing zones of democratic peace would certainly meet resistance on the part of the undemocratized.

Throughout the Cold War, realism was undoubtedly the dominant school of foreign policy at the theoretical level, and it has remained very influential since. However, only two presidents, Richard Nixon and George H.W. Bush, can really be considered to have made realism the basis of their foreign policy. All the others have practised a mixture of liberalism and realism, and have, to different degrees, incorporated within their policy a vision of American exceptionalism. Herein lies the fundamental irony of American realism: to dominate the theory of foreign policy but to be neglected and sometimes vilified by many foreign policy makers. On the other hand, as Brian Schmidt and Michael Williams (2007) have eloquently argued, neoconservatism has succeeded in tapping into certain major themes of American history and political culture, especially the notion of American exceptionalism. The latter has a deep resonance across the political spectrum and at all levels of American society. Deliberate attempts by realists to treat the United States as a "normal" great power and thereby to exorcise exceptionalism probably explain to some extent their modest influence on the actual practice of American foreign policy.

NOTES

1 There have also been attempts to establish closer links between realism and mainstream constructivism, but they have not led to anything lasting yet. See Barkin (2003) and Sterling-Folker (2002; 2004).
2 See Halper and Clarke (2004) and Heilbrunn (2008) for a critical account. See also M. Friedman (2005) and Ehrman (1995).
3 For an in-depth analysis of the neoconservative conception of the national interest and its fundamental importance, see M.C. Williams (2005) and Schmidt and Williams (2007).
4 This distinction is crucial. *Academic* realism belongs to the field of IR theory, whereas *conservative* realism is an integral part of conservatism as a political philosophy or ideology, and separates most traditional conservatives from neoconservatives. Clearly, some academic realists also identify themselves with the conservative domestic agenda, but many academic realists would agree with Kenneth Waltz, who claims that "there's no way to directly read from theory to policy conclusions. People who say realists are hard line conservatives are doing that" (quoted in Halliday and Rosenberg 1998, 373). In this same interview, Waltz said he thought "Carter was an especially good president on foreign policy" (ibid.), a view with which neither traditional conservatives nor neoconservatives would agree.

PART 2

CONSTRUCTING GLOBAL ORDER AT HOME AND ABROAD – THE CASE OF CANADA'S MISSION IN AFGHANISTAN

3

Managing Life in Afghanistan
Canadian Tales of Peace, Security, and Development

BRUNO CHARBONNEAU AND GENEVIÈVE PARENT

Canada is known as an international promoter and broker of peace. In Afghanistan, this peacekeeping tradition was often at the centre of the debates for and against the Afghan mission: Was the war in line with the tradition, or was it time to forgo the tradition in view of a transforming international security environment? Yet, in these discussions of Canada's role in the world, the *kind* of peace that Canada promotes is rarely debated.[1] Hence, "peace" takes a universal and idealistic form. This leads to a historical narrative of Canadian peacekeeping that is fraught with difficulty because it focuses on militarization, force, or coercion as an indicator revealing if Canada is making peace or war, if Canada is a true peacekeeper or a mythical one, or if Canada should wage war or promote peace. In Afghanistan, the Canadian mission was authorized and legitimized in the name of international security and stability first, but ultimately as a humanitarian war that linked Canadian security and prosperity to Canada's vocation in promoting peace, security, and development abroad (see Nossal's Chapter 4). In other words, the humanitarian and peace tradition was reinvented, reimagined, and rewritten in order to accommodate for the fact that Canada was engaged in war.

To understand this repackaging, though, it seems necessary on the one hand to unpack the concept of peace. A critical examination of peace unravels the simplistic and naturalized assumptions underpinning common perceptions about Canada's role in the world. That Canada wages war against "scumbags" (to use the expression of former Canadian chief of the defence staff General Rick Hillier for the Taliban) in the name of global stability is not a contradiction but goes hand in hand with "traditional peacekeeping"; with promoting a (kind of) peace, (some) security, and (a type of) development. By unpacking peace, we can locate Canada within a global order where it actively participates in the construction and management of a hegemonic, US-led, and Eurocentric world order. Our analysis underlines the complementary nature of what is often perceived as contradictory or paradoxical: the peacekeeper or peace-builder that wages wars. Examining the meanings of peace shows how the Canadian government can implicitly (re)define it in a self-interested manner (and rooted in a specific historical context) that is then promoted on the faith in Canada's traditional peaceful and universal vocation. When the concept of peace is implicitly defined in universal terms, no debate is required because its nature is unquestioned and unquestionable. To deconstruct peace suggests that Canada is fighting for a peace defined in self-interested and Eurocentric terms, one that participates in a so-called peace-building enterprise of global proportion rooted in a Western will to power.[2]

On the other hand, Canadian tales of peace, security, and development have a legitimating capacity that is ultimately linked to representational practices that hide or obscure the violence deployed in the name of peace, security, and development. In Afghanistan, we argue that Canadian peace-building efforts are grounded in gendered and orientalist representations, in a hegemonic imaginary of Afghan life (women and children in particular), that authorize and legitimize both the war and the humanitarian management and administration of Afghan life. That is, Canada's war is often represented as a peace-building mission to the benefit of an ideal Afghan individual who is in a perpetual condition of victimhood: the victim of the Taliban, of underdevelopment, of conservative Islam, of illiberalism; a victim that needs to be "saved" by the Canadian soldier of peace. Such images are inaccurate and misleading, for they conceive Afghan life as homogeneous in both condition and nature and thus transform it into a body-subject to be managed and governed by international peace-builders. Instead of allowing for multiple and intersubjective forms of peace, instead of allowing the Afghan "victim" to participate fully in its own peace and thus in its own political empowerment, Canada's war participates in the global management of peace and war, of victims of war, Afghans generally, and so resembles a post-colonial effort to impose a global order assumed to be universal.

Canadian Tales of Peace

It is essential to provide the international political context to the construction of Canadian tales of peace.[3] Considering the context of global order leads us toward a fundamental question: *What kind of peace* does the Canadian state promote, build, and wage war for? Indeed, war "has always been used to establish, expand, and objectify a specific version or conceptualization of peace that is just in the eyes of defenders or aggressors" (Richmond 2007, 249).

As Oliver Richmond argues, in Western political thought and policy framework, peace is often depicted as having "an ontological stability enabling it to be understood, defined, and thus created." Particularly observable within the orthodoxy of the discipline of international relations, peace tends to be defined as either the antonym of war or as a universal form that informs the "orthodox assumption that first the management of war must be achieved before the institutions of peace can operate, at a global, regional, state, and local level." In this mindset, the key instruments to achieve peace are militarization, force, and coercion, while peace itself is "imbued with a hegemonic understanding of universal norms, now increasingly instilled through institutions of governance" (Richmond 2007, 250). In the Canadian context, and despite a recurrent emphasis on peacekeeping and peace-building, the theorization of peace has been obscured historically by debates about war and conflict, more specifically about Canada's role in NATO and at the UN, and about its relationship with its American neighbour. Promoting and building peace, including the practice of peacekeeping, was mainly conceived as a Western practice resulting from the perceived necessities of Cold War power politics.

Peace, understood as simply the absence of overt (and largely state) violence, has roots in, and is reminiscent of, Cold War politics and attitudes.[4] Peace is thus very often synonymous with national defence and security. For instance, one of the basic assumptions that supported the wide consensus on the direction of Canadian policies during the Cold War "was that the most serious threat to international peace and global human welfare was international communism and that the strength of the United States was the primary bulwark against its spread" (Pratt 1983-84, 120). From this common assumption, we distinguish two general interpretations of the Canadian peacekeeping imaginary. First, the detractors argue that the image of the Canadian peacekeeper is largely an aberration, a historical misrepresentation of what is involved in peacekeeping, or sometimes even an obstacle to the pursuit of the national interest. It is often argued that Canada has a proud military tradition that is distorted by the myth and dream of peacekeeping-Canada. In the aftermath of 11 September, this viewpoint was defended fervently. As J.L. Granatstein (2007, 1) vehemently writes: "We are in a war against terror that will affect us even as Canadians hope in vain that it will not. It is Canada's war because we are a First World nation-state firmly within the Western tradition, and in this struggle (which is on the verge of becoming existential) we need to bolster our defences, military and ideological" (see also Maloney 2006-07). Afghanistan is understood as a war against an *enemy* and not as an enterprise in peace-building per se: "Canada is fighting in Afghanistan because an Afghan government supported those who planned and executed an attack against the World Trade Center and the Pentagon" (Stein and Lang 2007, 290). As the argument goes, to pretend that Canada is doing anything other than waging war is to be seriously mistaken and to undermine the mission, efforts, and sacrifices of Canadian troops.

The second interpretation is based on a strong belief in Canadian liberal values and peace expertise but is nonetheless intertwined with the same understanding of peace. For the advocates, the "myth locates Canada as an altruistic and benign middle power, acting with a kind of moral purity not normally exhibited by contemporary states and confirms Canada's premiere status as one of the most experienced peacekeeping countries in the world" (Whitworth 2004, 85). Within the myth, peace takes on an explicit universal and idealistic form that has its roots in liberal thought and that, in Canada in the 1990s, took the shape of "human security." The Canadian minister of foreign affairs, Lloyd Axworthy, defined human security in opposition to state security, claiming that

> human security is much more than the absence of military threat. It includes security against economic privation, an acceptable quality of life, and a guarantee of fundamental human rights. The concept of human security recognizes the complexity of the human environment and accepts that the forces influencing human security are interrelated and mutually reinforcing. At a minimum, human security requires that basic needs are met, but it also acknowledges that sustained economic development, human rights and fundamental freedoms, the rule of law, good governance, sustainable development and social equity are as important to global peace as arms control and disarmament. It recognizes the links between

environmental degradation, population growth, ethnic conflicts, and migration. (Axworthy 1997, 184)

However, as Mark Duffield (2007a) argues, beneath an apparent concern for human life and a cosmopolitan ethic, human security reframes geopolitics and redefines threats to the national interest in biopolitical terms of underdevelopment, environmental collapse, economic marginalization, pandemics, bad governance, and so on. Such factors identify underdeveloped peoples that can, in a globalized world, produce international instability. It also identifies the state as indispensable for guaranteeing human security. Duffield (2007b, 238) argues that human security reiterates the centrality of the state as the producer of security because it is built on "the humanitarian distinction between effective and ineffective states; some states are better than others at supporting the human security of their citizens." By distinguishing between effective and ineffective (failed or fragile) states (see O'Meara's Chapter 1), and thus by constructing an inequality of states, the idea of human security embodies the idea of the responsibility to protect where "sovereignty over the life of people living within ineffective states has become internationalized, negotiable, and contingent" (Duffield 2007b, 240).

For both the supporters and the skeptics of Canada's peace vocation, the target or potential targets of intervention are ineffective states. For the latter, ineffective states can harbour terrorism, while, for the former, these states also represent a moral obligation. Both supporters and skeptics articulate the necessities of limiting political life within the state by articulating the impossibility of political life outside the state. Despite debates over the practice of Canadian intervention abroad, over how peace can be attained (through waging war or peace-building), both groups share complementary assumptions and conceive of peace in the same manner. Peace is associated with the ideas of security, development, progress, and modernity as incarnated by the nation-state. Peace can thus be produced through nation- and state-building or, as Michael Ignatieff (2003) calls it, "empire lite." This kind of peace entails a Eurocentric vision of world order that suggests international management, tutelage, and trusteeship of ineffective states by effective states, whether through the use of force, coercion, or diplomacy. As Richmond (2007, 251) puts it, "Many assertions about peace depend upon actors who *know* peace then creating it for those that do not, either through their acts or through the implicit peace discourses that are employed to describe conflict and war in opposition to peace." Further examination of the historical relationship between liberal claims to universal reason and imperialism can reveal the liberal paradox underpinning the Canadian mission in Afghanistan: the desire to promote the ideals of life, liberty, and freedom while also authorizing the use of force, legitimizing death that is not murder, and accepting illiberal forms of political rule.

Imperial Wars of Liberal Peace

Within the liberal ideological and intellectual tenets that frame many arguments and debates about Canadian politics and foreign policy, it is anathema to many observers, politicians, and ordinary citizens to think of Canada's role in the world as having any part of an imperialist urge or will to power. Canadian liberal values and norms are assumed to protect the nation from such an urge. An important exception has been critical feminist scholars of Canadian foreign policy who have partly pointed to how liberalism and the values it carries can be reconciled and in fact intertwined with imperialist or illiberal impulses. For example, Ann Denholm Crosby argues that Canada's human security agenda, despite its humanitarian appearance, is supported by an understanding of security that "remains the face of power acting in its own interests behind the mask." By conceiving of the security of the world's peoples as dependent on a prosperous global market economy, she writes, the "human security agenda is meant to address the range of insecurities produced or exacerbated by global market forces even as the government's main foreign policy interest, the pursuit of prosperity and employment for Canadians through the global economy, serves to reinforce those forces" (see A.D. Crosby 2003, 90-107). Similarly, Sandra Whitworth's analysis of the Somalia Affair – where Canadian soldiers abused, tortured, and killed Somalis in 1993 – underlines crucial contradictions and suggests "how Canadian representations of nation and military depend on the benign and altruistic image of Canada as peacekeeper – an image that is fundamentally at odds with the roles soldiers are expected, and indeed were *created*, to perform." But more importantly here, Whitworth argues that at the same time as Somalia was destroying the myth of Canada as peacekeeper, the affair also reconfirmed the common conceptions of militarized manhood, agency, race, and civilization, especially through the federal commission that followed and mainstream media representations of the events. Once the contradiction of the morally superior soldier of peace was exposed, it had to be silenced, for it revealed the raced and gendered dynamics of peacekeeping: "Peacekeeping as a practice confirmed not only visions of the Canadian state but also the qualities possessed by the men of the Canadian military – appropriately masculine, exercising choice, sent from a country that helps others, coming from a civilized world of superior race" (Whitworth 2004, 85-109; see also Sjolander, Smith, and Stienstra 2003).

These examples of critical feminist analyses suggest that Canadian liberal values and norms, and their global projection on the basis of a claimed universalism, are not necessarily incompatible with illiberal practices. As John Gray pointed out:

> Liberalism, which in its applications to personal conduct aims for toleration and even pluralism, is in its political demands an expression of intolerance, since it denies the evident truth that many very different forms of government may, each in its own way, contribute to an authentic mode of human well-being ... *All non-liberal societies stand condemned*, together with the excellences and virtues which they harboured. (Cited in Greener 2007, 297, emphasis added)

B.K. Greener argues that this condemnation of non-liberal societies emphasizes the division between the domestic and international spheres and derives from a fundamental teleology of linear progress. The latter belief implies that "there are certain levels of civility within domestic and international society that are to be measured on liberal terms ... [The paradox that emerges] is that toleration is extended to others within the liberal sphere but is not necessarily offered to those without" (Greener 2007, 298). Consequently, as one can observe in the post-Cold War discourses of the end-of-history euphoria and the clash-of-civilizations gloom, key binaries (inside/outside, self/other, effective/ineffective, civilized/barbarian) can be construed, maintained, and reproduced to serve liberal forces and interests. In other words, liberal peace does not inevitably extend to non-liberal societies because "this notion of peace is not necessarily applicable to states that have not attained a certain kind of democratic representation. 'Uncivilized' nonliberal regimes may be seen as legitimate targets as they have no representative character in liberal terms" (Greener 2007, 310).

There has been a general lack of concern in studies of Canadian global policies for the historical links between the Canadian (liberal) internationalism tradition and imperialist practices, or even for the legacy of the colonial relationship in the contemporary workings of the international system. Technically, Canada was never a colonial or imperial power, which might explain why Canadian foreign policy is very rarely, if ever, conceived in imperial or post-colonial terms (except perhaps in its relationship with the United States). But Canadian actions abroad do not take place in a political or ideological vacuum, nor in a world of impenetrable borders where Canada can export peace outside. The kind of peace that Canada advocates has deep historical roots, and its nature can only be fully appreciated within the larger evolution of global order and American hegemony (see O'Meara's Chapter 1). Put another way, Canadian involvement in Afghanistan should be interpreted only through the historical construction and reproduction of the forms and means of American, Western, and Eurocentric hegemony. As Duffield points out, the general disregard in international relations for the links between liberalism, imperialism, and colonialism has worked to conceal the liberal paradox and, thus, the fact that the liberal order has divided nations and peoples into either biologically determined races or, more recently, politico-cultural civilizations: "The dichotomies that liberalism establishes between the civilized/barbarian; developed/underdeveloped; effective/ineffective, for example, are accepted as normal and unremarkable because, since the dawn of modernity, they have been experienced as a legitimate *developmental* challenge. Development is the essence of a specifically *liberal* imperialism and its associated politicocultural racism" (Duffield 2007b, 230, emphasis added). Canada's vocation to promote liberal values and norms, while in theory noble, has also the effect of promoting Eurocentric categories that work to pigeonhole, classify, and manage the peoples of the world.

Canada's War of Security for Development

After 9/11, security concerns overshadowed developmental ones, though the latter never disappeared. Indeed, it seems that security is uncritically linked to a developmental challenge. According to the Canadian government, the traditional security concerns of the Cold War disappeared with the Soviet Union, "only to be replaced by new and more complex threats that have proved difficult to address." In the new-found "fluid nature of the international security environment," the priority of Canada's "role of pride and influence in the world" (Canada, DFAIT 2005) has been unambiguously identified as ineffective states.

Failed and failing states pose, it is argued, a dual challenge for Canada. In the first instance, the suffering these situations create is an affront to Canadian values. Beyond this, they also plant the seeds of threats to regional and global security. They generate refugee flows that threaten the stability of their regions. More ominously, the impotence of their governing structures makes them potential breeding grounds or safe havens for terrorism and organized crime (Canada, DND 2005, 5).

In a nutshell, we observe the merger of Canada's peaceful vocation with its national interest in fighting global terrorism. Ineffective states represent a humanitarian challenge offensive to Canadian morality that, if left alone, could also threaten Canadian security and global stability. This merger needs the efficient/inefficient dichotomy in order to justify war as a tool for building a kind of peace and development.

This merger and associated dichotomy have two crucial and intertwined policy implications. First, it creates a de facto inequality between states: those that know peace and those that do not. The concept of the ineffective state is usually deemed important and commonsensical, but it is also recognized as poorly defined, vague at best, and indeterminate at worst. Broadly defined as a lack of state capacity, ineffectiveness embodies the idea that political problems are instead institutional, technocratic, and cultural and, thus, that solutions are to be found in the practice of state-building. Consequently, Canadian and international peace- and state-builders readily assume that "states and citizens can be capacity-built and empowered by correct practices of external regulation" (Chandler 2006, 56). The idea of ineffectiveness implies an inequality between states that justifies the intervention of effective states inside ineffective ones. It construes the sovereignty of ineffective states as contingent, negotiable, and internationalized (Duffield 2007a).

Second, in policy terms, the significance is that the concept of human security "is woven into the strategy for rebuilding failed and fragile states," and that the "*stable* state" is re-emphasized as "a crucial institutional framework for realizing and protecting individual human rights" (Welsh 2006, 916, emphasis in original). For Duffield (2007a, 80, emphasis in original), "Liberalism's recurrent dichotomy between civilization and barbarism reappears as the humanitarian differences between *effective* and *ineffective* states. This division, which highlights the differing capacities and political will of states, is the essential basis of human security and the responsibility to protect."

These two policy implications converge in the discourse around the "new security environment." The international security environment of the twenty-first century is summarized in the widely accepted truism that security without development is doubtful, and that development necessitates security (Charbonneau 2010). Within this ideological framework, peace is associated with international *stability* and redefined according to ideas of dangerousness and instability that can threaten the zone of peace. Whether or not one can point to a specific conflict or threat does not matter because one can always identify the world of underdeveloped and illiberal states as the source of (potential) threats. In this mindset, to promote peace is to wage war, and to wage war is to fight for peace. The Canadian Armed Forces fight wars to promote development and thus "will be called upon to perform wide-ranging tasks, from delivering humanitarian assistance, to separating warring factions, to establishing the conditions – even in the midst of conflict – for the rule of law, democracy and prosperity to take root" (Canada, DND 2005, 32). In practice, this means an emphasis on approaches and concepts that link security and development: 3-D (defence, diplomacy, and development), whole-of-government, and three-block war. For the Canadian military, these speak to the fluid and chaotic characteristics of the new international security environment (Charbonneau and Cox 2008). We suggest instead that when Canada promotes security for development, it participates in the humanitarian management of Afghan life.

The Management of Afghan Life

The rest of this chapter examines what it means, concretely, to promote peace, security, and development in Afghanistan. Tales of peace, security, and development can legitimize and authorize Canadian international interventions, notably in the context of Canadian domestic politics. More importantly, such narratives usually obscure the violence that is deployed where practices of peace, security, and development are enacted and enabled. By analyzing what has been done so far to "save" or "help" the Afghan people, we can better understand the meanings and effects of promoting security and development by means of waging war.

Canada's "ultimate aim is to leave Afghanistan to Afghans, in a viable country that is better governed, more peaceful and more secure" (Canada 2008, 3). Or as the Independent Panel on Canada's Future Role in Afghanistan put it, the objective "is not to create some fanciful model of prosperous democracy, Canadian objectives are more realistic: to contribute, with others, to a better governed, stable and developing Afghanistan whose government can protect the security of the country and its people" (Manley et al. 2008, 33). The key words are "more," "better," and "stable." There has been no attempt to make of Afghanistan a prosperous country such as Canada. Overall, in these official documents, it is made very clear on several occasions that development in Afghanistan means first and foremost global and regional stability, and security for Canada. Canadian efforts will continue to focus on supporting "a more capable Afghan national government that can better provide for Afghanistan's security, manage its borders and *sustain stability* and reconstruction over the longer term" (Canada 2008, 3, emphasis added). It is an enormous challenge, but so far Canadian efforts, and the military in particular, have allegedly met with "significant successes in their strategy of 'clear, hold and develop'" (Manley et al. 2008, 13). In this way, development is directly linked to the fight against insurgents. Development is made synonymous with counter-insurgency tactics and is defined as a technique of security.

This strategy to build a "more peaceful" Afghan state for guaranteeing security is rooted in liberal thought and its key binaries. It can be witnessed at two related sites. First, it is well known that Afghan women's rights and freedom were strategically used to authorize and legitimize the invasion of Afghanistan (see Byrne's Chapter 7; also Hunt 2002; Russo 2008; Whitworth 2002). But we go one step further. This focus on women (and children) produces a discourse of an *ideal Afghan victim* as the target of peace-building. This abstract construction of Afghan life is needed to fit with the conventional images and understandings of Western governments and societies about Afghan life, and women in particular. This ideological construction of the nature and condition of Afghan life renders it non-political, non-social, and powerless, thus susceptible to being helped and saved according to Canadian and international standards of civilized life. Hence, the help provided to such a fantasy is not only inappropriate but often symbolic and prone to strategic use and other political objectives. Second, the actual Canadian (and international) developmental efforts have yet to change significantly the condition of Afghan life. They have been strictly limited and defined to serve the war effort. Canada's signature projects are meant to win the "hearts and minds" of Afghans, argued to be necessary to support the military campaign and sustain a "more stable" security environment. We now turn to our analysis of these two sites of strategies for the management of Afghan life.

Women and Children: Innocence in Victimhood

Afghans are conceived of on Eurocentric understandings of the roles of men and women in liberal modern society. These pre-existing gendered narratives distinguish between women, children, and men and older boys. Specifically, explicit and purposeful images of women and children are referred to continuously in order to capture an abstract condition of *innocent victimhood*. Such imagery authorizes the protection of the "objectively innocent"

(Carpenter 2005) and participates in the construction of simplified understandings of the conflict and intervention. Innocence does away with the requirement of knowing the victim and her or his needs because it homogenizes the victim's nature and condition. The "victim must be seen as entirely lacking agency ... [and] must be unambiguously 'innocent'"; pure "victim status" or innocence is crucial to convince the saviour of the victim's inability to help her/himself (Carpenter 2005, 316). Women and children are powerful symbols to convey both innocence and victimhood (young men of draft age are usually excluded, as they are perceived as active or likely combatants) because they are implicitly identified through the dualism of civilization/primitiveness, good/bad, modern/premodern. The image of oppressed women is often interpreted as a powerful sign of premodernity or tradition (see Byrne's Chapter 7).

This image of the innocent victim is deeply rooted in gendered and orientalist assumptions, as it construes an innocent Other who needs to be saved and a guilty Other (the Taliban) who needs to be eradicated. Furthermore, for women and children, innocence means political apathy and irrelevance, as political activity is associated with men. The latter are politically active and often associated with the "combatants." The former are often innocent victims, that is, passive agents who are subjected to the horrors of war and sufferings of backwardness. Of course, Afghan women, like all women in war zones, are active socially and politically. Women engage in a great variety of roles, including "fighters, community leaders, social organisers, workers, farmers, traders, [and] welfare workers," with motives as varied as the men's (Pankhurst 2003, 158). This variation ranges from attempts at minimizing the effects of or at ending violence to participating directly or indirectly in combat (El-Bushra 2000; Jacobson 2000; Pankhurst 2003). However, to conform to victim status, the active role of women in war and in the peace processes must be silenced and left in the shadows of the men's actions, the men being the "doers" (Pankhurst 2003, 157). Furthermore, the association "of 'women and children' ... infantilizes the women of Afghanistan, denying them both adulthood and agency, affording them only pity and a certain voyeuristic attraction" (Shepherd 2006, 20).

This imaginary of premodern and innocent Afghan femininity also encapsulates all Afghan women without discrimination. Afghan women are perceived as a homogeneous group no matter how important the differences in their condition might be: rural versus urban, poor versus wealthy, Islamic versus secular, educated versus uneducated, from different social, age, and class backgrounds or regions, and so on. Consequently, more often than not, "the approaches adopted in the delivery of assistance have relied on standardised, 'one-size-fits-all' blueprint solutions, rather than seeking genuinely to understand and harness the traditional mechanisms that women have established for leadership in the past" (Barakat and Wardell 2002, 911; see also Farhoumand-Sims 2007; Zulfacar 2006).

The association of women and children with words such as "victim," "vulnerability," and "innocence" is not new or unique to Afghanistan. Because of deep-rooted gender beliefs, they make better symbolic victims. To elicit the sympathy or interest necessary to support an operation such as that in Afghanistan, the production of an acceptable victim is very useful. This strategic purpose of using the allegations of the maltreatment of women to justify military intervention should come as no surprise, as it is rooted in long-held gender beliefs. As Azarbaijani-Moghaddam (2007, 134) writes, the "decision to opt for military intervention against the Taliban ... continu[ed] a historical trend of using women's rights as a political pawn."

A popular and authoritative example of the effects of this innocence-in-victimhood status comes from the symbolic importance of the burka "problem." The Afghan woman is depicted regularly as a silent and passive victim of the burka who needs to be "liberated only by Western military intervention" (Rostami-Povey 2003, 267; Russo 2008). She is without initiative and almost incapable of finding ways to survive or to cope under Taliban rule. However, through decades of war, Afghan women have worked in groups and organizations building solidarity and cohesion among relatives, friends, and neighbours within their communities. Under Taliban rule, many women kept working and were engaged in income-generating activities (teaching, producing and exchanging goods and services, sewing, knitting, hairdressing, and much more), either overtly or clandestinely. Many Afghan women risked their lives to turn their homes into underground schools mainly for girls and women, but also for boys. They used their burka to hide notebooks, books, pens, and other objects. Many women were caught by the Taliban and were persecuted, jailed, and tortured, but a number of men also died because they supported women developing clandestine networks, associations, and organizations (Rostami-Povey 2003). Moreover, some Taliban policies were successfully softened, suggesting that change was possible through non-confrontational approaches (Barakat and Wardell 2002; Khattak 2004). For instance, the Taliban officially agreed to open schools for girls in Kandahar and Kabul in the last months of their reign. The Taliban were also aware of the clandestine schools run in Afghans' homes, and they allowed Afghan women to run bakeries (Khattak 2004).

In the end, we shall probably never know how many Afghan girls were being clandestinely educated before 2001, but we do not actually know either how many Afghan girls are being educated in Canadian-built schools now. All that we know is that there is more violence, war, and death than before (UN News Centre 2008a, 2008b).

The innocent Afghan victim is the implicit and often explicit target of Canadian and international peace-building efforts. In Canada, it is woven with the peacekeeping myth of the soldier who builds peace. It is a victim who has suffered from war, but mainly from backwardness and illiberal (Taliban) rule, and thus can be saved by soldiers of peace.[5] This gendered and orientalist construction allows us to see how Afghan life is implicitly defined in a self-interested manner that authorizes its management for purposes, objectives, and interests other than its betterment.

Development Efforts as Counter-Insurgency
Overall, we identify two key narratives supporting the peace-building efforts in Afghanistan that work to conceal development as a technique of security. First, the efforts are legitimized by inaccurate accounts of pre- and post-Taliban rule that, in particular, claim an unquestionable improvement in the condition of women since the US-led invasion. This discourse obscures the fact that, in the 1990s and prior to the Taliban coming to power, women's conditions worsened as they were kidnapped, raped, and murdered by the US-supported mujahedeen who fought the Soviet Union in the 1980s (AIHRC 2007; Zulfacar 2006). The same discourse masks and conceals that the government of Hamid Karzai has been responsible for human rights violations, has often been hostile to human rights and democracy, and is a government partly composed of fundamentalists and warlords who have long histories of animosity and violence (Ahmed-Ghosh 2006; Farhoumand-Sims 2007; Suhrke 2008). The second assumption is that of the passive innocent victim of the burka discussed above. We presume that the West's concern about the oppressive nature of the burka is the least of Afghan women's worries, if one at all. Indeed, their daily concerns relate mostly to their lack of access to housing, food, education, employment, health care, and safe childbirth conditions, and the removal of landmines (Miller and Gall 2002; Womankind Worldwide 2008).

This camouflage politics dismisses the many reports that show deteriorating conditions since the 2001 invasion. Afghanistan remains one of the harshest countries to live in, especially for women: it has the highest maternal mortality rate; it is the only country where suicide rates are higher among women than men; it has one of the highest rates of domestic violence in the world; it is a place where increasing numbers of women self-immolate to escape a dire life of domestic abuse and servitude, forced marriage, and other social customs; it is a country where girls as young as eight years old are married to elderly men; and it has a rate of 60 to 80 percent forced marriages (AIHRC 2008; CPHD 2007; UNIFEM 2008). A survey found that 82.7 percent of Afghan women experienced violence (psychological, physical, sexual, or forced marriage), and 62 percent "experienced multiple forms of violence" (Global Rights 2008, 1). Moreover, Afghan women experience prejudice and discrimination from the police and court officials. Women are jailed for adultery (where rape is defined as a form of adultery) and for fleeing home (Human Rights Watch 2009).

The 2007 *Afghanistan human development report* (CPHD 2007) points to the 2007 human development index (0.345), which fell slightly from 2004 (0.346). This is partly because of the following: life expectancy at birth was estimated at 43.1 in 2005, compared with 44.5 in 2003; the probability at birth of not surviving to age forty is estimated at 0.419; while levels of malaria and tuberculosis have decreased significantly, "health indicators for both women and children remain exceptionally low" (CPHD 2007, 1); as much as 68 percent of Afghans lack durable access to clean water; 50 percent of children under five are underweight; despite a remarkable rate of economic growth, it has not reduced extreme poverty and hunger in any significant manner, with 6.6 million Afghans not attaining their minimum food requirements and 24 percent of households suffering from poor food consumption (CPHD 2007, 18-34; see also Womankind Worldwide 2008). Moreover, while the gross school enrolment ratio rose to 59.3 percent in 2005, up from 45 percent in 2002, the boy-girl ratio remains largely in favour of boys (CPHD 2007, 19), and female illiteracy is estimated at 88 percent (CPHD 2007; Womankind Worldwide 2008, 41). The number of girls in secondary school also decreased by 4.7 percent per annum during 2004-05 (UNIFEM 2008). Attacks on schools, teachers, and students remain a significant obstacle to education, especially for girls. For instance, between April and August 2009, 102 schools were attacked (arson, explosives), 105 teachers and students were killed, and 200 students – 196 of them female – were poisoned (Human Rights Watch 2009). Sexual violence and harassment of girls attending school have also been reported (see UNIFEM 2008). In short, despite Canadian and international promises to improve life conditions and women's rights, and despite their claims to significant achievements, the vast majority of Afghans have yet to see the fulfillment of these promises and are worse off than before 9/11 (Donini 2007; Farhoumand-Sims 2007; Human Rights Watch 2009; Khattak 2004; Kitch and Mills 2004). Seeing a number of their short-term gains disappearing, Afghan women who advocate for their rights still have to put their lives at risk, especially outside Kabul or other major urban centres.

Many Afghan women have been the victims of a "backlash against any new-found freedoms" (Pankhurst 2003, 161). That is, as international donors work to rapidly transform Afghan society, the result is often strong cultural resistance that can exacerbate the level of violence against Afghan women. Social norms become entrenched, leading to even more prejudicial treatment of women. For instance, in 2006, the Afghan department for the promotion of virtue and the prevention of vice – initially established during Taliban rule – was reinstated without much protest from the international community (Amnesty International 2007; Asia Foundation 2006; CPHD 2007; Human Rights Watch 2007; Senlis Council 2006, 2008; Womankind Worldwide 2008).

The overall aid effort has also been criticized for its lack of coherence, its unsuitability or irrelevance to Afghan wants, its corrupted practices, and much more. For instance, there seems to be no or very little partnership between Western NGOs or contracting companies and local organizations in Afghanistan. Local organizations "are frequently sidelined in favour of better known, urban-based figures who speak the 'language' of Westerners and are able to connect with influential foreigners" (Womankind Worldwide 2008, 53). And while many projects could be accomplished at a much lower cost by Afghans, Western contractors are disproportionately privileged, "sometimes [even when they have] exorbitantly high bids" (51). In addition, many projects focus on non-material development that consists of short-term workshops or social projects such as those that aim at teaching Afghans "modern" gender relations and the workings of a market democracy. The limited resources and efforts involved are invariably taken away from the immediate needs of material development, including access to clean water, health care, and improved sanitation facilities (Cardozo et al. 2005; Donini 2007).

Despite numerous reports to the contrary, it is quite amazing how the Canadian government and its NATO allies have multiplied, with mainstream media complicity, claims of the substantial progress of "real" development in Afghanistan. It has been quite common to hear about the fast-growing Afghan economy, the millions of refugees who returned to Afghanistan after 2002, the millions of children (especially little girls we are told) who went back to school, and the roads, hospitals, schools, and other infrastructure that are being built. Antonio Donini (2007, 158) talks of a "perception gap ... the significant disconnect between how outsiders and local communities view what is happening in the country." He finds a deep disconnect between the aid community's understanding of peace and security and that of Afghans. He notes that the popular view among Afghans "is that 'the foreigners are here to get rich' ... Aid agencies turn up unannounced, make an assessment and then disappear without result. If they do turn up again, their work is often viewed as superficial and unsustainable" (165-66). According to Donini, the deep malaise among Afghans over the international mission reflects "significant levels of alienation ... [and] revolves around three Ds: disillusionment, disempowerment, disengagement" (163).

Conversely, in early 2008, the Canadian International Development Agency still maintained that "Canada has been helping [Afghans] ... to confront these challenges by supporting high-impact initiatives ... The results have been nothing short of remarkable: thousands of projects have been completed so far, providing wells, irrigation systems, power lines, rural roads, clinics, and other institutions and infrastructure."[6] But as the Senlis Council (2006, 2008) has repeatedly and flatly stated: Canada has little to show for the aid money it has spent in Afghanistan since 2002.[7] How can we account for such contradictions? How can we accept the claims of developmental progress in Afghanistan by the Canadian government and its allies despite abundant evidence to the contrary?

In June 2008, in its first report to Parliament, the Government of Canada recognized for the first time that the security situation had deteriorated and that development aid had not produced sufficient results.[8] Many recommendations of the Independent Panel on Canada's Future Role in Afghanistan were adopted. The overall solution was to bring the security and development agendas closer together in order to "rebalance" the military and civilian programs: "Diplomatic, development and security operations are being aligned more closely and altered for more immediate and lasting effect." The objective was "for better integration of security, governance and development operations" (Canada 2008, 3, 5). Despite such realignment, the main focus remained the war. For the period 2008-11, the government identified six priorities. First, $99 million was allocated to security (other than the war), that is, for training, mentoring, and equipping the Afghan army and police and to build the administrative, logistical, judicial, and correctional capacities to support the activities of the police and army. Second, $210 million was pledged to help the Afghan government provide basic services, including the two so-called signature projects to restore the Dahla Dam ($50 million) and to build and repair fifty schools in Kandahar ($12 million). Third, Canada promised $111 million for humanitarian assistance, including $60 million for polio eradication, the third signature project. Fourth, $32 million was targeted for strengthening Afghanistan's ability to manage its border with Pakistan. Fifth, $355 million was allocated to promote democratic development (financial and technical support of upcoming elections; collaboration with international donors to provide technical and financial resources to support the Independent Elections Commission; building institutions and technical expertise). Last, $14 million was allocated to building mechanisms for promoting national reconciliation. The total money projected for the building of a "more peaceful" Afghanistan amounted to $821 million over three years, compared with only $741 million over the fiscal years 2001-02 to 2006-07. However, all six of Canada's new priorities came with an important caveat: "Specific allocations are subject to adjustments in response to changes in the complex Afghan environment."[9]

If this money is indeed spent where it was intended, it will likely have an impact. But it does not compare to the financial cost of Canada waging its war in Afghanistan. The numbers are difficult to assess but are nonetheless revealing: $6.1 billion from fiscal 2000-01 to 2006-07 according to the Manley report (Manley et al. 2008, 32) or anywhere between $7.7 and $10.5 billion according to the Office of the Parliamentary Budget Officer (Canada, OPBO 2008).[10] More importantly, the intended impact of development projects seems oriented largely toward improving the conditions for military victory (or "sustainable stability") in a context described as political warfare over "the will of the people" where, it is said, insurgents use asymmetric warfare tactics, including the targeting of civilians. In other words, as then chief of the defence staff Hillier has often reminded the Canadian public, Afghanistan is first a battle for the "hearts and minds" of the population. In counter-insurgency warfare, the population is the last arbitrator, the target of military strategies, and the space where the "enemy" manoeuvres (see Stein and Lang 2007, 211-13). This mode of warfare "within population" emphasizes the perceived need for hearts-and-minds military campaigns. Such campaigns draw attention to the long-standing relationship between counter-insurgency and development because the military must be directly involved in activities that are construed as humanitarian or as part of developmental efforts (Duffield 2007a, 130). In this mindset, Canada's new emphasis, the so-called signature projects, is quite telling. They concentrate on Kandahar, where Canadian troops are deployed, and they symbolize the better and closer coordination between security, development, and diplomatic operations for the "strongest ... more immediate and lasting effect" (Canada 2008, 1, 4). They are construed as crucial tools to support the Canadian strategy of "clear, hold, and develop" and to help the Afghan government consolidate its power and authority in the face of a distrusting population (see Canada 2008, 1-4; Manley et al. 2008; Stein and Lang 2007, 210-29).

As Christian Olsson argues, counter-insurgency and the hearts-and-minds leitmotiv do not represent a tactical mode of operation as such, but a general strategy of governance and a rationale to authorize the modern use of force. Counter-insurgency and hearts-and-minds have a long colonial history inextricably linked to the political legitimation of the use of force through the diversification of the means of military actions (Olsson 2007). Put another way, Canada's policy priorities in Afghanistan (for 2008-11 and beyond) might promote development, but a type of development akin to a technique of security for building "more peaceful, better governed, and more secure" Afghanistan – akin to a technique of management of Afghan life.

Conclusion

Canadian tales of peace, security, and development are historical and political productions that can be (re)written with purpose. They usually serve the power, influence, and interests of various actors and can support multiple political projects. It is in this abstract but deeply political space that Canada can redefine, revamp, and reimagine its role in the world. Such tales, however, can be imagined only if Canada is theoretically separated from its global and historical context. The peacekeeping myth serves such a purpose very well. By distinguishing Canada from the United States, and by blurring the line between war and peace, and between security and development, it carries claims of political change while ultimately denying it. By obscuring Canada's role in the production and management of American hegemony and global order, and by merging Canadian tales of war with tales of peace, it can be claimed that Canada's war objectives in Afghanistan are "consistent with Canada's history of international engagement, and with principles that Canadians recognize as just and reasonable" (Manley et al. 2008, 20). Our critical analysis, on the other hand, takes us further than a simple re-evaluation of Canada's role in the world: it takes us toward a critique of Canadian liberal values, way of life, and political system.

NOTES

1 As discussed below, one of the key exceptions comes from critical feminist scholars of Canadian foreign policy.
2 Here, we are not concerned with whether most Canadians believe in the peacekeeping myth. This is another (empirical) question that Kim Richard Nossal examines in his chapter. Rather, we assume the standpoint that the myth is mostly an elitist project. That is, it is constructed and maintained by, and mostly for the consumption of, Canadian governing elites (especially political and military elites).
3 For an overview of the peacekeeping myth, see Whitworth (2004).
4 On the forgotten yet significant and broad impact of the Cold War on politics and society, see Nehring (2010).
5 In July and August 2008, we went through every single page of the official website "Canada's engagement in Afghanistan," and that of the Department of National Defence. Overall, we found that the Canadian government's narratives about the Afghan mission, both in texts and pictures, are overly romanticized, sometimes orientalist, and always very optimistic about the unquestionable good that Canada is building and doing in Afghanistan. See http://www.afghanistan.gc.ca; in particular, see the section "Stories from the field." See also http://www.forces.gc.ca, especially articles from "The Maple Leaf" section.
6 This quotation was taken from CIDA's website in March 2008 at http://www.acdi-cida.gc.ca/CIDAWEB/acdicida.nsf/En/NAT-11692710-JY2. Since then, however, such claims have been taken off the website.
7 One particularly harsh critique pointed to a hospital that CIDA was proudly claiming to be one of its most impressive accomplishments in Afghanistan. The Senlis Council claimed that the hospital was in fact an empty tent when it visited it; a tent that was nowhere to be found a few days later when the Senlis Council came back (Senlis Council 2007b, 24).
8 In speaking of the security situation in Afghanistan, the new chief of the defence staff, General Walter Natynczyk, was quick to dismiss the growing violence in Kandahar as "insignificant" (G. Smith 2008).
9 All numbers come from the Government of Canada's website, http://www.afghanistan.gc.ca/canada-afghanistan/priorities-priorites/.
10 Kevin Page, Canada's parliamentary budget officer, claimed that a lack of government transparency and consistency and the fact that some federal departments did not cooperate with his requests for information have made difficult to estimate the full cost of the Afghanistan mission (CBC News 2008).

4 Rethinking the Security Imaginary
Canadian Security and the Case of Afghanistan

KIM RICHARD NOSSAL

A hegemon, Dan O'Meara argues in Chapter 1, is able to socialize its allies with its "security imaginary" – the way in which "representations of states, of relations among states and of the international system are created" (Weldes 1999, 10). The implication, however, is that these patterns of socialization flow unidirectionally outward from the hegemon as it propagates and reproduces cultural practices that help entrench smaller allies into the hegemonic imperium. But is it possible for an ally to try to rethink the security imaginary and recast it in a way that challenges the hegemon's imaginary? My purpose in this chapter is to examine a period in foreign and defence policy when Canada's political leaders were openly encouraging Canadians to question dominant American assumptions about international politics, and to reconsider not only their country's role in the world but also its relationship with the hegemon. Between 1993 and 2006, during the prime ministerships of both Jean Chrétien and Paul Martin, Canadians were consistently encouraged by their governors to rethink their assumptions about the country's place and role in global politics, a rethinking that went well beyond the well-established rhetoric of internationalism and multilateralism that had been a staple of Canadian foreign policy discourse in the 1970s and 1980s (Keating 2002; Munton 2002-03). Of course, political leaders can encourage new thinking, but to what extent were Canadians actually moved to embrace such a new reconceptualization of Canada in world affairs? The case of the Canadian mission in Afghanistan offers us a useful way to assess the degree to which the efforts of Canadian leaders during this period had a longer-term political impact on the attitudes of Canadians. In particular, I argue that the case of the mission in Afghanistan presents us with ambiguous evidence about the longer-term effects of the efforts to recast the security imaginary. On the one hand, it is clear from opinion polls that Canadians have accepted much of the reconceptualization of security being articulated by the Chrétien and Martin governments. On the other hand, it is equally clear that efforts to cast the mission in Afghanistan in terms consistent with these new conceptions of security have been unsuccessful, since Canadian support for the mission remained consistently tepid, suggesting that the revisioning, such as it was, remained incomplete.

Rethinking the Security Imaginary

The so-called revisioning that occurred during the Liberal governments of both Jean Chrétien and Paul Martin had several distinct but interrelated elements. First, the idea that national interests – the selfish ends of the political community – should drive Canada's international policy was rejected. Indeed, the very term "national interest" was dropped from the government's lexicon (Granatstein 2003, 4-5; Nossal 2003; Gotlieb 2004b, 2). Lloyd Axworthy (2003, 3), Canada's minister of foreign affairs from 1996 until 2000, openly disparaged what he called the dominance of "naked self-interest" in world politics. In a similar vein, Paul Heinbecker, Canada's ambassador and permanent representative to the United Nations, dismissed the idea when he wrote in 2000: "Canadians are moved by humanitarian impulse, not by the cold-blooded or rational calculations of realpolitik ... Principles are often more important than power to Canadians" (quoted in Granatstein 2003, 12). Instead of naked self-interest, broader conceptions of interest were invoked: Axworthy (2003, 1, 5) argued that Canadians were "on the road to global citizenship" in articulating notions of a global "common good."

Second, Canadians were encouraged to see their country as a generous and activist contributor to the global good. Canada, it was commonly said, was a "norm entrepreneur" – an "innovative player" working to entrench global rules (Axworthy 2003, 4). In this view, Canada was also a selfless power, expansively seeking to "build lives of freedom for all people," based on "the fundamental human rights of every man, woman and child on earth" (Canada, DFAIT 2005, 20). To this end, Canada willingly contributed to peacekeeping and peace-building, deploying what Axworthy (2003, xii) referred to as "our blue-helmeted constabulary" on UN-sponsored missions, thus adding to and entrenching an already well-established "peacekeeping myth" that Canada was not only the inventor of peacekeeping but also the world's leading peacekeeping nation (Granatstein 1986; Hillmer 1994; Maloney 2002; Wagner 2006-07).

To be sure, such portraiture tended toward the narcissistic and self-congratulatory. Axworthy (2003, 6, 378) celebrated Canada as a "value-added nation" and an "agent of change." One of his successors, Bill Graham, minister of foreign affairs from 2002 to 2004, touted "our long-standing advocacy of human rights, the rule of law, democracy, respect for diversity, gender equality and good governance ... and [Canada's] unique opportunities to contribute to their realization in virtue of our population and our experience" (Canada, DFAIT 2003). For his part, Paul Martin took self-flattery to extraordinary heights, boasting, for example, that Canada was "a progressive force in the world" (Canada, DFAIT 2005, foreword). On more than one occasion, he cited, with evident approval, the slogan of Indigo Books and Music Inc. – "The world needs more Canada." And with Jennifer Welsh's idea of Canada as a "model power" (Welsh 2004; see also Cheung-Gertler 2007) as his cue, Martin frequently claimed that Canada had much to teach others: "We are an example to the world of what a country should be. Showing others the way is at once our destiny and responsibility" (Martin 2004). A year later he would claim that "we will set the standard by which other nations judge themselves" (quoted in Nossal 2005, 1031).

Third, in Axworthy's reconceptualization of Canada's position in world politics, historical approaches to strategic culture (Nossal 2004) were set aside. Canada was not portrayed as a *willing* partner and ally of the United States in global affairs; rather, if Canada was in the American orbit, it was because of American hegemonic power. In this view, the connection was therefore necessarily begrudged, and one could sense a deep frustration in Axworthy's description and analysis of American global behaviour. Anti-hegemonism and anti-Americanism overlapped: while in opposition in the late 1980s and early 1990s, Axworthy had demonstrated a deep vein of antipathy toward the power of the United States (Nossal 1994). As the Liberal Party's external affairs critic, he had contributed to the party's campaign platform in 1993 that promised that under a Liberal government Canada would cease to be a "camp follower" of the United States (Liberal Party of Canada 1993, 106; see also Axworthy 1992-93). During his tenure as minister of foreign affairs from 1996 to 2000, he left little doubt that his views about American hegemony and American unilateralism had not changed (Nossal 1997). Nor had his views about the inappropriateness of following the United States in global affairs: as he put it euphemistically – without actually naming the United States – Canada had little interest in associating itself with "the way of the warrior, using the immense reach of a military apparatus to seduce, shape and when necessary coerce compliance with its own set of goals, values and interests, increasingly disdainful of any international rules of restraint" (Axworthy 2003, 407). On the contrary: Canada was conceived of as an alternative to the hegemon, a country with the "strengths ... to take a special kind of leadership in helping manage a world dominated by the power and influence of our continental neighbour" (6). However, such views were not unique to Axworthy: Chrétien's decision not to join the United States in the 2003 invasion of Iraq, and Martin's decision in 2005 not to participate in the Ballistic Missile Defense scheme were motivated by comparable views of the proper relationship between Canada and the United States.

Fourth, and deeply connected to the concern about the growth of American hyperpower and American unilateralism, Canadians were encouraged to regard multilateralism – support for the United Nations and for international action to solve global problems – as the core and overriding principle for Canadian foreign policy. As Axworthy (2003, 235-36, emphasis in original) put it, "The UN is *vital* to Canada, affording us a place in which we can exercise influence, lessen our dependence on bilateral relations and help establish policies and practices consonant with our values and interests." Certainly, the Canadian campaign to create the International Criminal Court and the articulation of what Gotlieb (2004a) has called the Chrétien doctrine – the requirement that the United Nations approve any use of force before Canada would contribute forces – were both in keeping with the premium put on multilateralism and the United Nations during this period.

Fifth, Canadians were encouraged to rethink the nature of national security. When he came to office in 1996, Axworthy explicitly rejected the dominant fixation with the *state* as the traditional object of security. Building on critiques of national security that dated back to the paradoxes of security during the Cold War era itself (Ullman 1983; Mathews 1989; Buzan 1991), and following the tendency to adorn security with descriptive adjectives (see Nossal 1995), Axworthy championed the notion of human security – the idea that the proper focus of security policy should be on *people* rather than on *states* (Axworthy 1997, 2003; also G. MacLean 2000), arguing that Canada was willing "to take risks on behalf of victims of war in far-flung places" (Axworthy 1999). The concept was also formally enshrined in Canadian policy (Canada, DFAIT 1999; McRae and Hubert 2001), even if only briefly. Moreover, Axworthy put the idea into action, seeking to galvanize a global ban on anti-personnel landmines (Axworthy 2003, 126-55; Tomlin 1998) and pressing for global action on children affected by war (Sorger and Hoskins 2001), among other initiatives (see Shaw's Chapter 10). Human security was used to justify Canadian participation in the bombing of Serbia in early 1999 (Axworthy 2003, 177-99; Nossal and Roussel 2000) and in the intervention in East Timor later that year (Hataley and Nossal 2004). It was reflected in the increased emphasis on the role of women in Canada's development assistance policies (Keeble and Smith 2001). Under Axworthy, the Canadian government also sponsored the International Commission on Intervention and State Sovereignty (ICISS), a blue-ribbon panel of experts to examine the notion of national sovereignty and how it could be fitted to the requirements of human security (Welsh 2002; Thakur, Cooper, and English 2005; Welsh, Thielking, and Macfarlane 2005).

As Julie MacArthur (2008, 422) has noted, the notion of human security had "immense appeal for scholars and practitioners interested in the creation of a more just world order," and Axworthy's embrace of the concept spawned a considerable academic debate over both the meaning and the applicability of the concept in Canada's case (for example, Hay 1999; Stoett 1999; Owens and Arneil 1999; Paris 2001; Irwin 2001; Bosold and von Bredow 2006). Now, it is true that, as Furtado (2008, 420) has argued, human security "never became the animating concept of Canadian policy." Formally, at least, it did not even survive Axworthy's departure from politics in 2000: *Human security: Safety for people in a changing world* was quickly "disappeared" from the website of the Department of Foreign Affairs and International Trade almost immediately upon the minister's departure (and is now available only on an Organization of American States website). However, there can be little doubt that what Allan Gotlieb (2004b) has called the "romantic streak" in Canadian foreign policy under Axworthy continued to find expression in Canadian foreign policy. Certainly, when Paul Martin took over as leader of the Liberal Party and prime minister in 2003, he keenly embraced the focus on human security, promising, for example, that his government would "always express the concerns of Canadians about the poor and underprivileged of the world; the frightened and helpless victims of battle-torn societies" (Martin 2003b).

Finally, Martin carried forward Axworthy's efforts to rethink national sovereignty. In his acceptance speech as Liberal Party leader, Martin promised to embrace "new thinking about how the international community governs itself, and how sovereign nations take action together in tackling global issues" (Martin 2003b). As prime minister, he encouraged Canadians to rethink the deeply entrenched notion of national sovereignty. Eight months before taking over as prime minister, Martin (2003a) had argued in a speech that "in appropriate circumstances, and when consistent with our values, we should be prepared to use the means necessary to achieve our international goals [even] when full consensus on the right steps is not possible." Once in power, Martin consistently and explicitly supported the idea of humanitarian intervention, endorsing the main findings of the report of the ICISS (2001) that sovereign states had a "responsibility to protect" their citizens, rejecting orthodox views of state sovereignty. As he put it, "Failed states more often than not require military intervention in order to ensure stability," arguing that military intervention was "indispensable," though not enough to provide long-term security (Martin 2004). His government's International Policy Statement, released in April 2005, formally promised that Canada would "hold governments accountable for how they treat their people, and to intervene if necessary to prevent a humanitarian catastrophe" (Canada, DFAIT 2005, 20).

In sum, over a twelve-year period, Canadian leaders articulated a security imaginary – a fundamentally different vision of international politics and Canadian foreign and security policy – that was significantly at odds with orthodox American ways of conceptualizing a country's role in international politics. The refusal to conceive of international policy in terms of the national interest, the embrace of such ideas as human security and the responsibility to protect, the advocacy of the idea of Canada as a model power, and the willingness to denigrate the hegemonic power of the United States and defy the hegemon on issues such as the invasion of Iraq or the Ballistic Missile Defense scheme – these indicated what Axworthy (2003, 420) called finding "alternatives to the present ideological and conceptual straitjackets" on thinking about Canadian foreign policy.

To be sure, this revisioning received a mixed reaction within the Canadian state apparatus. The main opposition party, the Conservative Party of Canada and its predecessors – the Reform Party, the Progressive Conservative Party, and the Canadian Alliance – never bought into the reconceptualization being articulated by the Liberals. At the bureaucratic level, officials in the Department of Finance loved it because it was so cheap to implement and fitted well the overweening objective of reducing the deficit. Officials in the Department of Foreign Affairs and International Trade liked the increased prominence it afforded their department. But it was fundamentally at odds with the orthodox security imaginary in the Department of National Defence and the Canadian Armed Forces. If the Canadian Armed Forces recognized that peacekeeping provided them with considerable public support, they had little use for notions of a constabulary force, preferring to retain multi-purpose, combat-capable forces, and in particular those capable of interoperability with the armed forces of the United States (Charbonneau and Cox 2008). However, the relative power position of the Canadian Armed Forces and Department of National Defence in the bureaucratic firmament in Ottawa in the 1990s meant that the national defence establishment was unable to oppose some of these efforts at reconceptualization. The Somalia Affair had deeply discredited the military (see Bercuson 1996), and Chrétien himself left no doubt that he had little time for National Defence, whose budget was dramatically cut year after year (Bland 2003; Granatstein 2004). Even after 9/11, which radically transformed the security environment in Ottawa, the military had to watch in dismay as the Chrétien government's policies on Iraq and Ballistic Missile Defense threatened its relationship with its American military counterpart. Indeed, it was not until Paul Martin came to office in December 2003 that the military budget was dramatically increased, and not until General Rick Hillier was appointed by Martin as chief of defence staff that what Hillier took to calling "the decade of darkness" (Blanchfield 2007b) largely came to an end.

In addition, it is not clear that the revisioning being urged on Canadians by their governors was not driven largely by domestic political purposes. Stairs (2001, 44), for example, has argued that many of these policy initiatives appeared to be "guided by a domestic politics that had been manufactured by its own myths, or even that it had finally fallen victim itself to the spins that it had doctored." For Stairs (2003a, 503), the "inflated and self-serving rhetoric" of this era was "clearly designed to appeal to the preferences and prejudices of a population indoctrinated by its own myths." In a similar vein, I have suggested that we should see much of the discourse of this period as "ear candy" that had overt and barely disguised domestic political purposes: "Government ministers tended to speak about Canada's role in the world in terms that were so sweet-sounding to Canadians that not only did the rhetoric convince listeners that their government was actually doing something worthwhile in their name, but it also generated considerable political support for those engaging in the rhetoric" (Nossal 2005, 1018).

Several analysts (Cohen 2003; Stairs 2003b; Gotlieb 2004b; see also Nossal 1998-99) have noted that the "new vision" articulated for Canada's role in the world reflected the dramatic decline in the resources allocated by the Canadian government to international affairs in the 1990s as the Liberal government sought to reduce the huge deficit and national debt it had inherited in 1993. As Stairs (2003a, 489-90) has acidly argued, in times of financial restraint, "the vocabulary of values – always a cheap concoction – assumes a greater prominence. The premise is that it will warm the mood and cool the criticism. The spinning of tales – tales not false, perhaps, but certainly canted – becomes an increasingly valued and admired art as the policy establishment struggles to bridge the gap between what well-intentioned Canadians think and what the government really is doing."

We can certainly see the efforts of the governments of both Chrétien and Martin to distance Canada from the United States, and from American power, as an attempt to play to the deeply entrenched anti-Americanism that is evident in Canada, particularly English-speaking Canada (Granatstein 1996; Nossal 2007a). In 1997, Chrétien himself had admitted, albeit inadvertently, how he had made defying the United States "his policy" because "it's popular" (Nossal 2008, 136). Particularly after the election of George W. Bush as president of the United States, Chrétien and many of his ministers and backbenchers essentially encouraged anti-American sentiments in Canada for precisely that reason: because there are often clear electoral gains to be had from such a policy. And although Martin came to office promising a different approach to the United States, when push came to shove, he was too tempted by the electoral gains on offer: both the 2004 and 2005-06 election campaigns featured planks that were unambiguously designed to tap anti-Americanism in Canada (Nossal 2008).

Even though the Conservatives under Stephen Harper clearly had a very different outlook on Canadian foreign and defence policy when they were in opposition (Nossal 2007b), we cannot conclude that the January 2006 elections, which resulted in a Conservative minority government, was a rejection by the electorate of the Liberal attempts of the previous decade to reconceptualize Canadian foreign and defence policy. Rather, we can ask whether more than ten years of a very different articulation of foreign and defence policy goals might have longer-term effects on Canadian public attitudes toward security.

A Longer-Term Impact? The Case of Afghanistan

What longer-term impact did these efforts to get Canadians to reconceptualize foreign and defence policy have? There is some public opinion poll evidence that the campaign had an impact. In 2008, for example, the Department of National Defence commissioned Ipsos Reid to conduct an extensive public opinion poll, using both telephone interviews and focus groups, on Canadians' views of national defence. The poll, leaked to the media in September 2008 (Brewster 2008), revealed that Canadians largely rejected the idea that the purpose of the Canadian Armed Forces was to use force in international politics. On the contrary: 92 percent of those polled believed the purpose of the Canadian military should be to respond to natural disasters around the world. When focus group participants were asked about their image of the Canadian military, one responded: "I do not picture a Canadian soldier carrying guns." Only half of the participants believed that Canadian forces should participate in international security operations; the other half believed that Canadian troops should act as ceasefire observers.

Although the 2008 poll provides important evidence of the attitudes of Canadians toward the alternative security imaginary, another indication of whether the so-called revisioning had a longer-term impact can be found in the attitudes of Canadians toward the multi-dimensional Canadian mission in Afghanistan. This mission began in 2001 with Canada's contribution to the initial American-led Operation Enduring Freedom; it then shifted to the NATO-led International Security Assistance Force in Kabul from 2003 to 2005, and then to Kandahar in 2005 to head the Provincial Reconstruction Team in that province (for a history, see Stein and Lang 2007; Manley et al. 2008). Because the Afghanistan mission meets so many of the criteria that were being articulated as ideal characteristics of Canada's global engagement, it is a useful test of David S. McDonough's assertion (2007, 628) that "Canadian interventionism in Afghanistan appears to be informed by the human security agenda."

First, all phases of the Afghanistan mission have received the authorization of the UN Security Council. The original US-led invasion to overthrow the Taliban government by force in 2001-02 after the al-Qaeda attacks of 11 September was approved by the Security Council, which unanimously adopted the well-established code phrase authorizing the use of force – "all necessary steps" (UN Security Council Res. 1373, 28 September 2001). The invasion not only was aimed at removing a regime that had given al-Qaeda sanctuary but could also be painted as a humanitarian mission, since the Taliban had also engaged in a wide range of human rights violations, including well-documented atrocities and the systemic oppression of girls and women.

Second, the Afghanistan mission has been a deeply multilateral exercise. The elected government of Hamid Karzai that resulted from the overthrow of the Taliban in 2002 invited the international community to assist it in creating stability and generating economic development. In particular, the Afghanistan Compact of 31 January-1 February 2006 that provides the framework for international support for the Afghanistan government involves fifty-one "participating governments," including all five permanent members of the UN Security Council; thirteen "observer governments"; and ten participating organizations, including the UN, the World Bank, the International Monetary Fund, the European Union, NATO, the Organisation of the Islamic Conference, two development banks, and the Aga Khan Foundation (Afghanistan Compact 2006).

Third, although the initial invasion was led by the United States, the international effort to stabilize the Karzai government quickly morphed into an operation that was manifestly *not* dominated and run by the United States. Indeed, one measure of the lack of US control in Afghanistan has been the degree of blunt and open grumbling by Americans that the NATO-led mission is a "spaghetti sandwich" that needs to be "cleaned up" by the assertion of greater American control (Lubold 2008).

Finally, the Afghanistan mission has unambiguous humanitarian and development objectives that fit well with the precepts of human security. For example, the Afghanistan Compact outlines objectives to provide the people of Afghanistan with security, good governance, and economic development. The mission also has openly gendered goals: to prevent a return of the Taliban and thus a return of the discriminatory treatment of girls and women that was the mark of Afghanistan politics during the Taliban period. In short, if one considers the rearticulations of security being embraced by Canadian leaders from 1995 to 2006, and then looks at the Afghanistan case, one might readily conclude that this was a mission that would be eagerly embraced by Canadians if they had in fact bought into the reconceptualizations of security and foreign policy of their leaders (on the Canadian mission, see Charbonneau and Parent's Chapter 3).

However, this has manifestly not been the case. All the evidence available suggests that support among Canadians for the mission in Afghanistan has been tepid at best. Although there is considerable rhetorical support for Canadian troops in Afghanistan, manifested in such political phenomena as Red Friday/Vendredi rouge rallies, "Support our troops" stickers, and spontaneous public tributes to those Canadian soldiers killed in Afghanistan, public support for what the Canadian Armed Forces and the other agencies of the Canadian government are doing in Afghanistan is much less evident.

On the contrary: although the Ipsos Reid poll conducted for the Department of National Defence in the summer of 2008 revealed that two-thirds of respondents supported what Canada was doing in Afghanistan (Brewster 2008), every other public opinion poll taken between 2006, when the

Martin government committed Canadian troops to the Kandahar region, and September 2008, when Afghanistan was in essence taken off the political agenda, shows that Canadians are essentially split on the mission. For example, in a Decima poll in April 2006, 45 percent of Canadians polled approved of the mission; 46 percent were opposed (Angus Reid Global Monitor 2006). In February 2007, an Angus Reid poll showed that 46 percent wanted Canadian troops brought home. In May 2008, 54 percent of Canadians opposed an extension of the mission (Angus Reid Strategies 2007, 2008). Polls by the Strategic Counsel, which have asked the same question since 2006 ("Overall, do you strongly support, support, oppose, or strongly oppose the decision to send Canadian troops to Afghanistan?"), show that between 2006 and 2008, national overall support for the mission was never above 48 percent, while overall opposition ranged from 44 percent to 61 percent (Strategic Counsel 2008). Importantly, as Table 4.1 shows, the degree of "strong" opposition is clearly more marked than the degree of "strong" support: strong support ranges between 5 and 11 percent over this two-year period; by contrast, approximately 25 percent of respondents registered consistently strong opposition to the mission. Moreover, there is no clear trend line in public attitudes: the polarization has remained remarkably steady and has not changed with the large number of casualties suffered by Canadian troops in Afghanistan since March 2006 (Boucher 2010).

The split in public opinion revealed by polls is reflected in the marked lack of enthusiasm and the high level of doubt expressed in public discourse about the mission. There are notable exceptions (such as Blatchford 2007), but much of the commentary has been marked by a certain dubiousness about the mission, much of it expressed by mainstream voices. For example, in a 2007 report, Gordon Smith, a former Canadian ambassador to NATO and former deputy minister of foreign affairs, concluded that "current NATO policies and programs in Afghanistan are not on course to achieve that objective, even within a period of ten years" (G. Smith 2007, 4). Likewise, a blue-ribbon panel chaired by Chrétien's former deputy prime minister, John Manley, which was appointed by Stephen Harper in 2007 to advise the government on options in Afghanistan, recommended continuing the mission, but the tone of the report of the Independent Panel on Canada's Future Role in Afghanistan was cautious and measured, admitting that there were "no simple solutions," that there was a high degree of unpredictability, and that success was by no means certain (Manley et al. 2008, 30, 39). Finally, the Standing Senate Committee on National Security and Defence reported in 2008 that the Canadian mission was hampered by an "array of

TABLE 4.1

Canadian attitudes toward sending troops to Afghanistan, March 2006–August 2008

	Mar 06	May 06	Jun 06	Jul 06	Aug 06	Sep 06	Oct 06	Dec 06	Apr 07	May 07	Jul 07	Jan 08	Aug 08
Total support	55	40	48	39	37	43	44	35	36	40	36	39	35
Strongly support	11	6	11	8	6	11	10	5	6	10	7	7	9
Support	44	34	37	31	31	32	34	30	30	30	29	32	26
DK/NA/Ref[a]	4	6	8	5	8	8	3	4	7	5	5	6	4
Oppose	26	31	26	31	31	26	26	35	31	27	31	31	28
Strongly oppose	15	23	18	25	24	23	27	26	26	28	27	25	33
Total oppose	41	54	44	56	55	49	53	61	57	55	58	56	61

Question: "Overall, do you strongly support, support, oppose, or strongly oppose the decision to send Canadian troops to Afghanistan?" As Boucher and Roussel (2008, 151, fn 6) note, the Strategic Counsel polling sample was exceedingly small; individual provincial results are based on such a small n that the margin of error climbs to what they argue is an unacceptable 6.3.

a DK/NA/Ref: Don't know or refused to answer.

Source: Adapted from Strategic Counsel 2008.

disfunctionality [sic]" (Canada, Senate 2008a, 2). Perhaps not surprisingly, these doubts about the effectiveness of the mission were reflected in the editorial and columnist opinion of the mainstream press as well (for example, Simpson 2008; *Toronto Star* 2008; *National Post* 2008; Taillefer 2008).

Canada's national political parties were likewise split on the mission (for a full discussion of the party positions on the Afghanistan mission, see Nossal 2009). The Conservative government inherited the phase of the mission agreed to by the Martin government in 2005 (Stein and Lang 2007); indeed, units of the Canadian Armed Forces were arriving in the Kandahar region just as the Harper government was taking office. But the Conservatives remained both united and enthusiastic about the mission. Although it was a Liberal government that had approved the mission, the Liberal Party was essentially divided over the mission. During the contest for the party's leadership, two of the contenders, Bob Rae and Michael Ignatieff, supported the mission, while the eventual winner, Stéphane Dion, did not. As leader of the Opposition, however, Dion was essentially forced into voting for an extension of the mission to avoid having the Conservative government fall and calling an election the Liberals were not ready to fight.

For its part, the Bloc Québécois, reflecting not only its desire to avoid an election but also very high levels of opposition to the Afghanistan mission in Quebec, had what Boucher and Roussel (2008, 146) call a "quite nuanced" position. On the one hand, the Bloc favoured an end to the military mission. On the other hand, the Bloc argued that a "sudden withdrawal from Afghanistan would be irresponsible toward the people and the government of Afghanistan, as well as toward our allies, who are counting on Canada's collaboration until then" (Canada, House of Commons 2007).

The New Democratic Party was in the most awkward position. Like the other parties, it did not want to fight an election. On Afghanistan, the party's official position was that this was "the wrong mission for Canada" and that Canada should "support our troops" by bringing them home (CBC News 2006c). However, when in April 2007 the Bloc Québécois announced that it was voting for a Liberal motion to withdraw Canada's forces from Afghanistan in 2009, the NDP ended up voting with the governing Conservatives to defeat the motion, embracing the pretzel logic that they had to vote against any motion that would terminate the mission in February 2009 because they were in favour of bringing the troops home immediately (CBC News 2007).

Finally, one measure of the lack of public enthusiasm for the mission is the development of a small but robust peace movement dedicated to bringing the mission to an end. Without any evident irony, the Canadian peace movement appropriated as their catch-cry an American protest slogan for the Iraq war – "Support our troops. Bring them home" (repeating what previous generations of Canadian peace movements had done during the Vietnam War in the late 1960s and the Gulf War of 1991, when they adopted miniature-replica derivatives of protest slogans invented by Americans for those wars). The campaign to secure a Canadian withdrawal from Afghanistan was coordinated by several pan-Canadian advocacy groups, including the Canadian Peace Alliance, the Council of Canadians, and the Rideau Institute on International Affairs' Ceasefire.ca campaign. However, it also featured numerous local groups, ranging from the Canada Out of Afghanistan campaign (in Victoria) to the St. John's Campaign against the War (in Newfoundland and Labrador) and numerous local groups in between (for a directory of groups, see Canadian Peace Alliance 2008).

How can we explain this low level of support for an international mission that fit so well with the recasting of the security imaginary that had been pressed by the Liberal governments of Jean Chrétien and Paul Martin? Here we are confronted with a methodological problem, since not one of the public opinion polls that demonstrate so clearly the depth of opposition and the tepidness of support for the mission actually tries to plumb the reasons for Canadians' attitudes. Thus, we are left to offer plausible explanations.

One possibility is that Canadian attitudes toward the Afghanistan mission are a function of what might be called communications failure. One of the persistent criticisms has been that, as the Senlis Council put it in 2007, "the Canadian government has failed to make a clear, objective argument to the Canadian public for Canada's efforts in Afghanistan" (Senlis Council 2007a, 7). Likewise, the Manley commission's 2008 report argued that "governments from the start of Canada's Afghan involvement have failed to communicate with Canadians with balance and candour about the reasons for Canadian involvement, or about the risks, difficulties and expected results of that involvement" (Manley et al. 2008, 20). Certainly, when prompted by a pollster's question, Canadians in large numbers (61 percent) have not been hesitant to respond that they do not think that the government has explained the mission effectively (Angus Reid Strategies 2007, 3). In this view, if governments had only explained things more clearly, Canadians would support the mission.

The problem with this explanation is that Canadian governments *have* tried to explain the mission, particularly the phase that began with the movement of the battle group back to Kandahar. Since February 2006, there have been three extended parliamentary debates on the mission. In February and March 2008, for example, fully five parliamentary days were devoted to debate on the mission, with 128 MPs (55 Conservatives, 40 Liberals, 11 Bloc Québécois members, 20 NDP members, and 1 independent) contributing. Moreover, there have been numerous attempts by ministers to explain Canada's Afghan involvement, using a range of different arguments.

When he first came to power and visited Canadian forces in Kandahar, Harper sought to frame the Canadian mission in national interest terms. First, he argued that Canadian security depended on ensuring that Afghanistan did not again become an incubator for terrorist attacks, reminding his audience of the Canadians who had died in the al-Qaeda attacks on the World Trade Center and of the recent inclusion of Canada on the list of countries that al-Qaeda would seek to attack. Second, Harper argued that Canadian security was affected by the opium trade, which, he said, "wreaks its own destruction on the streets of our country." To be sure, the prime minister invoked three other justifications for the mission: the importance of a country such as Canada taking a leadership role in global politics, the importance of the humanitarian mission, and the importance of "standing up for Canadian values" (Harper 2006b).

Such a primary focus on the national interest was hardly unexpected, given that the Conservatives had come to power with clearly little sympathy for ideational initiatives closely associated with the Liberals, such as human security or the responsibility to protect. Thus, this general line of argument was sounded throughout 2006 on numerous occasions by the prime minister (Harper 2006a); Gordon O'Connor (2006), the minister of national defence; Peter MacKay (2006), the minister of foreign affairs; and Josée Verner (2006), the minister responsible for the Canadian International Development Agency.

However, as the polling numbers showed no sign of change (see Table 4.1), the Harper government increasingly sought to justify what Canada was doing in Afghanistan in terms that mirrored Liberal romantic discourse. Thus, for example, when O'Connor embarked on a cross-country tour in early 2007 to galvanize support for the mission, his speaking notes contained only a brief opening reference to the threat of terrorism but then immediately turned to a discussion of Canadian assistance for Afghanistan. "As a nation," O'Connor said,

> we identify ourselves by our desire to help others in need. Canadians recognize the dire straits of the Afghan people. Decades of civil war, years of

extremist rule, a severe lack of basic infrastructure and public services, drought, poverty, drugs and corruption all plague this population. Canada has a long history of helping those in need, and as part of this NATO mission, we are continuing this noble tradition. (G. O'Connor 2007)

Much of the rest of his address focused on how Canada was making a difference in Afghanistan, the positive consequences of Canadian assistance to the Afghan people, the consequences to those people of the return of the Taliban, and a tribute to Canadian forces. Apart from the two brief sentences about terrorism at the outset, O'Connor did not frame his justification in terms of national interests. He never once mentioned the United States. Indeed, the tropes he used to justify what Canada was doing in Afghanistan had a distinctly familiar timbre: his address could easily have been given by Paul Martin or Bill Graham – or even Lloyd Axworthy. By June 2008, when the government reported to Parliament on the progress being made in Afghanistan, there were no longer any references to the national interest, and only a brief reference to preventing Afghanistan from becoming a base for terrorism. Rather, the report indicated that "these are the objectives of Canada's engagement in Afghanistan – to contribute to Afghanistan's future as a better governed, more peaceful and more secure country" (Canada 2008, 16).

In short, the "communications failure" argument fails to account for the fact that the government *was* trying to find an explanation, moving from one rooted in national interest to one rooted in humanitarianism. Given this, we might reasonably conclude that there is another possibility: that the explanations being advanced were simply unconvincing to Canadians. This, in turn, raises the question why. I advance two plausible alternatives. One possibility is that Canadians saw the mission in Afghanistan as nothing more than an extension of the American global war on terror being waged by the administration of George W. Bush, and merely part of the broader American campaign in Iraq, and that their opposition to broader American policy drove attitudes on Afghanistan. That the two wars are deeply connected is a common assertion among opponents of the Afghanistan mission. For example, Steve Staples, the president of the Rideau Institute, reminded viewers in a welcome video that was posted on the institute's "Ceasefire.ca" campaign website during the Bush era that "right now our government has thousands of Canadian troops stuck in a war in Afghanistan. We're part of a NATO force, but we're really fighting for George Bush," his voice-over said to an unattractive image of Bush giving a speech against the backdrop of an American flag. The video reminded viewers that "we kept Canada out of Iraq, and we kept Canada out of missile defense," and concluded that "we can make Canada a voice for peace again" (Ceasefire.ca 2008). (The video was archived with the election of Barack Obama.)

There can be little doubt that the American push for the invasion of Iraq in the winter of 2002-03 was generally unpopular in Canada, and that Chrétien's decision to not commit combat troops to the invasion and to pretend that there was no Canadian contribution to that invasion – when in fact Canadian Armed Forces personnel *were* involved (Stein and Lang 2007, 86-90) – was extremely popular across the country. The reasons for the unpopularity of the Iraq war in Canada were many. They include the deep unpopularity of Bush himself among Canadians, an unpopularity to which the Chrétien government itself openly contributed (Boucher and Roussel 2008, 144; Nossal 2008, 136-37).

Likewise, there can be little doubt that there was a deep connection between the American war in Iraq and Canadian government decisions in Afghanistan. The Chrétien government's decision in early 2003 to deploy a battle group to Kabul and the NATO International Security Assistance Force was clearly linked to the impending war in Iraq. As Bill Graham, at that time the minister of foreign affairs, admitted to Stein and Lang (2007, 65): "There was no question, every time we talked about the Afghan mission, it gave us cover for not going into Iraq." A clear consensus emerged in Ottawa in early 2005 that a battle group deployed to Kandahar to what at that time was still the American-led Operation Enduring Freedom would be a good way of repairing the damage to the Canadian-American relationship that had been done by Chrétien's decision on Iraq and the decision of the Martin government to reject Canadian participation in Ballistic Missile Defense in February 2005. Although Martin was to claim later that he did not agree with this view (Stein and Lang 2007, 182), the fact is that the cabinet that he headed approved the deployment in May 2005.

An alternative explanation is that Canadians are not so much opposed to Afghanistan because they are opposed to the larger American project in the Middle East or even the global war on terror, but simply because neither of the justifications on offer from their governors make much sense to them. The national interest argument that has been floated – that billions of dollars in treasure and scores of Canadian lives are needed to keep Canadians safe from terrorists – is clearly not convincing. And while a national interest argument, couched in *realpolitik* terms, could be constructed for the Afghanistan mission, focusing on the geopolitical need for American control in the Persian Gulf region and the importance of a small country such as Canada contributing to those efforts, it is unlikely that any Canadian minister would articulate such an argument, at least in public, and equally unlikely that Canadians would find such *realpolitik* discourse compelling.

On the other hand, however, neither does the alternative security imaginary – the one rooted in humanitarianism, human security, global citizenship, multilateralism, and altruism – seem to appeal to Canadians in the Afghanistan case. For although there might be "good news" about the progress that is being made in Afghanistan in terms of development, education, public health, and gender equality (Pigott 2007, 134-35), it appears to make no difference when this progress is communicated to Canadians by their governors (for example, Canada, Senate 2008a). The polling numbers remain persistently flat and unenthusiastic.

So which of these two alternative explanations is more plausible? Did antipathy toward the Iraq war, antipathy toward Bush, or even a certain antipathy toward American military adventures colour Canadian attitudes toward the Afghanistan mission? Some *assert* this connection (for example, Charbonneau and Cox 2008), and take as a given that other Canadians think as they do, but in fact we cannot know, for there is no unambiguous evidence that the opposition to the Afghanistan mission has been driven by a perceived link to the war in Iraq. But by the same token, there is no clear evidence for the alternative proposition that Canadians have responded to the Afghanistan mission as they do because they find none of the explanations on offer convincing.

Conclusion

I have argued that we should question the usual assumption that Canadian state officials are simply the uncritical recipients of a security imaginary propagated by the hegemon. During the Liberal governments of Jean Chrétien and Paul Martin from 1993 to 2006, we saw Canadian political leaders encourage Canadians to rethink the orthodox verities of international relations: the standard (realist/American) lexicon of national interests, national power, national security, national sovereignty, and strong support for one's great-power ally. Instead, Canadians were encouraged to think in terms of global interests and multilateral methods for the management of global problems; new conceptions of security and new definitions of national sovereignty; and to question American hegemony and American power.

I have suggested that Afghanistan provides a useful case study to test how far Canadians bought this encouragement to see the world in ways that challenge American orthodoxy, since the mission in Afghanistan – from the initial campaign to overthrow the Taliban government in 2001-02 to the stabilization campaigns associated with the Afghanistan Compact of 2006 – can be seen as emblematic of the redefinitions that Canadians had been encouraged by their governors to embrace.

However, although polls suggest that Canadians have bought into some parts of this alternative security imaginary, it is clear that Canadians have not bought into the Afghanistan mission as it has been constructed for them, either by the Liberal governments that approved it or by the Conservative government that inherited it. Support for the mission has remained flat and tepid, and seemingly not affected by the growing casualty rate, by the mixture of positive and negative news from Afghanistan itself, or by anything that those who speak for government, the agencies of the Canadian state, or the Canadian Armed Forces might say.

The lack of clear and unambiguous evidence leaves us in the frustrating position of not knowing precisely why Canadians have taken the positions they have on the Afghanistan mission, yet one conclusion does seem appropriate: it would appear that Canadians have not been totally moved by the alternative vision of global politics articulated by Liberal leaders from 1993 to 2006, and adapted by the Conservative government to justify the Afghanistan mission since then. Canadians might enjoy the ear candy that has been fed to them about how generous they are, but they appear to be manifestly attached to an orthodox security imaginary when it comes to missions such as Afghanistan that involve putting thousands of their fellow citizens in harm's way and spending billions of dollars for outcomes that promise only limited direct benefits for Canada.

5

Constructions of Nation, Constructions of War
Media Representations of Captain Nichola Goddard

CLAIRE TURENNE SJOLANDER
AND KATHRYN TREVENEN

On 7 October 2001, Prime Minister Jean Chrétien addressed Canadians in a nationally televised broadcast, confirming that Canada would be contributing to the international coalition taking action against Afghanistan's Taliban regime. "We are part of an unprecedented coalition of nations that has come together to fight the threat of terrorism," Chrétien explained. "I have made it clear from the very beginning that Canada would be part of this coalition every step of the way" (*National Post* 2001). Almost five years later, on 17 May 2006, Captain Nichola Kathleen Sarah Goddard was killed in combat twenty-four kilometres west of Kandahar, Afghanistan, during a firefight with Afghan insurgents. The seventeenth Canadian killed in Afghanistan since 2002, Goddard became the first Canadian female soldier to be killed in action since the Second World War, and the first ever to be killed on the front lines of combat (CBC News 2006a). Through an examination of the media portrayal of Captain Nichola Goddard after her death, this chapter begins to explore the way in which media representations and manipulations of gender (and of implied gender roles) are deployed to effectively shape – and limit – the parameters of public debate over Canada's involvement in the Afghanistan mission. Both these gendered representations, and the representations of gender, contribute to the construction of the sovereign state as "protector." As many critical feminist scholars have documented, the protector/protected dichotomy that is instrumental in defining one aspect of gendered hierarchies also effectively depoliticizes state actions

(Peterson 1992). This gendered hierarchy, defining the state as masculine, confers upon it a responsibility to protect in the public sphere, just as the husband/father, responding to a gendered hierarchy within the private sphere, has a responsibility to protect. As defender of Afghan civilians (notably women and children), and as combat soldiers (who are really peacekeepers), the image of the Canadian state as protector becomes one against which political opposition becomes difficult to articulate. As protector, the Canadian state's participation in the Afghanistan mission is both "natural" (consistent with gender hierarchies) and an unquestionable good – conferring legitimacy upon the entire mission in the same breath. As Denis Stairs (2003b, 240) has critically argued, "Canadians have grown alarmingly smug, complacent, and self-deluded in their approach to international affairs ... They have come to think of themselves not as others are, but as morally superior. They believe, in particular, that they subscribe to a distinctive set of values – 'Canadian' values – and that those values are special in the sense of being unusually virtuous." Nichola Goddard's death, and the media representations of the tragedy of her death, provides an example of the ways in which Canada's "moral superiority" is popularly constructed, emphasizing the moral foundations of the Canadian nation and its international role, including its role in Afghanistan.

To examine the ways in which the state-as-protector construction is advanced, two portrayals of Nichola Goddard produced by newspaper coverage after her death are examined. The print media (often aided by military spokespeople) constructed representations of Goddard as both the "gender-neutral soldier" and the "(extra)ordinary peacekeeping soldier." We argue that these representations speak fundamentally to Canadians' conceptions of appropriate gender roles, the Canadian military, and Canadian foreign policy toward the war in Afghanistan. We further argue that the image of Nichola Goddard constructed by the media serves to reassure Canadians that on all of these issues (gender roles, military force, and the war in Afghanistan), Canadian society is not just ethically right, fair, and equal but actively laudable. We thus examine how the gendered representations of the war and its participants have circled back to reinscribe and reinforce certain foundational assumptions about Canadian society: that we are an equal and gender-blind society, that we are a peace-seeking and peacekeeping actor in the international system, and that Afghanistan represents "Canada at its best" (Blanchfield 2007a; see also the analysis in Charbonneau and Parent's Chapter 3). Through a focus on Nichola Goddard, a study of the gendered representations of the war can tell us not only about how war is promoted to an often skeptical Canadian public but also about the degree to which normative gender roles are used to reinforce particular images of the Canadian state on the international stage, and thus to construct a particular understanding of the nature of Canada's military intervention in Afghanistan.

To understand how gender affected representations and interpretations of Nichola Goddard after her death, we chose to examine the coverage provided by 268 articles (including letters to the editor) run in seven Canadian daily newspapers. This coverage begins in May 2006 with Captain Goddard's death and extends to February 2007. The seven newspapers were chosen because of their status as national or regional dailies, as well as for the specific role they played in the telling of the Nichola Goddard story. The newspapers are the *Calgary Herald,* which published 93 articles on Nichola Goddard; the *Winnipeg Free Press,* with 40 articles; the *Daily News* (Halifax), with 26 articles; the *Globe and Mail,* with 47 articles; the *National Post,* with 44 articles; *Le Devoir,* with 6 articles; and *La Presse,* with 12 articles. The *Globe and Mail* and the *National Post* are considered national newspapers in (English) Canada, while *Le Devoir* and *La Presse* are the most important French-language dailies published in Quebec. The remaining three papers were selected because of the special attention they paid to the death of Nichola Goddard. The *Daily News,* published out of Halifax, was chosen because Nichola Goddard spent her teenage years in Nova Scotia, hence the attentive coverage of her death. As the major daily in Manitoba, the *Winnipeg Free Press* paid special attention to Goddard's regiment, which was based in Manitoba. Finally, Goddard's parents resided in Calgary, the city where she was married, and which Nichola Goddard had adopted as her hometown.

Media representations of Nichola Goddard were constructed in part by the publication of portions of her letters sent to friends and family at home. We are privileged to have been able to read them, and we are conscious that this adds to our responsibility to treat her words and thoughts with particular sensitivity. What we seek to interpret and reflect on in this chapter is not the "truth" of Goddard's character, experience, or role in Afghanistan. Instead, we focus on the representations of her built by the media and assess what these representations reveal about Canadian society and normative gender roles. Although we turn a critical lens on the ways portraits of Goddard as an exemplary Canadian peacekeeper reinforce Canadian foreign policy goals, we do not question the integrity and thoughtfulness of her commitment to peacekeeping, nor the depth of her sacrifice.

The story of Nichola Goddard's death is characterized by the common – and even banal – brutality of contemporary warfare. The Battle of Panjwaii, which had been raging throughout the day, seemed all but over. Captain Goddard, a forward observation officer with the 1st Regiment Royal Canadian Horse Artillery based in Shilo, Manitoba, was in an armoured vehicle that was patrolling in a village in the Panjwaii district as coalition troops continued to look for the remains of the Taliban forces. Suddenly, the shooting started again, "blazing in from every direction" (Farrell 2006). "We were in the process of doing final searches in the village when one of our call signs came in 'ambush,'" recalled Lieutenant Colonel Ian Hope, the man who led the Canadian troops into battle (quoted in ibid.). Shortly before 7 p.m., Captain Goddard's column of vehicles was ambushed in the renewed fighting. Goddard, with her head and shoulders sticking out of the hatch of her vehicle, had been on the radio constantly, "directing artillery fire and aerial bombardment." Rocket-propelled grenade fire hit the turret of her vehicle, producing a "storm of shrapnel" that struck Goddard in the head. "'Her LAV [light armoured vehicle] was struck with rocket fire, at least two, and possibly three rockets, and unfortunately she was killed,' Hope said" (ibid.). Canadian brigadier general David Fraser, commander of the Canadian and coalition forces in Kandahar in 2006, offered his sympathies to Captain Goddard's family upon news of her death. "Our hearts, our prayers and our sympathies go out to the family of Nichola Goddard," said Fraser, standing in front of a Canadian flag at half-mast. "It's a hard day, but it's also a day of achievements here. The government of Afghanistan and the Afghan national security forces have had a good successful day. There was significant Taliban casualties both killed and captured. Unfortunately, the cost today was the life of Nichola" (quoted in *Halifax Daily News* 2006a).

"One of the Boys" Means "We're All Equal"

The media coverage and commentary on Captain Goddard's gender reveal several interesting contradictions. First, there is the fact that Goddard's gender was part of what made her death such a large news story: She was the first Canadian woman killed in front-line combat. Despite this starting point, however, the coverage overwhelmingly focuses on how unimportant her gender was to her role as a soldier. The Canadian public was effectively being told that it should pay attention to Goddard's gender for only as long as it took to disregard it completely. The second contradiction seems built into most claims to gender-blindness or gender-neutrality. Most accounts of Goddard's gender-neutral status as a soldier portrayed her as "one of the boys," "just like a man," or "as good as a man." In all these examples, gender-neutrality is not neutral at all – it assumes masculinity or maleness as the standard or default gender. Gender neutrality – and that neutrality as masculine – is critical in preserving the logic of the state-as-protector, however, for the protector has most usually been male; women have historically been excluded from the state-sanctioned roles of protector or defender (Peterson 1992, 53.) In this respect, women in the military challenge this model of the nation/state as a patriarchal, heterosexual family – one that is protected in the public sphere by the father. Women in the military reverse the normalized gender hierarchy. Goddard's gender becomes something that has the potential to disrupt this patriarchal construction of the sovereign state, unless her (female) gender is erased. In constructing Goddard as having no gender, the message being sent is a reassuring one. If the Canadian military – an institution frequently criticized for its sexist, racist, and homophobic discrimination – is gender-blind, then Canadians can stop worrying about gender-based oppression or structural discrimination. If Goddard's gender is erased to the point of irrelevance, then it is still possible to construct the state-as-protector and to preserve the dichotomies between protectors and protected that are fundamental to the domestic and international spheres.

For the Nichola Goddard presented by the media, gender was not something to be noticed, much less celebrated. Using comments from family, friends, military brass, and Goddard herself, the media insisted that Goddard be remembered as a soldier, not a female soldier. Goddard's family led the way in this. Her father, Tim Goddard, was quoted as saying that his daughter "believed a soldier is a soldier is a soldier and [that] she didn't think gender had anything to do with the job she was trained for" (McGinnis 2006). Goddard's husband, Jason Beam, was just as clear, saying his wife had never thought of herself as a "combat trailblazer." "I don't think she wanted to be perceived as a female doing a job. She felt she was just like one of the other soldiers and wanted to come across that way" (Giroday 2006). Beam went on to say that "it was one of her pet peeves; she wanted to be known for doing her job well and not be seen as a female" (O. Moore 2006). The *Herald* also quoted a friend of Goddard's sister, Alexandra Garigue, who remarked that "Nichola would have been furious" if she thought that one of the reasons Canadians were deeply affected by her death was that she was a woman killed in combat; "for Nichola, she was doing what she believed in, and she was helping people in the most concrete way" (Payton 2006).

The media depicted Goddard's colleagues as even more adamant that gender had nothing to do with her role as a soldier. Her former supervisor,

Major Reiffenstein, pointed out that Goddard would "want to be remembered as a really, really good soldier, not as a female officer, a female soldier or a first of anything" (O. Moore 2006). For Warrant Officer John Lannigan, Goddard was a "shining example for both males and females"; despite being in a "predominantly male trade ... people really respected her" (Williamson 2006b). Captain Harry Crawford went further: "Female soldiers play an equal role in today's Canadian army, he said. Soldiers are soldiers. They are brothers-in-arms" (York 2006). The official response of the Canadian military to Nichola Goddard's death and service supported the media image. Lieutenant (navy) Morgan Bailey was explicit: "I cannot stress enough that we view all of our fallen comrades, who pay the ultimate sacrifice in support of their nation, equally and regardless of gender. A soldier is a soldier, and we respect their service to Canada on equal terms" (Jaimet with Wattie 2006). The insistence by the military that Nichola Goddard had no gender other than "soldier" belies its history of highly publicized scandals involving rape, the sexual assault and abuse of women, and inquiries into sex discrimination, systemic racism, hazing, and the creation of a hostile environment for women and LGBT (lesbian, gay, bisexual, transsexual) people (Razack 2004; Winslow and Dunn 2002; see Kinsman's Chapter 6). In such a context, the portrait of Captain Goddard created by the media held the potential to assuage concerns that gender discrimination remained a substantial issue in the Canadian Forces – without gender, gender discrimination seems moot.

Throughout the coverage, it is striking the extent to which the very reason news of her death had so captured media attention – her gender – was dismissed as irrelevant. The *Calgary Herald* bemoaned that "it is perhaps unfortunate that the history books will remember Goddard as the first Canadian woman to die in combat. Because those who knew her say her sex was irrelevant. She was a soldier, plain and simple" (Williamson 2006b). Goddard's death had touched so many, not because "she was a woman who was leading a platoon of men" but because "she showed that gender did not matter ... [a fact] so evident in the respect and admiration ... coming from her male comrades" (Remington 2006b). The *Winnipeg Free Press* echoed the sentiment: "She was the first female soldier to die in combat since the Second World War, and that got people's attention, but she would not want to [be] remembered for that. Canada is one of only a few Western nations that put women into combat roles, and Capt. Goddard would have shared the attitude of her comrades in arms – a soldier is a soldier" (*Winnipeg Free Press* 2006a).

Nichola Goddard's own words, published after her death, also reflected a desire to be a gender-neutral soldier. Describing her forays outside the camp, she commented, "I have seen about 100 men in our trips and easily double that in children, but no women so far. I don't think they realize that I am a woman when we drive by, which is fine by me" (Fortney 2006a). Meeting for the first time with tribal leaders in Afghanistan, she recounted:

> We were in a village and were just getting on our kit to walk to the next town. I had attracted a crowd of five men aged 15-60 who were watching me ...
>
> Anyway, the interpreter came up and had a two-, three-minute conversation in Pashtu with the five men who were watching me. Then he turned to me and said, "Please excuse their staring. They are just very surprised that you are a woman working with all of these men. I have told them that you climbed over the mountain with us with your heavy bag and that you had no problems. They think that you must be very strong. I explained to them that you are just like the men, and that you can do everything that they can do the same as them."
>
> It was perhaps the greatest statement of equality that I have ever heard – and it was given by a Pakistani-raised, Afghan male in the middle of an Afghan village that is only accessible by a five km walk up a mountain. (quoted in Berenyi 2006)

Once she had arrived at the next community, Goddard was invited to participate in the meeting with the village elders, where the surprise continued:

> I am not sure how serious the discussion was before I got there, but once I arrived it quickly centred on my marriage status. The big shock was not that I was in the army, but that I was married and in the army. The fact that my husband was not also a soldier was even more disturbing ... The remainder of the discussion revolved around my inexplicable lack of children. The elder offered to go inside and get me some milk and bread, as diet was probably the issue. (quoted in Berenyi 2006)

The second time she was invited to participate in a meeting, the discussion focused on a different issue:

> Anyway, here the issue was not my lack of children, but my availability. My boss was apparently asked if I was available to marry one of the elder's sons who looked to be about 15. After we'd established that I was already married, the issue turned to the all-important one of baking bread. When I confessed that I could not make the delicious flat bread that they serve (like

a flat naan bread) the elder asked, "Can you at least boil water to make chai?" I was quite indignant in my response. (quoted in Berenyi 2006)

Throughout, Goddard seems intent on demonstrating that she was not preoccupied – or limited – by "the whole female thing," which she feared "would be a huge issue" (quoted in Berenyi 2006).

Gender concerns were present in the camp as well. Goddard explains that when she first arrived in Kandahar, she was sharing a small tent with nine other officers. She recounted: "This morning, I put my lock inside my combat boot. Then, I picked up my boots and yelled out 'Scorpion check' as I tipped my boot upside down beside my buddy's cot. There was a big 'thump' as the lock fell out. My buddy, Howard Han ..., shot out of bed like he'd been shot. It was pretty good. The good news is that I no longer need to worry about being the first one to scream like a little girl" (Fortney 2006a). Later, when she was moved into a tent shared by roughly two hundred soldiers, a decision was quickly taken to move the women out of the tent (only three soldiers were women). Captain Goddard wrote a letter protesting the move to the commanding officer. She argued, "I think that we have taken a benign situation and created a fantasy." The commanding officer wrote her back, agreeing to a compromise – the women could remain in the tent with the others but had to be segregated behind a tarp, isolated from the men (Fortney 2006a).

In all these examples, the strategies Goddard uses to deflect attention from her gender – humour, the assertion that she does have some feminine skills, and a determination not to be singled out – point to the highly gendered environment she lived and worked in. It seems possible that Goddard's own assertion of her gender-neutrality was not a simple affirmation of gender integration, as the military and press assert but, rather, a common and tactically smart response to the high cost of being a woman in a highly masculinized environment. Throughout the repetition of the refrain "a soldier is a soldier is a soldier," we are reminded forcefully that the original template of a soldier is male. Goddard is notable because she has risen to the male standard, not because the standard itself is neutral or ungendered.

This dynamic is made particularly clear in an op-ed by Barbara Kay, published in the *National Post*. Kay argues that

> Captain Goddard's courage and impeccable service record do not indicate a wider trend for women in the military. She was a "manly" soldier – I say that with great admiration and no irony – and the exception to a general rule.

Nevertheless, in 30 or so wars currently in progress, most uniformed women are still choosing the traditional (and honourable) path of their non-uniformed historical sisters – providing logistical, administrative and medical support to the men who kill and get killed. As competent and professional as Captain Goddard was, her attitude was unusual. There are about 8,000 women in the Canadian Forces (CF), of whom 225 actually occupy the "combat arms" trades. What have we spent to recruit, train and service women in order to deploy this low number? Don't ask (because they won't tell).

The government does not promote gender equity in nursing, teaching, library science or childcare, because these are all intrinsically female professional bastions. Intrinsically male bastions, however, are regarded as fertile ground for cultural "re-education," and now even military spokesmen docilely toe the feminist line as expressed by one retired woman lieutenant: "In this modern era of equality of the sexes, [soldiering] has no gender."

A pretty notion, but a falsehood nonetheless. The Forces need women in most occupations, but for combat purposes most women are inferior to men in both body and spirit; and most uniformed women self-select out of combat, just as most civilian women self-select out of other male-dominated high-risk professions.

By all accounts, Captain Nichola Goddard was a great combat soldier who defied such generalizations. But our recruiters and policy-makers would be well-served to understand just how exceptional this woman was. (Kay 2006)

Throughout this article, Kay highlights the idea that Goddard is an *exception* to the rule that women are inferior soldiers. Women and men are still "intrinsically" different and suited therefore to different domains of work. Kay's piece is explicitly misogynist and anti-feminist, while the assertion that a soldier has no gender is not, but both arguments destabilize the basic claim to gender equality found in most newspaper coverage by reinforcing the idea that the military male norm should remain unspoken and unseen. In this article, however, Kay also reinforces the idea that men are the protectors, that men are meant to assume the combat roles in the military, and that Goddard's presence represents a rare exception – with no power to fundamentally disrupt the sovereign order.

Interestingly, while denying or erasing the relevance of her gender, press reports also went to great lengths to point out that Goddard was, in fact, a woman. Commentaries were offered on her romantic history, her plans to have children, and her capacity for nurturing. Gabrielle Giroday (2006) in the *Winnipeg Free Press* explained that "Goddard doted on their pets – two dogs and two cats which had been rescued from the animal shelter – and it was her dream to open a boarding kennel when she left the army." The *Globe and Mail* also highlighted her love of animals: "'After the weekend I'd talk about my kids driving me crazy and she'd talk about her dogs,' Major Reiffenstein ... [recalled]" (O. Moore 2006). In the absence of children, her pets were an adequate substitute – the markers of her nurturing nature.

Goddard was portrayed as a girl in other ways as well. Her mother was cited as recalling that when the family lived in Edmonton, "Nichola was showing an interest in typical teenage girl pursuits, such as boys, short skirts and shopping ... She was very conscious of her feminine side. That was part of the beauty of who she was becoming, retaining her femininity while working in a masculine world" (Fortney 2006b). Her colleague, Sergeant Patrick Desbiens (with whom Goddard had helped fight the fires that tore through British Columbia in 2003) recalled that while Nichola Goddard was as fit as any man, she was more than that: "She could turn it off as quickly as she could turn it on. Sharing a tent with six or seven guys didn't bother her in the least ... she was just one of the soldiers. But outside of that, if you saw her at the mall, she was Nichola then" (Williamson 2006b). Here again, the need to "turn off" her gender while being soldier reinforces the norm of the military as masculine space. When not acting as one of the protectors, Goddard could return to her gender-"appropriate" role as one of the protected.

Finally, it is interesting that when reflecting on Goddard's successful career and noteworthy leadership style, many articles talked about traits that have been traditionally constructed as feminine. They revealed that Goddard "often fussed over her troops, keeping them occupied and entertained with maintenance duties, training films and games" (Brewster 2006). She had a calming voice when coordinating the artillery assets in her battle group and calling down artillery fire. To one of the reporters embedded with her unit, "she was The Voice, that warm, completely unflappable, calm voice on the radio that felt like balm to taut nerves and overactive imaginations" (Blatchford 2006b). Despite her absolute professionalism and the seriousness of her purpose, "she remained playful, spontaneous and remarkably open to the people and experiences that Afghanistan offered her" (Blatchford 2006a). Nowhere do the authors of these articles reflect that perhaps it was in part her more "feminine" qualities that made her so good at her job. The assumption throughout is that if she was a good soldier, it was because she was not defined by her gender, because she was not acting like a woman. Nowhere in the gendered representations of the military, of war, and of soldiers is there an acknowledgment that the so-called feminine traits of nurturing, compassion, creativity, and emotional openness might be skills that soldiers need. Protectors are not nurturers.

The portrayal of Goddard as "one of the boys" is crucial because it works against the disruptive potential of Goddard's gender; if she is indeed "one of the boys," she is not really a woman, and therefore, she can be easily integrated into the ideal of a (masculine) military. More powerfully, though, the erasure of Goddard's gender, and the insistence that she is a soldier just like any man, maintains a gendered construction of the Canadian state as "father knows best," as an international protector. Just as with Nichola Goddard, however, the gendered (male) image of Canada as international protector also depends for its success (and its domestic saleability) on qualities often ascribed to be feminine – notably, those qualities most often associated with international peacekeeping. The second portrayal of Nichola Goddard presented by the media provides just such a reading of gender roles.

Nichola Goddard: Portrait of the (Extra)Ordinary Soldier

The second media-driven portrait of Goddard offers a more complex and subtle reassurance to Canadians. If the gender-neutral military can represent a society that does not need to pay attention to gender discrimination, then the portrait of Nichola Goddard as both ordinary (just like any other soldier) and extraordinary – speaks to ongoing Canadian anxieties about the war in Afghanistan (see, for example, Nossal's Chapter 4). While all commentators agreed that Goddard was an excellent soldier, an extremely competent leader, and a thoughtful and caring person, they also continually reflected on Goddard's reasons for joining the military. They cited her commitment to peacekeeping, her thoughtful defence of the use of military force, and her caring nature more generally. All these qualities, while no doubt reflecting Goddard's personality and skills, feed into a long-held belief that women provide the moral anchor for their societies. While men compete, fight, and produce in the public realm, it is women's softer, peace-loving, and nurturing side that maintains and sustains society.

Thomas Paine, in his *An occasional letter on the female sex*, writes in a woman's voice to describe this difference between the sexes: "Our duties are different from yours, but they are not therefore less difficult to fulfill, or of less consequence to society: They are the fountains of your felicity, and the sweetness of life. We are wives, and mothers. 'Tis we who form the union and the cordiality of families. 'Tis we who soften that savage rudeness which considers everything as due to force, and which would involve man with man in eternal war. We cultivate in you that humanity which makes you feel for the misfortunes of others" (Paine 1775/1989, 9). Defined in such a manner, although without the rhetorical flourishes of the eighteenth century, Goddard's gender provides the backdrop for a subtle justification of the war in Afghanistan and creates a reassuring portrait of what the Canadian military is doing there. Here, gender is critical – both Goddard's and that of those Canada is protecting in Afghanistan. By personalizing Goddard – providing background about her childhood, her articulate defence of the mission, and her exemplary leadership – the media focuses our attention away from other, broader questions and anxieties, and constructs the Canadian state as a benign and laudable international protector. Goddard's whiteness is also necessary to the media portrait of her as civilized, moral, and rational. As Sherene Razack argues in *Dark threats and white knights: The Somalia Affair, peacekeeping and the new imperialism* (2004), "National and international mythologies of heroic white people obliged to make the world safe for democracy and needing to employ violence to do so flood our airwaves" (8). Although newspaper reports do not explicitly refer to Goddard's whiteness (the many pictures of her reproduced in both print and electronic media obviated the need to do so), following Razack, we argue that her racial privilege forms the background against which she is represented as the civilized peacekeeper opposed to the racialized and orientalized Afghan other.

Newspaper coverage of Captain Goddard's death in combat provided a detailed background picture of her childhood and personal life. Born in Madang, Papua New Guinea, in May 1980, Goddard spent her childhood living with her teacher parents and two sisters in numerous northern communities, from the Black Lake reserve in northern Saskatchewan to Pangnirtung on Baffin Island. Later, in La Ronge, Saskatchewan, "Nichola ... developed a taste for adventure and athletic pursuits," taking up cross-country skiing and subsequently racing for the Alberta and Nova Scotia junior Nordic teams (Fortney 2006b). While studying at Dr. John Hugh Gillis Regional High School in Antigonish, Nova Scotia, where Goddard was about to graduate with top honours, a representative of the Royal Military College came to the high school to meet with students. Nichola decided to apply, and her strong grades translated into an entrance scholarship to attend the college (MacEachern 2006).

In addition to the basic facts of Goddard's early life, newspaper coverage also offered a strong narrative about why Goddard had joined the military. According to at least one of her high school history teachers, Goddard's decision was a reflection of her early interests. Flipping open a Canadian history textbook to a chapter on the UN and Canada's role in peacekeeping, Brian MacNeil, a teacher at Dr. John Hugh Gillis Regional High School, recalled: "I remember even then Nichola was really keen on the military ... She was keen on helping people out in whatever aspect of life." MacNeil's sense that this was an appropriate career choice for Goddard was confirmed a year later when she returned to Antigonish to visit his class and to "enthusiastically share" what it was like to be in the forces (MacEachern 2006). Her biathlon coach at Royal Military College went even further: "To me, she is a hero; she wanted to be a peacemaker and a peacekeeper, she died doing what she loved and she served our country with pride. She was the kind of person that wanted to be on the front line of anything she was doing and she took a lot of pride in her work" (Beaupré 2006).

Goddard's commitment to peacekeeping was also revealed in an exchange she had with her father. In a debate over the role of military force in the world, Dr. Goddard argued that "education is the key to development for the poor and oppressed," whereas Captain Goddard "subscribed to the view that military force is required to permit the reconstruction of civil society." "Quick as a flash," Tim Goddard recalled, "she punctured my professorial balloon." "You can't do that when the bad guys run things, Dad," she said, "they just shoot you. You have to have peace and good government in order for the rest to happen. I do what I do so you can do what you do." "As always," Dr. Goddard said, "she was right" (quoted in Blatchford 2006a). These accounts of Goddard's education and experience of the military contribute heavily to a picture of Goddard as an exemplary Canadian soldier – a deeply reflective soldier – one who is thoughtfully committed to the ideal of peacekeeping.

Shortly before the mission that would lead to her death, Goddard was interviewed in Afghanistan by an embedded reporter for CTV News, giving her an opportunity to reflect on her decision to join the military. Like many young students, she commented, "I signed up to go to university. I needed a job, I had no money ... But somewhere along the way, I fell in love with it. I'm probably a lifer now" (Williamson 2006b). Once she graduated, she took on a job with the artillery, tasked to call artillery fire on enemy targets. The job was described as a "risky assignment, one of the most dangerous in the artillery" (York 2006), yet she was proficient enough that a colleague described her as "the most technically and professionally competent officer I have ever served with" (Captain Andrew Charchuk, quoted in Remington 2006b), a view echoed by her direct superior from 2002 to 2005, Major Anne Reiffenstein: "She was smart and funny and bright ... She worked extremely hard to be proficient; it's a combination of technical and tactical skills" (O. Moore 2006).

In addition to her skills as a soldier, Captain Nichola Goddard was known as "a strong leader who inspired loyalty and courage among the soldiers of her unit" (York 2006). This respect for Goddard's leadership was echoed by others upon hearing of her death. Major Liam McGarry, commanding officer of Goddard's regiment, read out one of the eulogies at her funeral: "Capt. Goddard was an outstanding leader and soldier. Her dedication to the soldiers under her command was unwavering ... Capt. Nichola Goddard was highly respected by officers and soldiers alike, throughout the regiment and across the Canadian forces" (Williamson 2006a). Captain Harry Crawford, a friend and chaplain at Camp Nathan Smith, the Canadian base on the outskirts of Kandahar, went further, reflecting that "they [the soldiers of her unit] would do anything for her ... The soldiers knew her. They would follow her into hell and back" (York 2006). Another colleague, who was in Goddard's squadron at the Royal Military College in 1999-2000, reflected: "She was just one of those people who were so pleasant and charismatic. She had a very radiant personality, and she was eternally optimistic ... In retrospect, yes, she had the qualities that make a great leader" (Williamson 2006b).

Defining the nature of her leadership abilities, Goddard was also remembered in the news as a compassionate and caring person. Captain Crawford was quoted recalling the day he first met Nichola Goddard. He "had just moved to Canadian Forces Base Shilo ... where Goddard was based. It was -40 that day, and Crawford, a Nova Scotian, was unprepared and hatless in the harsh Prairie winter. Goddard ... took care of that right away. 'When she noticed I didn't have any hats, she went right to her house and gave me some of hers. She would give you the toque off her head" (*Halifax Daily News* 2006b). Her generosity and concern for others manifested themselves in other ways as well. Captain Andrew Charchuk, a friend at the Shilo base, remembered how Goddard had "helped his wife when she was injured in a car accident. 'It was just in her nature to care,'" he said, reflecting that her "compassion and love for life always shone through everything she did" (Edmonds 2006).

Finally, the media published a family statement speaking to Goddard's caring and compassionate nature. "'Nichola had a huge smile, and an even bigger heart,' said a family statement [published after her death]. 'She was a volunteer scout leader and a faithful member of the Anglican Church. She was always a caring person. Once, during a ski race, a competitor became hypothermic and collapsed by the side of the track. Nichola stopped and helped him down to the finish, losing any chance of winning the race herself. After that, her friends all called her "care bear." At Shilo, she agreed to shave her head as part of a cancer fundraiser, and her men gleefully auctioned off the right to wield the razor. She raised a lot of money"' (*National Post* 2006). Importantly, though, the media reports of Goddard's qualities and values lead to an inescapable conclusion: If Nichola Goddard believed in the military and the mission in Afghanistan, then all Canadians should. The media reports also further create the impression that Goddard, although exceptional, represents the military very well – she is an ordinary soldier – a mark of what the Canadian military represents on the international stage. Canada truly is acting as the protector, and Goddard, as a white woman and as a soldier, protected women and children in Afghanistan – that is, those who, by reason of their gender, nationality, ethnicity, religion, or age (all suggesting their vulnerability) needed protection.

To create the image of an ordinary soldier, newspapers highlighted Goddard's own insistence that she was just doing her job. Despite her obvious skills and capacity for compassionate leadership, or perhaps as a reflection of them, Nichola Goddard insisted throughout her career that she was simply a soldier, like all the others. Writing a letter home after returning from a fifteen-day mission in the mountains north of Kandahar, Goddard observed: "I am always astonished at the way that the military acts as a great equalizer. It doesn't matter where you are from, or how much money you had growing up or the size of your family. It doesn't even matter what country you're from or your level of education. Once you're out with other soldiers, doing your thing, we are all the same" (Berenyi 2006). Warrant Officer John Lannigan, who met Goddard in 2003 during artillery training at Canadian Forces Base Gagetown, pointed to her as an example of the good soldier: "If I had to give you an example, prior to her death, of a good soldier, I would have given you her ... She had all the skills, and she loved her job" (Williamson 2006b). In many of her letters, the good soldier recounted how she felt participating in ramp ceremonies to honour the fallen: "Standing among thousands of soldiers watching caskets being loaded into planes was always 'very moving,' she wrote ... struck by the fact that those lost were regular soldiers, just like her" (McGinnis with Linn 2006). The ordinary soldier was present after her death as well. In February 2007, the governor general of Canada presented thirty-three Meritorious Service Decorations to individuals whose specific achievements brought honour to the Canadian Forces and to Canada. Among those honoured was Captain Nichola Goddard, who was presented the award posthumously. Her husband, himself a retired member of the armed forces, accepted the medal on her behalf. While pleased that Goddard was being honoured for her participation in the Afghanistan mission ("She definitely deserves it and definitely earned it," he said), Jason Beam reflected that Goddard might not have enjoyed the attention that came with the honour. "I'm not quite sure she would enjoy all this publicity about it and being up front and on stage and everything," he commented (CTV News 2007).

Publishing extensively from her personal letters, the newspaper media concluded that Nichola Goddard's death reflected the high but justified price of the war in Afghanistan. Goddard's own reflections and even ambivalence about the war seem to speak to this debate. Reflecting on the military presence, she writes:

> The kids all run out to watch us drive by. Sometimes they wave and smile, but other times they swear at us and throw rocks. I still find it pretty shocking to see young children so full of hate at us being here. But others wave and smile and seem to want us around. It is hard to know who is right. I just have to believe that we are doing a good thing. (Fortney 2006a)

> Understandably, they weren't too fond of us – at least not initially. It was really encouraging to see the difference between the locals' reactions when we first showed up to the last few days. Kids were starting to wave, and elders were coming forward of their own volition to talk to us – it was wonderful. (*Winnipeg Free Press* 2006b)

> I had never truly appreciated the awesome power of a democratic government before. We are here to assist that legitimate and democratically elected government. It is easy to poke holes in that statement and say that the system is corrupt and that violence and poverty make people easy targets for our own agendas. Those statements are true; however, we have to start somewhere. With the best of intentions, we have started in Afghanistan. There is nowhere else that I'd rather be right now. (Berenyi 2006)

These published reflections not only reveal Goddard to be a thoughtful and articulate commentator, they also draw her into a broader justification of military intervention. If Goddard is "every soldier," then Canada's peacekeeping efforts are in good hands. Goddard's obvious concern for the children feeds into the gendered bias of the state-as-protector. Despite describing herself as a "poster child for why people should join the military" (Berenyi 2006), it was not in shooting the bad guys that Nichola Goddard was portrayed as finding her purpose. As one reporter noted, "There was a lone protester on a side street outside Goddard's funeral holding a sign saying that Canadian soldiers should be 'peacekeepers.' To Goddard, that's exactly what she was doing" (Remington 2006a). Her role in combat, as part of a military that had been defined in the public imagination as anything but a combat army since the end of the Korean War, was powerfully driven by that imaginary. She might have worn a soldier's uniform, but Nichola Goddard's reflections on her role in Afghanistan reinforced a Canadian perception of the military as peacekeepers.

Goddard's thoughtfulness and clear compassion – her peacekeeper's sensibility – in the face of months of media debate about Canadian soldiers being killed in Afghanistan in a combat role played a part in sweeping the debate aside. Notably, on the day that Canadians learned of Goddard's death, the House of Commons was to vote on a government motion to extend Canada's commitment to the Afghanistan mission for another two years beyond the initial 2007 deadline. Goddard's death was announced within the context of that debate and prompted this commentary in the *Calgary Herald*:

> Soldiers aren't supposed to be deep thinkers. They are supposed to be automatonic grunts. That's been my impression, anyway, and, as usual, it's probably wrong. Maybe everybody in the Canadian Forces is like this. I don't know because I haven't met very many of them. But thanks to Goddard's family ... we know more today about the person that was Capt. Nichola Kathleen Sarah Goddard – and perhaps a little bit more about the 2,300 dedicated Canadian soldiers still in Afghanistan.
>
> We always hear that Canadian soldiers are different than Americans and other coalition soldiers. We are told they are more educated, more enlightened and more passionate about making a contribution in the world. True or not, I can't say. But if every Canadian soldier is half as dedicated and passionate as Goddard, how proud and inspired all of us can be. (Remington 2006a)

The self-described poster child for the Canadian military became the poster child for Canada's role in the world. As one letter writer to the *Calgary*

Herald put it, "Captain Goddard epitomizes the Canadian character, quietly doing heroic deeds" (Isaak 2006).

The Canadian imaginary was powerfully reinforced by sentiments like those expressed by a *Calgary Herald* reader: "A little part of every Canadian died the day Capt. Nichola Goddard died in battle. That part of our heart was replaced by pride for every member of the Canadian Forces" (Moody 2006). In the context of the debate holding sway in Canada, Nichola Goddard became a symbol of something better: "People back home have every right to criticize the mission. That's democracy. There are legitimate questions about how long to stay and how to measure progress. But before they dismiss Afghanistan as a fool's errand, they should listen to the people like Capt. Goddard who stand in the front lines. They believe in Canada's mission" (*Globe and Mail* 2006). With the exceptional Nichola Goddard onside, how could one not believe in the mission too? The depoliticization of Canada's role in Afghanistan made possible by the gendered representations of it becomes critical in a divisive political time. If Nichola Goddard believed that the mission was a peacekeeping one, if she had a commitment to the good that it could do, how is it possible to contest the mission's legitimacy, or to question Canada's role within it? Goddard as "any soldier" emphasizes the inherent good of Canada's military commitment; Goddard as a (female) soldier, committed to peacekeeping and conceiving of the mission in those terms, makes opposition to the mission appear churlish and mean-spirited – and unworthy.

On 18 May 2006, by a vote of 149 to 145, the Canadian House of Commons voted to extend Canada's mission in Afghanistan until 2009. Editorials in the *Winnipeg Free Press* and the *Calgary Herald* argued that this decision, although not a powerful political victory, at least showed Goddard some respect. "The day after Capt. Nichola Goddard died, Parliament had the grace and good sense to promise that her death would not be in vain – that Canada would continue the fight" (*Winnipeg Free Press* 2006a). "Those who complain of the meaninglessness of a soldier's death do not grasp how utterly vain such a death would be if Canada abruptly left Afghanistan because of it and the seeds of democracy languished, unwatered, in the volatile climate there. We will pay a far greater tribute to Goddard and to the other Canadian soldiers who have lost their lives there if we finish what they started" (*Calgary Herald* 2006). If someone as good as Goddard, who believed in the good of the mission, gave her life in the conduct of it, then to oppose Canada's intervention in Afghanistan would be to stand on the side of evil, against inherent good.

Members of Parliament, including two contenders for the leadership of the Liberal Party of Canada, argued the same thing. In a letter to the *National Post,* Scott Brison argued: "We have a responsibility to defend ... [human rights] at home and abroad ... Our country must be willing to stand up for the values that we espouse ... Following her death on Wednesday, Captain Nichola Goddard's husband said, 'We shouldn't tuck our tails behind our legs and run ... We've kind of got our foot in the door now to start making a difference. I think we need to follow through and carry on with the mission.' I couldn't agree more" (Brison 2006). Michael Ignatieff made the point even more starkly, saying that he could not, in all good conscience, vote against the government's motion on the same day as Nichola Goddard became the first female Canadian soldier to die in combat since the Second World War (*Le Droit* 2006).

Conclusion

In this chapter, we examine the two primary portraits of Nichola Goddard produced by newspaper coverage after her death. This discussion allows us to point out the extent to which the media constructed representations of Goddard as both the gender-neutral soldier and the (extra)ordinary peacekeeping soldier. Far from being disruptive to the military order in which Canada is participating, Goddard's gender is used to reinforce foundational assumptions about the Canadian nation and its international role. As Sandra Whitworth has argued, the image of Canada as peacekeeper is a central myth in the Canadian imaginary. In this myth, "Canada is an altruistic and benign middle power, acting with a kind of moral purity not normally exhibited by contemporary states" (Whitworth 2003, 76). This myth leaves the state-as-protector role intact, and representations of Nichola Goddard work to reinforce it.

The representations of Goddard the media provided in the days and months following her death speak fundamentally to Canadians' conceptions of appropriate gender roles, the Canadian military, and Canadian foreign policy toward the war in Afghanistan. Goddard's gender and its erasure foreclose some of the space for political debate over the merits of the Afghanistan mission: If Goddard stood for it, how could anyone be against it? After her death, these representations continue. Prime Minister Harper's surprise visit to Afghanistan in May 2007 famously included a visit to a school for orphans. Nichola Goddard, the poster child for the military, becomes the ultimate representation of the Canadian imaginary. As a reader from Whitby, Ontario, wrote to the *Calgary Herald:*

I am proud of Canada's place in peacekeeping and helping make a better world for everyone. Nichola is the perfect example of Canadians everywhere willingness to go the distance for others. I did not know her, but I will remember her contribution to her family, her regiment and her country. (Henry 2006)

PART 3

CONSTRUCTING GLOBAL ORDER AT HOME – CONCEPTUALIZATIONS AND PRACTICES OF NATIONAL SECURITY

Against National Security
From the Canadian War on Queers to the "War on Terror"

GARY KINSMAN

National Security as Hegemonic Ideological Practice

"'Security' is a sacred cow of a word in the name of which highly dictatorial and sweeping actions are possible for which no explanation can be forced." Thus wrote Harold (1960-61, 1-2), who was purged from the Canadian Navy when the Royal Canadian Mounted Police and Naval Intelligence determined him to be a homosexual, in the late 1950s.[1] In contrast to the hegemonic "common sense" that uncritically defends national security, this is a critical "good sense" observation growing out of Harold's experiences with the military and the national security regime.[2] Harold was among thousands of suspected gay men and lesbians purged from the government and the military as so-called national security risks.

This entry point signals the taking up of the social standpoint of those most detrimentally affected by this national security campaign, in this case lesbians and gay men. From this place, we can see more and move further beyond the ideology and practice of national security. Crucial to the theory and method proposed here is a general social standpoint shift to those most directly affected in critically interrogating national security.[3]

National security is both social and historical, and is an ideological practice or code. We tend to forget this, given the normalization of national security as hegemonic common sense. I use "ideology" in the sense of a social form of knowledge production that attends to the management and ruling of people's lives and that is uprooted from people's everyday social experience.[4] This focus on ideology critique is based on the previously mentioned standpoint shift. This leads us to ask critical questions about national security – including which nation is being defined and whose security is being defended (Kinsman, Buse, and Steedman 2000). Rather than simply accepting or taking for granted constructs of the "national interest" and national security, we need to always ask whose national security is being articulated and who is doing the defining.

Those defined as national security risks are Otherized (Bannerji 1995) as threats to the nation and are coded with danger. Within national security discourses and practices, the concept of national security has been defined in opposition to actual and perceived threats from communists, socialists, peace activists, trade unionists, women's union auxiliaries, feminists, immigrants, high school and university students, First Nation activists and scholars (especially the American Indian Movement but also including Native Studies programs), supporters of Quebec sovereignty, black activists in Nova Scotia and elsewhere, and "sex perverts" (Kinsman, Buse, and Steedman 2000). Later, in the 1990s and since, there has been a focus on other subversives in global justice and anti-poverty movements and now in the expanding category of "terrorist" used against Muslim- and Arab-identified people and other people of colour (see Byrne's Chapter 7).

The ideology and practices of national security both exclude and include (Corrigan 1981, 313-16). Those *excluded* either can be cut off from their human and citizenship rights (D. Smith 1990a, 30-32, 43), or these rights become increasingly precarious, with these groups being afforded fewer rights than those at the centre. In contrast, those who are *included* are positioned at the centre of the nation-state. This is a relational process of exclusion and inclusion that expels some groups from the fabric of the imagined nation while simultaneously placing other groups at the centre of this nation. This is what national security as an ideological practice is all about.

By asking who is being excluded from the fabric of the nation and who is being included at the centre of this nation we are prevented from taking constructions of the nation and national security for granted. We have to ask whether national security encompassed the security of working-class people, indigenous peoples, women, lesbians and gay men, immigrants, and others during these years. Or was this national security directed against these groups by the security regime?

This chapter is drawn from joint work with Patrizia Gentile (the "we" I sometimes refer to) for the *Canadian war on queers: National security as sexual regulation*.[5] Based on interviews with lesbians and gay men directly affected by national security campaigns, this research takes up their social standpoints to critique official national security texts released through access to information requests and the interviews we have undertaken with security officials. Practices of national security are sometimes narrated in reference to an enemy located outside state relations but rarely from the perspective of those who are dominated and marginalized within a hierarchically organized political order such as the Canadian state. The stories of the dominated are rooted in social and political power relations, but these stories are also very much the fabric of the construction of national security and of what is being referred to as "global order" in this book. This points to how the ideology and practice of national security *and* resistance to it participate in the construction *and* deconstruction of global and local orders.

The Social Organization of Forgetting and the Resistance of Remembering

For most of us, this process of national security is not very visible. In the face of the official story of Canadian politics and history, we do not always have the social and historical literacy to remember these experiences of exclusion and inclusion.[6] I am suggesting that capitalism and oppression rule in part through what we call the *social organization of forgetting,* based on the annihilation of our social and historical memories that leads to forgetting our pasts, and especially past struggles and resistance (Corrigan and Sayer 1985, 195; Dunbar-Ortiz 2008; Radstone and Hodgkin 2003a, 2003b; Ross 2002). There is a major lack of the critical historical and social literacy that C. Wright Mills (1959) wrote about and a need to develop our sociological and historical imaginations to counteract this. Remembering earlier national security campaigns can help us in addressing the current ones we face. Remembering can be a basis for resistance.

As David McNally (2001, 191) points out, drawing on the work of cultural and social theorist Walter Benjamin, "Rather than something laid down once and for all, the past is a site of struggle in the present." This is very much the case for struggles over national security. There are important stakes in these struggles. Struggles over the past are part of our struggles in the present, and we are also searching for resources in the past for our current struggles – and for our possible futures.

In hegemonic constructions of Canadian nationalism and national security, the nation-state is portrayed as a monolithic, unitary entity, despite the actual multinational character of Canadian state and social formation. All nations are imagined communities (Anderson 1991), but this takes a particular form in Canadian state formation. Social differences, and struggles organized by oppressed groups around them, can easily get defined as problems of national security. The concept of national security rests on notions of the interests of the "nation," which in the Canadian context is defined by capitalist, racist, heterosexist, and patriarchal relations. Canadian state formation is historically a racializing and class-based project founded on the colonization of the indigenous peoples (Bannerji 2000; Thobani 2007). It also includes the subordination of the Québécois and the Acadians, in alliance with the British Empire and later with American imperialism.

In 1994, a Treasury Board report on information management and security, which played an important part in coordinating security information and procedures within state relations, defined "national interest" as concerns relating to "the defence and maintenance of the social, political and economic stability of Canada."[7] Social, political, and economic stability is seen here as inherently in the national interest. This gives us a clear sense of the pro-capitalist character, of this construction of the national interest with any challenge to capitalist, social, sexual/gender, political, or economic relations being defined as a challenge to the national interest of Canada. We will see later how this definition of national interest is mobilized against anti-poverty and global justice protestors and "subversives" of various sorts who disrupt the stability of capitalism in Canada. We also see here the ways in which a unitary, monolithic character of the nation is constructed that denies the many social differences, inequalities, and relations of exploitation on which "Canada" is constructed.

Queering National Security in the Context of the War on Terror

One of the more insightful aspects of queer theory, a discourse-focused approach often influenced by postmodernism and post-structuralism, is the notion of *queering* aspects of social life from the standpoints of queers.[8] "Queer" is taken up here as a way of reclaiming a term of oppression; to assist in developing a broader framework for social and political resistance than lesbian, homosexual, or gay; as a term that can include bisexual and transgender experiences; and as a place from which to critically interrogate ruling sexual and gender relations. From being marginal, as in most mainstream social theorizing, the experiences of queers become central in this process of queering social discourses and relations. Although in queer theory this is most often done on cultural or discursive terrains, we wish to give this insight a more historical and materialist basis to make this insight more relevant to critical historical and sociological investigations and to activist concerns (Kinsman 1996, 13-14, 23-40). I use this perspective to queer (or render strange) national security. We place the social experiences of queers at the heart of our critical analysis of national security. From this standpoint, it is the practices of national security that have created problems in the everyday lives of queer people.

As I wrote this chapter, not only was I looking at the historical past but I was doing this in the historical present of the war on terror. In this context, I was amazed that many accounts (even critical ones) of the war on terror view it as entirely new and distinct from earlier national security campaigns. This fetishism of 9/11 created through the mainstream media and the construction of the post-9/11 world as "new" prevents us from seeing the relevance of earlier national security campaigns to our critical understanding of the current war on terror. Here, I focus on important continuities between earlier and current national security campaigns, but there are also significant discontinuities and something that is very new in national security post-9/11, which other chapters in this book explore in detail. Our critical investigation of the national security campaigns against queers is intended to wrench open the fabric of national security and to push forward critical questions about the current deployment of national security.

Queer Anti-Racist History and Sociology from Below

This critical work draws on a number of sources and inspirations. These include the work of E.P. Thompson (1968) and the articulation of history from below (E. Wood 1995, 13, 49-107). This involves looking at the world from the standpoint of workers and has served to inspire other histories from below, including anti-racist, women's, and queer histories. We also draw on currents within autonomist Marxism (Cleaver 2000; Dyer-Witherford 1999, 62-90; Kinsman 2005a) that focus on the activity of workers and a refusal to portray workers as simply victims and give all power to capital. This approach maintains our focus on resistance, the social relations of struggle, and the possibilities for transformation. We combine this with the Marxist-feminist work of Dorothy E. Smith (1987, 1990a, 1990b, 1999) in developing sociologies for women and the oppressed, and her important critique of ideological practices and the textual practices of ruling. We draw on her institutional ethnography approach, which turns the skills and capacities of critical ethnography against ruling institutional relations (such as national security) in our society (Campbell and Gregor 2002; Devault 1999; D.E. Smith 2005).

These approaches all have a relation to historical materialism, but this tradition has unfortunately not been very developed in relation to critical gender and sexual politics. This is why we propose developing a historical materialism for queers that includes a queering of historical materialism. I reject the often hegemonic academic way of viewing Marx as an economic determinist where the economy determines all. Instead, Marx's work needs to be seen as a profound critique of how economics operates as a form of reification (Cleaver 2000; Holloway 2005) – obscuring the importance of social relations and practices. Marx's project was to constantly disclose the social relations between people hidden behind the power and appearance of things.

Developing this historical materialism for queers is at the same time a queering of historical materialism growing out of queer resistance and lesbian/gay/queer movements. Queer resistance through seizing and expanding social spaces partially opened up by capitalist social relations has created spaces to develop queers' own desires and needs and a basis for resisting the various forms of oppressive sexual regulation mobilized against them.[9] This queering requires shattering the natural and ahistorical appearances of heterosexual hegemony and the present gender system; disclosing the oppressions lying beneath the "natural" appearance of these hegemonic practices; excavating the socially made character of sexualities and genders; and putting heterosexuality and the current gender regime into question. This points us toward the possibilities of overturning heterosexual hegemony and transforming erotic and gender relations, through linking this to the transformation of state, class, gender, and race relations. Marx's work and method still have a lot to tell us about the dynamics of capitalist social relations and how these shape the lives of queers and others.

This needs to also be thought through and redefined by the critical work on racialization and Otherization by such theorists as Edward Said (1979) on orientalism, and Himani Bannerji (1995, 2000), Sherene Razack (2004, 2008), Nandita Sharma (2006), Andrea Smith (2005), Sunera Thobani (2007), and others. Through the historical and social practices of capitalism and imperialism, some groups get homogenized as supposedly sharing the same ahistorical "essence," and they then get Otherized as different and "deviant," compared with those placed at the centre. Otherization is always a relational process in which some are Otherized while others are constructed as the normal group at the centre. We need a mediational social analysis (Bannerji 1995) that grasps how race, gender, class, sexuality, and other social relations are made in and through each other in concrete social history.

The War on Queers

From 1958 on (with earlier roots), within the Canadian state there was a major campaign against suspected gay men and lesbians, since their "character weakness" supposedly made them vulnerable to blackmail by enemy agents. In contrast, many of those we have interviewed report being blackmailed only by the RCMP, which attempted to get them to give the names of gay men and lesbians. Thousands of suspected homosexuals were spied on, interrogated, or purged from their jobs during these years. The Canadian state even tried to develop a detection technology – which came to be dubbed the "fruit machine" – that attempted to identify queers so that they could be denied employment.[10] These campaigns continued in the military, the RCMP, and the Canadian Security Intelligence Service on an official level into the late 1980s and early 1990s.

A central aspect of the Cold War in Canada was therefore gender *and* sexual regulation, and the campaigns against queers were key to this. The focus on queers was not simply a mistake, nor was it simply about individual homophobia.[11] The anti-queer aspects of the Cold War were not an epiphenomena of little importance but were central to the deep-rooted mediated social character of the Cold War. By the later 1960s and 1970s, these continuing anti-queer mobilizations were attempts to contain the re-emergence of gender and sexual political struggles.

A key objective of the continuing Cold War mobilizations was the making of the "normal," as Mary Louise Adams (1997) and others have persuasively argued. Moral regulation (Brock 2003; Corrigan 1981, 1990) was always a key feature of these mobilizations, as certain forms of social practice were defined as moral and normal, while others were constructed as immoral and deviant. This making of the normal was always constructed against Others, dangers, and risks. A central and continuing feature of the Cold War was the construction of both sexual normality *and* sexual deviance. And key to this was the mobilization against queers and *for* heterosexual normality. Queers were thrown outside the fabric of the nation. But this is also a relational social process. The other side of these mobilizations is that the Cold War mobilization of national security is fought *for* heterosexual hegemony – producing heterosexuality, as in the national interest, as "loyal" and as "safe." Heterosexuality becomes the national sexuality. In the military and the security police, this was a defence of a narrow hegemonic heterosexual masculinity against various queer threats that were seen as undermining the masculine character of state relations, the military, and the police. National security was both an exclusionary device, expelling queers from the fabric of the nation, and an inclusion device, constructing the Canadian state as heterosexual.

Queer Resistance
But queer people refused to cooperate with the security police. David reports that

> we even knew occasionally that there was somebody in some police force or some investigator who would be sitting in a bar ... And you would see someone with a ... newspaper held right up and if you ... looked real closely you could find him holding behind the newspaper a camera and these people were photographing everyone in the bar.

David is speaking about his experiences of police surveillance in the 1960s in the basement tavern at the Lord Elgin, one of the major gathering places for gay men in Ottawa. Surveillance such as this was one way the RCMP collected information on homosexuals. David's story is a remarkable example of resistance against police surveillance strategies by the men in the bar:

> We always knew that when you saw someone with a newspaper held up in front of their face ... that somebody would take out something like a wallet and do this sort of thing [like snapping a photo] and then of course everyone would then point over to the person you see and of course I'm sure that the person hiding behind the newspaper knew that he had been found out.

Rather than diving under the tables or running for cover, these men exposed the police and turned the tables on the undercover agents. David's story reveals not only the national security surveillance regime but also the resistance to it in the 1960s. This resistance obstructed and forced shifts in national security practices, since many of the RCMP's previous informants were no longer talking to or willing to give the names of other queers to the RCMP. The basis for this resistance was in growing forms of queer talk and solidarity. Queers were put under surveillance because of a "character weakness," but gay and lesbian resistance to this security policing provoked police surveillance of queer organizing itself.

In the 1970s, as gay and lesbian liberation and then gay and lesbian rights organizing emerged, they became obstacles to the national security campaigns, since these movements targeted the anti-queer national security practices of Canadian state formation. In response, the RCMP tried to understand this growing resistance through conceptualizing "gay political activists" and "radical lesbians" as national security problems. The perspectives of queer organizing based on coming out, being public, and building movements and communities undermined the secrecy and relations of the closet that the national security campaigns against queers were based on.

Numerous reports on gay groups we have accessed for the 1970s are in response to a request for information from the Montreal Security Service prior to the Montreal Olympics in 1976 (NGRC 1976). This request was made in response to queer organizing against the pre-Olympic "cleanup" campaign in Montreal. It was common for cleanup campaigns against "vice," including against the gay scene, to be organized before major public events, and it was explicitly stated that this was the case with this particular campaign. This coincided with a growing police response to the public visibility of gay establishments, of gay community formation, and of gay sexualities. In 1975-76, many gay and lesbian bars and gay bathhouses in Montreal were raided by police as part of the attempt to "clean" gays out of downtown bars and "public" places.

The Montreal police were encountering a new problem in gay activist organizing. They wanted information from across the country on this movement so that they could figure out how to deal with it. We also see important connections here between national security, social and moral "cleansing" (the surveillance or harassment of groups considered undesirable), and sexual policing that was also relevant to the organizing of the 2010 Olympics in the Vancouver area, where anti-poverty activists, homeless people, indigenous peoples, and anti-Olympic protesters themselves were targeted (No One Is Illegal Vancouver 2008; Olympic Resistance Network 2008; Spirit of Warrior Harriet Nahanee 2008).

On 19 June 1976, more than three hundred gays, lesbians, and supporters joined in the largest gay rights demonstration up to that point within the Canadian state. Demonstrators marched through downtown Montreal chanting, "À bas la répression policière" [Down with police repression]. As a result, the cleanup campaign was largely halted, and this helped lay the basis the next year for two thousand people taking to the streets to protest the police raid on the Truxx bar, which in turn helped lay the basis for human rights protection for lesbians and gay men being established in Quebec in 1977 (T. Warner 2002, 148-49).

The National Security Campaigns against "Subversives"

Queers, along with other groups, were constructed by the security regime as subversives. Queers were put under surveillance because of who they were perceived to be and because of what they did in building liberation movements. Subversives more generally are put under surveillance because of what they do. The adaptability of the concept of subversion is a key ideological conceptualization for national security. As Grace and Leys argue in relation to state definitions of subversion:

> Many writers on subversion have complained that the term refers to a "grey area" and is difficult to define. Our view is that it has always referred to a fairly clear reality: legal activities and ideas directed against the existing social, economic and political [and I add sexual, gender and racial] order ... Any radical activity or idea with the potential to enlist significant popular support may be labeled "subversive" ... [Subversion] is invoked ... to *create* a "grey area" of activities that *are* lawful, but will be denied protection from state surveillance or harassment by being *declared* illegitimate, on the grounds that they *potentially* have unlawful consequences. In capitalist societies the targets of this delegitimation have been overwhelmingly on the left. (Grace and Leys 1989, 62-63, emphasis in original)

For indigenous people in what is now called Canada, there has always been a major security response to their militancy, from Kenora, Grassy Narrows, Kanesatake, and Kahnawake, to Ipperwash and the murder of Dudley George, Gustafsen Lake, and the current struggles in Caledonia and Tyendinaga. Most often, but not always, white protestors were addressed in a less repressive fashion.

This seemed to shift in the fall of 1997 when the campus at the University of British Columbia became the site of the Asia-Pacific Economic Cooperation (APEC) meeting. Activist groups among students and in the community were put under RCMP surveillance. There were major violations of people's democratic rights, and the publicized use of pepper spray against young demonstrators engaging in non-violent direct action. The mobilization of national security at the APEC summit involved the RCMP defending the foreign leaders who were the target of protest, including Indonesian dictator Suharto. Canadian national security in this context was defined by the Canadian state's commitment to APEC as one vehicle for capitalist globalization and by Canadian state and corporate support for the

Indonesian Suharto and other regimes. This is what led the RCMP to defend Suharto, other foreign leaders, and their undemocratic and secret meetings. The designation of Suharto and others as "internationally protected persons" under the Canadian Criminal Code and the 1973 Convention on the Prevention and Punishment of Crimes against Internationally Protected Persons led to their protection becoming part of Canadian national security (Okafor 2000, 185-86; Pearlston 2000).

The use of pepper spray, which was controversial in 1997, has now been normalized as part of the repertoire of police action against global justice and anti-poverty protestors. Their arsenal of pain-inflicting equipment also includes plastic and rubber bullets, tear gas, and sometimes Tasers. In June 2000, pepper spray was used against global justice activists protesting the Free Trade Area of the Americas (FTAA), and more than fifty protestors were arrested in Windsor, Ontario, at the meetings of the Organization of American States (Windsor Peace Committee 2001).

In this context, militant political dissent and protest was increasingly read by officials and the mainstream media as not only subversion but terrorism. In June 2000, the police responded to an anti-poverty demonstration with a major attack when they cleared Queen's Park in Toronto of protestors. Following this, the level of police surveillance and policing of actions organized by the Ontario Coalition against Poverty (OCAP) increased significantly, with some authorities identifying OCAP as a terrorist organization for its direct action anti-poverty work. OCAP activist John Clarke was charged with a series of offences, including incitement to riot, as a result of his participation in organizing this demonstration. In 2001, a Crown attorney labelled Clarke a terrorist for an action involving a mock eviction of a cabinet minister who was responsible for the evictions of many people living in poverty across the province (Gadd 2001; Shantz 2003).

The largest security mobilization against global justice protestors took place at the third Summit of the Americas, organized to discuss the proposed FTAA, in Quebec City in April 2001. Police used tear gas (5,192 canisters in a forty-eight-hour period, and peaking at a rate of thirty canisters per minute), pepper spray, and rubber and plastic bullets (903 of them), injuring at least one hundred protestors, and arrested more than four hundred people (Chang 2001; Moreau 2006, 3; Swift 2002, 11). The police were even authorized to use lethal force against those protestors perceived as posing a danger to any of the thirty-four state leaders gathered at the summit (MacKinnon and McKenna 2001). In defence of the security "wall of shame" and the meetings of state and corporate leaders, the police engaged in major forms of violence against protestors, especially when activists were successful in pulling down the security barrier. Unfortunately, government officials and much of the mainstream media labelled the limited and targeted corporate property destruction that some groups engaged in and the breaches of the security fence as instances of violence, deflecting attention away from the much more profound violence of the police and the violence of the daily generation of poverty, homelessness, and hardship in people's lives that permeates capitalist social relations. Despite the police violence and some of the mainstream media coverage, activists were successful in disrupting the start of the meetings, exposing the secrecy of the meetings, and drawing attention to the problems of the FTAA (Chang 2001).

In response to challenges to police actions at the summit, the justification for the violence was the protection of internationally protected persons (IPPs) and the security threat that the demonstrators supposedly represented. As Katherine Moreau (2006, 78) points out, "The 'security' of these IPPs was placed above the individual rights of the demonstrators in the name of 'national security.'" In response to the so-called subversion of anti-poverty and global justice protesters, "anarchists," and "radicals" are read out of the fabric of nation. This builds on the mainstream media association of anarchism with disorder and with violence, which obscures that anarchism is a critique of state relations and violence (Day 2008; McNally 2002, 244-49). At the same time, a commonsense support for capitalism (or at least the presumption that there is no alternative to it) is placed at the centre of the nation-state.

The War on Terror

The national security "war" on Arabs and people identified as Muslims did not start with 11 September 2001. The racialization and Othering of Arab- and Islamic-identified peoples, including that directed at Palestinians resisting the occupation of their land, has a long history. During the 1991 Gulf War, this racialization grew in Canada, which led to heightened surveillance and discrimination against Palestinians, Iraqis, Iranians, and others. This included the Canadian Security Intelligence Service (CSIS) holding intimidating interviews with more than five hundred Arab Canadians and showing them photos of people taken at anti-war demonstrations and other places for identification purposes (Kinsman, Buse, and Steedman 2000, 256-63). These practices directed against Arab- and Muslim-identified people have been intensified since 11 September 2001. CSIS regularly conducts "interviews and interrogations with hundreds of Arabs and Muslims across Canada at their work places, homes and in the vicinity of local mosques" (Christoff 2007).

In the aftermath of 9/11, the Canadian state moved quickly to introduce new anti-terrorism legislation in response to the Bush regime's initiative for a war on terror, in an attempt to harmonize relevant legislation with the United States and other Western powers and also for its own domestic reasons in terms of perceived internal threats. Multiple aspects of the Canadian national security war on terror cannot be traced out here (but see elsewhere in this book); I therefore limit myself to two areas: rendition and national security certificates.

Rendition is the practice of seizing a person in one country and moving him or her to another for the purposes of interrogation, torture, or prosecution. The most famous example of this is that of Canadian citizen Maher Arar, who in 2002 was interrogated by FBI and immigration officials in New York City, held in custody for twelve days, and then sent to Jordan on a plane, where he was shackled and chained most of the time. He was then driven to Syria and tortured for nearly a year until he was finally released. It is now clear following the official inquiry into what happened that this rendition was initiated by and sustained by the RCMP giving erroneous information about Arar (2006) to US security officials (Thobani 2007, 244-46; Webb 2007, 9-24).

Arar is one of numerous people who have gone public with similar stories, including Benamar Benatta, Abdullah Almalki, Ahmad El Maati, and Muayyed Nureddin. Benatta, who was illegally transferred to the United States and tortured and held for five years by US authorities, is calling for a public review of his case. Benatta, an Algerian refugee claimant, was handed over to the Americans on 12 September 2001. Canadian officials wrongfully identified Benatta as a suspect in the terrorist attacks of 11 September 2001 based solely on prejudicial suspicions – he was a Muslim man who knew something about airplanes. Without a hearing, without legal counsel, and without conducting proceedings in his first language (French), Benatta was unceremoniously driven over the border in the back of a car and handed over to US officials. On 20 July 2006, Benatta was finally allowed to return to Canada and has resumed his claim for asylum.

The national security certificate procedure is part of the security provisions of immigration legislation. Following 9/11 and the passage of the anti-terrorist legislation in 2001, there was an overhaul of the immigration system with the passage of Bill C-11 in 2002. As the People's Commission on Immigration Security Measures points out, this legislation:

> reframed migrants without Canadian citizenship, including Permanent Residents, under the new category of "foreign nationals." It also introduced mandatory detention of non-Permanent Residents named in a security certificate, on information provided by CSIS, before any judicial review whatsoever of the allegations. This has meant years of detention for refugees such as Mohamed Harkat, who spent two years in an Ottawa jail before the certificate was even reviewed by a judge. (People's Commission on Immigration Security Measures 2007, 24-25)

The security certificate process is set in motion when the minister of citizenship and immigration and the solicitor general of Canada, at the request of CSIS, sign a certificate naming an individual as a threat to national security. The certificate is reviewed by a federal court judge, but the standard of proof is "reasonable grounds to believe," which is not as rigorous as the criminal law standard of "beyond all reasonable doubt"; the detainee and his or her lawyer are not given access to the information against the detainee; and the key terms, including "national security," "terrorism," and "membership," remain undefined. The certificate then becomes a deportation order with no regard given to whether the individual might be tortured if deported to their country of origin (People's Commission on Immigration Security Measures 2007, 24-25; Razack 2008, 25-58).

National security certificates have been used against five Muslim-identified men: Mahmoud Jaballah, Mohammad Mahjoub, Hassan Almrei, Mohamed Harkat, and Adil Charkaoui. All were released from custody, most with very stringent home arrest conditions (Shephard 2007). They had previously been held at the Kingston Immigration Holding Centre – a $3.2 million facility within Millhaven penitentiary specifically constructed for security certificate detainees. After a series of hunger strikes for basic health and living conditions at what came to be dubbed "Guantanamo North," a Supreme Court decision on 23 February 2007 challenged the heart of Canada's secret trials regime, deeming the security certificate procedure to be unconstitutional. The Supreme Court gave the government one year to respond to the decision before the law was to be nullified. Yet, all five detainees remained in indefinite, arbitrary detention or house arrest conditions, under threat of deportation and possible torture, under a law recognized as illegal.

The Conservative government introduced new security certificate legislation in 2007, which was passed with the support of the Liberal Party in 2008. It is based on the special advocate model (where a special advocate but not the detainee is allowed access to the secret information used against the detainee), which continues the injustice of security certificates while further entrenching the use of secrecy in the immigration and justice systems. The new legislation provided a minor reform but holds the main features of the security certificate procedure in place – including placing arbitrary power in the hands of spy agencies and politicians; replacing precise charges with vague concepts; and relying on secret suspicions, profiling, and association instead of evidence – and it has no purpose not covered by criminal law except deportation to torture (Neigh 2008). In practice, it assumes that Muslim immigrants are potential threats to national security. This also writes these Muslim refugees and immigrants out of the fabric of the Canadian nation (Razack 2008). More recently the national security certificate regime has fortunately begun to crumble. In December 2009 the federal court quashed the security certificate against Hassan Almrei (Tibbetts 2009).

Those excluded in the context of the war on terror are Muslim- and Arab-identified people and other people of colour, including queer people of colour, while those included at the centre are white, and largely Christian-derived. This is one of the reasons, despite official denials, that the racist "clash of civilizations" discourse permeates so much of the popular discourse of the war on terror.

The State of Exception or the Rule of Law in National Security

As mentioned, the focus on 9/11 has led to the decontextualization of the current war on terror from earlier national security campaigns, leading some theorists and activists to interpret the war on terror as a state of exception where the regular rule of law has been suspended. This leads to focusing on the horrors of the Abu Ghraib prison in Iraq, Guantanamo, rendition, Canada's national security certificates, and the erosion of civil rights in the context of the war on terror. It is imperative we focus on these, but it is sometimes suggested that all we need to do is get rid of this state of exception and restore the rule of law. The "state of exception" is an expression used by Carl Schmitt and taken up in the work of Giorgio Agamben (2005, 1998). For Agamben, the modern operation of power is based in an almost permanent state of exception in which the regular rule of law is suspended, as in the Nazi concentration camps. A central image in this view is the camp, and in this context we are no longer so much citizens as detainees. The central form of power becomes the state of exception, and the rule of law comes to be based on it. Although this captures something crucial about the mobilization of national security in the context of the war on terror, it leads us away from seeing how the deployment of national security measures is also rooted in the normal relations and routine operations of power and the rule of law. As Michael Hardt (2004) points out, "My hesitation with this view is that by posing the extreme case of the concentration camp as the heart of sovereignty it tends to obscure the daily violence of modern sovereignty in all its forms. It implies, in other words, that if we could do away with the camp, then all the violence of sovereignty would also disappear" (see also Huysmans 2008). As we suggest, doing away with the violence of the national security state requires a much broader project of social transformation that challenges the social roots of racializing, colonizing, heterosexist, patriarchal, capitalist, and state relations, including the rule of law itself.

Agency and Resistance

As in the war against queers and against so-called subversives, people are fighting back against the racism, fear, and insecurity produced by the war on terror. The wars abroad, such as the Canadian participation in Afghanistan, and the national security campaigns at home, including security measures against Arab- and Muslim-identified people, are being resisted. People's actions can make a difference. The large anti-war mobilizations in 2002-03 against the Iraq war, especially in Quebec, played an important part in keeping Canadian troops out of the Iraq war, even though Canadian corporate and state support for that war has still been significant (Fenton 2007). More recently, people's organizing has challenged the legitimacy of the national security certificates and the wide-ranging anti-terrorist legislation, creating the basis for important legal decisions that the government has been forced to respond to.

We are never simply passive victims or people without agency, and we have the power to act. Through our actions we can subvert and undo national security – through carrying out popular education and building powerful social movements and alliances among the various groups facing national security onslaughts, and through activating what is currently relatively passive opposition to war, occupation, and racism. This is the way we can move toward a world in which there is no Othering and we can appreciate and celebrate the social differences between people. Now is the time to get to work against national security. We need to resist the forgetting of the Canadian war on queers and participate in the resistance of remembering through continuing to queer and challenge national security. Through increasing our resistance, we weaken the hold of national security over our social worlds.

NOTES

1 Harold is a pseudonym to protect his confidentiality.
2 I use the terms "hegemony" and "hegemonic" in Gramsci's (1971) sense to refer to the bringing together of the moment of coercion and force with the manufacturing of consent in the relations of ruling. On the statist focus that continues with many Gramscian-derived uses of hegemony, see Day (2005). Both hegemonic common sense and oppositional good sense grow out of the contradictory character of social experiences in a social world defined by exploitation and oppression and the struggles against them.
3 On this use of standpoint as a transformer of social knowledge see Frampton et al. (2006, 1-17, 38, 44-70) and D. Smith (2005).
4 I do not use the term "ideology" as it is commonly used in sociology and political science, as a biased form of knowledge or as knowledge from a particular point of view. As Roslyn Wallach Bologh (1979, 19) suggests, "Ideology refers to all forms of knowledge that are divorced from their conditions of production (their grounds)."
5 Published by UBC Press in 2010. We use the term "war" as in "war on queers" in a parallel way to how anti-poverty movements have used expressions such as opposing the "war on the poor." Without in any way trivializing the experiences of actual warfare and colonialism, we wish to point to the seriousness and the systematic character of the national security campaigns against lesbians and gay men and the devastation these created in thousands of people's lives. At the same time, notions of war as in the "Cold War," the "war on drugs," and the "war on terror" have often been inflected by and colonized by right-wing deployments of this term. Thanks to Dan O'Meara for raising this point in discussion at the conference.
6 I am using the term "literacy" here not in the formal sense but in the sense that Paulo Freire uses it where it is always tied up with relations of social power and resistance to them. Developing social and historical literacy is developing the means to name and transform the social worlds we exist within and produce (Freire 2006; hooks 1994).
7 Treasury Board of Canada, "Information and Administrative Management Component, Security," 09-06-94 (Ottawa: Treasury Board), C6.
8 Queer theory can be used in a number of ways. Here I am using queer theory in a narrow sense to refer to the theory, influenced by post-structuralim and post-modernism, that emerged in the later 1980s and early 1990s. This queer theory can lead queer theorists to veer off in the direction of a discourse reductionism that

reduces the complexities of social practices and relations to the discursive domain alone (Hennessy 2000; Jagose 1996; Sedgwick 1991; M. Warner 1993).
9 This approach learns from but moves beyond both John D'Emilio's (1983) one-sided emphasis on capitalist social relations and wage labour as key to the emergence of the homosexual and Michel Foucault's (1978) one-sided emphasis on the moment of labelling in official discourse as key to the emergence of the homosexual to develop a more relational and mediational approach that grasps the coming together of capitalist social relations, sexual resistance, and sexual regulation in the emergence of the homosexual, the lesbian, *and* the heterosexual (Kinsman 1996, 23-81).
10 This is documented in G. Kinsman and P. Gentile's *The Canadian war on queers: National security as sexual regulation* (Kinsman and Gentile 2010).
11 On the individualist and psychological limitations of homophobia, see Frampton et al. (2006, 40-41).

Framing Post-9/11 Security
Tales of State Securitization and of the Experiences of Muslim Communities

SIOBHAN BYRNE

Following the terrorist attacks of 11 September 2001, Western governments hastily passed legislation designed to protect the state and its citizens from the ubiquitous threat of global terrorism. Examples include the Patriot Act in the United States, the Anti-terrorism, Crime and Security Act in the United Kingdom, and the Anti-terrorism Act in Canada. These security measures enabled governments to respond to the external threat of global terrorism by targeting individuals and communities within state borders through the application of new domestic security strategies. Ironically, these so-called *security* strategies have not advanced the security of some citizens and residents and, in some instances, have contributed to their *insecurity*, leaving them vulnerable to stereotyping, racial profiling, and acts of intimidation.

Further, an increasing climate of Islamophobia in the West reflects and reinforces the orientalizing myths that inform state securitization processes and the broader "civilizing" mandate of the war on terror. In this environment, Muslim women are more likely to experience harassment and discrimination – especially those women who are easily identified by cultural practices related to dress (Hamdani 2005, 8-9; also Canadian Federation of Students 2007, 14). Such experiences of insecurity and the fear that they generate suggest that we need to unpack state-based conceptions of security, particularly as they have evolved since 9/11, and understand the concept of security as it is operationalized and experienced locally, inside the state. Feminist interrogations that begin by examining *how* security is experienced by the most vulnerable and marginalized communities reveal a gendered security discourse that perpetuates racialized conceptions of citizenship and belonging.

The experiences of Muslim, Arab, South Asian, and other ethnocultural communities in Canada are particularly telling in this regard because these communities are very often perceived to be threats to national security and values. An examination of Canadian government policy changes and media reports demonstrates how a changing Canadian security landscape impacts Muslim (or presumed to be Muslim) Canadian residents and citizens. High-profile security debacles such as Project Thread and Canada's role in the detention and deportation of Canadian citizen Maher Arar reveal the orientalist mythologies at work in the new security agenda. Such an analysis highlights the gendered impacts of the national security discourse and policy changes on Canadian Muslim women, especially the ways in which the war-on-terror script continues to frame Muslim women as subjugated victims of a tyrannical religion and, indeed, in need of "saving" (see Charbonneau and Parent's Chapter 3).[1] Women who did go off-script and were critical of the civilizing mandate of the war on terror were publicly reprimanded by politicians and in the popular press. Similarly, the gendered constructions of Muslim men who were characterized by the state as at risk of radicalizing were construed as posing a threat to national security.

Canada is pursuing a new global security agenda at the same time as gendered and xenophobic constructions of *Muslim-man-as-terrorist* and *Muslim-woman-as-oppressed* are coming to the fore in national and local popular discourses. These policy pursuits and discursive constructions are not mutually exclusive; rather, they work together to reinforce the orientalist myths on which they rest. I argue that this post-9/11 national security discourse, developed and enforced by the Canadian state in the name of protecting all Canadian citizens from the threat of global terrorism, and reiterated and reinforced through the media, undermines the experience of belonging, the guarantee of civil liberties, and ultimately, the security of these identity communities.

A Critical Feminist International Relations Approach

The third debate in international relations (IR) in the 1980s and 1990s opened up the largely elite-focused and state-centric field to critical, feminist, and post-structuralist approaches, where different agents, locations, and levels of analysis were prioritized (Sylvester 2007, 553). However, the post-9/11 return to familiar state-centric analyses, concerned with the central war *problématique* and accompanying statist conceptions of security, presents a particular challenge for scholars who have been working within a critical feminist IR tradition (Pettman 2004, 90). Jan Jindy Pettman (2007, para. 17) observes that, despite the work of feminist IR theorists, a renewed emphasis on terrorism and security undermines "all that careful unravelling of simplistic, naturalised understandings and the tracing of the complexities, contradictions, shifting alliances and multiple identities, contesting and reconfiguring power relations." The post-9/11 climate is coercive, she argues, because it regulates "what can be asked, or said, and makes us politically suspect – even before we get to explicitly engage in gender talk" (para. 17).

Feminist IR approaches establish how those hierarchies of power, based on hegemonic conceptions of gender and other classifications, affect those actors who are otherwise overlooked in mainstream analyses (Tickner 2006, 40). Further, some feminist IR treatments rethink what counts as knowledge by observing political events from the perspective of women's experiences (Kronsell 2006; Tickner 2006). Nearly two decades ago, Cynthia Enloe (1990) asked, "Where are the women" in international politics? Hilary Charlesworth and Christine Chinkin (2002, 600-1) remind us that most of the central actors in the immediate aftermath of 9/11 were men: the hijackers, the brave firefighters and heroic police officers, the rescue workers, the men in the White House, and most of the major actors on the international stage. In matters of national urgency and security, women's voices are rendered unimportant.

Similarly, post-colonial feminist interventions consider not just the location of women in international politics but how privilege and power are also constructed along gendered and racialized lines. In the post-9/11 context, such interventions reveal how "security," as enacted by state governments in response to the global threat of terror, works to demarcate the boundaries between Self and Other. Yasmeen Abu-Laban (2002, 476-77) reminds us that in Canada, the post-9/11 period parallels other historical periods in which racist practices were justified on the grounds of national security, such as Canada's policies of internment during both world wars. Following the events of 9/11, Western states have drawn on a long history of orientalist imaginings of the Other to construct threat along culturally and religiously essentialized lines (Abu-Laban 2002, 477-78; also Naghibi 2007, xii-xiii).

Abu-Laban (2002) argues that, in Canada, the kind of cultural essentialism that informs such representations undermines Canada's celebrated model of inclusive citizenship. She writes: "Addressing the problem of essentialism in turn requires also de-masking and keeping central the myth of the neutral state, the myth of the unblemished record of liberal thought and scholarship, and holding an anti-essentialist view of 'culture' and 'cultural groups'" (Abu-Laban, 2002, 478; for more, see Kinsman's Chapter 6).

By focusing my analysis on the Muslim community, it becomes possible to draw out some of these gendered and racialized conceptions of belonging that inform the new Canadian security agenda in the context of the global war on terror (D'Costa 2006, 129; also Pettman 2004, 91). In this sense, I attempt to map what Anna M. Agathangelou and L.H.M. Ling (2004, 534) term a "majority-based" or inclusive conception of human security. Just as the Arab- or Muslim-man-as-terrorist trope seems evident in the treatment of Canadian residents and citizens under the Anti-terrorism Act, so too do other similarly orientalist and gendered tropes, such as Muslim-woman-as-oppressed.[2] These racialized and gendered representations of both Muslim men and women are upheld by the state and representations in the media and popular discourse – reflecting a national security discourse that constructs who belongs and who is excluded. Moreover, these representations reflect a broader global ideological context in which a "clash of civilizations" serves to legitimate discriminatory national security policies that target Muslim communities (Abu-Laban 2002, 459).

The Changing Canadian Security Landscape

Not unlike other Western governments, the Canadian government began instituting a series of security measures designed to protect Canadians from acts of terrorism in the aftermath of 9/11. Many of these measures have come under criticism from community organizations that claim these measures specifically target, and therefore unnecessarily harass, Canadian citizens and residents who are visibly of Middle Eastern or South Asian descent. Far-reaching changes were enacted three months after the 9/11 attacks through Bill C-36, now called the Anti-terrorism Act. The act introduced amendments to the Official Secrets Act (becoming the Security of Information Act), the Canada Evidence Act, the Proceeds of Crime (Money Laundering) and Terrorist Financing Act, the Canadian Security Intelligence Service Act, the National Defence Act, and the Charities Registration (Security Information) Act. The act also provided for the creation of the Public Safety Act to amend the Aeronautics Act and allow the government to, for example, collect and use information on airline passengers (Canada, Department of Public Safety, 2005). A controversial no-fly list was also introduced in June 2007 to alert airlines to people the Canadian government considers a threat to security.

In 2004, the government issued Canada's first comprehensive national security policy. It earmarked $690 million for new security initiatives, including the creation of the Integrated Threat Assessment Centre and a new Department of Public Safety and Emergency Preparedness, now simply called Public Safety Canada (Canada, Privy Council Office 2004). The Integrated Threat Assessment Centre, housed in the Canadian Security Intelligence Service (CSIS), was formed in response to Auditor General Shelia Fraser's report on the lack of intelligence-gathering coordination. It brings together a variety of security agencies and departments, such as the Canada Border Services Agency, CSIS, the Department of National Defence, the Privy Council Office, Public Safety, and the RCMP.

These sweeping legislative and institutional changes create unprecedented powers of investigation, detention, and prosecution. Some legal observers and other critics argue that these changes represent a knee-jerk reaction to the events of 9/11 and not a sound national security policy. For example, Kent Roach argues that what these legislative changes may do, in fact, is deflect attention from the adequate enforcement of laws that already exist. He maintains that the Canadian Criminal Code was sufficient to prosecute any of the 9/11 hijackers if the terrorist attacks had occurred in Canada (Daniels, Macklem, and Roach 2001, 7). On the Anti-terrorism Act, the Canadian Bar Association (2001, 13) recommended that "the federal government make a concerted commitment to funding law enforcement agencies, intelligence gathering agencies and the military to levels that allow full use of existing law enforcement tools for the protection of national security and public safety." Legal scholar Lesley Jacobs (2003, 376-82) argues that the Anti-terrorism Act was not intended to be an emergency measure to investigate acts of terrorism, evidenced by the fact that the act is not subject to a sunset clause. Instead, the act entails *preventative* measures, through risk assessment, that necessarily involves criminal profiling. As Jacobs (2003, 382) writes, the problem with risk profiling is that "the security and freedom of those deemed to be risks is compromised for the security and freedom of those people who are not." Indeed, as then justice minister Anne McLellan remarked in the wake of the 9/11 attacks, the "balance" between the rights of the individual and collective security considerations has shifted (Leblanc 2001).

In addition to the new laws and policies, other controversial security tools that the state uses include the security certificate program. This program, part of the Immigration and Refugee Protection Act, allows the state to detain foreign nationals and permanent residents. Since 9/11, six certificates have been issued. All of the outstanding certificates are for men of Middle Eastern origin. Amnesty International (2006) finds that the security certificate process "falls far short of international standards for fair trials and may result in arbitrary detention and violation of the right to liberty. Detainees are effectively denied their right to prepare a defence and mount a meaningful challenge to the lawfulness of their detention. The right to appeal is also denied." Although detainees can choose to be deported to their country of origin, this is not an option for those who would be under threat of torture or death if they are returned (see Zerrougui, de Biedermann, and Hashemi 2005). In a landmark Supreme Court ruling in February 2007, the court gave Parliament one year to address the part of the process that allows confidential information to be used in court. Although the federal government has recently tweaked the process by creating a special advocate system whereby court appointees will be privy to some of the secret information, the Canadian Bar Association and the Federation of Law Societies of Canada agree that the changes still leave the program unconstitutional (Foot 2008).

Canada's track record in implementing these new or revived security measures has generated some skepticism. Two of the most controversial cases are the preventative detention of twenty-three men from Pakistan and India as part of Project Thread, and Canada's role in the deportation of Canadian citizen Maher Arar from the United States to Syria, where he was imprisoned and tortured. In the case of Project Thread, although security officers stated that there was "no known threat" (Jimenez, Freeze, and Burnett 2003), many of the men were subsequently deported – not as a security threat but for fraudulent student visas. In the case of Maher Arar, Justice Dennis O'Connor (2006), head of the Commission of Inquiry into the Actions of Canadian Officials in Relation to Maher Arar, found that there was no evidence to suggest that Arar is or ever was a threat to national security. O'Connor's damning report finds that information provided by the RCMP very likely informed the US authorities' decision to detain and then deport Arar to Syria. Further, Canadian officials deliberately tried to discredit Arar by leaking false information to the press. Given Canada's hurried enactment of far-reaching legislation and the extent of several high-profile national security investigation fiascos, I suggest that Canadian state practices of national security are informed by, but also reproduce, racialized conceptions of belonging that clearly render the safety, security, and freedom of some Canadian residents, such as the deported students and Maher Arar, more vulnerable (for more, see Kinsman's Chapter 6).

The War-on-Terror Script: Constructing Muslim Women Post-9/11

The Canadian state's national security practices rest on racialized and gendered constructions of belonging that are evident in popular representations of the Other in the broader war on terror. In the weeks that followed the attacks, women were introduced into the subsequent war-on-terror script as oppressed Muslim women in need of saving by the West. This script was repeated in the popular press and came to inform public dialogue on the Western Muslim women who may also be in need of saving. As Pettman (2004, 89) writes, "They figured in a familiar guise, as symbols of difference, of Otherness, as border guards of the boundaries between Us and Them, marking their culture/religion, lack of civilization, barbarity, and unreformed religion." Suddenly, Laura Bush and Cherie Blair were making public pronouncements and organizing social projects in support of Afghan women. For example, Laura Bush used the entire time slot allotted for one of President George W. Bush's weekly radio addresses in November 2001 to deliver her message: "Afghan women know, through hard experience, what the rest of the world is discovering: The brutal oppression of women is a central goal of the terrorists" (quoted in BBC News Online 2001). On the same day as Laura Bush's unprecedented radio address, the US State Department released a report entitled *The Taliban's War against Women*. Women were clearly scripted as victims and in need of rescue by US-led forces (Charlesworth and Chinkin 2002, 602-3).

Similarly, Cherie Blair launched a campaign for Afghan women's rights and education, stating to the press: "The women of Afghanistan still have a spirit that belies their unfair, down-trodden image ... We need to help them free that spirit and give them their voice back, so they can create the better Afghanistan we all want to see" (quoted in BBC News Online 2001). Krista Hunt (2006) describes this process of including women as victims as the "(en)gendering of the war on terror." She argues that the Bush administration "embedded feminism in the war in Afghanistan in order to favourably shape public perception that this was a war of liberation and to gain strong support for the project of 'civilizing' Afghanistan" (52-53). Other states picked up on this narrative and added women's rights and human rights to their list of reasons to support the war on terror. In the Canadian context, Prime Minister Stephen Harper, along with former prime ministers Paul Martin and Jean Chrétien, affirmed this part of the mission. In a speech delivered by Harper (2007) to Canadian troops in Afghanistan in 2007, he remarked: "Because of you, the people of Afghanistan have seen the institution of democratic elections, the stirring of human rights and freedoms for women, the construction of schools, healthcare facilities and the basic infrastructure of a functional economy."

The hijab, or Muslim headscarf, in particular, was popularly characterized in media reports as both symptomatic and emblematic of the oppression of women in Afghanistan. For example, shortly after the war in Afghanistan began, *Globe and Mail* columnist Marcus Gee (2001) remarked: "It would be embarrassing for Britain and the United States, and a tragedy for Afghan women, if the new regime in Afghanistan were to keep women imprisoned behind the veil." Such narratives about Muslim women are not new. As Cynthia Enloe (2006, ix) writes, the veil was "taken off the nineteenth century imperial shelf, dusted, polished and put to new use, especially by officials of the US administration of President George W. Bush and their international allies in order to wrap its 'war against terror' in the justifying banner of 'women's liberation.'" Clearly, the mission in Afghanistan was understood in those early days as not just about rooting out terror but as a social, political, and civilizing mission designed to emancipate the people.

Where Muslim women spoke out against their use as symbols of oppression to justify the war on terror, they were criticized in the press and by politicians in Canada for going off-script. For example, University of British Columbia professor Sunera Thobani came under attack for her October 2001 speech at the conference entitled "Women's Resistance: From Victimization to Criminalization" in Ottawa, where she said: "US foreign policy is soaked in blood. And other countries of the West including shamefully Canada, cannot line up fast enough behind it. All want to sign up now as Americans and I think it is the responsibility of the women's movement in this country to stop that, to fight against it" (Thobani 2001). Thobani's speech was publicly admonished by the prime minister in the House of Commons, by federal opposition parties, by the premier of British Columbia, and in the press. For example, columnist Diane Francis (2001) called Thobani a "mouthy and intolerant woman" and reasoned that "letting people say what they want can lead, quite simply, to the beginning of the end of civilization." *Ottawa Citizen* columnist Dave Brown (2001) wrote: "It's war, folks. Ms. Thobani and her sisters are operational revolutionaries hell bent on rebuilding western society."

She received death threats, hate mail, and calls for her dismissal from teaching at the University of British Columbia. In an unprecedented move, the RCMP publicly announced that Thobani was the subject of an investigation of hate crime – ostensibly for her perceived anti-Americanism. Even though the complaint was dropped, Thobani (2003, 401-3) says the RCMP's statement was personally, and financially, damaging. Of the press reports and public statements about her speech, she writes:

> by repeatedly reconstructing my status as a non-White, immigrant woman, the media reiterated – in a highly intensified manner – the historically racialized discourse of who "belongs" to the Canadian nation, and hence has a right to "speak" to it. This racialized discourse constructed me as an outsider to the nation, part of the "enemy" within its territorial boundaries, against which the ideological borders of the nation had to be defended. Repeated calls for me to be fired from my teaching position, and to have me "go back to where I come from" (and in a good number of cases for me to "go back" to Afghanistan!) reconstituted – in a moment of crisis – the vulnerable and constantly "under surveillance" status of Third World immigrants in Canada. (Thobani 2003, 401)

Thobani, a prominent woman of colour, did not parrot the refrain of Laura Bush and Cherie Blair. Because she went off-script, arguing that "escalating militarization would serve neither the interests of women in Afghanistan, nor those of women in North America" (Thobani 2003, 403), her personal as well as her professional security was compromised.

The limits to dissent and to what can and cannot be said were evident with the treatment of Thobani. In contrast, those women who do "speak out" against Islam are rewarded for their courage. For example, speaking of Dutch MP Ayaan Hirsi Ali, who was screening a film critical of Islam, the *National Post*'s Robert Fulford writes:

> Today, she comes across as articulate, passionate and elegant, as well as clearly secular. She has a kind of vertical beauty, a long face perfectly shaped. Apparently, a profound strength of spirit makes her appear serene, even after nearly three years of living under police protection. She makes her points with exceptional clarity in a subtle, Africa-accented English, one of her six languages. It would be hard to imagine a more persuasive advocate for Muslim women. (Fulford 2005)

Fulford also reports that Irshad Manji, journalist and author of 2005 bestseller *The Trouble with Islam Today,* was at the screening and told the audience that critical voices about Islam are not heard – either because religion is a sensitive topic or because people fear being labelled racist.

When Muslim women are not being constructed as oppressed and in need of saving, they are being characterized as mysterious, dangerous, and threatening to national security. Indeed, a 2006 report published by the Integrated Threat Assessment Centre (ITAC), entitled *The female jihadist*, warns that women in the "Islamic world" and the West "have had the advantage of greater mobility and have traditionally been used for reconnaissance missions, as facilitators, as couriers and even as bombers. Women have also assumed leadership roles in groups" (see S. Bell 2007a). In a *Montreal Gazette* column, Peter Bergen and Paul Cruickshank (2007) suggest that Muslim women in the West are using the principles of gender equality to increase their participation in acts of terrorism: "The main way women have played a greater role in such operations is in auxiliary functions: running websites, handling finances and logistics, urging on their husbands." In their column they suggest that this means that women can play dangerous roles as "'stay-at-home' wives." Women are using the liberty they have in the West, and their position as housewives, to threaten the security of Westerners. Similarly, the *Globe and Mail* (El Akkad and McArthur 2006) ran the story "Hateful chatter behind the veil," condemning the inflammatory anti-Canadian comments the spouses of some of the men arrested on suspicion of terrorism had written in chat rooms.

Bannerji reminds us that such characterizations of women mythologize their victimhood:

> The dehumanization involved in converting a person, an embodied socio-historical being, into a sign or symbol implies much more than an epistemological violence. It is based on the same principles that enabled a physical, social, and symbolic violence to be visited upon [J]ews in pogroms and the holocaust, on various indigenous peoples in colonial genocides, and on Africans in slavery. (Bannerji 2000, 169-70)

In both characterizations of Muslim women, whose oppression or malevolence is both marked by and hidden behind the veil, women are rendered as symbols of a backward, primitive, and barbaric Islam.

Risk Profiling and the Radicalization of Canadian Muslim Men
Just as the gendered and orientalizing discourses have framed women as either feeble and oppressed or duplicitous, Muslim men (and those presumed to be Muslim) are also constructed by gendered and orientalizing discourses. Part of what informs new preventative security strategies is a

fear of the potential radicalization of young Muslim men. This fear, perpetuated in popular discourses and by the media, is evident in the policy documents and statements from Canadian security agencies. The *National Post*'s Adrian Humphreys (2007) recently detailed a 2006 CSIS document that finds that "while there is a certain understanding of the radicalization process, there are still many questions about how an individual changes from 'the kid next door' to a suicide bomber or an extremist staging a terrorist attack against a civilian target." Similarly, Humphreys outlines a report from the ITAC, which states: "One of the shared features seems to be that at some stage they come to be 'seekers' of greater knowledge about Islam, and through this process may become radicalized, depending on the ideological influences to which they are exposed." Speaking of such radicalization, Mike McDonell, the RCMP officer responsible for National Security Criminal Investigations across Canada and co-chair of the Canadian Association of Chiefs of Police Counter-terrorism and National Security Committee, reported to the Special Senate Committee on the Anti-terrorism Act in January 2008: "Allow me to reiterate a well-used refrain: It is not a matter of if, it is a matter of when. The threat is there, casting a shadow at the heart of our society. Local level radicalization is happening in Canada" (Canada, Senate 2008b).

In this sense, the preventative risk profiling comes to the conclusion that every Muslim is a potential terrorist, even the kid next door. Controversially, the Anti-terrorism Act amended the Criminal Code to define terrorism as an act committed "in whole or in part for a political, religious or ideological purpose, objective or cause." Legal scholars such as Roach (2006, 421) have argued that this leaves the state vulnerable to the charge that it is actively using religious profiling in its attempt to establish motive.

Islamophobia in a Canadian Context

The 2006 national census reports that more than 58 percent of the 6.2 million new immigrants to Canada come from Asia, including the Middle East, compared with only 12 percent in 1971 (Statistics Canada 2006). As the ethnocultural map of Canada is changing, racial, ethnic, and religious profiling draw clear distinctions between those who "count" as Canadians and those who do not. The net effect of characterizing Islam in general and Muslims in particular as potential threats to national security necessarily establishes that the security agencies are engaging in racial profiling. Indeed, Justice O'Connor in his 2006 report found that since 9/11, certain religious and ethnic groups have been targeted. He recommended that "the RCMP set down in writing its policy directing that investigations not be based on racial, ethnic or religious profiling. Moreover, it is important that all aspects of national security investigations pay appropriate attention to the human rights and interests of those who may be affected" (D. O'Connor 2006, 521). As well, Julian Fantino, then the chief of the Toronto Police Service, spoke to the issues of increasing hate crime at the 2004 Hate Crime Conference, held in Toronto. He reported that there was a 66 percent increase in the number of reported hate crimes in 2001. Of the 338 hate crimes reported, 121 were directly related to the 9/11 terrorist attacks. Religion accounted for 36 percent of the reported hate crimes, with Jewish and Muslim communities being the most affected groups. Fantino warned that statistics are difficult to compile and interpret because "a large number of hate-motivated crimes remain unreported for fear of nothing being done or drawing more attention to themselves and in turn, attracting further violence" (Fantino 2004). These numbers are indicative of broader national trends in hate crimes in Canada (Dauvergne, Scrim, and Brennan 2008) and international trends in hate crimes in the United States and Europe (Diène 2003).

It is in this context of gendered and orientalizing characterizations of Muslims in Canada that negative perceptions of institutional practices of cultural accommodation are growing. For example, the 2008 report of the Consultation Commission on Accommodation Practices Related to Cultural Differences in Québec identified a period of intensified anxiety and public turmoil over issues related to the "reasonable accommodation" of cultural minorities following 11 September 2001. The report found that for some members of the public, accommodation practices were understood as an attack on society's core values, such as gender equality, fairness, and secularism (see Bouchard and Taylor 2008). This turmoil was evident in several highly publicized incidents in Canada. For example, in January 2007, the Quebec town of Hérouxville passed a resolution detailing a code of conduct and instructing new immigrants that women were allowed to drive and that the public stoning or dowsing of women in acid was prohibited (Bonnell 2007; also Gyulai 2007). The resolution advised newcomers that "we drink alcoholic beverages ... and at the end of every year we decorate a tree with balls and tinsel" (see Ha 2007). This "advice" is clearly directed at Muslim immigrants and makes assumptions about the content of cultural practices – that the treatment of women in Islam is necessarily oppressive. To be sure, this code of conduct was lambasted in the Quebec press and the subject of satirical portrayals, such as Rock et Belles Oreilles' year-end comedy sketch "Hérouxtyville." However, the passage of the resolution in the post-9/11 climate, during a period in which the social and political parameters of reasonable accommodation continue to be hotly debated, indicates the extent to which Canadian minority communities and Canadian Muslim communities are under particular scrutiny.

The veil was similarly politicized in recent debates concerning voting in Canadian elections. Stephen Harper challenged the election commissioner's decision to allow women to vote with their faces covered. Other political leaders concurred, including Liberal Leader Stéphane Dion, who asked Elections Canada to change its diction "to require veiled women to unveil their faces to confirm their identities" (Offman 2007). Certainly, this has not been a political flashpoint for those Canadians who vote by mail ballot. We have to ask why this issue related to voting has captured the attention of party leaders now.

These kinds of discussions put Muslim women in a vulnerable position vis-à-vis the rest of Canadian society. Salima Ebrahim (2008) of the Canadian Council of Muslim Women argues that Muslim women felt integrated and comfortable as part of the broader "Canadian mosaic" prior to 9/11. However, following the attacks, an increasing climate of suspicion and racism against Muslims and Arab Canadians left Muslim women particularly vulnerable because they experienced discrimination based on their colour, religion, and gender. The Canadian Council of Muslim Women completed a community research project on this very issue. Its 2002 report entitled *Voices of Muslim women* (Hussain 2002) argues that women who wear the hijab are easily recognized as Muslims, and they are therefore often identified as sources for information about Islam at school and in the workplace. The report notes that although some women welcomed questions about Islam from teachers, friends, and colleagues, others felt "forced into a more vocal position, one that they did not necessarily want to assume" (Hussain 2002).

Similarly, participants reporting to the Task Force on the Needs of Muslim Students, an initiative of the Canadian Federation of Students, which looked into the needs of Muslim students at Canadian post-secondary institutions, explained that Muslim women are asked to speak to contentious questions related to Islam more frequently than men. The report states: "In addition to having to defend their religion generally, the Muslim value of modesty has resulted in women, particularly those in hijab, having to defend themselves against the allegation that they are self-oppressed" (Canadian Federation of Students 2007, 14). Other university women reported being both physically and verbally harassed on campuses. For example, the task force reports that a woman at the University of Windsor was pushed onto the street and called a "stupid Paki," and other women reported being called "witches" and "nuns." These Islamophobic and sexist attacks on campuses are not isolated, and faculty members have also been the victims of such abuse. For example, vandals spray-painted McMaster University professor Muriel Walker's office door with anti-Islamic messages. Walker says she was targeted because she organizes and supports events on campus such as "Hijab Day" (Gandhi 2007).

Marie Chen, the then acting director of legal services at the African Canadian Legal Clinic, described the experiences of Somali immigrants to the Proceedings of the Special Senate Committee on the Anti-terrorism Act (Canada, Senate 2005): "We have received anecdotal accounts from Somali women who have experienced added humiliation at border crossings, who have been asked to remove their hijab during searches and who also have endured the pat-down when you go through the airport." As such, Somali women are particularly vulnerable because of their race, colour, status as newcomers, religion, and also their gender.

In 2003, the National Organization of Immigrant and Visible Minority Women of Canada (NOIVMWC) and the Canadian Research Institute for the Advancement of Women held focus groups across Canada in six languages on behalf of Status of Women Canada on the impact of the new security agenda for Muslim women (Bose and Johnson 2005). In the focus group sessions, women reported that they were interrogated by security guards in airports and on cross-border train trips. One woman described being strip-searched at Pearson International Airport. All of these incidents led NOIVMWC to conclude that racial profiling is taking place in Canada: "These incidents and many others recounted to us by the women in the study lead NOIVMWC to believe that racial profiling is alive and well in the aftermath of 9/11. Many of the focus group participants were traumatised by the publicity generated around Operation Thread" (Bose and Johnson 2005, 6). Muslim women reported that they were more easily profiled than Muslim men because of their appearance and mode of dress. As a result, some women indicated that they were therefore choosing not to travel to the United States and beyond (Bose and Johnson 2005).

Conclusion

Since 9/11, new national security measures, along with racialized and gendered conceptions of belonging, have created an environment of insecurity for many Canadian citizens. The securitization of Canadian policy is designed to protect Canadians from foreign (and domestic) threats. Particularly in light of the fact that this legislation is a direct consequence of the 9/11 attacks on the United States, and because it is designed in such a way as to identify threat based on adherence to ideology or religion, we can see how it is informed by racialized and gendered conceptions of threat. The new security agenda works with popular constructions of *Muslim-man-as-terrorist* and *Muslim-woman-as-oppressed* to reinforce orientalist myths.

Critical feminist scholars tell us to look beyond a restrictive state-level analysis and consider the experiences of marginalized actors and communities within the state. Certainly, the Canadian state does not exist within a vacuum. The 9/11 attacks on the United States and the ensuing global war on terror also marks a shift in national security strategies in other Western states. The Canadian state, through the implementation of the Anti-terrorism Act and the controversial usage of the security certificate process, is responding to a perceived international security crisis. What feminist interventions reveal in this case is the way in which the Canadian state, as a response to the US-led global war on terror, implements security policies that actually "render the lives of their most powerless citizens insecure" (Tickner 2006, 41). In this analysis, I have focused on the experiences of those Canadians most likely to be the targets of the new security measures – Muslim (or presumed to be Muslim) Canadians – and evaluated the interplay between ideas or tropes as well as state institutions and security policies.

Discursively, Muslim women are constructed as oppressed victims of antiquated and misogynist communities and therefore emblematic of the so-called anti-democratic and illiberal impulses of the so-called Islamic world. These same gendered constructions also place Muslim men at risk, especially if every Muslim "kid next door" is at risk of "radicalizing." When we consider the arrests of the twenty-three foreign students in 2003 and the role of CSIS in the detention and deportation of Maher Arar, it is clear that the pre-emptive anti-terror net is being cast too broadly.

To be sure, such constructions of Muslim, Arab, Middle Eastern, and South Asian communities are rooted in a long history of orientalist imaginings of the Other. However, it is the pursuit of the terrorist lurking in our suburbs, radicalizing in the Mosque, and tyrannizing women that has created a culture of permissibility whereby every Muslim, particularly women, is answerable in an imagined national multicultural dialogue. Fantastically, Muslim women are called upon as the spokespersons for the cultural practices of an entire religion in newspaper features, television programs, and university interfaith panels. Women are thrust to the fore to defend Islam – an incredibly risky burden in a period in which Islam is on trial.

By examining the intersections of race and gender from a feminist IR perspective, we open up our analyses to additional actors, communities, and interests. This can help us to build our understanding of the ways in which national security agendas can perpetuate racialized and gendered conceptions of citizenship and belonging – conceptions that are, in this case, rooted in a broader post-9/11 ideological context. When we consider the orientalizing discourses that are part of this post-9/11 context and the ways in which such discourses inform national security policies such as Canada's anti-terrorism legislation, we can see how Abu-Laban's "myth of the neutral state" evaporates. In this sense, understanding how national security strategies are experienced within the state and developed in relation to broader global discourses can allow us to better theorize a more inclusive conception of human security. After all, to what end is security sought?

NOTES

1 Here, I use the word "saving" to identify the moment of imperialist subject-production captured by post-colonial critic Gayatri Chakravorty Spivak's (1988) statement "White men are saving brown women from brown men." Spivak is referring to the nineteenth-century British abolition of widow sacrifice. I have appropriated Spivak's use of the word "saving" to capture the contemporary American imperial justification for war as a civilizing mission.
2 These are not the only tropes that continue to frame representations of Muslim men and women. For example, Evelyn Alsultany (2007) identifies other powerful tropes operating in American advertising campaigns after the attacks of 11 September 2001, including the moderate Muslim, the "good" Western Muslim (juxtaposed with the "bad" Eastern Muslim), the patriotic Muslim, and the "moral" Muslim who is committed to *heterosexual* family values.

Re-Conceptions of National Security in the Age of Terrorism
Implications for Federal Policing in Canada

T.S. (TODD) HATALEY

Many would agree that during the Cold War Canadian national security interests were defined largely as military in nature. National security goals were pursued through collective military agreements and various international organizations, all with the strategic goal of keeping the threat outside the territorial boundaries of the state. The post-Cold War period has seen, in the words of former deputy US attorney general Jamie Gorelick, "both conceptually and on the ground ... a real shift in the paradigm of national security" (quoted in Andreas and Nadelmann 2006, 158). The threats are no longer primarily military in nature, nor are they easily contained outside the territorial boundaries of the state. Asymmetrical transnational threats such as terrorism have changed the nature of security threats, while at the same time threatening the capacity of the state to pursue its own interests.[1] Transnational terrorism has emerged as a real concern for Canadian security agencies. The dynamic nature of terrorist organizations means that terrorist strategies continue to evolve, challenging Canadian security agencies to respond with suitable policy changes. This challenge has become increasingly clear as terrorist organizations, in the absence of state support, have turned to criminal activity as a means of supporting their operations.

From a policing perspective, the shifting paradigm suggests an increased demand for police agencies and policing strategies in combating threats against the state. Peter Andreas and Richard Price (2001, 31-32) have argued that during the 1990s, there was a growing convergence between the functions of the police and the military, such that, in the United States at least, this shift has been reflected in a "militarization of policing and a domestication of soldiering" (see also Andreas 2000; Dunn 1996; Payan 2006). Since the beginning of the war on terror, there has been an endless stream of academic and policy-oriented writing on strategies for waging a war on terror, many of which include an increased role for police in combating terrorism (see Bowman 2007-08; Deflem 2006; Dolan 2005; Olson 2007).[2] I seek to contribute to that body of literature through arguing that in the Canadian case the most effective method for combating terrorism, and thus ensuring the security – and more importantly the stability – of the Canadian state, must include a domestic policing function and the strategies used for combating criminal activity.

The first part of this chapter discusses the main concepts of terrorism and criminality. Defining such terms can be controversial, notably in the context of a "war on terror" that has worked to define and redefine global terrorism. It is thus crucial to assess the meanings of these terms. The second part provides empirical evidence illustrating a convergence between terrorist and transnational criminal organizations, both in association and method, and more importantly demonstrates the need to fundamentally rethink where threats to the stability and security of the state are found and combated.

Terrorism, Crime, and National Security

Theoretically framing any political investigation presents several issues. Although the goal of conceptualizing any political issue is to move beyond the descriptive, to explain the phenomenon in question in a normative context, and in doing so to provide some degree of predictive capacity, all theoretical lenses present some degree of bias. Here, I begin by providing definitions of contestable terms used in this chapter. I then illustrate that a constructivist analysis incorporating a framework based on timing, path dependence, and critical events can be useful for explaining the changing dynamic of modern terrorism and the need for Canadian security agencies to modify their respective security policies in response to this shifting dynamic.

Jerrold Post (2007, 3) defines the central concept of this chapter, terrorism, as a type of "political violence or threat of violence against noncombatants or property in order to gain a political, ideological, or religious goal through fear and intimidation ... the act is designed to have an impact on an audience that differs from the immediate target of the violence." In Post's view, terrorism is a strategy employed by diverse groups with equally diverse goals. Anthony Marsella (2005, 15-16) maintains that defining terrorism is an "endless debate." Despite the multitude of definitions, however, most carry several common characteristics. Marsella suggests that five conditions are useful for identifying and defining terrorism: (1) the use of force or violence by (2) individuals or groups that (3) is directed toward civilian populations, (4) is intended to instill fear, and (5) is used as a means of coercing individuals or groups to change their political or social positions. Here there are two important points to note. First, terrorism is a violent behaviour and as such consists of a set of expectations. Second, broadly defined, the act of terrorism is perpetrated for the purpose of coercing change, which can include, but not exclusively, change in state behaviour.

Two qualifying adjectives are often used with terrorism. The first is *inter*national terrorism, which simply means terrorism involving citizens and/or territory of more than one country (Marsella 2005, 15-16). The second is *trans*national terrorism, meaning terrorism that crosses international boundaries. This is in contrast to domestic terrorism, which suggests terrorism initiated and perpetrated by citizens on their own territory. Part of the difficulty in defining transnational terrorism, however, is accounting for the importance of ideas and the movement of ideas unencumbered by state boundaries. In my view, ideas are as important as physical entities such as terrorist training camps.[3] I would argue, for example, that a citizen of the United Kingdom who learns to make bombs on the internet is no less a transnational terrorist than a UK citizen who trains as a bomb maker at a terrorist camp in another part of the world.

Given that one of the central theses of this chapter is that terrorist organizations have begun to rely on criminal organizations and methods as a means to continuing their activities, it is paramount that crime be distinguished from terrorism. Simply put, crime can be defined as "the intentional commission of an act usually deemed socially harmful or dangerous and specifically defined, prohibited and punishable under the criminal law" (Schmid 2004, 198). As instructive and comprehensive as this definition may be, it does not really separate crime from terrorism, simply because terrorism can be defined by the state, and certainly is in Canada, as a criminal offence.[4] Tamara Makarenko (2004) further argues that crime and terrorism can be placed on a continuum, with crime existing on the far left and terrorism on the far right. In this theoretical framework, criminal enterprises are motivated by economic gain, and terrorist groups by political goals. Cooperation between groups is considered a naturally occurring event, given that each group stands to gain through cooperation. Theoretically, she maintains, the two can converge into what she refers to as the black hole syndrome, where civil or regional war is promoted as a means of securing both economic and political power (Makarenko 2004, 138). Chris Dishman (2005) agrees with Makarenko's concept of a criminal-terrorist convergence. However, he argues that convergence results in a leadership vacuum within terrorist networks, creating increased opportunity for low- to mid-level terrorists and criminals to cooperate in the interest of advancing their respective goals. What both authors point to, however, is what Shelley and Picarelli (2002) refer to as the feature that distinguishes between terrorism and organized crime: while some of their methods may look the same, criminal activity is primarily about economics, whereas terrorism is a political pursuit.

Furthermore, the word "crime" is frequently used in conjunction with two qualifiers: "organized" and "transnational." Organized crime as defined in section 467.1(1) of the Criminal Code of Canada states that "criminal organization" means a group, however organized, that (1) is composed of three or more persons in or outside Canada; and (2) has as one of its main purposes or main activities the facilitation or commission of one or more serious offences that, if committed, would likely result in the direct or indirect receipt of a material benefit, including a financial benefit, by the group or by any one of the persons who constitute the group.[5] Transnational crime, as with transnational terrorism, refers to organized criminal activity that crosses international boundaries.

"National security" is another highly contestable term (see Kinsman's Chapter 6). Buzan, Waever, and de Wilde (1998) have argued that the term has been largely defined in the context of power and more precisely within the framework of the state. National security, in keeping with the realist tradition, has come to mean protecting the state from external threats (Liotta 2002, 475). In contrast to this traditionalist approach to understanding security, I opt for a broader, more inclusive definition of the term for several reasons. First, in the contemporary world order, states face a number of threats that cannot be confronted by traditional military responses. These non-traditional issues, be they economic, health, or criminal in nature, can have the effect of limiting the political choices available to states and non-state actors, and by consequence reduce the quality of life (see Ullman, quoted in Katzenstein 1996, 8). Second, and more importantly, tying national security to the security of the territorial state fails to take into account what makes the "state." Alexander Wendt (1999, 215-45) argues that states exist as actors only because of a corporate or collective identity, made up of the individuals who hold a common conception of what the "state" is or is not. Threats to the state, I would therefore argue, also have to be threats to the individuals who compose the collective structure that holds the state together. As a result, understanding national security moves us beyond the territorial mould and becomes deeply rooted in the domestic sphere, or as Richard Ullman (1983) argued more than twenty-five years ago, national security has to be broadened to include issues that limit political choice.

This approach to defining and understanding national security is consistent with the definition of national security found in both the Canadian Security Intelligence Service Act (Canada, Department of Justice 1984) and *Securing an open society: Canada's national security policy* (Canada, Privy Council Office 2004). According to the latter, "National security deals with threats that undermine the security of the state or society" (3). Furthermore, the National Security Policy states that Canada's national security can be understood as a three-part process: (1) it protects Canada and the safety and security of Canadians at home and abroad; (2) it ensures that Canada is not a base for threats to our allies; and (3) it contributes to international security.

The Canadian Security Intelligence Service Act, which was written well before the war on terror began, is even more specific in defining threats to the security of Canada:

(a) Espionage or sabotage that is against Canada or is detrimental to the interests of Canada or activities directed toward or in support of such espionage or sabotage;
(b) Foreign influenced activities within or relating to Canada that are detrimental to the interests of Canada and are clandestine or deceptive or involve a *threat to any person;*
(c) Activities within or relating to Canada directed toward or in support of the threat or use of acts of serious violence against persons or property for the purpose of achieving a political, religious or ideological objective within Canada or a foreign state; and
(d) Activities directed toward undermining by covert unlawful acts, or directed toward or intended ultimately to lead to the destruction or overthrow by violence of, the constitutionally established system of government in Canada. (Canada, Department of Justice 1984, Interpretation Section; emphasis added)

In sum, limiting the definition of national security to a territorial or state-bound framework fails to provide an adequate definition. Such a definition fails to address the security of the individuals, whose collective identity makes the existence of the state possible. It furthermore fails to incorporate not only the spirit of national security in the Canadian context but also the definition of national security as outlined in Canadian policy documents.

The Crime-Terrorism Continuum

Recent scholarship on the relationship between crime and terrorism has noted an increased relationship between organized criminal operations and terrorist groups. Thachuk (2007, 16) claims, however, that from a policy-making perspective, the two entities continue to be treated as separate, resulting in policies that are ineffective in combating international terrorism.[6] Swanstrom (2007, 6) echoes this concern, arguing that the dialogue on security needs to be widened to include transnational crime issues such as drug trafficking. Saul (2003) has taken this argument one step further by arguing that law enforcement and criminal justice responses have played a lesser, secondary role to the military in the war on terror, which has resulted in a disjointed, if not weakened, strategy in combating terrorism. The convergence of criminal and terrorist activities refers to a number of separate yet related issues. At the very core is a debate as to whether or not terrorism, specifically a terrorist act, can even be considered a criminal activity. The debate is further complicated by the fact that a generally agreed-upon definition of terrorism does not exist. Here, however, I am more concerned with what the United States Congress has termed "precursor criminal activity" (United States, Congressional Research Service 2007, 2). Precursor criminal activity can be defined as "unlawful acts undertaken to facilitate a terrorist attack or to support a terrorist campaign" (1). Lucrative criminal operations such as trafficking in contraband goods, extortion, fraud, gambling, identity theft, money laundering, and any number of other crimes have all become a means of funding for terrorist organizations. And although these types of criminal activities have traditionally been the domain of organized crime, terrorist organizations are increasingly becoming not only affiliated with criminal groups but also moving wholesale into the business of crime, independent of the expertise held by organized criminal groups (Hutchinson and O'Malley 2007, 1096). In citing a study done by Mark Hamm in 2005, McGarrell, Freilich, and Chermak (2007, 147) maintain that a clear pattern of precursor activity exists across a diverse number of terrorist organizations. Hamm's study shows that all terrorist organizations require "money, material, transportation, identity documents, communications systems and safe havens to accomplish their aims," and that crime finances many of these operations.

Nowhere is the convergence of crime and terrorism more clearly articulated than in the international drug trade, where the linkages between terrorist groups and drug cartels have even given rise to new terminology to describe the activity: "narco-terrorism." Dolan (2005) goes so far as to argue that since 2001 there has been a convergence between drug and terrorist policy in the United States. In 2007, the US State Department's List of Foreign Terrorist Organizations linked eighteen of forty-two terrorist groups to illegal drug trafficking.[7] The Fuerzas Armadas Revolucionarios de Colombia (FARC), for example, were reported to have entered into alliances with criminal groups inside and outside of Colombia, including with Mexican drug trafficking groups. This arrangement reportedly sees cocaine shipped to Mexico in return for weapons. Similarly, Russian crime groups have allegedly sent arms to Colombia in exchange for cocaine (Makarenko 2004, 132). Terrorist organizations have also actively lent support to Afghan drug cartels to aid in the movement of heroin out of the region and into Europe in exchange for weapons and financial support. The Islamic Movement of Uzbekistan and al-Qaeda have both been implicated in the smuggling of heroin from Afghanistan to European locations (Makarenko 2004, 132). Less sensational criminal operations are also exploited by terrorist organizations to fund activities. The terrorist cell responsible for bombing the Madrid trains in March of 2004 raised support through petty crime. Hezbollah received financial support from a criminal operation involved in smuggling cigarettes from states with low taxes (North Carolina) to states with higher taxes, notably Michigan (Hutchinson and O'Malley 2007, 1097). A more recent and increasingly lucrative source of income for terrorist groups is the sale of counterfeit goods, such as designer clothing and accessories, pirated CDs and DVDs, and fake medications (*Sunday Times* 2005).

In Canada, crime reportedly has been used by various suspect groups to fund terrorist activities. The Tamil community in Toronto has reported incidents of extortion by members of the Liberation Tigers of Tamil Eelam seeking funds to continue the conflict in Sri Lanka (CBC News 2005b). Hutchinson and O'Malley (2007, 1097) claim that an estimated $1 million a month flows from the Tamil diaspora in Toronto to the Tamil Tiger organization. In a separate incident, three Canadians were among nine individuals arrested in 2006 and charged by US officials for crimes including conspiracy to provide material support for a designated terrorist organization and bribery. The arrests were related to an incident in which the nine men attempted to purchase surface-to-air missiles for the Liberation Tigers of Tamil Eelam (CBC News 2006b). More recently, the Canadian Integrated Threat Assessment Centre reported that some or part of the proceeds derived from the illegal sale of a drug called Khat (*Catha edulis*) within the Canadian Somali community is possibly used to finance terrorist activities in east Africa (S. Bell 2007b). Finally, it is not possible to talk about terrorist activity in Canada without reference being made to the millennium bomber, Ahmed Ressam. Ressam was reported to have supported his day-to-day existence through criminal activities, including credit card fraud, pickpocketing, shoplifting, and stealing identity documents for resale to terrorist groups (United States, Congressional Research Service 2007, 20).

Although Canada has initiated strategies to combat transnational terrorism both at home and abroad, Canadian participation in a group known as the Egmont Group of Financial Intelligence Units illustrates policy changes in response to political demands. The Egmont Group, which is currently composed of 108 member states, was initiated in 1995 as a mechanism to combat international money laundering.[8] In July 2000, in response to strong international demands to better control international money laundering operations on its soil, the Canadian government joined the Egmont Group with the creation of the Financial Transactions and Reports Analysis Centre of Canada (FINTRAC), the Canadian financial tracking agency (Colapinto 2004). FINTRAC's initial mandate was combating money laundering; however, that was expanded in December 2001 to include terrorist financing. In 2002, FINTRAC reported to Parliament that suspected terrorist financing with Canadian origins amounted to $22 million (CBC News 2003). In 2006, the amount had jumped to $209 million. In reality, the numbers presented to Parliament by FINTRAC represent first-time efforts to track terrorist financing, better allocation of resources for doing so, and the ever-changing list of terrorist organizations. However, at the same time, the efforts to track such spending represent a Canadian government policy response to what the government has perceived as a threat to Canada's national security. The politicization for the first time of foreign remittances (money going abroad from Canada to support nationalist initiatives is nothing new) serves to illustrate not only the salience of this issue to the Canadian government but also the type of feedback event that provokes organizational shifts. In the end, though, tracking money transferred from a host country such as Canada to a terrorist group is difficult given the unregulated nature of the informal money transfer systems such as hawalas and other unregulated measures used to transfer wealth abroad.[9]

Explaining the Convergence

The most cited explanation for the convergence between crime and terrorism is the decline in state support for terrorist organizations. Terrorists have traditionally been able to exploit the sovereignty of states, receiving financial and material support from state sponsors, while at the same time being allowed a safe haven for training and recruiting.[10] In the post-9/11 world, pressure from the international community, increased efforts in tracking and controlling money destined for terrorist organizations, and the invasion of Afghanistan had the cumulative effect of restricting state-sponsored money and territory for terrorist organizations (Dishman 2005, 238). This is one explanation for the growing convergence, and although the argument has also been made that the links between organized crime and terrorism have always been present, the phenomenon of globalization has served to accentuate and strengthen those ties.

International organized criminal groups have benefited substantially from globalization (Glenny 2008). The liberalization of global markets, rapid spread of information technology, and increased global mobility have provided them with more opportunity and manoeuvrability (Thachuk 2007, 7), while also mitigating some of the risk involved with criminal activity (Picarelli 2006, 8). Information technology and international borders have enabled criminal organizations the ability to put layers of anonymity between themselves and the regulations of state-bound actors. At the same time, the internet has allowed for the development of criminal networks that can operate with little to no centralized leadership across multiple jurisdictions (Picarelli 2006, 8). This expertise, developed and exploited by organized crime groups, became particularly important to terrorist organizations, especially in the context of the post-9/11 world, where international efforts to control the financial and logistical networks of terrorist groups put pressure on their survival. The skills developed and perfected by criminal groups, such as document forgery, smuggling of contraband, money laundering, and cyber crime, all became skills necessary for terrorist organizations willing to change and wanting to flourish in the post-9/11 climate. Criminal groups have benefited to a great degree from the war on terror, providing services required for terrorist groups to survive in the post-9/11 climate.

A second reason cited for the convergence of terrorist and criminal activity is the decentralization of terrorist cells. The flattening of the organizational structure has been made possible by the increasing usage of technology and the development of autonomous cells. These developments have meant that operational cells have had fewer links to the central command structure, leaving those cells semi-autonomous and responsible for much of their own respective fundraising (Dishman 2005). The net result is that in the absence of centralized financial and strategic support, smaller cells have opted for less sophisticated and less expensive terrorist attacks while turning to criminal activity to fund these operations. The 7 July 2005 bombings of the London Underground are estimated to have cost approximately US$15,000 – money raised by the cell through criminal activity (United States, Congressional Research Service 2007, 4). Although the terrorist attack carried out by Timothy McVeigh and Terry Nichols was entirely domestic in nature, that they used theft to fund and support the bombing of the federal building in Oklahoma City (Hamm 2007, 9) clearly illustrates the effectiveness of this type of strategy.

A third reason for the convergence of terrorist and criminal activity is the increase in counterterrorism measures in the post-9/11 context. Central to this, of course, has been the successful freezing of terrorist funds and closer tracking and monitoring of suspicious financial transactions. The result of shutting down the international financial system to terrorist funding has been a shift toward criminal methods for raising, laundering, and smuggling money. And although petty criminal activity forms part of this phenomenon, large-scale transfers of money from source countries via hawalas and other types of informal money transfers or smuggled as cash or other high-value goods have become more prevalent. Wealthy Western states, in particular, have become host countries for terrorist fundraising.

Domestic (Local) Policing and Terrorism

With the convergence of terrorism and criminal activity come additional challenges for domestic police agencies, as police are now the first point of contact in combating terrorist financing and precursor criminal activity. Clarke and Newman (2007) argue that police agencies play a critical role in the fight against terrorism, given that police play the front-line role in the gathering of ground-level intelligence and the development of criminal databases used to support investigations into both criminal and terrorist activities. "Intelligence-led policing" provides policing agencies with the framework for the collection of information fundamental to combating terrorism.[11] Because of their day-to-day presence in the community, front-line, general duties, policing officers are in the best position to identify and document individuals involved in criminal activity, in particular criminals and criminal activity that fall outside the norm for their respective communities. This is not to say that front-line police officers will be able to identify terrorist suspects and cells based on observed behaviours within the local communities but, rather, that police are in the best position to observe the presence of newcomers within the community and, more importantly, the presence of new individuals or groups involved in criminal activity. In other words, intelligence-led policing means that front-line police officers, as clichéd as it may sound, are the eyes and ears of the community and are in the best position to see change within the makeup of the community and the activity in the community, criminal or otherwise.[12]

Intelligence-led policing, however, is not without limitations. Clarke and Newman (2007, 12) argue that one of the problems with the model is the assumption that all information is good information and that some of that information can form the basis of useful intelligence. As a result, not only are police officers encouraged to input as much information as possible but programs such as Crime Stoppers and Community Watch further encourage community members to provide additional information to be inputted into police databases. The utility of police information systems, however, is only as good as the information entered into the respective systems – the garbage in, garbage out phenomenon. Accuracy of information is paramount in the development of useful intelligence for combating terrorism. This poses substantial challenges for front-line police officers and their agencies. The issues can be as simple as entering data accurately into the system, including the proper spelling and order of names, dates of birth, addressees, and so on, and as complex as being able to identify forged or false documents. Terrorists, not unlike criminals, have little to no interest in having their true identity documented on any government or police records management system. As was illustrated in the case of Ahmed Ressam (United States, Congressional Research Service 2007, 20), identity theft becomes part of the precursor crimes that facilitate terrorist activities. Being able to identify these types of criminal activity not only is difficult but requires constant training as new technologies and techniques make document fraud and identity theft increasingly difficult to detect.

The utility of the information is further limited by the capacity police agencies have for sifting through and providing thorough analysis of the inputted information. Turning information into useful intelligence requires the expertise of people with the appropriate skills and technology for converting the information into a format that has a utility for investigators. Intelligence analysts are a critical component in the production of operational intelligence. And although in the post-9/11 period most police forces have increased their capacity for the generation of intelligence, the relationship between those that generate intelligence and those involved in law enforcement is not without problems. Two issues stand out with regards to this relationship. First, for most police forces, hiring an intelligence analyst means less money available for putting officers on the street. In communities where policing is still locally controlled and police visibility is still valued as a deterrent to crime, arguing for another civil servant sitting behind a desk collating information often falls on deaf ears. Second, in police culture the bonds of trust between police officers are often reason enough to have the confidence to share information with other officers. Most analysts, however, are civilians, outside police culture, and therefore less likely to have the confidence or trust of police officers. This is further complicated by the differing security clearances of police officers and intelligence analysts, further marginalizing the function of intelligence analysts.

At the local level, probably the greatest deterrent to the effective use of intelligence is dissemination of intelligence. Nowhere is this more evident than in multi-jurisdictional areas, both in a geographic sense and an organizational one. In situations where the police force of a local jurisdiction is different from the police force responsible for the enforcement of federal statutes, sharing of criminal databases is not a foregone conclusion.[13] Protectionism, rivalry, and a lack of political will have resulted in many police records management systems being restricted to single-agency use, thereby effectively limiting the dissemination of information and potential intelligence to other agencies operating within the same geographic jurisdictions. A similar problem exists between agencies operating with overlapping enforcement mandates. In Canada, most federal government agencies now have some type of in-house intelligence-gathering capacity – for example, the Canada Border Services Agency, Transport Canada, and the Canada Revenue Agency. The information gathered and analyzed by these agencies tends to be in support of the enforcement mandate of each respective agency, but overlapping mandates do exist. This type of situation appears most often because most criminal organizations are not involved in only one type of criminal activity. For instance, the Customs Act provides the Canada Border Services Agency with the mandate to investigate cigarette smuggling. However, the organization being investigated may also be involved in using the proceeds of this particular criminal activity to finance terrorist activity (see, for example, Hutchinson and O'Malley 2007, 1097). This creates a situation where the sharing or integrating of intelligence databases is all the more important for effective policing of potential terrorist activities.

Hamm (2007) has argued that the best strategy for combating terrorism is the detection and investigation of criminal activities committed to support and facilitate terrorist activities. In concurring with this position, I have argued here that, at the local level, police agencies are in the best position to gather information that can be translated into effective intelligence in the fight against terrorism. This is not without its challenges. These challenges at the local level include the need to gather accurate information and to develop the skills necessary for recognizing criminal activity that may facilitate terrorism, the use of professional intelligence analysts as partners in law enforcement, and the development of data networks that allow for the timely sharing of information and intelligence between law enforcement and other intelligence-gathering agencies. If indeed the intelligence-led policing model is to be effectively used in policing terrorism, then intelligence needs to be effectively generated and shared within and among police and other enforcement agencies in a timely manner.

Internationalization of Domestic Policing

The last section focused on the local dimensions of policing terrorism; this section departs only slightly from that by expanding on the need for domestic policing to have also an international focus. This is not an argument for the development of an international police force for hunting down terrorists but, rather, for local police agencies to learn from the terrorism experiences of foreign police agencies and to develop and apply best practices within their home jurisdictions. As terrorist networks span international boundaries, police agencies need to reach out to other foreign police forces – for sharing intelligence, but also for sharing enforcement practices and lessons learned.

The phenomenon of criminal activity being used to support or facilitate terrorist activity is a global issue, as evidenced by the terrorist attacks in London in 2005 and Madrid in 2004. In both cases, the funding for the operations was linked to criminals involved in weapons trafficking, drug trafficking, and fraud (Bennetto 2004; Hamilos 2007). From a policing perspective, not only are these two attacks examples of the use of precursor crimes to support terrorist activities, but they also represent actual case studies that can and should be used by policing agencies as a means of informing and educating front-line police officers. McGarrell, Freilich, and Chermak (2007, 147) maintain that the arrests made in the London and Madrid bombings demonstrate that intelligence information gathered from various sources was key in the post-event investigation that led to the arrest of numerous suspects.

In Canada, where terrorist attacks and threats of attacks are still a relatively rare occurrence, attacks such as those in London, Madrid, and Bali are opportunities for Canadian police agencies to learn investigative methods to better be able to detect terrorist cells in advance of an attack by looking for precursor crimes. Liaising with police agencies in other countries does not need to be a costly endeavour but simply requires the development of some mechanism whereby the lessons learned in one jurisdiction can be passed to the front-line officers in another jurisdiction, irrespective of international boundaries.

When we look closely at the London and Madrid bombings, however, there is another link that speaks not only to the critical nature of police information sharing between international jurisdictions but also to the change in the strategic operation of terrorist groups brought about, I would argue, as a reaction to state actions. Besides the evident link between the Madrid bombers and financing from London-based extremists, the attacks were very similar in the manner in which they were carried out. In both cases, the perpetrators were not foreign-born radicals; rather, with the exception of one person, all were born in the country in which they carried out the attack. The internet was used as the primary source of communication, directions, and inspiration, illustrating the importance of "ideas." These local terrorist cells were not directed by a "terrorist hierarchy" but were inspired to action by choice (Van Natta and Sciolino 2005). As crime scenes such as those in London and Madrid are deconstructed by investigative teams, the information gathered becomes important intelligence that needs to be shared between agencies. Too often, however, this information and intelligence makes its way to only anti-terrorist units. This information must be disseminated to the front-line general duties police officer, who seems to be in the best position to observe interactions in the community. In the case of the London bombers, none of the individuals involved in the bombings was under surveillance by British intelligence or anti-terrorism units (CBC News 2005a). And although front-line police officers armed with both intelligence and training may not have made a difference in this case, they can be an important source of bottom-up information for anti-terrorist and intelligence units, especially when information on what types of behaviour and characteristics to be aware of flows from the top down.

The sharing of information and intelligence between police agencies of different countries, whether based on best practices, lessons learned, or drawing links between groups operating across international boundaries, speaks strongly to the need for greater interstate police dialogue. The argument here is not to create an international version of Europol (see Deflem 2006) but, rather, a greater dispersion of information gained from the daily operations of community policing, as well as through the investigative process. How such dialoguing is done is dependent on several variables, central to which are cost and security. Clearly it would not be financially viable for small police forces to forward-deploy liaison officers to major international cities. However, just as international criminals and terrorists use the internet to communicate, so too can police forces from around the world use secure internet to share information. In North America and Europe, most police officers have, at a minimum, access to secure internet. The simplest and most efficient way to share information down to the level of the frontline officer and back up the police hierarchy is through the internet. In a world of globalized crime and terrorism, police forces need to be prepared to share information across international boundaries, and to look for valuable and pertinent intelligence within that information.

Conclusion

Increasingly, in the global world, the local has become more important. Efforts by the international community to restrict terrorist organizations' access to territory and money have resulted in strategic changes to how terrorist organizations operate. The ideas and methodologies that define terrorist organizations move freely across international boundaries. The training ground is the internet, and funding is provided in many cases though local criminal activity. To fight the war on terror means law enforcement agencies must take action at the local level, where the recruitment, planning, and funding of operations start.[14] And although governments are willing to commit more and more resources to fighting terrorism "over there," the agency best suited to fighting terrorism is the local police agency. Police officers are in the best position to observe, document, and investigate activities in the community. However, all that information needs further processing – formulated into intelligence and shared with other policing agencies, both nationally and internationally. A piece of seemingly random information in Toronto may, in context, be the key to disrupting a terrorist cell in Rome. Moreover, there needs to be a complete circle, a mechanism by which intelligence, best practices, and lessons learned make their way back to the community police officer, providing indicators of what types of behaviours and characteristics are most significant. In Canada, the implications for federal policing are clear: solid partnerships for the purpose of information gathering and sharing need to be established with municipal, national, and international police agencies. Moreover, the synthesis of raw information by trained intelligence analysts into useful and shared intelligence will further facilitate the degree to which community police officers and national security investigators are effective.

NOTES

1 There is a substantial literature examining the changing nature of state security threats, led in many cases by critical security studies. See, for example, Buzan, Waever, and de Wilde (1998); Grayson (2008); Krause and Williams (1997); Liotta (2002).
2 Many commentators consider the war on terror a post-9/11 initiative by President George W. Bush. Richard Clarke (2004) suggests, however, that a war against terrorist targets was well underway during the Clinton administration.
3 On the importance of ideas in international relations, particularly the relationship between ideas and agents, see Ruggie (1998b) and Wendt (1992).
4 The Criminal Code of Canada lists terrorist- and terrorism-related offences under section 2.1 of the act. See http://laws.justice.gc.ca.
5 See http://www.rcmp-grc.gc.ca/organizedcrime/what_e.htm.
6 From the perspective of war fighting, Olson (2007) argues that modern war needs to include threats from non-traditional militaries. A strategy for war fighting has to include threats from asymmetrical non-state actors.
7 See http://www.whitehousedrugpolicy.gov/publications/policy/ndcs07/chap3%5Fpref.html.
8 The Egmont Group is named for the location of the first meeting at the Egmont-Arenberg Palace in Brussels on 9 June 1995.
9 "Hawala" is the Arabic word for "transfer," but is more often used to describe the informal transfer of value (money or otherwise) without the physical conveyance of money. See Viles (2008). "Other unregulated measures" include the smuggling of regulated monetary instruments (cash, diamonds, gold) and the export of high-value items such as cars and electronics.
10 Contrary to this position, Edward Newman (2007) argues that terrorist groups emerge not only in regions absent of regulation and authority but also in strong states. The reason for a convergence between criminal and terrorist groups is that both have a common goal of being able to operate free of the limits and restrictions of states, thus providing one motive for cooperation.
11 "Intelligence-led policing" is defined as "a strategic, future-oriented and targeted approach to crime control, focusing upon the identification, analysis and 'management' of persisting and developing 'problems' or 'risks'" (de Lint 2006, 1).

12 For example, a Turkish police investigation following the November 2003 suicide bombings that killed 68 people and injured over 700 in Istanbul found that nearly 300 people had some prior knowledge of the suicide bombings. Of that, only 48 were viewed as ideologically committed terrorists, leaving approximately 250 community members who were not ideologically committed but had some knowledge of the impending attacks. Accessing this information could have potentially prevented the attacks (McGarrell, Freilich, and Chermak 2007, 151).

13 In Canada, most major urban areas are policed by locally controlled municipal police forces. The most visible exception to this is the Lower Mainland of British Columbia, where the RCMP does the bulk of the municipal policing. Provincially, the RCMP does all the provincial and territorial policing, with the exception of Ontario and Quebec, with their respective provincial police forces. Federally, the RCMP is the only police force of jurisdiction, though joint forces operations, which include members from other police agencies, are increasingly more common.

14 According to a 2006 study published by Smith, Damphousse, and Roberts (2006), which examined sixty-five terrorism case studies, nearly one-half of all terrorists lived within thirty miles of their targets and all their preparatory work took place within this radius. In addition, there was on average a two- to three-month time lapse between planning and commission.

Biosecurity in Canada and Beyond
Invasions, Imperialisms, and Sovereignty

PETER STOETT

In an age of superpower military assertion; nuclear, chemical, and biological weapons; mass state murder; and terrorism, it may seem trite to worry about invasive bullfrogs. Yet, there are serious concerns over the ability of delicate ecosystems to withstand the onslaught of bullfrogs "the size of dinner plates" as they spread rapaciously across British Columbia. Apparently, the frogs were introduced in the 1930s by an enterprising restaurateur, who released them after realizing they would not become fashionable menu items, and the population has exploded in recent years throughout large portions of Vancouver Island and the southwestern part of the mainland (Read 2004). They have a wide-ranging appetite for other amphibians, ducklings, garter snakes, songbirds, and even mice. Similar fears surround the potential introduction of the Asian carp, which escaped from Arkansas catfish farms in the early 1990s and eats almost half of its weight in plankton and vegetation every day; and of the hydrilla weed, originally from Asia but a more recent escapee from Floridian aquariums, which is apparently on its way northward, wiping out local plants and choking "lakes and rivers in thick mats of tough stems and leaves" (Gorrie 2004). Even Canadian beavers are running amok in Chile and Argentina.[1] Such species, and even smaller microbial actors, are agents of change in the theatre of biosecurity, eluding the simplistic friend/foe dichotomization on which the initial thrusts of the war on terror depended.

Invasion, counter-invasion, containment, infiltration, and imperialism: all of these conventional terms, so common in the study of international relations (IR) and foreign policy, can be employed – for better or worse – in a contemporary discussion of ecology. Indeed, the threats to environmental security and biosecurity are tangible and expanding. I distinguish the two in the following way: while they both entail the protection and conservation of biota, including human life, from threats to habitat and health, "biosecurity" refers also to the construction of the mental images we utilize to pursue that protection, which in turn at least partially define what it means to be biota – in our case, human – and how this is situated within a particular social context.[2] That context, in IR, has assumed the Hobbesian anarchic dilemma, with its attendant ubiquitous survival threats and a universalizing, limited ethics that reproduces its own validity. It is quite possible to imagine a context that instead focuses on what, borrowing from a long line of extra-paradigmatic thought, I have referred to as the *glocal condition*, whereby the nexus point between local needs and traits and global forces (including competing conceptions of order) and imperatives defines the political and biological space of our time (Gore and Stoett 2009). Not surprisingly, this has emerged as a central theme of this book: to conceive of security in terms of the inside/outside dichotomy makes as much sense as treating atmospheric pollution by building very large, thick, self-containing bubbles in which we can live our terrified lives.

The language of invasion and counter-invasion may be better suited to traditional security analysis than to those pursuing biosecurity concerns, yet the similar semantics should hardly surprise us in this post-9/11 world, where securitization has become a common approach to most issues. For my purposes, "securitization" refers to the militaristic response to problems that are perceived or repackaged as threats to more traditional conceptions of security, including national and economic security (both combining toward some rustic notion of "our way of life.") Thus, Kelle (2007, 218-19; borrowing from Waever 1995) argues that public health has been securitized in the face of bioterror. Although we need to deal with the invasive nature of threats to biosecurity, we need also to avoid what I refer to as reflexively securitizationist responses. Famously, Foucault (1991) made reference to the growth of the biopower of the state; present threats to biosecurity afford a historically unparalleled opportunity for its continued expansion, even at the level of global governance. Canadian leaders, in their search for Canada's place in the present world order, run the risk of making a regrettable contribution – not regrettable because we need to do nothing about biosecurity threats but because a securitizationist response will not challenge us to do enough.

Below I offer a broad survey of several principal threats to biosecurity, all easily applicable to Canada, and all of which may solicit securitizationist responses but demand instead a much more cohesive and reflective critical examination of our way of doing things within a glocal conception of structure and agency. Arguably, the most common terms denoting traditionally revered threats are "invasion," "infiltration," and "balance of power." I use these terms here to connote the threats to environmental and human security that may well render other security considerations moot in the future. I then offer a brief discourse on the meaning of biosecurity within the context of a post-9/11 security climate, suggesting it should provoke serious critical reflection instead of reflexive securitizationist responses, and invoking two other terms used with regular promiscuity in international studies: "imperialism" and "sovereignty."

Invasion: Alien Species

The most commonly accepted definition of bioinvasives is probably "widespread nonindigenous species that have adverse effects on the invaded habitat" (McNeely et al. 2001; see also Colautti and MacIsaac 2004), though IR specialists might note with humour that the term "invasive species" has such a negative connotation that it has been charged with over-emotionalizing, thus betraying the standards of dispassionate science (Theodoropoulas 2003). Of course, the ultimate invasive species, and the one with the uncontested claim of most "ecological damage done" in the process, is humankind.

For several centuries, bioinvasion has been a global affair. Such species displacement is often referred to as human-mediated global dispersal. There are, of course, non-human mediated dispersals, such as ice flows in the Arctic, changing wind patterns, and even "kelp rafts" in the Antarctic (S. Smith 2001). But these are not known to cause lengthy migrations; this takes human intervention. Some of the species introductions have been deliberate, in efforts to affect bio-pest control, or for hunting and fishing purposes (for example, game species). Most notoriously, perhaps, the Nile perch has destroyed biodiversity in the Lake Victoria region of central Africa. The North American Great Lakes (after being ravaged by the invasive sea lamprey) have been populated largely by introduced species, and terrestrial species such as ring-necked pheasant and sika deer have been introduced for hunting purposes (G. Cox 1999). The Asian carp was originally introduced to clear vegetation from fish farms. An electric barrier between the Chicago Sanitary and Ship Canal and Lake Michigan is the last line of Great Lakes defence against this ravenous fish. The most damaging invasions, however, have been incidental: in general, human-mediated transport is the most important factor for the range of invasive species, though conducive temperatures, competitive ability, and lack of enemies is more important once generous transportation services have been provided by unwitting economic actors.

According to one estimate, since the completion of the St. Lawrence Seaway in 1959, at least forty-three non-indigenous species have been established in the Laurentian Great Lakes, including the dreaded sea lamprey, an ocean-going predatory parasite that devastated the Great Lakes fisheries. US-Canadian bilateral efforts to combat the lamprey resulted in the Great Lakes Fishery Commission, which has made some impact on mitigating its harm (Abramovitz 1996, 47). The majority of invasive species have arrived courtesy of ballast water from commercial ships (Grigorovich et al. 2003). In 2008, almost fifty years after the seaway began operation, the United States and Canada have finally agreed on an (unimplemented at this stage) inspection system for incoming ships. Arguably, what is perhaps the most infamous example of transoceanic bioinvasion in Canadian history, the inedible *Dreissena polymorpha*, or zebra mussel, was the main impetus. The mussel invasion has had a significant economic impact, clogging intake valves in ship engines and power plants. In the words of one analyst, the clogging caused by zebra mussels is akin to "an acute hardening of industrial arteries" (Bright 1998, 181). Some environmentalists might argue this may be good for the environment (the mussels filter water as they consume), but it is decidedly bad for biodiversity.

In areas where they are highly concentrated and the technology permits, zebra mussel colonies can be eradicated. This involves using chemical agents (known as molluscicides), freezing and boiling (through steam injection), acoustical vibration, electrical currents, and the introduction of biological agents (such as predators, parasites, and disease). All of these techniques present obvious problems for the greater aquatic environment and may in fact cause more problems than they solve. As van Driesche and van Driesche (2000, 74) remind us, "No examples of successful biocontrol of aquatic invertebrates exist." Manual removal is possible for small boats but presents an enormous challenge (in terms of safety and labour) for large ships and underwater pipelines. Reporting the sighting of mussels in non-contaminated areas is vital so that protected areas (such as clam grounds along the Mississippi River) can receive immediate attention. But there will be no large-scale eradication program. Like the purple loosestrife, which spread inexorably across Canadian fields after its introduction from Europe (White 1993), the zebra mussel is here to stay. It would seem that coexistence, rather than counter-invasive warfare, is the only reasonable response.

Indeed, zebra mussels are but one problematic invasive species that have been specifically linked to ballast water discharges by the International Maritime Organization, Global Environment Fund, and UN Development Programme, which have together instituted an international Global Ballast Water Management Programme. The others include cholera, the cladoceran water flea, various sources of toxic algae, and the self-fertilizing hermaphroditic North American comb jelly. Many of these species have literally crisscrossed the globe as a consequence of the expansion of trade – secure in freshwater ballast tanks and emptied in awaiting ports.

Although many bioinvasions take place on the local scale (such as the spread of the pine beetle in British Columbia and Alberta), the problem is clearly international in scope. The Global Invasive Species Programme (Ruiz and Carleton 2003) is an effort to catalogue and recommend remedial action for thousands of invasive species identified so far, but such efforts face all the usual problems of global environmental governance (see Stoett 2007). One of those problems is lack of public and elite concern, but – even if we overlook the severe threat to human health posed by cholera, and the impact of such species on economic activities such as fishing, hunting, and agriculture – it is churlish indeed to ignore this threat to biosecurity. Alien species do more than challenge competitors; they can even change the ecosystem itself, fundamentally altering its characteristics (Beisner, Ives, and Carpenter 2003). For example, there is ample concern that the large numbers of introduced salmonine fish stock in the Great Lakes – in excess of 745 million fish between 1966 and 1998 – have also fundamentally altered the recipient ecosystems (see especially Crawford 2001). When invasive species actually transform ecosystems, they also can create hybrid taxa, or "genetic pollution" resulting from introgression, and this can be studied only at the level of gene analysis (Petit 2004; see also Hengeveld 1989). This becomes even more important with the agricultural introduction of genetically modified organisms, invasive species in their own right when they pollinate adjoining farmland, leading to vigorous calls for precaution, as well as related bioterrorism fears.[3] Fixing the problem with natural predators can lead to even greater problems: the deliberate introduction of so-called biological-control agents can release them from the constraints imposed by their natural enemies, further homogenize the world's biotic communities, and affect non-target species. They can also lead to unpredictable evolutionary changes (Edwards 1998). Indeed, containment measures are especially counterproductive when biodiversity conservation efforts in fact demand more connectivity between bioregions and transborder conduits for species migration (Sanders and Stoett 2006).

There is also evidence that warming trends will induce species migration northward (Hughes 2000). Such unassisted migration will prove difficult for rare species of plants and trees, and adaptation or extinction is as likely (Iverson, Schwartz, and Prasad 2004). Not so for insects. Warming patterns, for example, have vastly extended the range of the mountain pine beetle, ravaging Yoho National Park in British Columbia and threatening forests in Washington state and Banff. We are likely to see further zebra mussel northward migration as relevant reproduction temperatures become more common, and flooding could expand zebra mussel territory even further. It is believed that "climate change will affect the incidence of episodic recruitment events of invasive species, by altering the frequency, intensity, and duration of flooding ... [in turn] allowing aggressive species to escape from local, constrained refugia" (Sutherst 2000, 224; see also Kolar and Lodge 2000). Thus, the discourse on bioinvasion must now be seen as nested within the broader global debate on the mitigation of, and adaptation to, climate change. As importantly, it challenges the logic of placing trade in the global marketplace on an unassailable pedestal.

Infiltration: Biosafety and Infectious Disease

Invasive species are not always visible to the naked human eye, and it is often more accurate to describe them as infiltrating as they penetrate biota and begin to spread their own habitats from within. Indeed, the most pernicious and dangerous to human health live at the microbial level, escaping untrained detection, threatening animal and human life, and capable of amazing rates of infection as they leap from one organism to another. Any casual student of history is familiar with the Black Death (bubonic and pneumonic plagues originating in the Eurasian steppes that killed roughly a quarter of the European population in the fourteenth century), the impact of viral infections on Native Americans during colonization (A. Crosby 1986; Lovell 1992), the advent of tuberculosis and other diseases during industrialization, the flu pandemic of 1916-20 (Collier 1974), and other incidents that demonstrate the ability of infection to spread with alarming and deadly speed. Arguably, however, in an age when security concerns are heightened by the fear of bioterror, we are more conscious of the microbial threat than ever before, and the acute economic impact of disease detection in agricultural operations makes this even more evident. A securitizationist response will keep us in perpetual fear of the murderous use of infectious disease for the strategic gain of our enemies, but the overwhelming threat from the spread of HIV/AIDS and other microbial agents has little to do with terrorist attacks and much to do with public and animal health provision.

On the farm, foot-and-mouth disease, mad cow disease (or bovine spongiform encephalopathy – BSE), and the avian flu H7N3 have had immeasurable kill totals in many countries, including Canada (Stoett 2006). Similar concerns are expressed over the spread of viruses in the aquacultural industry, particularly among net-pen-reared Atlantic salmon in British Columbia (St. Hilaire et al. 2002). The larger fear, however, is that such pathogens will make the species leap and begin infecting humans at uncontrollable rates.

In late 2004, influenza experts warned of a possible perfect storm of infection that could easily kill millions. Certainly, the experience of the so-called Spanish flu, which killed some 40 to 50 million people during and after the First World War, suggests that another such catastrophe is possible.[4] As of June 2010, according to the World Health Organization (WHO), the H5N1 avian influenza virus has killed nearly 300 people, most of them in Asia.[5] Scientists worry that the flu could mutate into a strain that can spread rapidly among humans, which would make SARS, which took Canadian public health officials by surprise in 2003, look innocuous in comparison. Meanwhile, threats of a major influenza (H1N1) breakout in Canada in 2009-10 were avoided after a major vaccination campaign across the country.

Although a hot topic in the 1990s (Preston 1994), infectious diseases (microbial pathogens) have received increasing attention by security analysts since 2001 (Heymann 2003), though much of it is fixated on the bioterrorist threat (Chyba and Greninger 2004). However, the main threat here to human health and industry stems not from deliberately released anthrax spores or smallpox but the incidental spread of disease in a highly interconnected global economy. The securitizationist response has already been on full display. Then US president George W. Bush made it clear in 2005 that the proper response to any serious outbreak would be quarantine, and that the military would be employed to enforce such measures, though the Posse Comitatus Act of 1878 bans the military from participating in police-type activity on American soil. Indeed, money to stockpile a potential antiviral drug was enveloped in a Pentagon spending bill. Subsequently, the North American Plan for Avian and Pandemic Influenza was announced after the

2007 Security and Prosperity Partnership of North America meeting of the American, Canadian, and Mexican leaders. It contains reasonable measures and relies on multilateral approaches such as that advanced by the WHO but also makes it clear that the departments of Homeland Security and Defense will have substantive roles to play in the event of major outbreaks. Feminist analyses on the appropriation of rights and freedoms by the "bioterror industry" might well be adding the pharmaceutical-military industrial complex to the list in the near future (Kane and Greenhill 2007).

The fear that avian flu could be the next major pandemic is quite justified, but we need not look to the future for a deadly epidemic, since we are in the midst of one. It can also be argued that global bioapartheid is already here. "Global bioapartheid" is a dystopian term referring to a world in which people with access to immunization, either through avoidance of infection or medical attention, are strictly separated from the many more without. HIV/AIDS has claimed over 20 million lives in recent decades, most of them in Africa but with increasing numbers in Asia, Russia, and elsewhere. Worldwide, some 40 million people live with HIV/AIDS, more than half of them in sub-Saharan Africa (UNAIDS/WHO 2003), many of whom are co-infected with tuberculosis or other pathogens. Trends toward safe-sex behaviour have reduced the spread of HIV/AIDS in Canada, though there are fears it is again increasing among men who have sex with men, and its spread among heterosexually active young women and intravenous drug users continues to rise.

There are endless disputes over the exact numbers involved in this pandemic. Yet, anyone travelling in southern Africa, where HIV seroprevalence runs as high as 35 percent, cannot help but notice the preponderance of fresh graves in local and even makeshift cemeteries. The only thing comparable is the wartime cemeteries of armed conflict zones. Humans have achieved considerable success in the past against infectious diseases such as cholera, smallpox, polio, and leprosy (though even here the application has been uneven), and advances in the fight against HIV/AIDS have been as remarkable but even less egalitarian in their distribution, as tireless campaigners such as Stephen Lewis remind us.

We should not forget that fighting infectious diseases is a learning process and will be a cumulative effort. As Ronald Glasser (2004, 42) reminds us, "It is no exaggeration to say that the billions of dollars so reluctantly pushed into viral research as a result of the efforts of AIDS activists in the 1980s and 1990s enabled the WHO to quickly find the cause of another viral plague [SARS]. And it was the ability to share accurate information in real time via email and the Internet that allowed the WHO to hold the disease in check." The reality, of course, is that there will never be an end to such work, since the microbial world is an endlessly adaptive one. As is the case with invasive species such as zebra mussels, the emphasis must be on prevention, early detection, the development of alternative responses in the event of emergency, and the humane treatment of those affected. International co-ordination is essential (Zacher and Keefe 2008), and the educative effort is of unprecedented significance. But we must also be concerned with the biosecurity threats presented by the very lifestyle we wish to protect, and it is to that more introspective theme I turn next.

The Balance of Power: Environmental Change

If natural disasters remind us of the sheer power of nature, we may well be on the cusp of an astonishing intellectual leap in which we finally acknowledge that a major perceived (but quite unreal, in scientific terms) shift in the balance of power vis-à-vis the human-nature relationship is taking place with the advent of accelerated climate change. Environmental change is, of course, unavoidable, and it would be as futile as disingenuous to refer to this in itself as a threat to biosecurity. It is the rapid rate of humanly induced change that is at issue, and we are making unprecedented alterations at both the macro and micro levels that present incalculable risks to human, animal, and plant life, prompting geologists to speak of entering the "Anthropocene" age, which is essentially a "no-analogue" condition, incomparable to any before it (Dalby 2006, 21). With this age, however, comes even greater unpredictability of natural events and a diminishment in our ability to creatively respond to the resultant threats to the crafted self-image of the liberal utilitarian ideal (see Laferrière and Stoett 1999).

At the macro level, biodiversity is challenged by the centuries-long process of agricultural production, since it moves us toward homogenous ecosystems and is reliant on unnatural inputs, especially fossil fuels, for increased yields. According to the US Department of Agriculture (USDA), biosecurity is about the protection of the food supply and, specifically, responses to food safety emergencies. After 9/11, the USDA formed the Food Biosecurity Action Team in order to assess "potential vulnerabilities along the farm-table continuum."[6] The implied threat here is, in essence, terrorism – more specifically, terrorists – and though attacks on the "farm-table continuum" are not undreamt of, they are far less realized threats to human habitat than the agricultural production system itself, heavily reliant on oil products, pesticides, antibiotics, and land-erosive practices. Urbanization and suburbanization also threaten biodiversity, and industrialization has introduced a wide array of carcinogens and other contaminants to the water supply; extensive increases in atmospheric pollution, including greenhouse gases; and geopolitical risks related to the pursuit of energy security. A holistic view is needed to measure our impact today.

The extensive use of antibiotics, both by people and on farms, is an example. Excrement containing antibiotic residue gradually finds its way into the water system, including the Great Lakes, increasing the risk of waterborne infectious diseases. According to an International Joint Commission report, "Some experts believe that the massive and largely unregulated use of antibiotics in agriculture, coupled with the increasing number of antibiotic-resistant pathogens found in nature, may present the greatest risk," resulting in the evolution of "superbugs" we would be unable to resist (Spears 2004). As Price-Smith (2002, 168) puts it, there is a "link between temperature increases and a shortened extrinsic incubation rate coupled with increased biting activity of many arthropod vectors ... Since global environmental change is expected to generate significant long-term shifts in abiotic phenomena (temperature, humidity, water resources, etc.), we can reasonably expect attendant shifts in pathogenic virulence" (see also Ewald 1994; McMichael and Bouma 2000).

Beyond this, it has even been suggested that some 80 percent of all cancers are likely due to environmental factors that could be reduced or even eradicated, including toxic industrial and agricultural chemicals, excessive sunlight, and nuclear radiation from power plants and military operations (Burdon 2003). The UN Environmental Programme asserts that "some 25 percent of all preventable ill-health, with diarrhoeal diseases and acute respiratory infections heading the list" is directly attributable to poor environmental quality.[7] Of course, these linkages are all controversial in the causal sense, but the point is that, in pursuing economic and military security, environmental security for the common citizen is compromised. This may lead to a rethinking of priorities. Arguably, the largest single threat to biosecurity is the unprecedented global reduction in biodiversity, itself an essential environmental condition (P. Wood 2000, 34-84), we have witnessed over the last several decades (Norgaard 1988). Canada is not immune to the prospect of species extinction (Boardman and Beazely 2002). Habitat protection is the most important element of species conservation, and environmental change is the greatest threat to habitat.

It is increasingly difficult for northern governments to avoid these public policy questions, or the suffering of millions of victims in the South.

Biosecurity threats, referred to as neglected diseases by the WHO and other UN agencies, "affect almost exclusively poor and powerless people living in rural parts of low-income countries," including Chagas' disease (a sleeping sickness) and river blindness (WHO 2002, 96). Malaria and yellow fever, among other tropical diseases, remain serious health threats in many states also struggling to deal with the AIDS pandemic, land and forest degradation, and civil or international military conflict. Indeed, in international law, there is an increasing recognition of the right to a healthy environment (Schrijver and Weiss 2004). For example, members of the UN Economic Commission for Europe recently signed the Aarhus Convention, which not only pledges signatories to pursue sustainable development paths but also guarantees greater citizen input (see Giorgetta 2002). Of course, this is but a formal convention, and security specialists are under no illusions about the actual enforceability of conventions. Yet, some scholars have even argued that proper environmental impact assessment should now be considered an element of customary international law, a position based largely on the widespread rhetorical acceptance of the precautionary principle (DiMento 2003, 172-74; see also Hunter, Salzman, and Zaelke 2006).

Climate change presents a wide range of challenges to the contemporary discourse on biosecurity, including the need to rethink dominant (and ultimately false) assumptions about just who is in charge: perhaps the presumptive balance of power is shifting back toward an abandoned awareness of our high vulnerability to things natural. But this shift is accompanied by centuries of collected wisdom, culture, science, and policy analysis, suggesting we can do better. We need ethical guidelines, however, and these must emerge from the discourse as well.

Imperialism, and toward a Sovereignty of Biosecurity?

Bioimperialism generally has referred to the purposeful or incidental spread of biota from core to peripheral states and/or regions (A. Crosby 1986; Paterson and Dalby 2006). Others stress the intellectual violence inherent in the process of forcing conceptions of human-nature relations on Native populations, part of the broader pattern of campaigns of cultural imperialism (Shiva 1993). We must also consider the idea that governance efforts (global and otherwise) to manage the myriad threats to biosecurity further entrench the biopower of states and corporations and create obstacles to the realization of environmental justice (Dobson 2003; Illsley 2002). This question is rarely raised when discussions of policy responses to biosecurity threats take place, yet it is vital, as justice is coming to play a much more central role in our evaluation of global environmental governance efforts (see Adger et al. 2006; Roberts and Parks 2006), including the development of international law (Rajamani 2006). Finally, the pursuit and maintenance of biosecurity provides what is perhaps the ultimate example of the need to apply the precautionary principle (see Burns 2006; Whiteside 2006), raising further ethical dilemmas and demands related to the construction, social distribution, and prevention of risk (Beck 1992; Leiss 2001). At the most basic level, since Canadian biosecurity cannot be viewed in national isolation, we are forced also to consider not only Canada's relatively privileged place in the world but the discrepancy between the health risks endured by people in peripheral regions, such as the Inuit, and the average suburban Canadian as well. Sovereignty assumes a new, perhaps more urgent (and yet, in a naturalistic manner, perhaps timeless) meaning in this context: the ability to pursue strategies of self-protection, for both humans and natural (if forever altered by human activity) ecosystems. Although Litfin (1998) and Eckersley (2004) have both discussed the greening of the state and the subsequent transformation of sovereignty, IR theorists need to look beyond traditional notions of sovereignty as well (Laferrière and Stoett 1999).

Ethics entails obligations, and though most of the securitization discourse revolves around states and armies, and verges into the non-state world mainly because of the presence of terrorists and rebel groups and insurgencies, the private sector is instrumental in both spreading and containing the invasions, infiltrations, and system changes discussed in this chapter. Likewise, private military and pharmaceutical firms and NGOs are involved in efforts to protect the wealthy from their impact. Agricultural corporations are surely as responsible, both causally and ethically, for threats to biodiversity as are aquafarmers, shipping lines, and suburban developers. Securitizationist responses tend to overlook the causal significance and ethical obligations of the private sector. Environmental politics has always served as a corrective to this tendency and will continue to do so. Just as legal sovereignty entails certain rights and obligations on the part of state governments, a sovereignty of biosecurity demands respect for basic human rights and restraint on behalf of those who profit from the more harmful forms of exploitation.

This book centres on the notion of a world order that is still framed by the universalizing discourse of American power and the reverberate effects this has on people within states such as Canada. The securitizationist response to biosecurity threats is surely an instance of hegemonic, if ultimately futile, discursive evolution. As Weber (2006, 112), borrowing from Foucault (1991) and Darier (1999) suggests, a post-structuralist approach would deny the legitimacy of constructing normalizing master discourses, including those defining the abnormalities inherent in natural evolution as fixable or preventable problems. Contemporary efforts to deal with biosecurity issues through either global governance efforts that, although often laudable in their own right, are also perceived as unjust impositions on peripheral states or regions, or by militarized approaches emphasizing containment and counter-invasion, will not suffice. They will be seen largely as yet further links in the historical chain of an unfolding imperialistic narrative. To avoid this, and to have a concrete impact on life without disdaining liberty in the process, is indeed a magnificent challenge.

Conclusion

None of this is to argue that physical threats posed by terrorist activity or warfare are insignificant. Both the United States and Canada are fertile ground for enterprising terrorists determined to threaten biosecurity. A *New York Times* editorial referred to the 123 chemical plants that could, if attacked, endanger a million lives each: the threat of "dirty bombs" (which disperse radioactive material without an explosion), suicide attacks on nuclear power plants, lax port security, hazardous waste transport, and bioterrorism, or the use of agents such as smallpox, anthrax, or plague (Garrett 2001).[8] Surreptitious attacks on food supplies are always a possibility. Small amounts of contaminants, such as polychlorinated biphenyls (PCBs, which are both carcinogenic and neurotoxic) could be spread throughout the food system with a concerted stealth attack on grain silos (Homer-Dixon 2002, 59). Water can be purposefully contaminated (though the Walkerton, Ontario, scenario of neglect is far more likely). Similarly, the threats posed to human and non-human life by military activity cannot be overlooked. In Canada, the environmental legacy of the Cold War Distant Early Warning lines is of great concern to local communities. Abroad, the use of depleted uranium has become a hot topic, often quickly linked with cancer and infant malformations, and provoking a special UN task force. At the global level, the Biological Weapons Convention and similar arms control agreements have the protection of human health as their ultimate aim. But, in general, Canada has been fortunate to escape the biosecurity threats of military conduct and preparation, even if it has historically contributed to them elsewhere.[9]

But the threats this chapter describes are scratching the very fabric of life. Again, we will always live with the uncertainties posed by the imperative of biosecurity. As Robert Clark (1997, 544) writes, "Diseases are part of the price we pay for globally spreading ourselves and the other living things on which we depend for food," as are invasive species and environmental alteration. But there is no need for complacency either, and several points may be stressed at this time. We need three levels of action to become organizing principles. First, in the biosecurity issue realm, the front-line worker has become an essential element in the chain of response. As we now have a small cadre of wildlife management experts monitoring invasive species, health professionals experienced in dealing with highly contagious pathogens, and many farm workers experienced with avian flu and mad cow containment, we can perhaps begin to build upon this resource for future generations both within and outside Canada, making sure we incorporate indigenous peoples' knowledge in the process.

Second, governments and private sector decision makers must act preemptively, committing resources commensurate to the magnitude of these threats. This does not entail the inducement of panic but, rather, steadfast dedication to developing the expert community and reaction forces necessary to stem outbreaks. This should not be an ephemeral electoral issue but a recognized function of the state. We cannot bomb our way out of this mess, increasing military budgets and engaging in propaganda warfare.

Finally, civil society must be engaged not only to educate the public but also to increase its direct participation. There is an awkward yet inevitable tension between the science and politics of these issues, since they evoke ethical and moral considerations. This cannot be overcome by reliance on technocratic means of governance. On the contrary, such debates can open the door to the broader introspection necessary to reassess the values and directions of our society, as well as Canada's role in the world. Indeed, we might ask how we can utilize such security threats to broaden civic participation and reduce structural inequities, instead of lowering and reinforcing them respectively. For example, Thomas and Weber (2004, 188) argue that the contemporary global health debate offers an opportunity for interested actors to "reintroduce the wider social concerns constitutive of a more integrated approach to health care, which would locate specific interventions within a broader project of socio-economic transformation."

Ultimately, the management of these issues will be a function of their presentation, representation, and misrepresentation by media, government, NGOs, and multinational corporations alike. Prevention and preparedness are obviously necessary. With invasive species and infectious disease, we can predict patterns of prevalence but would be foolish to believe we can do so with great accuracy, or enough to eliminate the element of very unpleasant surprise. Environmental change is even less manageable. But what may be needed, more than ever, is a healthy dose of introspection. Many of the invasive species we face today are approaching Canada because of economic processes that need to be tightly regulated if we stand a chance of controlling further spread. Similarly, the processes of mass industrialized agriculture – the feeding of bovine spinal matter to cattle, the close quarters in chicken coops, the water contamination resulting from excessive untreated farm excrement, the "massive application of antibiotics to livestock that would otherwise perish in the lethal miasma created by industrial agriculture" (Glasser 2004, 36) – are responsible for the speed with which biosafety can be compromised. Our eating, driving, and recreational habits, all consumer activities, have a profound effect on human health but also on ecosystem maintenance capacity. In short, the glocal condition frames our personal lives, and the pursuit of a sovereign biosecurity begins at the kitchen table.

Eric Laferrière and I have argued elsewhere (Laferrière and Stoett 1999) that both radical ecology and critical IR theory follow many similar intellectual trajectories. Indeed, the more critical school views the global ecology agenda as little more than a transformation of northern security concerns.[10] Critical theory is more than an attack on the dominance of positivism in the discipline of international political science. It takes us toward a critique of modernity, though some of its postmodern linguistics often obscures the path. If we take the plunge and consider the contemporary global industrial and agricultural system an ecocidal one, it becomes apparent that the greatest challenge to biosecurity continues to be the dominant mode of thinking. The greatest threats to Canadian biosecurity come not from proliferative parasites, anthrax-wielding terrorists, or Spanish fishers with illegal nets. They are a function of the agricultural and industrial processes on which the Canadian society and state have become dependent, making bioinvasion a permanent feature of the ecological, and political, landscape.

NOTES

1 See J. Ross, "Beavers too eager for their own good," *Miami Herald*, 22 December 2005, http:www.miami.com/mld/miamiherald.
2 There are reasonable limits to this definition. "Biosecurity" should not refer to the protection of all living things from any type of infectious agent (viral, fungal, bacterial, parasitic). This would even be unhealthy, since we need certain infections and parasites to survive, and the psychological implications are as obvious.
3 For a good description of the science on genetically modified organisms (GMOs) see Leiss and Tyshenko (2002). Risks associated with GMOs include human health

(such as allergens) and environmental risks (such as crossing GMOs with wild relatives, the acceleration of insect resistance, and effects on non-target species). For a good discussion of how industry and the Canadian government mismanaged the optics of GMOs see Leiss (2001). For an engaging discussion of the international biosafety regime, see Mulligan (2000). Note, however, that there are measures in place to outlaw the hostile use of GMOs. The African Union has put forth a Model Law on Safety in Biotechnology, related to the Cartagena Protocol on Biosafety, and the possibility of deliberate release of GMOs to cause harm cannot be overlooked. However, in the African Union case, this may apply more to fears of eco-imperialism, and subsequent demands for legal reproach, than to armed conflict situations, and there would seem little relevance to Canada here (see Sunshine Project 2002).

4 "Flu experts warn 'perfect storm' of infection could kill millions," *Montreal Gazette*, 21 November 2004. There were in fact three influenza pandemics in the twentieth century – 1918-19, 1957-58, and 1968-69 – of which the first was by the far the deadliest.

5 See WHO's website at http://www.who.int/csr/disease/avian_influenza/country/cases_table_2008_06_19/en/index.html.

6 From the USDA website, http://www.usda.gov (2004). This is linked with the Office of Homeland Security.

7 "Globally, 7 per cent of all deaths and diseases are due to inadequate or unsafe water, sanitation and hygiene. Approximately 5 percent are attributable to air pollution" (UNEP 2002, xxvi).

8 "The District of Columbia Council recently adopted a temporary ban on [hazardous waste] shipments after a Naval Research Laboratory scientist warned that if a 90-ton tanker car carrying chlorine crashed during a Fourth of July celebration at the National Mall, it could kill 100,000 people in 30 minutes." "An insecure nation; Our unnecessary security," *New York Times*, 20 February 2005.

9 Canada was in fact a little-known contributor to the largest ecocidal campaign of all time, the American "Operation Ranchhand" in Southeast Asia, for which defoliants were tested in New Brunswick at Canadian Forces Base Gagetown in 1966 (Levant 1986: 204-5). For broad treatment of ecocide, see Stoett (1999, 51-72).

10 According to Wolfgang Sachs (1999, 23), the entire development framework has been redefined as a policy problem: how can northern dominance be maintained so as to control the spread of southern insecurity? This is, of course, an overgeneralization, but the sentiment is indicative of northern refusal to compensate for its own externalities.

PART 4

CONSTRUCTING GLOBAL ORDER ABROAD – CANADA'S POLICIES IN AFRICA

Canada, Africa, and "New" Multilateralisms for Global Governance Before and After the Harper Regime in Ottawa?

TIMOTHY M. SHAW

The illegal trade in drugs, arms, intellectual property, people and money is booming. Like the war on terrorism, the fight to control these illicit markets pits government against agile, stateless and resourceful networks empowered by globalization.

– Moisés Naím, "Five Wars of Globalization," 2003

Fragile states cannot or will not deliver what citizens need to live decent secure lives. They cannot or will not tackle poverty. As such, they significantly reduce the likelihood of the world meeting the MDGs [millennium development goals] by 2015 ... There are wider reasons why we need to work better in fragile states. They are more likely to become unstable, to destabilise their neighbours, to create refugee flows, to spread disease and to be bases for terrorists.

– United Kingdom, DFID, *Why We Need to Work More Effectively in Fragile States*, 2005b

The Secretary-General fully embraces a broad vision of collective security. The threats to peace and security in the 21st century include not just international wars ... but ... organized crime and civil violence. They also include poverty, deadly infectious disease and environmental degradation ... Collective security today depends on accepting that the threats each region of the world perceives as most urgent are in fact equally so for all.

– UN, *In Larger Freedom: Towards Development, Security and Human Rights for All,* 2005

This chapter examines the "new" multilateralisms as analytic and applied framework with specific reference to what they can provide for a state such as Canada in the post-9/11 world order. Specifically, what can such new multilateralisms offer Canada in terms of its inter- and non-state relations with Africa? As other chapters in this book discuss, our current world order is one that has been most recently redefined and shaped by US hegemony and a US preoccupation with its own national security in the current war on terror. However, this chapter suggests that (1) Canada's emerging role within the US-defined and US-led securitization of first/third world relations is at least a partial reversion away from an already successful track record in taking a leadership role in multilateral interstate and state-civil society relations, and that (2) the new multilateralisms can prove to be effective in dealing with security and economic issues that are important to both Canada and Africa. Multilateralism has been an aspect of Canadian foreign policy with which Canadians are comfortable, so much so that it has become a very part of the way that Canadians see themselves and their role in world politics. New multilateralisms have also proven to be extremely effective at adaptation to the changes brought on by globalization, especially in regard to the inclusion of non-state actors, in dealing with issues that are not easily defined in state terms but are at the heart of African development.

Analytic and policy frameworks are in flux, especially around notions of development (Haddad and Knowles 2007; Harcourt 2007), governance (Cashore, Auld, and Newsom 2004; McGrew 2005), and security (Böge, Fitzpatrick, and Paes 2006; United Kingdom, DFID 2005a; Klare 2002; MacFarlane and Khong 2006), even if the former tend to lag behind the latter. This chapter juxtaposes a range of both literatures and levels to advance analysis of the diversity of global coalitions with a focus on the more to less successful – that is, from the Ottawa and Kimberley processes through small island developing states (SIDS) and the International Criminal Court (ICC) to small arms and child soldiers. It is done so with relevance for Canadian interstate and non-state "foreign policy," especially toward Africa. I reflect on foreign policy before and during the mid-decade Harper government, one that has outlawed previously rather uncontroversial notions of human security and public diplomacy, at least for national diplomatic and civil society, if not defence establishments.

I attempt to build on the work of Hubert (2000), Murphy and Yates (2009), O'Brien et al. (2000), Thérien and Pouliot (2006), and Weiss (2000) on governance and multilateralisms, applying their frameworks to the range of multi-actor coalitions over contemporary global issues with relevance and resonance for "Canada's" global agendas. I also reflect in the conclusion on any implications for the disciplines of political science, international relations, foreign policy, and others, both trans-Atlantic and north-south, with a focus on the emerging debate over whether "African" international relations is different (W. Brown 2006; Lemke 2003), again with particular relevance for Canada's purported special connections to the continent. In short, I analyze such contemporary heterogeneous coalitions in terms of their impact on the definition and advancement of human development, human rights, and human security, with relevance to both the past and future foreign policy directions emanating from non- and intergovernmental Canada.

Specifically, I seek to identify and contrast a set of contemporary global issues that have led to a range of international coalitions seeking to ameliorate them, with relevance to Canadian debates and policies in particular and current analyses and discourses of Canada's good international citizenship role. As indicated in the first epigraph that opened this chapter, the highly uneven incidence and impact of "globalizations" has led to a proliferation of pressing global issues that impact non- and interstate foreign policy: child labour and child soldiers, drugs, forced migration, fundamentalisms, global warming, mafias, money-laundering, resources, small arms, terrorism, and so on (UN 2004). Globalizations have generated a range of international actors and networks leading to new space(s) for novel forms of mixed-actor coalitions, as those generated over landmines and conflict diamonds, which represent the salient aspects of a foreign policy global governance that has involved non-state as well as state and interstate actors (Conflict, Security and Development 2004; Hubert 2000; Keating and Knight 2004; McRae and Hubert 2001; Ramsbottom, Bah and Calder 2005).

However, despite Canada being an animator of such directions at the end of the last century (largely a function of the activist diplomacy of then foreign minister Lloyd Axworthy), under the current Harper regime it has abandoned "human security" and its parallel of "public diplomacy." At a time when unprecedented resources are being poured into the analysis of global issues and Canadian policies – from CIGI (Centre for International Governance Innovation)/Balsillie School of International Affairs at the University of Waterloo and Wilfrid Laurier University, to the Munk Centre for International Studies at the University of Toronto and the new Graduate School of Public and International Affairs at the University of Ottawa – it is ironic, if not depressing, that the present government in Ottawa should be so disinterested or deaf, preoccupied as it is with the challenging Afghanistan question. This is particularly worrisome, as Canada is hosting the G8 in mid-2010 at Huntsville in the district municipality of Muskoka, north of Toronto, when its hitherto global, cosmopolitan legacy should be celebrated rather than denied, including invitations to the Outreach Five: the B(R)ICs (Brazil, [Russia], India, and China) plus Mexico and the Republic of South Africa have been invited to each such summit, now part of Heiligen-damm Process established by the Germans (Cooper and Antkiewicz 2008).

Here, I suggest to go beyond the well-established and relatively successful cases of coalition attention, formation, and activism, such as the Ottawa and Kimberley processes (associated with the Axworthy legacy), to the more intractable instances, such as child soldiers or small arms, SIDS and the ICC, in addition to recognizing less high-profile incremental developments, such as the Extractive Industries Transparency Initiative (EITI) and the Diamond Development Initiative (DDI) (see Chapter 11 by Black and Savage). In this regard, the Bonn International Center for Conversion (BICC) brief on "The business of private, public and civil actors in zones of conflict" (Böge, Fitzpatrick, and Paes 2006) is instructive, as it juxtaposes the emerging and usually isolated genres of "corporate social responsibility" and "the political economy of conflict" with the codes of conduct for resource extraction companies in fragile states (see Thérien and Pouliot 2006 on the United Nations Global Compact).

In turn, then, I seek to begin to abstract a parsimonious set of factors that might explain why some global issues at certain times attract notice and generate continuing responses (for instance, the Ottawa and Kimberley processes), whereas others languish without significant or proportionate analytic or political attention (for instance, child soldiers and small arms). In so doing, I attempt to develop the comparative framework proposed by fellow Canadian Don Hubert, though I am less state-centric and more pro-international NGO (INGO) than him. While he privileges state and inter-state agencies, I place more attention on contexts, scale, and eminent advocates.

First, the larger context of global order has rapidly evolved from bipolarity to unilateral American power, from pre-9/11 and pre-7/7 (when the London bombings took place) to post-9/11 and post-7/7, from post-Cold War to the war-on-terror era, and so on. Moreover, distinctive crises such as the 2004 Christmas tsunami reinvigorated SIDS and related concerns of global order and governance, such as rising sea levels and declining global fish stocks. Second, it is important to consider whether the issue generates an extensive coalition in terms of numbers and diversity of associates, and especially whether the corporate sector is engaged. For example, the World Commission on Dams was the first such global commission to bring companies as well as international organizations, INGOs, and governments to the table. Third, given the influence of global media, does the issue attract the attention and support of global icons, such as Princess Diana's around landmines or Bono and Bob Geldof's about Africa (see Cooper 2008 on global stars and public diplomacy)? These three elements draw attention to the complexity and continuously evolving character of the global environment in which the "new" multilateralisms for global governance have developed. They also suggest crowded locations that call into question the relevance and influence of Canadian global policies, especially toward Africa.

The above, of course, brings up numerous considerations. Is the lessoning of the human security agenda, the emergence of the impact of globalization, and the impact of 9/11 the primary set of considerations that have led to the new multilateralisms, or has the change of governments in Canada been a larger factor? Recently, the Conservatives have made Afghanistan their primary security, defence, and foreign policy issue. One must consider whether this has come at a cost to Canada's multilateral policy initiatives. The emphasis on Canada's role in a US-led mission in Afghanistan has clear implications for Canada's role within the new global order. However, prior to this, the Ottawa and Kimberley processes had both resonated with Canadians and proven that the new multilateralisms could be an effective instrument of Canadian foreign policy. As Kim Richard Nossal argues in his chapter, the emphasis on either a close working relationship with the United States or Canada's leadership with the new multilateralisms is clearly reflective of the policies of the government of the day.

Global Governance

The contemporary global governance genre has evolved from the earlier, more formal and interstate perspective. Although it has been based on the traditions of idealism and international law and organization, it also consists of advocacy, as well as analysis (Thérien and Pouliot 2006). Like them, global governance has its roots in early postwar decolonization and multilateralism, as captured by the United Nations Intellectual History Project (Jolly, Emmerij, and Weiss 2005; also see MacFarlane and Khong 2006). Like the new multilateralisms, rather than the "old" multilateralism of states alone, it embraces a catholic range of heterogeneous actors in addition to a wide variety of states, including failing and/or failed ones (Dunn and Shaw 2001).

The emerging global governance approach to analysis is insightful in regard to such new multilateralisms, but it tends to lag behind public policy. The twenty-first-century foreign policy agenda in the Organisation for Economic Co-operation and Development (OECD), including Canada, is increasingly set by think tanks and global agencies rather than by national politicians or international scholars. Such a trend has reinforced the development of so-called public diplomacy by the leading foreign offices in the OECD states (Copeland 2005; Potter 2002). Even if the Harper government has seemed disinterested, the collaborative activities of state and non-state actors in advancing national as well as human security (or brand) are an essential element of the contemporary global order (see the controversial historical and conceptual overview by MacFarlane and Khong 2006).

One of the leading scholars in the field of globalization studies, Anthony McGrew, defines global governance as

> the evolving system of (formal and informal) political coordination – across multiple levels from the local to the global – amongst public authorities (states and IGOs) and private agencies (NGOs and corporate actors) seeking to realize common purposes or resolve collective problems through the making and implementing of global or transnational norms, rules, programmes and policies. (McGrew 2005, 25)

Another of global governance's leading advocates, albeit with a more international development and organization orientation, Tom Weiss similarly characterizes it:

> Global governance implies a wide and seemingly ever-growing range of actors in every domain. Global economic and social affairs have traditionally been viewed as embracing primarily intergovernmental relationships, but increasingly they must be framed in comprehensive enough terms to

embrace local and international NGOs, grassroots and citizens' movements, multinational corporations and the global capital market. (Weiss 2000, 810)

Weiss identifies a spectrum of emphases depending on analytic perspective or institutional connection – from global to good and on to humane governance emphases – his overview taking into account the Commission on Global Governance (1995) but preceding that on Human Security (UN 2003). He includes but does not overly advance UN and World Bank approaches. By contrast, Québécois Jean-Philippe Thérien privileges but three perspectives to world poverty, which could also be extended to governance with other foci: the traditional north-south approach, the Bretton Woods paradigm, and the UN paradigm. Indeed, as he suggests, "in explaining the differences between the Bretton Woods paradigm and the UN paradigm ... [I seek] to contribute to a better knowledge of the dynamics of multilateralism and global governance ... as the struggle against poverty is central to any strategy aiming to promote human security" (Thérien 1999, 725).

In practice, of course, all three approaches evolve over time, and there may also be distinctions of emphases within the Bretton Woods and UN paradigms – that is, between, say, the International Monetary Fund and the International Bank for Reconstruction and Development (IBRD) or between the UN Development Programme and the UN Children's Fund. We could also, perhaps, identify a further NGO or civil society approach, though again it would be rather heterogeneous given the somewhat broad spectrum of constituencies, concerns, and preferences among the myriad international, intermediate, and indigenous NGOs and social movements.

Finally, Canadian Robert O'Brien and his colleagues have focused on the relations between the Bretton Woods institutions and global civil society. They suggested that this encounter has served to transform global economic governance in the direction of greater plurality, what they call "complex multilateralism." The "old" multilateralism was more exclusive, top-down, and state-centric. They conclude that "complex multilateralism is ... broadening ... the policy agenda to include more social issues. Multilateralism is complicated not just because there are more actors, but because some of these actors are pressing for a new agenda" (O'Brien et al. 2000, 210).

I assume that such approaches present implications for global issues and policies, including for a range of actors within and around Canada. They constitute frameworks by which responsive, mixed-actor coalitions can be generated and advance their respective causes internationally, but outside established intergovernmental institutions. In other words, they suggest a new global policy context that is moving beyond state-centric diplomacy or the old interstate multilateralism. They might even represent a promising perspective of co-regulation that has been recently outlined, for example, in an original juxtaposition of the political economy of resource conflict with corporate social responsibility, certification, and regulations by BICC analysts (Böge, Fitzpatrick, and Paes 2006; see also Chapter 11 by Black and Savage).

Security and Development

In the 1990s, the dominant discourse on "new wars" had become about "the political economy of conflict" (David and Gagné 2006-07) or about the effects of greed and grievance, especially around resources such as diamonds, gold, and oil but also coltan and tropical timber. The dynamics of security and development was captured in the pioneering work of Will Reno (1999) in not only very difficult but also increasingly dangerous environments, and in the original juxtaposition by Mark Duffield of the analyses, literatures, and debates about development on the one hand and security on the other; hitherto two distinct "solitudes" (Muggah 2009). As Duffield (2001, 7) argues, "The focus of the new security concerns is not the threat of traditional interstate wars but the fear of underdevelopment as a source of conflict, criminalized activity and international instability." And Canada's unexpected, unhappy, and seemingly endless experience in Afghanistan will colour its notions of conflict, peace-building, and elusive development for decades to come. It serves to reinforce its reluctance to undertake further problematic R2P ("responsibility to protect") humanitarian interventions in African contexts such as Darfur (MacLean, Black, and Shaw 2006).

By the start of the new millennium and only momentarily diverted by 9/11 (at least in the world of donor policy), the dominant discourse on "new wars" encouraged the explicit juxtaposition, even integration, of "conflict/security and development" (United Kingdom, DFID 2005a) along the lines anticipated by Duffield and his colleagues (Conflict, Security and Development 2004). From a concern with security sector reform (OECD), this determination to connect these two genres mutated not only into "fragile states" (United Kingdom, DFID 2005b) but also into "difficult environments" (UK Department for International Development), "difficult partnerships" (OECD), "investing in prevention/stability" (United Kingdom, DFID

2005b), "low-income countries under stress" (World Bank 2002), Post-Conflict Reconstruction Unit (UK), "weak states" (Center for Global Development), and so on, with NGO coalitions being very active in helping to formulate acceptable policy in this not uncontroversial area. In turn, such formulations spawned a set of rankings of such "failed states." BICC proposed co-regulation among a range of compatible yet heterogeneous actors, particularly corporate and civil society responses to resource conflicts (Böge, Fitzpatrick, and Paes 2006). And Canada has proceeded from all of government task forces on Darfur to one on Afghanistan.

With relevance for Canadian concerns, especially on Africa rather than Afghanistan, the European debate about security at the policy level reflects a profound discourse at the more abstract, analytic level between "old" and "new" security (although, of course, these so-called levels are inseparable in reality). The new security perspective is more interdisciplinary and non-state in inclination and recognizes the irreversible character of globalization; put another way, it is more compatible with human than national security (UN 2003). Such a post-realist and pro-human approach became more feasible with the end of the state-centric bipolar nuclear Cold War (Shaw 2006). However, it took the UNDP (1994) to popularize it before the middle of the 1990s (MacLean, Black, and Shaw 2006). It was subsequently developed and reinforced through its espousal by, among other things, Canada's foreign minister Lloyd Axworthy. His advocacy of the anti-landmine treaty, the erstwhile Ottawa Process, was highly symbolic in this regard (Hubert 2000; McRae and Hubert 2001). In turn, the embryonic human security network of the mid-1990s led to the International Commission on Intervention and State Sovereignty (ICISS 2001) before the end of the century, even if its report – "The responsibility to protect" (R2P), as a generic framework through which to respond to the new security challenges and humanitarian crises – was overshadowed by 9/11. Meanwhile, a coalition of like-minded states and INGOs established a Global Center for R2P in New York City in 2008.

The "responsibility to protect" (ICISS 2001) represents an attempt to go beyond state-centrism and orthodox security toward a redefinition of "humanitarian intervention" in a world where a significant proportion of states cannot really advance their citizens' development and security, as in Darfur, Rwanda, and Uganda: "Where a population is suffering serious harm, as a result of internal war, insurgency, repression or state failure, and the state in question is unwilling or unable to halt or avert it, the principle of non-intervention yields to the international responsibility to protect" (ICISS 2001, xi). While the horrors of 9/11, then 7/7, and the subsequent war on terror diverted attention away from ICISS, its underlying theme of structural violence arising from uneven globalization (or "underdevelopment") is increasingly salient. This was reflected in the UN (2004) high-level panel on global security, which was something of a return to an earlier, somewhat "glorious," Canadian period, albeit without its "prince," Lloyd Axworthy. Its suggestions for "a more secure world" were followed by the secretary-general's ready endorsement: "The threats are from non-State actors as well as States, and to human security as well as State security ... The central challenge for the twenty-first century is to fashion a new and broader understanding ... of what collective security means" (UN 2005, 11). In turn, there is an ongoing, lively, albeit somewhat "Canadian" (Keating and Knight 2004; MacLean, Black, and Shaw 2006), debate over whether human security means the narrower conceptualization of "freedom from fear" or the broader, more cosmopolitan notion of "freedom from want," which embraces cultural, ecological, gender, health, and related freedoms and rights (contrast Andrew Mack, Lloyd Axworthy, and Don Hubert among the twenty-one contributions to the compilation by Burgess and Owen 2004). The long-anticipated *Human security report* (Human Security Report Project 2005) from the now-defunct Canadian Consortium on Human Security and the Liu Institute for Global Issues at the University of British Columbia (now based at Simon Fraser University) emphasizes the narrower formulation (see MacLean, Black, and Shaw 2006; and Shaw 2006 for overviews of the first – only? – decade of "human security").

Meanwhile, in the post-9/11 and post-7/7 period, countries and communities have been concerned to understand and respond to the causes of (Islamic) fundamentalisms. This has led networks such as the Commonwealth into new areas such as "security" broadly defined. Between the Malta and Kampala summits, a Commonwealth commission investigated how to advance "respect and understanding," calling for further development of the "tradition" of "multilateralism," using dialogue and discussion to discover and define "civil paths to peace" (Commonwealth 2007, passim, esp. 5-14). The prior Commonwealth commission had anticipated such directions or possibilities:

> The Commonwealth has already made important contributions to supporting both democracy and development ... the Commonwealth must make more of its comparative advantage with respect to other regional and

global bodies. The Commonwealth is a unique microcosm of global social and ethnic diversity, and of North and South ... the state, the market, civil society and the international community each has a vital role to play in delivering development and democracy. (Commonwealth 2003, ix)

Canada as part of the Commonwealth (Berns-McGown 2007-08) can contribute to, as well as benefit from, its increasingly multicultural and multiracial heritage, as in Australia, the Republic of South Africa, the United Kingdom, and others. Post-9/11 and -7/7, reinforced by traumas in the hitherto pragmatic Netherlands, which was rocked by high-level violent attacks mid-decade, there is growing concern about tolerance in multireligious communities; hence the prestigious commission chaired by Amartya Sen (Shaw 2008, 92-95), with its focus on multiple identities and networks (Commonwealth 2007).

Canada advanced African development as a central focus when it last hosted the G8 a half-decade ago at Kananaskis. Its legacy from the Halifax summit of the mid-1990s is the continuing Halifax Initiative; in Kananaskis, it advanced an African agenda that has since been taken up by many subsequent summits. In 2010, however, given the trauma of Rwanda and tragedy of Darfur, will Canada really claim to have a lingering, sentimental concern with Africa? Moreover, what will the implications be for continuing heterogeneous coalitions for global governance?

The Ottawa and Kimberley Processes, ICC, and EITI

An interesting and not insignificant debate is emerging over why some new global issues get attention and lead to effective global coalitions and negotiations, as in the Ottawa and Kimberley processes (McRae and Hubert 2001), while other arguably equally compelling campaigns, such as child soldiers, explosive remnants of war (ERW; see http://www.theworkcontinues.org), and small arms nexuses are ineffective (Hubert 2000; O'Dwyer 2006). As Hubert writes:

> While much of the credit for the successful banning of landmines has deservedly gone to the ICBL [International Campaign to Ban Landmines] and to NGO advocates, the success of the campaign can be explained only through an examination of three other sets of actors: the ICRC [International Committee of the Red Cross], the UN, and key governments ... a model for effective humanitarian advocacy is emerging with three broad dimensions. They are the pursuit of stringent standards with widespread

but not necessarily universal support; political coalition building among NGOs, states and international organizations; and negotiating environments that allow for voting rather than consensus decision-making, access for NGOs and the selection of a supportive chairperson. (Hubert 2000, xviii)

So why did the Ottawa and Kimberley processes rather than the ICC, let alone small arms and child soldiers campaigns, achieve momentum and some degree of attention and resolution as policy directions for global to local state and non-state actors? Similarly, one can ask, why has SIDS seemed to have peaked at the turn of the century, only to be revived by the postponed Mauritius Barbados +10 conference of early 2005 that followed the terrible South Asian "regional" tsunami at the end of 2004? Furthermore, what were the respective inputs from Canada, both state and non-state, corporate and civil society actors?

Central among contemporary global issues are landmines and conflict diamonds. Yet, within these campaigns, the question of corruption through resource revenues from oil, gas, and other natural resources is also increasingly telling. The first two foci arose from non-state actor coalitions – ICBL and Partnership Africa Canada (PAC), respectively – which advocated their resolution (Hubert 2000). By contrast, the Extractive Industries Transparency Initiative (EITI) was more a function of the Blair regime in its second term, and its association with British and European multinationals, albeit encouraged by a significant NGO lobby – the three hundred–plus NGOs in the established, high-profile, and vocal Publish What You Pay coalition (see http://www.publishwhatyoupay.org), which now has a Canadian office, co-located with PAC and DDI in Ottawa. The explicit objective of these effective coalitions is the management of revenues from natural resources (largely energy and mining) to promote poverty reduction, economic growth, and development, instead of exacerbating conflicts. They operate along the lines and represent instances of the security/conflict and development nexus analyzed above.

The Diamond Development Initiative (DDI; see http://www.ddiglobal.org) is based in PAC's offices in Ottawa. It constitutes an extension of the successful PAC animation of the Kimberley Process, which has involved both the private and public sectors. Launched in 2008, it progresses from the regulation of supply via the Kimberley Process to the enhancement of production, entailing more sustainable conditions for artisanal miners, especially in Africa. The board of DDI includes directors associated with De

Beers and the diamond industry's manufacturing and marketing associations, as well as official development assistance agencies such as the United Kingdom's Department for International Development and experts in development and the environment. Its advisory council includes a broad range of international agencies, such as the International Bank for Reconstruction and Development and the United Nations; INGOs; and consultants from Africa, Europe, and North America. Moreover, the Publish What You Pay network serves to advocate the EITI initiative though national chapters, such as that in Canada, also co-located with PAC:

> The DDI seeks to establish, through a new system of interconnecting partnerships, a developmental and regulatory environment in which rough diamonds can be mined and marketed for the benefit of artisanal miners, local communities and governments and the wider diamond industry, thus giving meaning to the expression "development diamonds." It is a logical outcome of the effort to halt "conflict diamonds." (PAC 2008, 5)

Given the legacy of empire, now metamorphosed into distinctive globalization facilitated by the anglophone Commonwealth connection (Shaw 2008), many energy and mining companies have roots in Australia, Canada, and South Africa, with headquarters in Britain; hence the genesis of EITI, even if much of the mining sector in Canada is now owned by Brazilian (Vale), Swiss (Xstrata), and other non-Commonwealth companies.

The Ottawa Process arose in the post-Cold War period from a global campaign to outlaw landmines: the International Campaign to Ban Landmines was a coalition of 1,400 NGOs from ninety countries and winner of the 1997 Nobel Peace Prize. By contrast, the Kimberley Process was somewhat less global or visible, as diamonds are not a mass-market product. Nevertheless, the blood or conflict diamond campaign forced a multi-stakeholder response in part to avoid an expensive Nestlé/Nike/Shell-type public relation fiasco (Klein 2001). The current and parallel Diamond Development Initiative is a promising compatible spinoff, seeking to augment transnational regulation via the Kimberley Process through micro-level local artisanal development. As a result, it removes or reduces the need for mafias and militias. It seeks to be a novel mix of multinational corporations, international financial institutions, Development Assistance Committee member countries, local government ministries, and NGOs (DDI 2005). By contrast, the EITI coalition was more of a macro-level unilateral British government initiative, albeit in response to global NGO (for example, Global

Witness, the Catholic Agency for Overseas Development, Oxfam, Save the Children Fund, and Transparency International) and other pressures, given the potential for massive corruption presented by oil, gas, and comparable commodities (David and Gagné 2006-07). This is especially so given the rise in prices for commodities and energy exacerbated by the impressive economic growth in China and India.

Launched in the early twenty-first century, EITI picked up on related ethical/fair trade, accountability/transparency, and corporate social responsibility initiatives. The International Organization for Standardization (ISO) began in early 2005 a three-year process of developing an ISO standard for social responsibility – ISO 26000 – partly in cooperation with the International Labour Organization, for application to the mega-dollar energy sector in particular. This holds popular interest, but it also has some of the world's biggest corporations as players, unlike in the other relatively successful, efficacious processes. Moreover, because we all need petroleum products, the character of this sector is unlike those in the earlier Ottawa and Kimberley processes. This is especially important in a period of economic growth and high energy prices, which has been exacerbated by the expansion of the Chinese and Indian economies. In other words, consumer or popular opinion is likely to be less salient, as a boycott of oil and gas is not sustainable, even if targeting one or two brands is not impossible or improbable. Indeed, oil and gas, like fresh water, are likely to become the focus of conflict in the new century due to scarcities rather than boycotts (Klare 2002). Hence, the relevance of the BICC brief (Böge, Fitzpatrick, and Paes 2006), which contrasts a range of codes, certification, and regulation formulation (for instance, EITI; Forestry Stewardship certification; Kimberley Process; OECD Guidelines for Multinational Enterprises; UN Global Compact; and so on; see Thérien and Pouliot 2006) with the political economy of conflict and of resources literatures. It suggests a future world order of coregulation (Böge, Fitzpatrick, and Paes 2006, 26-45).

The United Kingdom's Commission for Africa endorsed EITI and called for "strong political and financial support" from the international community:

> EITI is a multi-stakeholder agreement under which oil, gas and mining companies agree to publicly disclose all payment they make to developing country governments and governments agree to publish what they receive. Published information is audited independently, and there is a clear role for civil society, who participates actively in the design, implementation and overview of the disclosure process. (Commission for Africa 2005, 147)

Clearly, EITI can be contrasted with the International Criminal Court in terms of advocacy, animation, organization, and impacts. The Coalition for the ICC (see http://www.iccnow.org) celebrated its first decade in 2005. Now constituted of over two thousand NGOs, like-minded states, and international organizations, the coalition led to the ICC being inaugurated in mid-2000 after sixty states had ratified the Rome Statute. The ratification was encouraged by the horrors of and temporary tribunals enquiring into Yugoslavia and Rwanda. Now one hundred states have so ratified the ICC. Despite the de facto veto of Washington, several American NGOs continue to advance the cause (see http://www.amicc.org, http://www.unausa.org, and http://www.usaforicc.org). However, by contrast to other coalitions, how efficacious (let alone appropriate) is the ICC when dealing with central Europe, northern Uganda, or with the Sudan over Darfur? Efforts at implementing ICC practices have encountered numerous political obstacles, to say the least.

Conclusion: Canada, Global Coalitions, and Governance, and the Study of Global Order

I conclude by suggesting that foreign policy for Canada, other countries, and other political communities in an era of global governance involving state and non-state actors is increasingly about networking for human development, rights, and/or security (Shaw 2006). New multilateralisms of mixed-actor coalitions facilitate the identification of and reaction to new issues. However, as noted at the outset, some global issues attract more attention and momentum than others. Furthermore, as Humphrey and Messner (2006, 108) write, "The emergence of China and India as powerful actors in global governance arenas and in global politics poses a series of questions for development policy and the future of global governance." This should also provide pause: We may lament the impact today, especially for an overshadowed neighbour such as Canada, of US unilateralism on, say, the ICC or small arms, but we should already recognize the roles and begin to factor the interests and impacts of emerging economies such as China and India into such equations (Shaw 2006), in addition to the OECD and even the G8. This rings especially true for increasingly marginal states such as Canada.

Such features of contemporary world order, globalizations, and new regionalisms present profound challenges to orthodox disciplines such as political science, international relations, foreign policy, and so on (see W. Brown 2006; Lemke 2003), and even for interdisciplinary fields such as development and security studies (see Mychajlyszyn and Shaw 2005). To understand and to locate, let alone to respond to myriad global issues, we need to transcend established frameworks and be prepared to recognize and juxtapose novel perspectives along the lines suggested. In turn, this means contemplating going beyond established approaches, assumptions, and debates (especially, perhaps, the state-centric ones) to novel, interdisciplinary perspectives appropriate for a global order characterized by over two hundred states, multiple non-state actors, and myriad global issues.

11

Mainstreaming Investment
Foreign and Security Policy Implications of Canadian Extractive Industries in Africa

DAVID BLACK AND MALCOLM SAVAGE

It is trite to say that the international political and security environment has changed substantially in recent decades. Change has occurred in the threats states face, how they perceive and respond to these threats, and in the number of salient actors on the international stage, most notably the rise of international civil society groups and the increasingly prominent political and security roles of corporations. Less clear is how states can effectively adapt to these changing circumstances. With this in mind, this chapter examines Canada's foreign policy efforts in Africa as they relate to extractive industries. Although the Canadian state has faced adaptive pressures in all areas of foreign and security policy, Canadian policy toward Africa highlights key changes in the policy environment and how the Canadian state has attempted to address these changes.

Our central argument is that there has been a classic tension in Canada's involvement in Africa between an official "brand" that emphasizes Africa as a site of humane and humanitarian engagement, and official support and assistance for Canadian extractive industries whose activities are often seen as counterproductive to humanitarian efforts. Although this tension has to some extent always existed in Canadian foreign policy, civil society groups have increasingly brought into focus potential and real contradictions between humanitarian goals and the negative effects of extractive industries. This increased publicity, which threatens to expose Canada's Janus-faced approach toward Africa, underscores both the challenges faced by Canadian policy makers and the changes the Canadian state has had to make in response. Chief among these changes is the acceptance of civil society groups as substantial players in foreign policy debates both as stakeholders and as potential monitors and whistleblowers concerning Canada's involvement in Africa. Similarly, in the ubiquitous "partnership" mould of foreign, security, and development policy making, private sector actors have become increasingly prominent and active participants in policy processes. As we argue here, these changes can be seen as an example of what John Ruggie has conceptualized as the "new global public domain," in which private (civil society and corporate) as well as public actors have actively engaged in new arenas "of discourse, contestation, and action concerning the production of global public goods" (Ruggie 2004, 504).

Any discussion of contradictions in Canadian foreign policy needs to address how policy goals are defined. This is so because contradictions will depend on how a state defines its goals and whether these goals are truly internally contradictory. It has always been the Canadian government's position that economic, development, and security policies complement each other. "Official" Canada has traditionally seen economic development (in this case through the promotion of extractive industries) as essentially complementary to broader developmental goals. This assertion is contained within a conception of human security that sees economic growth as essential in securing better living conditions. However, as this chapter seeks to demonstrate, one of the impacts of Ruggie's "new global public domain" is that the Canadian state has lost a significant measure of control over the definition of its own conceptual premises and policy goals. In other words, regardless of how elements within the Canadian state have defined the government's policy objectives in relation to human security, the images highlighted by national and international civil society organizations of environmental destruction and human rights abuses associated with extractive industries call into question Canadian efforts to pursue humanitarian and human security objectives on the continent (no matter how these goals are defined). In this respect, the Canadian state has been compelled to respond to the demands of civil society and, indeed, seek to incorporate both civil society and corporate actors in policy processes. The Canadian state has defined human security in essentially neoliberal terms, presuming the complementarity of liberal economic, political, and security objectives, but it must also respond to claims that its policies have effectively undermined human security goals as understood in more critical and transformative formulations of the concept.[1]

In advancing this argument, the chapter is divided into six main sections. Following this introduction, the second section discusses the nature of the extractive sector in Africa, highlighting its economic importance and key difficulties faced in developing the sector. The third section focuses on developmental and economic links between Canada and Africa. The traditional image (however mythologized) of Canada as a developmental champion for Africa is challenged in light of the extensive presence of Canadian mining companies on the continent. The fourth section illustrates the systematic and robust ways in which the Canadian state has supported and protected Canadian corporations, and its comparatively feeble efforts to promote corporate social responsibility (CSR). The fifth section scrutinizes the developmental and human security implications of the investments it has encouraged. Finally, the sixth section discusses the impact of civil society organizations on Canadian extractive sector policy toward Africa. In particular, we consider the ramifications of the "multi-stakeholder" National Roundtables on Corporate Social Responsibility and the Canadian Extractive Industry in Developing Countries, whose advisory group issued its final consensus report in March 2007, and whether these could transform Canada's historic role from a truncated and weak one to a position of leadership in promoting CSR and long-term developmental benefits from extractive industries.[2]

Mining and Development, Security, and the Environment

The importance of extractive industries to the future of many African countries cannot be overstated. The economies of industrialized nations such as Canada, the United States, and Australia have benefited greatly in terms of aggregate growth from resource extraction, and Africa's vast mineral reserves have generated hope for similar contributions. According to one UNCTAD (United Nations Conference on Trade and Development) report, "Geography has bequeathed the continent an impressive endowment of mineral wealth, including near-global monopolies of platinum, chromium and diamonds; a high proportion of the world's gold, cobalt and manganese reserves; and extensive reserves of bauxite, coal, uranium, copper and nickel" (UNCTAD 2005, 6). Mining and minerals have been leading sectors in the economies of resource-rich African countries, especially in terms of export earnings. According to Magnus Ericsson, "Mineral exports contribute between 25 and 90 percent of annual export earnings of 13 countries: Botswana, Ghana, Guinea, Liberia, Senegal, Mauritania, Namibia, Niger, Central African Republic, Sierra Leone, Zaire, Zambia and Zimbabwe" (quoted in B. Campbell 1999). Given the importance of foreign exchange earned through exports for government revenues, balance of payments, and debt servicing, it is not surprising that resource extraction has become a priority sector in many countries. This is especially true in the context of market-oriented structural adjustment reforms over the past two decades stressing the importance of exports and comparative advantage.

It is the sheer size of the continent's extractive sectors in relation to its overall economy that has fuelled the neoliberal common sense that increased extractive industry investment is surely good for Africa. Supporters emphasize that resource extraction has the potential to contribute to economic development by generating government revenues that can be used for development policies and projects, but also through the creation of jobs, the development of infrastructure, and in spinoff growth through forward and backward linkages in the economy (Di Boscio and Humphreys 2005).[3] Such claims have been strongly contested, however. Although all relevant controversies cannot be fully explored in this short section, some key issues are highlighted.

One set of concerns that has gained prominence because of the advocacy of local communities and international NGOs is the environmental and social impacts of mining activities (Earthworks/Oxfam 2004; Tienhaara 2006). Resource extraction has long been recognized as relatively harmful to the environment because of the destruction of natural surroundings, as well as the use of harmful chemicals, including cyanide and mercury, that are frequently leaked into local water sources. The destruction of natural surroundings and arable land has also been a source of community unrest, destroying livelihoods that depend on the natural environment, such as farming and fishing, and dislocating communities living close to mining concessions (Oxfam America 2006).

Extractive industries have also been linked to problems concerning governance, transparency, the distribution of resources, and security (the "resource curse"). Connected to the enclave nature of resource extraction, problems often arise because most of the revenues from extractive industries are provided to the state through taxes and royalties. Once in the hands of government officials, how these revenues are deployed depends on the quality of governance as well as the priorities and probity of state power holders. However, it has been noted that African governments often lack the capacity to effectively reinvest these funds into productive activities, and in many cases may not intend to use them for the benefit of their citizens. Frequently, the use of revenues generated from extractive industries has been opaque and poorly monitored, though international efforts such as the Extractive Industries Transparency Initiative (EITI) are seeking to rectify this situation.[4] In worst-case scenarios, extractive industries have been linked to profound human insecurity, with resource revenues financing military and para-military endeavours and sustaining protracted conflicts in the Sudan, the Democratic Republic of the Congo, Angola, Sierra Leone, and Liberia, among others (B. Campbell 2006; Freedman 2006-07; Le Billon 2006-07). The ensuing competition between rivals will often destabilize a country or region as groups seek to gain access to the rents generated by extractive industries.

Such issues remain matters of intense debate. Although it is true that extractive industries have been a source of conflict, insecurity (both large and small scale), social disruption, and environmental degradation, many argue that this need not be the case (Ascher 2005; Pedro 2006). If extractive industries are to play a greater role in development and minimize negative impacts on local communities, however, strategic interventions will be required from national and local governments (see Pedro 2006). Yet, as Bonnie Campbell (2003) points out, the ability of governments to perform such roles has been sharply constrained because of the restructuring of the state under the neoliberal principles of structural adjustment – precisely the same principles that have fostered the current mining boom in many African countries.[5] In short, the potential for extractive industries to negatively affect African countries is very real, while positive and sustainable contributions are elusive.

Reassessing Canadian Links with Africa: The Presence of Mining Companies

The previous section focuses on the developmental and security issues associated with mining activities, but the economic and social malaise of the African continent runs much deeper than the problems associated with resource extraction. Although it is important to recognize the diversity and richness of the "African experience," Africa has nevertheless been the locus of some of the worst manifestations of poverty, drought, war, and general human suffering in the world. For this reason, the continent has attracted much attention from the international community in terms of global developmental efforts, and Canada has been eager to demonstrate leadership, at least intermittently, in this salient diplomatic arena (see Black 2007). For instance, Jean Chrétien when prime minister exerted great personal effort to place Africa at the top of the agenda for the 2002 Kananaskis G8 meeting, prior to which Canada launched the high-profile Canada Fund for Africa, designed to support initiatives in trade and investment, as well as governance, peace and security, health, agriculture and environment, and information and communication technologies. His successor, Paul Martin, made great fanfare of supporting efforts to address the humanitarian disaster in the Darfur region of Sudan (see Matthews 2005; Nossal 2005). These prime ministerial initiatives were preceded by Canada's outspoken advocacy of the "human security agenda" under then foreign affairs minister Lloyd Axworthy (see Grayson 2004 and Nossal's Chapter 4). Such high-profile efforts were subsequently reinforced by strong official statements of support for African development and security in the 2005 International Policy Statement. Although the current Harper government has reduced the level of emphasis on African issues, history suggests that it may yet be moved to "rediscover" the continent (see Black 2009).

This is at least partly because, while such historic efforts reflect a degree of genuine concern for the developmental and security challenges facing Africa, it is no secret that these initiatives also serve important political functions. In particular, they have contributed prominently to the branding of Canada as a good international citizen in the global political arena. As Kyle Grayson (2006, 480) argues, "Canada is a country that relies heavily on its expertise in public diplomacy in order to cultivate a positive global brand image that greatly contributes to its soft power capabilities." By cultivating an image as a leader in human security and development, especially in relation to Africa, Canada has been able to earn diplomatic currency that serves several key functions, including differentiating itself from American foreign policy, assuming leadership in multilateral initiatives associated with the G8 and the United Nations, gaining diplomatic support in such multilateral forums, and appealing to domestic constituencies concerned with promoting global justice.[6]

In light of such concerted foreign-policy branding efforts on the part of Canadian governments, it is no surprise that from the perspective of the Canadian public, Canada's best-known links with the African continent are through ethically-oriented development assistance and human security efforts. However, as Peter van Ham (2001) notes, the advantage of branding is that cultivating the right brand can surpass the actual "product" of a country's assets, or in other words, mask the reality of Canada's relationships with Africa. The conventional wisdom has highlighted Canada's development and security efforts in Africa, yet such a perception largely ignores the enormous investments that Canadian companies have made in the extractive sectors of many African countries, with ambiguous security and development repercussions. Understanding the range and scope of Canadian mining companies' presence is therefore crucial to gaining a more accurate picture of Canada's role in Africa.

Given Canada's own mineral wealth and extensive experience in resource extraction, it is no surprise that Canadian companies are at the forefront of the global mining industry.[7] Lemieux (2005) notes that in 2005, 155 of the world's 304 larger companies (51 percent) were based in Canada. Furthermore, using figures from 2002, Ericsson (2005) notes that of the 25 largest mining companies in the world, 6 are Canadian, with one (Barrick Gold Corporation) in the top ten. Thus, while Canada is sparsely represented in the top ranks of global companies, Canadian companies of relatively smaller (but still large) size represent a major force in the global market. In 2005, the value of exploration by Canadian companies represented 40 percent of larger company programs worldwide (Lemieux 2005).

In Africa, larger Canadian companies have also been major players. In terms of mineral production, in 2000, Canadian companies held interests in almost forty projects in Africa. In terms of exploration, larger Canadian companies in 2005 planned to spend $195 million in Africa, representing 22 percent of all exploration activity on the continent and placing Canada second behind only South Africa (Lemieux 2005; B. Campbell 1999). Lemieux further notes that at the end of 2005, companies of all sizes listed on Canadian stock exchanges held interests in 660 mineral properties located in thirty-two African countries. In all, Natural Resources Canada estimated that total cumulative Canadian mining investment in Africa had reached $6 billion by 2005 and projected continued growth to $16 billion by 2010 (CCA 2007).[8] To put these projections in perspective, total Canadian official development assistance to Africa reached $2.1 billion in 2008-09, fulfilling the Martin government's commitment to double aid to Africa from 2003-04 levels (CIDA 2009b). In terms of geographical concentration, Canadian companies have been particularly active in exploration in South Africa, with 100 properties; Burkina Faso with 60; Mali with 75; Ghana with 55; and Tanzania with 75 (Lemieux 2005). The minerals of greatest interest have been gold and to a lesser extent diamonds, though Canadian private sector activity spans a range of other resources as well. With the exception of South Africa (which is a strategically important African "partner" for other reasons), each of these countries was included among the fourteen African countries identified as strategic development partners by the Canadian International Development Agency (CIDA) in the context of Ottawa's 2005 International Policy Statement.[9]

This strong presence in Africa can be attributed to two factors. First, Africa's mining industry has experienced a renaissance in recent decades (Martineau 2004). Beginning in the 1980s with the imposition of structural adjustment programs (SAPs) on much of the continent, African countries were strongly encouraged to liberalize their mining codes to attract foreign investment. Canada has played an active role in advocating liberalization of Africa's mining sector. For example, it was common practice for Canada, along with other OECD (Organisation for Economic Co-operation and Development) countries, to make its development assistance contingent on the acceptance of structural adjustment packages that required the liberalization of markets, including the minerals sector. With Ghana leading the way in 1984 by implementing a reformed mining code that protected property rights, streamlined concession processes, lowered taxes and royalties, and guaranteed the repatriation of profits, Africa has experienced an investment boom in the minerals sector. In 2004, US$15 billion was invested in mining, representing 15 percent of the global market, compared with 5 percent in the mid-1980s (FIDH 2007; UNCTAD 2005).

Second, the opening up of African markets has been accompanied by a fundamental shift in the structure of the global mining industry, toward consolidation through mergers and acquisitions accompanied by the rise of junior exploration companies (Ericsson 2005). Responding to intense competitive pressures in the global market, mining companies have responded by seeking growth through the rationalization of existing assets, rather than developing new ones (D. Humphreys 2005). According to Ericsson, over $150 billion has been spent on mergers and acquisitions since 1995. Despite such consolidation, however, the fundamental composition of the mineral industry remains highly fragmented, with larger companies controlling only 25 percent of the market (Ericsson 2005). With very few monopolies in mineral markets, the industry is still highly competitive, with companies seeking to increase their size and visibility in the marketplace. As larger companies gain advantages in terms of access to capital for exploration and development, the poor representation of Canadian companies at the very top of the spectrum (top ten) accentuates their vulnerability. This is particularly the case given that smaller companies are generally prone to hostile takeover bids (Ericsson 2005) – a trend highlighted by the foreign takeover of such Canadian "champions" as INCO, Falconbridge, and Alcan. Such foreign takeovers, while decreasing Canadian control of such companies, only create a greater incentive for Canada to promote the sector, particularly through the activities of Canadian-owned junior exploration companies, as discussed below. At the same time, they underscore the difficulty of securing the cooperation of major extractive companies in collaborative, state-based policy-making processes orchestrated by the Canadian government.

More important for the African market and in explaining Canada's strong presence in the region, however, is that this period of consolidation and rationalization has been accompanied by a sharp decline in larger company exploration budgets. In particular, between 1997 and 2001, following the Asian financial crisis and the scandal created by Bre-X's fraudulent claims of gold finds, mineral exploration fell by 55 percent (D. Humphreys 2005). Exploration has recovered in recent years, but such drastic alterations point to the intense competitive pressures faced by mining companies in the global market. Paradoxically, market competition has also placed pressures on mining companies to expand their assets and diversify their risks. As David Humphreys (2005) notes, investors in the mineral industry have demanded safer and more reliable returns, forcing mining companies to diversify their geographical base by entering new markets, and their product base by mining more than one mineral. However, rather than engage in the risky business of exploration where millions can be spent with little or no return, larger companies have instead preferred to rely on the activities of junior exploration companies (Ericsson 2005; B. Campbell 1999). Such companies are generally more creative and entrepreneurial in their exploration activities. On the other hand, as Bonnie Campbell (2005, 7) points out, they also "tend to be less subject to controls, less prone to apply best practices and [more inclined] to operate in high risk [areas] and at times zones of conflict." Upon discovery of a deposit, larger companies are then able to acquire concessions with known mineral reserves, thus reducing risk in expanding their assets.

It is in the rise of junior exploration companies that Canada has stood out globally. As Bonnie Campbell (1999) highlights, exploration companies have been extremely successful in raising capital on Canadian stock exchanges, with more money raised in Canada than in Australia, the United States, and South Africa combined. Thus, Canada has become a hotbed for growth in mineral exploration activity in recent years, with important implications for Africa. It is innovative junior exploration companies that first took advantage of the newly liberalized economies of African nations and thus contributed to the boom in mining investment on the continent (Martineau 2004). Before the 1980s, Africa's mineral wealth had remained largely unexplored because of the limited resources of African governments and the unattractive investment climate that prevailed. This changed with the rise of the juniors – a development in which Canada has been instrumental – in parallel with the implementation of structural adjustment reforms.

Canada's presence in the African mineral market is strong, but it is not necessarily secure. In particular, Canadian companies have faced stiff competition from companies based in developing countries. Latin American companies have greatly increased their presence. Companies from India and China are also increasingly prominent competitors, though their activities are concentrated in the energy sector. Although India is in the process of privatizing its state-owned mining companies (Ericsson 2005), there appears to be no such trend among Chinese companies. Thus, these companies remain important instruments of China's foreign policy and have been used extensively to increase its presence in Africa. Furthermore, the competitive pressure from countries such as India and China is exacerbated when issues of sustainable development are brought into the picture. According to Pring and Siegle (2005, 129), "[one of] the biggest factors to be faced by mining and other economic development efforts is the reorientation of international and national laws and regulatory frameworks to comply with the paradigm of 'sustainable development.'" Although Canadian and other Western companies have faced increasing pressure to conform to principles of sustainable development and corporate social responsibility, with potentially significant implications for their profit margins, Chinese and Indian companies remain largely insulated from such demands.

Thus, Canadian extractive industries have become major players in both the global and African mineral markets. Indeed, in contrast to the developmental branding efforts of the Canadian government, they are likely to be this country's dominant public face in many areas of the continent (Canada, SCFAIT 2005; Grayson 2006, 481). Yet, for most observers, much remains obscure or even unknown about the activities of Canadian and other countries' mining companies. It is relatively easy to track larger companies, which generally attract more publicity and for which official statistics are kept, but the activities of smaller and junior companies are largely left to estimates and speculation. Yet, it is in the activities of such smaller companies that Canada's relationship with Africa is perhaps strongest and certainly most rapidly growing.

Canadian Government Assistance to the Mining Sector in Africa

The forces of economic globalization, market liberalization, and intense competition in commodity markets provide the basis for increased activity of Canadian mining companies in Africa. In addition, however, the Canadian government has played a key role in enabling Canadian companies to secure a leading position in African markets (B. Campbell 1999). There are a number of ways in which agencies of the Canadian state provide robust support for Canadian extractive and other industries in Africa and elsewhere, as well as to related exporters in mining equipment and services. These include, first and foremost, Export Development Canada (EDC), which provides various support services, including export finance, risk insurance, and market information and analysis. CIDA has also provided support for the mining sector in African countries (notably Zambia and Zimbabwe) in the context of its support for private sector development – identified as one of five thematic priorities for the agency in the 2005 International Policy Statement, and carried forward in the emphasis on sustainable economic growth announced in May 2009 (CIDA 2009a). It also provided funding, through the Canada Fund for Africa, for the establishment of the Canada Investment Fund for Africa (CIFA), launched in April 2005, with total capital subscription of $212 million raised jointly from the federal government and private sector investors. CIFA's stated aim is to provide risk capital for private investments in Africa that generate sustainable growth. Of its initial eight investments, totalling US$35 million, three were in the mining sector and a fourth in energy. By early 2009, CIFA had invested in six extractive sector projects, four of which were operated by Canadian or Canadian-listed companies (Canada, DFAIT 2009, 12). Finally, the $17 billion Canada Pension Plan has been a significant investor in Canadian extractive industry operations overseas, including Africa.

In addition to financial and technical support, other federal agencies are very active in supporting the marketing and commercial branding efforts of Canadian extractive and mining supplies and equipment companies. For example, Natural Resources Canada, Foreign Affairs and International Trade Canada, EDC, Team Canada Inc, and the Brand Canada Program have supported the promotional efforts of large delegations of Canadian firms at major trade shows and on trade missions. EDC and the Government of Canada – through the Department of Foreign Affairs and International Trade (DFAIT) and CIDA – have also provided both financial and advisory support to the Canadian Council on Africa, an energetic lobby group promoting business links between Canada and Africa.

All of these sources of support and financing for Canadian investors, with the exception of commercial branding efforts, articulate formal commitments to the promotion of CSR principles (though the Canada Pension Plan Investment Board's "Policy on responsible investing" was only issued in

February 2007). Yet, none gives clear indications of *how* these commitments are to be discharged, beyond (in the case of CIDA, for example) encouraging compliance with the (voluntary) OECD Guidelines for Multinational Enterprises (see Blackwood 2006, 96; also Advisory Group Report 2007, 19). Similarly, EDC is now reportedly committed to "working with the Government of Canada and other stakeholders to identify best practices, and to incorporate into its due diligence those practices that are relevant to the mandate of a financial institution" (Canada, DFAIT 2009, 13). These are vague and weak reeds, especially given the lack of transparency surrounding many of their disbursements and the decision making behind them (EDC, for example, is not required to disclose its disbursements to the public). Although legitimate considerations of commercial confidentiality must be taken into account, these practices reflect a high level of official reluctance to actively foster CSR. Historically, then, when developmental and security objectives have been threatened or compromised by Canadian commercial interests, the Canadian state has for the most part prioritized the needs of industry (see Freeman 1985).

Particularly in the era of the "competition state" (Cerny 1997), such state-based efforts to champion and brand its own globally-oriented enterprises and investors are inevitable and arguably necessary adaptive responses. However, as the next section outlines, many of these efforts can be linked to mining activities that have impacted negatively on security and development in various African localities. Given the concomitant lack of robust provisions to foster improved corporate social and environmental behaviour, there is thus a real danger that the Canadian brand will be tarnished in ways that negatively affect its commercial interests. Moreover, its broader foreign policy brand, which, as outlined above, is closely associated in the recent past with the promotion of human security and a "new deal" developmentally for Africa, is also at risk of being seriously harmed by a lack of action on corporate behaviour that directly contradicts its stated development and security objectives (see Grayson 2006).

Key Controversies Surrounding Canadian Companies in Africa

Despite (and partly because of) the lack of clear and reliable information on Canadian mining companies in Africa, their operations have attracted a good deal of controversy and criticism, on human security, environmental, and developmental grounds. Indeed, one of the defining features of the new global public domain as articulated by Ruggie (2004) is that new regimes of accountability are emerging in which various civil society and multi-stakeholder initiatives are more systematically holding private sector actors to account for the social and environmental effects of their activities. Corporations, for their part, are becoming more sensitive and responsive to this broader conceptualization of their roles and responsibilities. Whether or not the specific controversies highlighted by Canadian civil society organizations are representative of widespread problems, they have tended to taint the sector as a whole, both within Canada and in Africa. It is worth highlighting several of these controversies, as they are a key stimulus to recent multi-stakeholder efforts to agree on a much more advanced and robust approach to CSR issues in this country. In addition, the following examples demonstrate the activities of transnationally networked civil society organizations in bringing extractive industry controversies to light, thus threatening Canada's security and development branding efforts while exposing the Canadian state's propensity to privilege corporate interests.

By far the most celebrated controversy concerning Canadian resource companies in Africa is the case of Talisman Energy, which owned a 25 percent stake in the Greater Nile Petroleum Operating Company (GNPOC) between 1998 and 2002, along with the state-owned oil companies of China (40 percent), Malaysia (30 percent), and Sudan (5 percent). Talisman was operating in the energy sector, but the lingering effects of this controversy have had a major influence on subsequent debates over CSR in all extractive industries. Talisman's role, in the context of the GNPOC, bears directly on the relationship between extractive industries and conflict, as GNPOC operations were widely seen as effectively helping to fuel the ongoing civil war "both by contributing to conflict over oil fields and by generating, for the Sudanese regime, revenue used to bankroll the war" (Forcese 2001, 41, 43). Indeed, the report of the Harker Commission, appointed by then foreign minister Lloyd Axworthy to investigate the situation, concluded in 2000 that

> there has been, and probably still is, major displacement of civilian populations related to oil extraction. Sudan is a place of extraordinary suffering and continuing human rights violations, even though some forward progress can be recorded, and the oil operations in which a Canadian company is involved add more suffering. (Harker 2000, 15)

Despite this finding, and an earlier threat by Axworthy to impose economic sanctions "if it becomes evident that oil extraction is exacerbating the conflict" (quoted in Drohan 2003, 266), the Canadian government ultimately retreated from this threat and merely exhorted Talisman to "ensure that their operations do not lead to an increase in tensions or otherwise contribute to the conflict" (Forcese 2001, 46; also Blackwood 2006). Craig Forcese argues that two interrelated factors explain the government's retreat from a more forceful response. The first was "the potentially damaging [domestic political] consequences for the government of taking on, and possibly wounding, a key Canadian company." This political logic was reinforced by a narrow interpretation of the Special Economic Measures Act, authorizing economic sanctions only on the basis of a decision by a multilateral organization to which Canada belongs or on the basis of a cabinet decision that the situation in question constitutes a "grave breach of international peace and security ... that has resulted, or is likely to result, in a serious international crisis" (Forcese 2001, 49-50; see also Drohan 2003, 267).

In the end, Talisman divested because of a diffuse combination of factors, including sustained negative publicity, a battered share price, and pending legal action under the Alien Tort Claims Act in the United States (for which no analogue exists in Canada). But the case highlights several enduring lessons. First, at the level of the Canadian political and bureaucratic establishment, there are still powerful disincentives to bring meaningful pressure to bear on Canadian corporations. Conversely, the bases for promoting CSR have been vague and weak, being principally voluntary in nature and hampered by low levels of transparency and the absence of mechanisms for accountability. Third, sustained controversy orchestrated largely by highly motivated civil society organizations and coalitions, such as the Sudan Inter-Agency Reference Group and the Canadian Network on Corporate Accountability, has created a political and public relations climate in which major Canadian extractive industries have become far more amenable to stronger and more transparent CSR measures, even if their strong preference continues to be for voluntary versus legislated ones. More broadly, the Talisman case illustrates how, in a few instances at least, Canadian private sector roles may be considerably more significant for national and regional security prospects than the role of the Canadian state. Particularly where the presence of the Canadian state is weak, then, Canadian corporations need to be understood as key foreign and security policy actors in their own right, interacting with other firms, states, and non-state actors (Stopford and Strange 1991).

Similar conclusions can be reached in relation to a second case bearing directly on high-intensity conflict. In 2002, the UN Security Council's Panel of Experts on the Illegal Exploitation of Natural Resources and Other Forms of Wealth in the Democratic Republic of the Congo named eight Canadian companies among eighty-five cited for violating the leading international standard for CSR – the OECD Guidelines for Multinational Enterprises. These and other companies protested vigorously, and their cause was taken up by their governments, which brought pressure to bear on the Security Council. The council then recommended a six-month renewal of the expert panel report to "verify, reinforce, and where necessary, update the Panel's findings, and/or clear parties named in the Panel's previous reports" (cited in Freedman 2006-07, 112). Most named companies were subsequently taken off the list and the expert panel was stood down. Despite NGO efforts to pressure home governments to carry the investigations forward, the Canadian government disregarded all but one of the eight dossiers brought to its attention (see Freedman 2006-07, 111-14).

It is beyond the purview of this chapter to probe the accusations made against these Canadian companies operating in the midst of what has been one of the most disastrous conflicts in the world. The general point, however, is that there was no clear and robust basis for investigating these allegations and that, in the absence of such provisions, the Canadian government effectively came to the defence of its corporate citizens without any apparent attempt to seriously probe the charges against them. Ironically, the ultimate impression created by this case, of somewhat vague but serious allegations and of a government that appeared unwilling to probe and pressure its own corporations, has reinforced the popular notion that wrongdoing is commonplace and that more serious measures are required.

It is not surprising that the lion's share of attention regarding potential corporate misconduct has focused on the most extreme cases, operating in situations of armed conflict (see BICC 2006; Drohan 2003). Yet, there are many more "routine" cases that, while less dramatic, bear directly on the controversies noted above concerning the social, developmental, and environmental implications of Canadian extractive industry investments in Africa. Moreover, because the latter are often linked to social and economic polarization, rising criminality, and community disruption and dislocation, they can be seen as undermining human security in its broader and more diffuse sense, as well as the more acute examples noted above.

Several controversial cases are to be found in some of the most reputedly successful of African countries, and core Canadian development partners, such as Ghana, Tanzania, and Mali. For example, a 2005 report of the Third World Network – Africa Secretariat highlighted several Ghanaian cases and controversies. These included the precipitous liquidation of Bonte Gold

Mines in 2004, "leaving behind un-reclaimed degraded land, unpaid compensation, and a debt of about US$18 million" (Darimani 2005). This closure, the report went on, resulted in a triple loss for local communities through environmental degradation, uncompensated destruction of farms and land, and the failure to engage in any social responsibility projects in the vicinity of the mine. More broadly, the report highlighted the role of Canadian mining companies in successfully lobbying the Ghanaian government to allow surface mining in the country's dwindling forest reserves. More broadly still, the policy environment that has helped foster the country's current mining boom, in which Canadian companies have been major players, is so liberal and beneficial to the foreign-owned companies that dominate the sector that some scholars have argued it has been of no help in addressing poverty at either the community or country-wide level (Amevor 2007).

Similarly, Tanzania has experienced a mining boom over the past fifteen years in which Canadian companies have been major players. It too has sought to advance this boom with the adoption of a highly liberalized mining code incorporating very favourable terms and conditions for foreign-owned companies (B. Campbell 2003). And it too is the site of controversy, notably surrounding the Bulyanhulu Gold Mine, now owned by one of Canada's largest mining corporations (Barrick Gold Corporation), with massive commitments from the government's Export Development Corporation ($173 million in political risk insurance) and the Canada Pension Plan ($351 million). Under previous owner Sutton Resources (also a Canadian company), artisanal miners were forcibly evicted from the concession area by Tanzanian troops in 1996, and allegations of large numbers of deaths continue to swirl around the initial development of this lucrative mining operation (Halifax Initiative 2006). On a smaller scale, the Sadiola Gold Mine in Mali, owned by IAMGOLD Corp. and supported by a significant ($38 million) investment from the Canada Pension Plan, resulted in the displacement of two villages with inadequate replacement land, scarce water resources, and environmental degradation from the mine. These costs have been exacerbated by rising social problems (prostitution, alcoholism, drug use, and the spread of HIV/AIDS) related to the arrival of the mine and its workers (Halifax Initiative 2006). Indeed, a thorough report on the impact of the gold mining industry in Mali by the Fédération Internationale des Ligues des Droits de l'Homme (FIDH 2007) provides a detailed analysis of how and why, despite the wealth generated by this industry, Mali remains one of the poorest countries in the world, while the impact of the most important mines has been largely detrimental in human rights and environmental terms.

Finally, the Third World Network – Africa Secretariat report cited above reflects the widely held view that Canadian government representatives in African countries are in effect advocates and facilitators for their country's mining companies, with no mandate and little inclination to investigate claims of corporate misconduct in a determined and even-handed way. The author of the report, Adbulai Darimani, writes: "The foreign missions of the Canadian government are believed to be stop-shops for corporate lobby and it is now an open secret that CIDA has been playing the role of clearinghouse for negotiating investment deals through technical and financial support" (Darimani 2005).

Without much more extensive research and analysis, including specific case studies, it is impossible to assess conclusively these reports of corporate irresponsibility and governmental complicity – or to determine how widespread these tendencies may be. But it is precisely the inability and unwillingness to probe such allegations, and hold Canadian mining companies accountable for their social, developmental, and environmental records, that feed the impression that problems are widespread and that the government as well as many mining companies have something to hide. These examples also demonstrate the virtually complete disconnect between foreign economic policy (in particular, investment and trade promotion) and a putatively human security–focused development agenda. Although Canada's official position has been that market-friendly economic development is a key condition for enhancing human security and development, it is hard to see how the above examples can be reconciled with the people-centred emphasis of the human security idea. In this light, developments in the new global public domain have led to more systematic pressures (mainly from civil society) to address these crucial regulatory and accountability gaps, a more responsive disposition toward these pressures from leading corporate interests, and a growing willingness on the part of at least some governmental interests to support and codify these non-state instigated trends.

Toward, and Away From, a New Leadership Role? The Roundtables Process and Beyond

In June 2005, the Canadian Parliament's Standing Committee on Foreign Affairs and International Trade (SCFAIT) issued a short report entitled *Mining in developing countries – Corporate social responsibility.* Having been exposed through its hearings to various instances in which Canadian mining companies had been connected with insecurity, environmental destruction, and social disruption in the developing world, the committee's report made numerous recommendations for stronger incentives, strengthened monitoring, new legal norms, and enhanced governmental support for improved corporate social responsibility. Predictably, given its historic predisposition on this issue, the federal government rejected all but one of the committee's recommendations. This one, however – that the government "put in place a process involving relevant industry associations, non-governmental organizations and experts, which will lead to the strengthening of existing programmes and policies in this area and, where necessary, to the establishment of new ones" (Canada, SCFAIT 2005, 2) – contained the seeds of a potentially substantial reorientation of the Canadian approach in this area.

Drawing on this opening, officials within the Department of Foreign Affairs and International Trade moved to establish an interdepartmental steering committee involving representatives of eight government agencies plus DFAIT as chair.[10] A parallel non-governmental advisory group was also created. Its seventeen members included leading representatives of civil society organizations associated with the Canadian Network on Corporate Accountability, influential representatives of the private sector (including senior executives of the Prospectors and Developers Association of Canada, the Mining Association of Canada, and Talisman Energy), representatives of ethical investment funds, and leading scholars in the area. The steering committee then collaborated with the advisory group to organize four national roundtables, in Vancouver, Toronto, Calgary, and Montreal (the major centres for extractive companies in Canada), from June through November 2006. These roundtables focused on five themes arising from the SCFAIT report: CSR standards and best practices, incentives for implementation of CSR standards, assistance to companies to implement CSR standards and best practices, CSR monitoring and dispute resolution, and capacity-building for resource governance in developing countries (Advisory Group Report 2007, 1). Finally, in March 2007, the advisory group (independent of but with support from the intragovernmental steering committee) issued a consensus report – no small feat given the very different interests involved. This report was to form the basis for a memo to cabinet, jointly submitted by CIDA, DFAIT, and Natural Resources Canada, with cabinet taking the final decision on how to respond to the advisory group's recommendations. One of the report's recommendations, that Canada join the Extractive Industries Transparency Initiative (EITI), was adopted by the government prior to its release, reportedly over the objections of at least one senior official in Natural Resources Canada.[11] There was thus a sense of excitement and momentum surrounding the advisory group's report in the weeks after it was issued, though the long subsequent delay in any substantial response from the government dampened this.

Substantively, the report made a wide range of recommendations that, in the view of the civil society–based Canadian Network on Corporate Accountability, "would establish Canada as a global leader in Corporate Social Responsibility" (CNCA 2007). At its heart was the proposal to establish a Canadian CSR framework that would set clear standards and reporting obligations for Canadian companies; reference international human rights standards and provide for the creation of human rights guidelines for the application of CSR standards; create an ombudsman's office, overseen by a tripartite monitoring and advisory group, to receive complaints regarding the operations of Canadian companies and assess corporate compliance with the standards; and include a provision for withholding government services from companies in cases of serious non-compliance. Among the other significant recommendations of the advisory group were: proposed steps toward greater transparency and fuller disclosure of support for Canadian companies by agents of the Canadian government, such as CIFA, EDC, and the Canada Pension Plan; support for industry association tools and civil society capacity-building, within Canada and in host countries; and initiatives to support contributions of the extractive sector to host-government development priorities, through governance and judicial system support and engagement with regional and multinational instruments and initiatives. Finally, the report advocated a process for ongoing study, scrutiny, and refinement through, for example, a proposal to create a government CSR centre of excellence and a Canadian extractive sector advisory group. In principle, then, these proposals would have had the potential to, at least, hold Canadian companies accountable for significant human rights and human security abuses arising from their operations in developing countries and, at most, promote more broadly based, sustainable, and developmentally-oriented results from their investments.

Several distinctive features of both the process and outcome of the national roundtables are noteworthy in analytical and theoretical terms. First, the process provides a good illustration of what Dashwood (2007,

133), following Ruggie (2004), highlights as the "reconstituted global public domain" shaped by the interaction between civil society actors and multinational corporations, alongside states.[12] The roundtable process, aimed toward the production of a new public good (enhanced CSR) among both Canadian companies and host governments but also closely attuned to transnational trends and demonstration effects, *required* the full participation of corporate, civil society, and state participants. In this regard, the roundtable process revealed the emergence of a substantial degree of common ground between some larger mining companies and their representatives, and civil society organizations that have been sharply critical of corporate misconduct.[13] While it would be a mistake to overstate this common ground, and to understate the degree of apprehension and mistrust that persists, the process revealed substantial movement on both sides.[14]

In particular, major mining corporations have increasingly come to an understanding that their long-term self-interest, including secure access to resources, depends on their ability to "demonstrate good corporate conduct": "While there has been a distinct emphasis on minimizing the negative environmental impacts of extractive-sector activities, in recent years the sector has begun addressing social issues. A number of companies have started referring to their need for a 'social license' to operate" (Advisory Group Report 2007, 7). To some extent, this has resulted from the punishing experiences of negative exposure to which some firms have been subject. It is surely no accident, for example, that a senior Talisman executive was a stalwart participant in the roundtable process. But it is also a reflection of a longer-term process of dialogue and learning among mining majors that, on the analysis of Hevina Dashwood, has been unfolding (albeit unevenly) among a handful of Canadian mining companies for at least a couple of decades (Dashwood 2005, 2007).

At the intragovernmental level, the roundtable process highlighted the old lesson that one needs to pay close attention to the varying interests and orientations of different government agencies, and fractions within them, in order to understand both processes and outcomes (Freeman 1985). It also highlights, however, a new willingness among some in government to accept a more expansive conception of the state's responsibility in relation to its corporate citizens. In this case, the initiative was taken by officials within the Global Issues Bureau of DFAIT – a particular corner of this department with a strong focus on human security issues and with ongoing responsibility for Canadian involvement in the Kimberley Process regarding "conflict diamonds." Given the other eight government departments and agencies involved in the roundtable process, a wide range of perspectives were brought to the table – some quite supportive of a stronger approach to CSR issues, others (according to first-hand accounts) taking positions that were considerably more recalcitrant than the industry representatives in the advisory group. In particular, and predictably, EDC and Natural Resources Canada tended to take far more skeptical and status quo-oriented positions. However, the ability of civil society and industry representatives in the group to arrive at a consensus position clearly increased the political impact of their report. It also indicated that, consistent with Ruggie's (2004) conception of the new public domain, initiative and leadership have increasingly shifted away from state-based institutions toward diverse combinations of non-state actors.

Finally, it is noteworthy that the advisory group recommendations were closely attuned and complementary to important transnational trends and instruments. For example, the report recommended that the Government of Canada adopt two widely supported codes – the Performance Standards developed by the World Bank's International Finance Corporation and the Voluntary Principles on Security and Human Rights developed in 2000 through a multi-stakeholder process involving the US and UK governments, companies in the extractive and energy sectors, and NGOs – as its initial framework standards. It further recommended the development of guidance notes and efforts to promote the further evolution of principles, guidelines, best practices, and measurable performance criteria in relation to both the Canadian CSR framework and international multi-stakeholder initiatives. Similarly, it advocated adopting the non-governmental Global Reporting Initiative (GRI) or GRI-equivalent reporting as the Canadian CSR framework reporting component, while supporting the development of GRI sector supplements where necessary – for example, regarding the oil and gas sector and junior exploration companies (Advisory Group Report 2007, iv-vi). In short, the Canadian process was strongly influenced by, and aspired to influence, key transnational, multi-stakeholder initiatives to promote and deepen CSR norms, standards, and procedures. In this sense it can be seen, once again, as firmly nested within the "reconstituted global public domain" referred to above.

The roundtable process and advisory group report can therefore be seen as innovative and promising. However, the government's response, when it finally came some two years after the report, in March 2009, put this promise in perspective. *Building the Canadian advantage* (Canada, DFAIT 2009) eschewed the adoption of clear Canadian CSR standards, instead committing only to promote various international CSR performance guidelines with Canadian extractive companies operating abroad; while the advisory group's proposed accountability process involving an ombudsman with robust investigative authority was replaced by an extractive sector CSR counsellor who "will only undertake reviews with the consent of the involved parties" (11; see also CNCA 2009). The overall approach shifted from one of even-handedly assessing and enhancing the CSR performance of Canadian extractives to supporting and facilitating the (taken-for-granted) entrepreneurial advantage and CSR "leadership" (Canada, DFAIT 2009, 3) of these companies and their industry associations. In sum, the government strategy marked a clear retreat from the most important accountability mechanisms recommended in the advisory group report and clearly indicated that the default position for government continues to be one of supporting and enabling the international operations of Canadian corporate citizens, enhancing their "competitive advantage" by improving "their ability to manage social and environmental risk" (Canada, DFAIT 2009, 4).

Conclusion

Even before the government's retreat in *Building the Canadian advantage*, the civil society–based Canadian Network on Corporate Accountability, although supportive of the advisory group report and its recommendations, called for additional steps to entrench and extend them, including incorporating them into binding legislation – a move that private sector representatives forthrightly opposed (Canadian Chamber of Commerce 2007; CNCA 2007; Grayson 2006). Moreover, there were important ambiguities in the recommendations – for example, concerning the circumstances under which Canadian government services would be withdrawn: "In cases of serious non-compliance where the Compliance Review committee determines that remedial steps have not been or are unlikely to be successful" (Advisory Group Report 2007, vii). Simply put, the language of the report was so vague and slippery on this point that it remained altogether unclear whether material sanctions for corporate misconduct (as opposed to the social or image-based sanctions arising from a protracted investigation) would eventuate. Despite these ambiguities, however, the roundtable process was an important example of both the growing controversy over Canada's sometimes contradictory approach to Africa with regard to development and extractive industries, and the "reconstituted global public domain" that has raised the political salience of such controversies. In short, this process illustrated the growing salience of both private sector and civil society actors in the making of Canadian foreign and security policy, and the complex interplay between them and disparate elements within the Canadian state, all in the context of shifting transnational norms and pressures – bringing into question the ability and willingness of "the state" to lead in this arena. Indeed, the controversy arising from the government's watered-down 2009 CSR strategy in *Building the Canadian advantage* set the stage for new initiatives from both the private sector and civil society aimed at advancing their own preferred visions of CSR – voluntary and legislated respectively.[15]

The logic and recommendations of the advisory group report and similar initiatives will be challenged from at least two perspectives. From the right, advocates of market liberalism, in mining and elsewhere, will express doubts about the negative effects of a more intrusive regulatory regime for CSR, whether legislated or not. As Philip Crowson argues, for example, "Mining is primarily an economic activity and a form of wealth creation ... Codes of Conduct to regulate how mining companies behave ... might create new problems, stultifying innovation and freezing corporate structures" (Crowson 2005, 607-8). From the left, scholars in the tradition of radical political economy will be, at best, highly skeptical of a framework that holds out the promise of enhancing the social and political legitimacy of foreign-owned mining and energy industries in Africa which, on historical evidence, have extracted vast wealth from the continent while leaving a legacy of large-scale ecological degradation, social dislocation, and the enrichment of despotic elites (for example, see Bond 2006). From this perspective, initiatives such as the roundtable process should be understood as corporate bluewash effectively masking the fundamental continuities in webs of exploitation – particularly so if they serve, in effect, to produce delay and prevarication.

Indeed, even if a Canadian CSR framework were to be effectively implemented, and to become a model for similar arrangements elsewhere, it remains uncertain whether such a multi-stakeholder middle way would contribute to sustained improvement of development and security outcomes in Africa. At least, in the Canadian context, the advocacy for such a framework highlights the historic incoherence of this country's Africa policies that have articulated various progressive human security and development objectives while remaining largely oblivious to the real-world implications of extensive, officially supported extractive industry investments on the continent. As the advisory group report highlights, there is a need to carefully integrate the role of extractive industries into the framing of CIDA's and DFAIT's development and security policies, especially given the privileging of governance and private sector development as core development policy themes.[16]

In the final analysis, then, the roundtable process embodies the possibility of a historic reorientation of the Canadian tradition of passivity and neglect in an area where this country's role in Africa is undeniably important, and where a leadership role is therefore clearly appropriate. Despite the setback of the government's response, what comes of this opening will bear watching in years to come.

NOTES

1. For a discussion of alternative views of human security, distinguishing more mainstream and "official" versions with more critical understandings, see Black (2006) and Grayson (2004).
2. As discussed below, the government's long-awaited March 2009 response to the advisory group report, *Building the Canadian advantage,* is not encouraging in this regard.
3. Although the latter contributions are admittedly smaller in the mineral sector relative to other economic activities such as manufacturing because of the capital-intensive and enclave nature of resource extraction, the real contribution of mining activity lies in its ability to add value in the context of conditions of relative underdevelopment in the economy as a whole. Thus, mining activities may provide a trigger for economic development where few other prospects exist.
4. The EITI is a multi-stakeholder initiative designed to support "improved governance in resource-rich, developing countries through the full publication and verification of company payments and government revenue" (DFAIT Backgrounder, http://www.fin.gc.ca/n07/07-012-eng.asp). For a detailed description see the EITI website at www.eitransparency.org.
5. The term "structural adjustment" refers to a set of economic policies advocated – indeed, imposed – by the International Monetary Fund and World Bank based on neoclassical economic principles. These policies advocate free markets and require the downsizing of state bureaucracies and the removal of government regulations on and intrusions into economic activity. Although the approach to structural adjustment conditions by international financial institutions and other Western donors has softened over the past decade, the core consensus on the importance of so-called market-friendly reforms has remained firm.
6. In the context of Canada's image as leader, we will leave aside the question of the substance and adequacy of its developmental and human security leadership efforts, though see Black (2006). Regarding diplomatic support, Canada's positive image in Africa, for instance, resulted in its gaining the support of all African member states in its successful bid for a non-permanent seat on the Security Council in 1999-2000.
7. Generally, mining companies operating internationally can be divided into three categories. The first two consist of large and small companies, with the former spending more than US$3 million on exploration and the later spending more than US$100,000

but less than US$3 million (Lemieux 2005). Companies in both of these categories are engaged in the production of minerals (mining, smelting, and processing), as well as in exploration. The final category comprises junior exploration companies that engage only in exploration versus production (Ericsson 2005).

8   An additional $3.9 billion was invested in oil and gas (CCA 2007).
9   Although one, Burkina Faso, was dropped from the streamlined list of seven African priority countries announced in February 2009.
10 The other departments and agencies represented were Natural Resources Canada, Industry Canada, Environment Canada, CIDA, Indian and Northern Affairs, the Department of Justice, the EDC, and the Privy Council Office.
11 Interview with author, Ottawa, 30 March 2007. The Canadian government provided an upfront contribution to the EITI Multi-Donor Trust Fund of $750,000, with a commitment to provide a further $100,000 annually. This buys it a "seat at the table" with other major supporters, including France, Germany, the Netherlands, Norway, and the United Kingdom.
12 Another useful way to think about the process, and its nascent outcomes, is as an emergent form of "governmentality," in which both corporate representatives and civil society groups are subjects as well as objects of governmental practices. See Sending and Neumann (2006).
13 A point highlighted by participants in the process.
14 The extent to which corporate representatives on the advisory group were ahead of the more recalcitrant attitudes in much of the private sector is revealed by the responses to the advisory group report from umbrella organizations such as the Canadian Chamber of Commerce (2007). These intra–private sector differences, which are echoed by intra-state differences (see below), seem to be a major reason for the government taking two years to respond to the report. See also Evans (2007).
15 The Prospectors and Developers Association of Canada introduced its e3 Plus voluntary "comprehensive ... CSR guidelines for mineral exploration" in March 2009. Meanwhile, members of the Canadian Network on Corporate Accountability promoted Liberal MP John McKay's private member's bill on Corporate Accountability of Mining, Oil and Gas Corporations in Developing Countries Act (Bill C-300), introduced in February 2009. See Baird (2009) and Lambert (2009).
16 See, for example, the development chapter of the 2005 International Policy Statement (IPS). The IPS has been formally disavowed by the Harper government, but the emphases on governance and private sector development have been effectively retained through the latter's emphasis on "sustainable economic growth" (CIDA 2009a, 5).

12 Peace-Building between Canadian Values and Local Knowledge
Some Lessons from Timbuktu

JONATHAN SEARS

As several chapters in this book demonstrate, durable peace in the contemporary neoliberal world order is intimately linked to the reconstruction of identities in post-conflict contexts. These reconstructions constitute both the "interveners" and "intervened upon." Indeed, as noted by Byrne (re. Muslims), Kinsman (re. queers), and Charbonneau and Parent (re. Afghans), the "target" groups are often problematically represented as being acted upon, rather than exercising agency onto themselves. In 1998, the United Nations published *A peace of Timbuktu* about the case of peace-building in north Mali between 1994 and 1997, and detailed the events that precipitated a conflict that was primarily between speakers of Tamashek and Songhay, and with the Malian military. *A peace of Timbuktu* describes the innovative peace-making that ended the fighting and points to the bases on which subsequent peace-building initiatives were begun. This succeeded largely for over a decade. In the 1990s, the combatants were disarmed through community-based negotiation, or *peace-making*. However, the process of *peace-building* began with combatants' reintegration into their home communities, and it further envisioned comprehensive initiatives to ground durable longer-term peace. International intervention, or traditional *peace-keeping* forces, were never needed in Mali to establish the conditions conducive to the peace talks (Poulton and ag Youssouf 1998). More recent violence in north Mali (2006-07), however, and the similar strategies of conflict resolution draw our attention back to the central place that grass-roots actors did and do play in successful peace-making and peace-building (BBC News Online 2006; IRIN 2006, 2007). There are many lessons in the Malian experience for peace interventions into the twenty-first century, that is, in a world of heightened security concerns and the global war on terror. The dominant role of the United States, for example, in the further militarization and securitization of development cooperation risks underplaying the important roles of those very groups that have a stake in the conflict and in rebuilding peace.

When we consider the inclusive peace-making processes and the role played by key actors in Mali, it becomes clear that lasting peace can be built only with a balance between extending universal norms and practices by the donor-interveners, as well as valorizing local capacities and values. I argue here that this success was only possible because of the inclusionary activities (and by that I mean through the inclusion of those local groups that played key roles in the conflict itself) and engaged decision making by key actors such as multilateral organizations, international NGOs, and bilateral cooperator states such as Canada. Indeed, valorizing local knowledge partly mitigates the neocolonial role that peace interventions have played in constructing developing countries as "voids" needing to be filled with effective institutions, viable markets, liberalism, and above all, order (Whitworth 2004; see Charbonneau and Parent's Chapter 3). Contrast such renewed "civilizing missions" with the north Mali case, however, and it is more necessary than ever to envision an internationalism that pays close attention to local knowledge, identities, capacities, and mechanisms of conflict resolution. Indeed, this "local knowledge internationalism" offers possibilities through which Canada might find a future role in the global order that can be more effective than bilateral and multilateral peace interventions.

At the heart of north Mali's lessons for Canada is the fact that at least a part of global order is located where identities are reconstructed at the grassroots level. This is, of course, complicated. As other contributors have noted, Gramscian theoretical approaches can help conceptualize hegemony and identity in the global context, as well as in terms of how legitimacy is built and contested within the domestic dynamics of both donor-intervener states and the intervened-upon milieus (O'Meara's Chapter 1; Neufeld 1995). At a moment when the discourses of building institutional *capacities* for lasting peace are being complemented by discourses of extending *values* (Canadian or American or French) as ostensibly universal values, a corresponding emphasis is also occurring on domestic or local values, or in the case considered here, Malian values.

Canadian internationalism has historically emphasized peacekeeping, humanitarian intervention, and multilateralism as the vehicles for the expression and embodiment of distinctly Canadian values. Multiculturalism, tolerance, democracy, idealism, and selflessness have all been woven into this mythology about Canada, Canadians, and what Canada contributes globally. Canadian bilateral interventions and multilateral cooperation occur in the historical moment of extending political and economic liberalization to developing countries. The contexts of intervention are increasingly complex. New conflicts will require new capabilities to meet the shift from peace enforcement toward cooperative peace-building (Cox and Sjolander 1998). Indeed, the broader political economy of bilateral and multilateral trade, development aid, and peace-building cooperation tends to reproduce neoliberal hegemony, and donor-interveners' imperatives increasingly edge out the participation of local actors and the inclusion of local priorities. In such scenarios, where the accountability of national governments in matters of justice and governance is drawn toward the priorities of multilateral agencies (for example, the World Bank poverty reduction strategy papers, or PRSPs) and the dominant bilateral donor-intervener states (for example, the United States and France), the legitimacy of developing country states is further undermined as their governments tend toward "preapproved" programs. This is often regardless of domestic priorities emerging from broad social consultations (Bretton Woods Project 2003; Degnbol-Martinussen and Engberg-Pedersen 2003; M. Moore 1998).

In a neoliberal world order, the emerging emphasis on local knowledge, along with indigenous identities and practices, as fundamental to lasting peace begins to recognize the changing global conditions of intervention since the 1990s. Canada's military-training assistance to developing countries is incorporating more skills than simply core combat readiness, with a special emphasis on culture-specific training and local customs (Treasury Board of Canada Secretariat 2007; UNAC 2007). The Pearson Peacekeeping Centre, which is funded by the Department of National Defence (DND) and the Canadian International Development Agency (CIDA), leads multinational, multidisciplinary training exercises and promotes capacity-building through partnerships in Africa and other regions.

Most relevant to the increasing complexity of intervention, the requirements for training actors in developing countries include taking local knowledge seriously. This is reflected in its emphasis on civil-military cooperation, cultural engagement, and capacity-building through local partnerships. Indeed, as peace intervention is better understood as a cooperative endeavour, there is greater potential for the integration of multiple actors both inside and outside traditional peace operations personnel. The coordination of direct and indirect action in sustainable peace-building is increasingly understood beyond the short term, and into the medium- and long-term time scales. Approached with appropriate modesty, then, Canadian expertise in engaged local capacity-building provides a foundation upon which to improve collaboration between Canadian government departments and agencies (for example, the Canadian Forces/DND, the Department of Foreign Affairs and International Trade, CIDA, the RCMP, the Department of Justice, and Elections Canada). This further integrates these Canadian state actors into non-state actors (southern domestic, northern domestic, and international NGOs) working for post-conflict peace-building (UNAC 2007).

Reconciling Values in a Neoliberal Moment

Promoting liberal so-called Canadian values also means engaging with so-called Malian values. Recently, this has been accompanied by political and economic liberalization, as manifest by the measures imposed by international financial institutions. Canadian values are extended by Canadian state, non-state, corporate and NGO actors, and they range from the relatively progressive to the centre-liberal to the neoliberal (Neufeld 1995). More specifically, in sub-Saharan Africa, so-called universal values are increasingly adopted by urban elites as they comply with political and economic liberalization. Conversely, culturally specific conceptions of well-being, citizenship, political participation, and economic activity often reside in the indigenous cultures of rural populations (Coulibaly and Diarra 2004). Often there are convergent interests among the Canadian (and other donors') liberal internationalist values and the urban ruling classes in sub-Saharan Africa. Contemporary Malian political cultures are thus born by a heterogeneous urban ruling class, its client actors in the upper-middle and the petty bourgeoisie classes. These actors have had formal or opportunistic interests in the political and administrative reforms (or socio-economic change), and often many actors remain that have been recycled from the authoritarian state structure into post-*apertura* state and non-state organizations. Thus, they straddle both civil society and the state (Amselle 1992; Bagayogo 1999; Benoist 1998; Fay 1995; François 1982; Harsch 1993; Manning 1998; Z.K. Smith 1997).

Grassroots peace-building must also negotiate the national (Malian) values discourse, itself part of domestic elites' struggles to unify the national ruling class. Peace-building is thus embedded in local and national hegemonic struggles. This adds to the functional aspects of the processes of peace-building. Such politics include a socio-cultural and values-based attempt to legitimate the Malian ruling class' drive to secure its own unity. This legitimation accumulates and deploys the cultural and discursive resources needed to "educate" the mass population into a "common sense" and often will not challenge the elites' entitlement to wealth and power. In doing so, it represents inequalities as natural and obvious, with a view to being widely accepted (Berman 2004). Because struggles over identity are often also over legitimacy, state and society actors are sometimes adversaries and at other times allies in competitions for power (Giddens 1993). Without strong differentiation of state and non-state spheres in contexts such as north Mali, the multiple formulations of state and/or military actors and civil society are a staging ground for each other. In short, they are spaces for the mutual recruitment and recycling of elites. Consent, then, is "drawn out," as "every relationship of 'hegemony' is necessarily an educational relationship" (Gramsci 1971, 350) in the dynamics between the state and society, and among the domestic and international actors situated in this site of cultural and political struggle. Education about peace, then, is a key part of this process. Hegemony is constructed through explicit and implicit intergenerational and inter-class negotiations, reproductions, and struggles. The possibilities and pitfalls of educational relationships demand sufficient sensitivity to their inherent power dynamics. Without such sensitivity, peace education will remain a form of hegemonic control and preserve the type of liberal internationalism that seeks to further globalize relations of production and trade that appeal to urban-based, cosmopolitan class actors. This process tends to reinforce the wealth and power of Malian elites. Valorizing so-called Malian values runs the risk of exacerbating rather than mitigating tensions between experiences in urban and rural Mali. This also plays into the tensions between the more remote and underdeveloped north and comparatively developed south. In Mali, communitarian norms and identities certainly are conducive to establishing and maintaining order, as the case of peace-making demonstrates. Thus, the valorization of local knowledge may reinforce existing patriarchal or patron-client relations and inequalities as part of the price of order and the cessation of violence (Grémont et al. 2004; Marty 2007). Since the 1990s, domestic discourses of democratization and peace-building have converged on the central state-formation issue of a crisis in legitimacy. Legitimacy is not merely a state attribute but a feature of the relationship between state and society. This type of legitimacy is to be sought and nurtured among a broad range of stakeholders in sustainable peace-building (Ball 2005). Indeed, the relationships between legitimacy, peace-building, and durable democracy extend beyond the official and formal spheres. They play into the dualistic thinking about tradition versus modernity typical within the modernization debates. This duality is still a characteristic found in the policies of political and economic liberalization. As such, non-formal norms and practices (for instance, local knowledge) can only compromise legitimacy (Ellis 1999).

A further barrier to imagining a dialogue of values rather than transfer, Canada's historical support role for US internationalism has been given new impetus since 2001. Canadian bilateral interventions and multilateral cooperation that support internationalism amenable to a US-led war on terror are also conducive to an international system of investment and trade that supports more narrowly national or corporate Canadian interests in reproducing relations of capitalist production. Thus, the myth of selflessly pursuing the common good, which is a characteristically neoliberal good, is such that Canadian values, like those of Canada's allies among the OECD (Organisation for Economic Co-operation and Development) countries, are represented un-problematically as fitting a universal good. The mythologizing of Canada's selfless, liberal internationalism that has framed the discourse of peace intervention in the past has certainly been criticized (Black and Sjolander 1996; Neufeld 1995; Neufeld and Whitworth 1997). The main observation made here is that local knowledge internationalism represents a potential way beyond narrowly neocolonial peace interventions.

Local diversity, complexity, and contestation in social relations may be taken seriously at key moments when relatively small-scale interventions can have significant impact (Poulton and ag Youssouf 1998).[1] Such localism in the model of north Mali's post-conflict peace-building points to more modest, low-profile, nuanced, and knowledgeable forms of intervention and cooperation. A key Canadian strength here is its preference for multilateralism, its emphasis on "quiet diplomacy," and its "constructive engagement" with civil society actors (Black 2001). To cooperate effectively in such ways requires new partnership strategies that have stable medium- and long-term financing to improve continuity and coherence of development institutions' initiatives. This encourages domestic NGOs to work their way out of dependency relations with donor organizations (Poulton, ag Youssouf, and Seck 1999). Indeed, as a scenario of twenty-first-century Canadian internationalism, localism could encompass a loose grouping of approaches that could help to anchor a reconstituted like-minded group (LMG) among those donor-intervener states most willing to approach peace interventions along the lines of decentralized, "quieter," and longer-term cooperation with domestic actors. This would challenge multilateral institutions to be less exclusionary and less dominated by the narrow interests of the OECD. By concentrating on support for decentralization and local empowerment, Canada might foster a more politically responsive, and inclusive internationalism (Black and Sjolander 1996; Neufeld and Whitworth 1997).

Indeed, there are profound differences between building and enforcing peace. As such, there are also differences between those conditions on the ground that make each the appropriate choice in an attempt to resolve a given conflict. On the one hand, peace-building must take the ideas and concerns of the stakeholders in a conflict into consideration and attempt to build upon this in order to create a lasting environment of cooperation. In this sense, it is bottom-up. On the other hand, peace enforcing is more often about the imposition of an order by outsiders (usually with the use or threat of force) and, as such, it is top-down. Peace enforcing usually does not consider or address the root causes of conflict for those stakeholders on the ground. In a world order in which the United States (and other dominant powers) has set a precedent of imposing "order" or claiming to have the right to change regimes, the local is lost. As a result, the ability to implement lasting peace built upon the concerns of those involved in conflicts is also lost.

Training, Capacity-Building, and Normative Peace Education

In engaging the transformation of political subjects' identities involved in peace-making and peace-building, more than simply technical operational skills are needed. Canada has been involved in supporting peace-building in Mali through both bilateral and multilateral involvement with Economic Community of West African States (ECOWAS) countries. These programs have engaged in community-based security sector reform and capacity-building, as well as in post-conflict resolution and reconstruction. ECOWAS countries have partnered with the Department of Foreign Affairs and International Trade's (DFAIT's) Glyn Berry Program for Peace and Security (formerly Human Security Program), which forms a part of the Canadian peace-building initiative. Canada also contributes to UN agencies operating in Mali, including the UN Development Programme (UNDP), UN Institute for Disarmament Research (UNIDIR), United Nations High Commissioner for Refugees (UNHCR), United Nations Children's Fund (UNICEF), UN Food and Agriculture Organization (FAO), and UN World Food Programme (WFP) (Canada, DFAIT 2002; Poulton and ag Youssouf 1998). In the past, Canada has recognized that conflict-prone social divisions not only are products of material conditions (reactions to unequal access to resources) but also are linked to changing identities, norms, and practices. This recognition has come through partnerships with Mali in the Projet de développement des capacités en maintien de la paix et sécurité, the Royal Military College of Canada, the Pearson Peacekeeping Centre, and CIDA. Indeed, the rich and varied experiences of instructors in multilateral, bilateral, and NGOs include the UNHCR, UNICEF, CARE Canada, the Pearson Peacekeeping Centre, and the Centre canadien d'étude et de coopération internationale (CECI). CECI's partnership with UNHCR in reintegrating returning north Mali refugees deserves emphasis. The level of trust in and effectiveness of CECI, especially in small-scale agricultural outreach (for example, supporting market gardens), enabled it to participate, beginning in 1999, with the Republic of Mali and a range of organizations, including Action contre la Faim, Agence des Musulmans d'Afrique, Aide Médicale Internationale, Croix-Rouge malienne, and Vision Mondiale (PPC 2006; Poulton and ag Youssouf 1998; UNHCR Global Appeal 1999). This activity further illustrates that effective peace cooperation links international humanitarian organizations, specialized government structures, national civil society groups, and international NGOs working on a range of programs, from humanitarian relief to capacity-building (P. Walker 2008). When the Pearson Peacekeeping Centre delivered peace operations training to 320 participants in Mali, Cameroon, and Ghana in 2005-06, the percentage of civilian participants in the francophone Africa training sessions nearly doubled the percentage overall: 42 as compared with 22 percent. This clearly indicates the emphasis placed in West Africa on non-military actors' engagement with peace-making and peace-building operations. Incorporating civilian, military, state, and non-governmental actors helps to address the problems inherent in the divisions between state and society interests in Mali and in other countries in sub-Saharan Africa (Chabal and Daloz 1999).

However, the straddling of spheres by actors involved in peace-making can complicate the restricted (and often) technical skills imparted through training and implementation. Even state-centred and relatively narrow or bounded interventions draw in actors and initiatives (such as the Red Cross) that straddle "relief" and "development" (Poulton and ag Youssouf 1998). As such, the technical aspects of peace-building might be consistent with interveners' ("Canadian") interests and values. However, these efforts are not entirely value-free and as such also reflect the donors' preferences toward a certain version of what are acceptable human rights and democratic governance initiatives (UNDP 2002). They may not be consistent with what is deemed acceptable human rights and democratic governance initiatives by all parties involved in the conflict. The educative stance adopted by multilateral and bilateral actors encompass training in technical competencies of peace operations, including peacekeeping techniques, related peacemaking skills, and some peace-building discussions. These work to bring the sometimes diverse concepts of what is acceptable together. The Peacekeeping and Security Capacity-Building Project for Francophone Africa has educational partnerships with the Kofi Annan International Peacekeeping Training Centre in Ghana and with the École de Maintien de la Paix, the École militaire d'administration, and the École militaire inter-arme in Mali. In goals and outputs, such education partly recognizes the normative sociocultural project of peace-building cooperation (Ball 2005; PPC 2006). Thus, post-2001 peace-building emphasizes local culture more than ever as its anchor. Indeed, effective membership in meaningful communities (cultural, occupational, and religious), economic exchange relationships, men's and women's age-grade associations, and local decision-making structures (state and non-state) are all a part of dynamic grassroots cooperation (Fatton 1995; Grémont et al. 2004; Konaté et al. 1999).

The search for Malian national characteristics by Mali's national political classes is key in the consolidation and legitimation of post-*apertura* democratization. On the one hand, accepting diversity and institutionalizing group autonomy recognizes and partly reconciles the relatively autonomous power bases at work in this country. On the other hand, discourses of Malian unity stress that the contemporary Mali nation-state draws its unity from *Maliba* and *Malikoro* (Great and Old Mali). This dates back to the eleventh century, when the society was dominated by large-scale political communities, including Ghana, Mali, Songhay, and Aksia empires (Adriamirado and Adriamirado 2001). The discourses of the so-called Malian value of ethnic harmony that are deployed by political elites form a part of the discourses of reconciliation (historical and regional) as part of the ongoing post-colonial, nation-building exercise. Indeed, the reconciliation discourses are linked to those of moral recovery, as well as cultural and religious revival. Thus, economic and political neglect of north Mali has a counterpart in the marginalization from being a site/bearer of the Malian values. Through symbolism and identity, north Mali peace-building is an ongoing struggle of subregional self-definition within the nation state. It negotiates a place in the national Malian values imaginary, along with a more important share in national wealth (Poulton and ag Youssouf 1998; Sears 2007). Although scholars recognize that reconstructing identities is part of the peace-building process, they pay less attention to the potential for resistance. In particular, the educational dimension of Canada's activities in post-conflict peace-building and security sector reform in Mali remain based on a limited understanding of the anxieties produced by, and potential for resistance to, its sociocultural transformation.

The Conflict and Its Resolution

Without telling the whole chronicle of the Malian conflict and its resolution, there are certain elements of the north Mali story that are important to highlight. The bases of conflict were the types that made localized conflict resolution a highly effective response. Years of state neglect and misrule exacerbated social inequalities. Along with this, recurring severe droughts in the mid-1970s and mid-1980s caused crises in the Kel Tamashek herds that had devastating effects on the livelihoods of many (McKeon 2003; Smaldone 1999). Remote and perennially excluded, both socially and economically, the Tamashek adapted to the colonial and post-colonial concepts of stateness and acceptable political behaviour in their own way. They adapted to, but did not submit to, this form of rule. Importantly, the colonial imposition and post-colonial reinforcement of Jacobin republicanism undermined, but did not erase, indigenous identities, norms, and practices (Wälzholz 1997; C.M. Warner 2001; Young 1994).

Indeed, the socio-economic interdependence proved resilient and conducive to the mediation and participatory decision making held in the facilitation groups (discussed below) that were formed to aid peace-making and lay foundations for peace-building. Crucial to grasp relative to the Kel Tamashek (Tuareg) crisis is that the different populations of north Mali have constructed their identities in multiple political and economic communities, not only through local and regional interdependencies but also in struggles with unresponsive, exclusionary outside rulers. Those outsiders included both the French colonial and the post-independence governments. A variety of traditional activities, including farming, livestock herding, fishing, trade, and commerce, have linked seven ethnolinguistic communities in the remote desert zone of north Mali through the long-standing bonds of social, cultural, and economic interdependence (Grémont et al. 2004; Marty 2007). Such interdependence was produced by north Mali's history of the past rule of different groups over one another, and pastoralists' and farmers' cohabitation and cooperation. Hence, neighbours' interdependence was as key a socio-cultural foundation for peace as links among clans. Songhay and Tamashek speakers share the concept of mother sibling-hood (called *fafa* and *ehaf* respectively). This is not only a family relationship among brothers born of the same mother but also describes relations of social cohesion and solidarity. Moreover, it extends to the cosmological realm, describing struggles in the material and spiritual realms between the forces of destruction and cohesion (Bailleuil 1996; Konaré 2000; Poulton and ag Youssouf 1998; Sears 2007).

In addition to the resilient socio-cultural interdependence, democratization prompted a shift from dictatorship to more responsive governance. This shift partly responded to the north Mali conflict itself, and to its more general national socio-economic and political context that was supported by actors inside and outside Mali's borders. In 1990, reacting to the history of economic and political exclusion, a small group of Kel Tamashek attacked military and government compounds. Then president General Moussa Traoré's twenty-three-year military regime reacted brutally. This, with other protests and crackdowns around Mali, precipitated a coup in March 1991 led by then lieutenant colonel Amadou Toumani Touré.[2] A transitional civilian and military government signed the Pacte National with the United Movements and Fronts of Azaouad (MFUA). A new constitution preceded elections in 1992 when Alpha Oumar Konaré become Mali's first civilian president in a generation. The leadership of responsive presidents (Touré in transition and Konaré from 1992 to 2002) is hard to overemphasize. Konaré's ability to withdraw civilian and military state functionaries from the front lines in north Mali allowed non-state, non-military actors to engage in peace-making with both combatants and non-combatants in their own communities. However, the slow pace of peace and democracy in north Mali contributed to renewed local conflict that erupted in spring 1994 between Tamashek-speakers and a counter force of mainly Songhay-speaking farmers (McKeon 2003; Smaldone 1999).

By September 1994, the crisis prompted north Mali civil society leaders to establish facilitation groups to solicit and encourage proposals for local development initiatives in anticipation of the peace-building process. Supported by a well-respected international NGO (Norwegian Church Aid), they convened intercommunity meetings and initiated a fund for reconciliation and peace consolidation in north Mali. This fund was in turn supported by more of Mali's partner-donors. In a significant break with past administrative practice, local state elites were given merely observer status in order to give other community members (such as elders, religious and civil society leaders, women, and youth) opportunities and space to renew traditional mediation practices. For its part, the Republic of Mali (GRM) further expedited administrative decentralization in order to grant real autonomy and decision-making power as promised. This was expected and needed in north Mali. Not only did this improve the capacity of state institutions, it also strengthened the crucially important moral authority of the Malian state by better engaging the dynamic production and reproduction of legitimacy in state–society relations. In this sense, key state and society actors built a lasting bottom-up arrangement to encourage community-driven initiatives for socio-economic development (McKeon 2003). Decentralization further promoted downward rather than upward accountability. The leaders of religious groups, local community leaders, and women's groups (to name a few) were able to integrate their respective social and cultural values, as well as relationships of economic exchange, into the peace process. Collaboration among multilateral, bilateral, and NGO actors (grassroots and international) enabled local leaders (including religious leaders and community elders) to negotiate ceasefires of limited scope and play a successively greater role in resolving the conflict. Hostilities came to an end by April 1995. Multilateral involvement included the UNDP, UNIDIR, UNHCR, UNICEF, FAO, and WFP, and the UN Department of Political Affairs, which collaborated with key bilateral, GRM, and NGO actors. It was only through such inclusiveness that this bottom-up, socially-based legitimacy was established (Macamo and Neubert 2002; Klute and von Trotha 2002; Rose 1996; Demante 2005; McKeon 2003).

Beyond state structures, bilateral and multilateral actors were able to grasp the importance of local involvement, decentralization, and devolved decision making in their own organizations. Key in these innovations was the ability and willingness to "think decentralized" (which is also characteristic of Canada's own cooperation in Mali). By working within civil society in relation to the decentralizing state, donor-interveners' partnerships with multiple Malian actors cultivated a rich awareness of political dynamics and empowered an already emboldened civil society. Most effective were bilateral donors, including the French, Dutch, Swiss, Canadians, Americans, and Norwegians, all of whom were able and willing to learn from the advantages and achievements in the non-governmental sector. A good example of the success enjoyed by NGOs was that of the Red Cross/Crescent and its domestic partner NGOs (Poulton and ag Youssouf 1998). UN and bilateral actors (including those from Germany, the Netherlands, Switzerland, and Canada) were open to decentralized decision making and indigenous mechanisms of dispute resolution. Donor-interveners should indeed give priority to strategies that decentralize decision making and that further embrace new ways of understanding the human condition as it is experienced in conflict zones.

The process was successful for the following reasons. First and foremost, the selection of community organizers was done in such a way that the participants in this process had an established track record of making decisions with integrity, and their respective positions were derived from their recognized honesty and ability to keep meetings focused on manageable problems and on solutions connected to the real needs of the interdependent communities. North Mali's facilitation groups were carefully constructed, inclusive of national and foreign non-state actors, supported materially and politically by national and multilateral and bilateral state actors, and leveraged local norms, practices, and institutions.

Second, the most important lesson for future peace interventions (especially for Canadian actors' demonstrated ability with devolved decision making) is the role of vital actors in key places at key moments with key (but limited) funding.[3] The discretionary authority of actors, from the presidency to the grassroots level, and especially within the bilateral and multilateral organizations, allowed them to take risks, access funding, and build relationships, as well as make and keep commitments with relevant stakeholders.

Also important for the north Mali success were appropriate partnerships among insiders, "insiders partial," and "outsiders" (McKeon 2003). Clearly, not all non-local participants and practitioners need to (or ultimately can) have as sophisticated an understanding as do locals of the complex and contested indigenous histories, identities, norms, and practices that inform Malian values. "Insiders partial," however, were crucial to north Mali peacebuilding, and their position is central to lessons for future peace-building cooperation. The practical partnerships characteristic of the north Mali processes were embodied in relationships among engaged, sensitive, and knowledgeable representatives. For example, R.I. Fung, from the UN Regional Centre for Disarmament in Africa of the United Nations Office for

Disarmament Affairs, acted in a specially created role of political adviser to the resident coordinator, (Norwegian) Tore Rose. Fung's supervisor, Prvoslav Davinic, then Malian president Konaré, and the UN Department of Political Affairs (UN/DPA) provided the administrative, financial, and moral backing to enable important actors such as Mahamadou Diagouraga, GRM Commissaire au Nord, to take calculated political risks that would have been judiciously avoided by UN actors in the past. Fung proved to be a model of foreign cooperation and was flexible, capable, humble, and effective (Poulton and ag Youssouf 1998). The UNDP–UN/DPA field-level collaboration was an innovative first, and it brought the theoretical links between security and development into front-line practice of peace-making, as well as laid the foundations for subsequent peace-building. Complementing the peace-making and peace-building initiatives, Canada supported similarly flexible cooperation and innovation in the 1992 initiative of D. Baudouin, along with Abdourahmane Niang (the Malian interior ministry), who arranged election observation with additional support from USAID and the Netherlands one election cycle before Mali's independent electoral commission was established in 1996-97 (Poulton and ag Youssouf 1998; Smaldone 1999).

The "insiders partial" figures (such as Fung) exemplify the locally engaged actors who made multilateral cooperation useful in catalyzing the existing capacities for peace-making and peace-building in north Mali. All these elements converged so that a sophisticated, sphere-straddling, and locally engaged understanding was able to grapple with the complex links between economics, politics, and culture. In doing so it was able to bridge the security/peace and development/well-being worlds of bilateral and multilateral intervention and discourse. Indeed, as much as the UN approach of "security first" for development (Poulton and ag Youssouf 1998, 193) partly describes the peace-making processes in north Mali, the foundations for peace-building were laid simultaneously by the existing energies and initiatives seeking development for comprehensive, sustainable security.

Lessons from Timbuktu

Because the north Mali case shows the necessity of a political economy perspective on security and development, an important element of the story is the historical moment of the neoliberal global order. As discussed by Charbonneau and Parent, Shaw, and Black and Savage in other chapters in this book, twenty-first-century multilateralism reconstructs security as part and parcel of supporting the basic needs of transnational production and trade. Often the result is declining attention to security and well-being on a human scale. In a world of heightened security concerns and a global war on terror, the case of Mali reminds us that lasting solutions to the problems of violence and challenges to claims of legitimacy lie in the ability of the interveners, such as the Canadian state through bilateral and multilateral cooperation, to bring local experiences and knowledge into the processes of rebuilding legitimacy and peace. Indeed, narrowing security toward hard rather than soft human security concerns is neither best nor inevitable. Undoubtedly, the Axworthy-era concept of human security innovatively reframed the mythology of Canada-as-peacekeeper, which may currently be losing traction. Nevertheless, a micro-level focus on the discourse of human security makes possible (as the Canadian Peacebuilding Coordinating Committee noted in its submission to DFAIT) "a long-overdue shift from a culture of reaction to conflict to one of prevention" (CPCC 2003, 6). This is consistent with Canada's engagement with community-based security capacity development of the recent past. It is what is here called "local knowledge internationalism."

There is no doubt that localism has been undermined by the war on terror, which tends to narrow rather than expand the conceptualizations of security in donor and partner countries. The case of north Mali suggests that comprehensive peace-building needs to remain at the forefront of an otherwise increased emphasis on hard security. The management of dissent and opposition, silencing of diverse voices, and undermining indigenous actors' own struggles and initiatives (Development Assistance Committee Network on Conflict, Peace and Development Co-operation 2004) has proven to be key to sustained peace-building. Moreover, indigenous conceptions of security in Mali, and across sub-Saharan Africa, have tended to be more comprehensive than merely the absence of physical harm or threat. In addition to provisions for seasonal drought, and to protect health and food security, access to basic services (whether provided by state or social networks) complements peace of mind in broadly spiritual and psychological senses (Hutchful and Fayemi 2004). Because of such complexities, peace-building should be built on mutual learning so that interventions respond not only to the immediacies of local conditions, actors, and dynamics but also to local conceptualizations of the issues at stake in transforming political subjects' identities. To qualify the extension of ostensibly "Canadian" values as ostensibly universal values is, indeed, salutary. It takes seriously the identities and agency of the intervened upon. Notwithstanding this apologia for "local values," however, what the "local values" are and as articulated by whom should remain at the forefront of understanding peace interventions. Indeed, as the political economy of liberal reform parallels that of liberal internationalism, developing countries' social policy occurs within the process of economic liberalism, and this often limits state and community resources for peace-building. International financial institutions' macro-economic stabilization and restructuring programs may insist on reduced public spending precisely when increased spending for security and development initiatives is needed. Furthermore, at the grassroots level, the impacts of economic restructuring may undermine the social economies essential for peace-building by destabilizing patron-client networks and increasing tensions among social groups. This can precipitate more violent reaction against slow or non-fulfillment of peace dividend promises (Poulton and ag Youssouf 1998; Chabal and Daloz 1999).

As other contributors to this book have noted, mainstream international relations' orthodoxies are being rethought in the post-2001 global context. Lessons from north Mali–style peace-building highlight the particular insights that may be drawn from sub-Saharan Africa in this connection (see Dunn and Shaw 2001). More specifically, the ongoing peace-building in north Mali, situated in its national, regional, and global contexts, can help reconceptualize the roles and relationships among state, non-state, and military actors, as well as the manifold structures and organizations that shape how donor-interveners and their domestic partners understand and seek peace.

NOTES

1 Canada's engagement with Mali in the 1990s was small. In north Mali through the mid-1990s, Canada contributed 3.5 percent of the US$214 million for "projects supposed to contribute to peace and development in northern Mali," and 7.7 percent of US$9.6 million to the "UN trust fund to support the peace process in Northern Mali" (Poulton and ag Youssouf 1998, 163).
2 Now president, General (retired) Touré was elected and re-elected in 2002 and 2007.
3 "Depending on how one defines the various programs supporting the peace process in Mali, its cost has been as little as $10 million to $12 million" (Smaldone 1999, 145).

Conclusion
Relocating Global Order

BRUNO CHARBONNEAU AND WAYNE S. COX

The intent of this book is ambitious. The chapters were selected with specific goals in mind, and with the intention of making the collection greater than the sum of its parts. Our starting point was a premise that much of the literature in international relations (IR) that deals with issues of security and global order is often left hanging in space. This is understandable because global order and associated references to international security, global stability, and global peace are rather lofty ideas that attempt to connect a series of disparate experiences of political order(s). In worst-case scenarios, the concepts of global order and American hegemony/power are used almost interchangeably. As a result, theorizations of political order(s) operate at such a high level of abstraction that generalized assertions about global politics are often so non-specific as to be of only limited value to case-study research. High levels of abstraction have significant effects on what is seen and unseen because they draw on conceptions of what it means to know and what it means to be in the world. One of the key themes in this book is the idea that global order is not disconnected from local experiences and that, in fact, the local is often the location of how people experience global order, and often the location where we find those ideas and experiences that inform the global order itself. Local practice involves social and political practices that maintain, reform, and/or transform global order. Both the theoretical and the case-related chapters in this book were selected to highlight various aspects of these complex interrelationships.

This book is an attempt at demonstrating that neither the local nor the global has primacy. This demonstration extends to a concern with claims about the spatial assumptions of IR theorizing, and the practical representations of space, political activity, and political conflict. An emphasis on locating global order underlines how the terms that refer to the "international" and political authority (sovereignty) are grounded primarily within a specific *temporality*. Claims about the possibilities and problems of a spatially defined global order of states are based on linear and teleological accounts of modernization, that is, upon linear and teleological accounts of how modern society and the modern state evolved (Inayatullah and Blaney 2004). It is in such temporal accounts of modern politics that hegemonic claims about a specific (state-centric) spatiality are enabled. The exploration of the relationship between location and politics challenges the usual articulations of space and time. It highlights how and where the "international" in global relations is the site of constant political practices and struggles over political authority and legitimacy. Indeed, studying global order means examining ever-evolving relations and processes of integration and interdependence, but also of fragmentation and disparity, and thus of ever-changing global/local boundaries and identities. The state seems to always pop its head out wherever we look; that is, it always seems central to experiences of global order. This is not, however, because it is the most important actor but because the state expresses and symbolizes the location of those social relations and practices that define and redefine the crucial national-international boundary that informs our perceptions of what is local and global. As several chapters in this book suggest, the state and those social forces in whose interest the state (or key aspects of the state) often acts usually represent the interests and perspectives of those empowered elites whose very empowerment is preserved by the status quo. As such, state-centric conceptions of global order can work politically to maintain or reform global order. Claims to legitimacy are often built upon a reference to "common sense," suggesting that theoretical strength comes from an ability to describe "the world as it is," but we suggest that an emphasis on state-centric perspectives cannot fully capture the local-global dynamics of, and changes to, global order in the post-9/11 era. The local is a very part of the construction and maintenance of global order itself, and thus presenting case research that examines the various and multi-levelled experiences of global order is crucial to understanding theoretically what and where global order is, in all its complexity and multiple locations. Consequently, this collection includes the work of several scholars whose central research encompasses a variety of issues and levels of analysis in order to offer a broad spectrum of locations where the roots of global order can be found, maintained, reformed, resisted, negotiated, and/or imposed. Security is a core theme because it seems to us that, especially after 9/11, this is where we find the stake to crucial questions about local and global boundaries and identities, social practice and political authority, interstate relations, state-society relations, and limits to the political imagination.

To begin, we included a short but necessary discussion of American power. This we believe to be essential, not least because the Canadian state has historically defined its global role in reference to its relations with the United States, and because of the unparallel global reach and power of the American state. The context of Canada-US relations is a significant site at which the limits to the political imagination are produced, notably in terms of Canadian security. Claims that the present global order is equivalent to American power/hegemony are misleading and overly simplistic, but the latter has important effects on the relationship between location and politics. In the words of John Ruggie:

> The world would look very different today if the Soviet Union or Nazi Germany had ended up as its hegemon after World War II. Indeed, important things would have been different even if Great Britain had done so. Accordingly, contra neorealism, I suggest that the fact of *American* hegemony was every bit as important as the fact of American *hegemony* in the shaping of the post-World War II order. (Ruggie 1998a, 14, emphasis in original)

Therefore, the chapters by Dan O'Meara (Chapter 1) and Alex Macleod (Chapter 2) examine the specificity of an American-shaped structural and ideational global order and the politics within American government and society. These chapters address some of the key questions and debates over how to shape and what shape should take the contemporary world order under the leadership of the United States. Both chapters focus on American conceptions and practices of security and militarism with the intent to demonstrate how they influence the structures of global order. Dan O'Meara argues that the historical development of the specific form of American militarism as a social project was a key moment to the establishment of American power globally because militarism permeated the American self-image and American conceptions of the United States' role and responsibility in shaping global order. Alex Macleod examines the changes in emphasis brought on by the American neoconservatives, and how this shift in emphasis changed American conceptions of security and the use of military force in the post-9/11 world order. His analysis raises important questions about the relationship between theory-building and political practice in American foreign policy.

This American specificity is essential to recognize for any analysis of our central case study: the role and place of Canada within that order. By virtue of its geographic location and of its degree of economic and social integration within the apex of world power, Canadian security is not operated, defined, or determined because of some systemic imperative attributed to international anarchy or global capitalism. We argue that Canadian security is grounded in social-historical practices of various actors at various levels (within Canadian civil society, within parts of the Canadian state, as a part of Canadian relations with other states and their respective institutions, and as a part of those international institutions and non-state actors that play a role in or influence Canadian foreign and defence policy). It is within these multiple locations of social practices that we locate Canada's and Canadians' role in constructing, maintaining, reproducing, and transforming global order. Although we can not offer a complete overview of the United States as a global power, interpretations of American power in this respect nevertheless need to be addressed or at least acknowledged. Thus, the focus on American militarism and security is a logical choice given the book's subject matter. American power (both state and social) has long been a central component of the context from which Canadian politics, and Canadian security specifically, has evolved (see also Charbonneau and Cox 2008; R.W. Cox 2005).

The rest of the book seeks to provide a wide range of situations where the Canadian state or Canadians participated in and experienced the consequences of this evolving global order. In some cases, the groups studied in these chapters acted to support American power and the status quo; in other cases the groups were indifferent to American power; and in some cases these groups sought to challenge US hegemony and the status quo. The actions of all groups studied in this book were not always considerate of the broader implications that their activities had on global order and on the role of the United States in (re)defining global order. More importantly, global order is not, we argue, simply about American power and the American state. It is about a more extensive set of institutions, mechanisms, practices, and ideas that transcend any single state in global politics, and as such, the role of the Canadian state and various aspects of Canadian society in global order are a very part of its definition and functioning. Once the consequences of the changes in roles that occur for a state such as Canada in the war on terror are debated and judged, some groups may view the Canadian role in Afghanistan as a continuation of an internationalist tradition, others may view the changes in domestic security policy and its implications on ethnic minorities as a domestic debate about fundamental rights, and others still may view the loss of Canadian soldiers in Afghanistan as a consequence of Canadians playing a role in American empire.

What we are elaborating on here, through case research, is a far more complex understanding of state and society, and how these interrelationships play into the Canadian participation in a global order under US hegemony. In this sense, Canada and the United States' "power" as actors in world politics is not an attribute but is conditional on complex sets of transnational social relations. What is understood as the state and the variety of groups and institutions that represent state interests (including many state-centric theories in the study of IR) might be in a position to attempt to define world politics in purely state-centric terms because it is often in their interests to do so. For those empowered and socialized into thinking of global politics in state-centric terms, the idea of a state-centric world becomes not only a part of how they see themselves but also of how they act. So state-centrism becomes practice, and it is a practice most effectively used by those in the best position to maintain the global order "as it is." However, for those individuals and groups more removed from the interests of a hegemonic state-centric set of interests (many of the groups discussed in the case chapters of this book), the identification and politicization of acting in support of, indifferent to, or against the interests of the Canadian state, or more broadly a Canadian state that plays a role in US hegemony, is almost impossible to see at the local level. Those who are engaged in domestic policing services in Canada and who have become the front line in the Canadian version of the war on terror simply might not view it as such – and nor should they. In a practical sense, it simply becomes a part of who they are and what they do. Passing a political judgment on the consequences of their activities, and pondering how their new roles are connected to larger and/or global interests is simply beyond the parameters of what domestic law enforcement agencies are designed to do, or how their members are trained to think. Moreover, if there is any critical self-reflection by many of the groups and institutions studied in this book, the popular consensus would be to try to understand their changing roles and environments within Canada – not as a part of an ever-changing global order.

So, Part 2 of this book emphasizes the Canadian mission in Afghanistan. In Chapter 3, Bruno Charbonneau and Geneviève Parent argue that the de/dislocation of Canada from its close relationship with the United States has helped to form myths about Canadian policies. When Canada is taken as a self-contained territorial unit (seen in most approaches that analyze the Canadian mission), the Canada-as-state-actor can be said to be separate from, and located elsewhere than within the orbit of, American power. The myths of the peacekeeper, of the international good citizen, and of the noble warrior are possible only if disassociated from Canada-US relations. When such relations are brought front and centre, it becomes possible to see the effects of the merging discourses on security and development and of its policy implications. Canadian tales of peace, security, and development merge for the purposes of managing Afghan life. In Chapter 4, Kim Richard Nossal notes that Canadian political leaders openly encouraged Canadians to rethink American assumptions about world politics. A conscious attempt was made to recast the Canadian role in global order based on Canadian values and assumptions. By focusing on how Canadian foreign and security policies were at odds with American understandings and conceptions of global order, Nossal argues that Canada has and can still maintain a specific location within global politics. In Chapter 5, Claire Turenne Sjolander and Kathryn Trevenen examine the ways in which the combat death of Captain Nichola Goddard was represented in the Canadian media. Their analysis suggests how manipulations of gender, the role of women, and nationalist pride can shape and limit the parameters of legitimate public debate. They highlight how the connections made between gender and nation in media representations created and disseminated knowledge that had ontological commitments to specific understandings of gender and nationalism. In short, the chapters of Part 2 focus on and assess how and *where* Canada/Canadians have worked, in the specific case of Afghanistan, to create and reproduce an *American*-led/defined order on the one hand, and to reform or change it according to Canadian values and ideals on the other.

Part 3 includes four chapters that examine both how local and national politics are informed by global politics and how global order is rearticulated and rewritten in various local practices and locations. Gary Kinsman in Chapter 6 and Siobhan Byrne in Chapter 7 consider the extent to which knowledge about Canadian security is committed to the preconceived and intertwined notions of gender, race, and nationality. Such ontological commitments, Kinsman argues, work to exclude and marginalize Canadians that are deemed different, thus identifying them as potential national security threats. His examination of the Canadian national security campaigns against queers, against anti-establishment groups, and against alleged Muslim terrorists underlines how general conceptions of Canadian security and of Canadian identity are intertwined, define each other, and include judgments about gender and race. Kinsman also points to how the exploration of the practical strategies of the marginalized and repressed can suggest other ways of understanding Canadian security and identity. Byrne looks at how the events of 9/11 and the wars in Afghanistan and Iraq have affected Canadian Muslim communities. She shows that the racialized and gendered representations of the war on terror generated insecurity for many Canadian citizens, leaving many vulnerable (especially Muslim women) to racism, machoism, and other acts of intimidation. The post-9/11 global script of Muslim vilification came to Canada, Byrne shows, to question the Canadian identity of Canadian Muslim citizens. In short, both chapters suggest that where you look is increasingly important. Examining Canadian security from the viewpoint of the marginalized and/or minorities, Kinsman and Byrne's case studies indicate the ways in which the local and global connect to write and rewrite, to confirm and reconfirm, and to sanction or challenge a specific understanding of Canadian security *and* identity.

After this focus on the effects and reactions to Canadian security policy, the other two chapters of Part 3 look at Canadian security from the perspective of policy making and governance. These two chapters suggest, albeit from completely different theoretical perspectives and focusing on unique issues, how Canadian "policy" cannot be practiced, devised, or implemented properly and effectively if it relies on a strict local-global distinction. In Chapter 8, Todd Hataley examines the changing roles of federal policing since 9/11 to argue that Canadian security begins with small, local, and on-the-ground police forces. Hataley contends that, although better multi-level coordination between Canadian police agencies and between Canadian police and global police agencies is desirable and necessary, contemporary terrorism requires local resources and frameworks to respond to threats that emerge in local neighbourhoods and settings. Global connections between national police agencies alone cannot promote Canadian security locally. In Chapter 9, Peter Stoett argues that the territorialized logic of Canadian security makes little sense where it is confronted with the transnational nature of the global ecology. The Canadian ecology cannot be protected conventionally from environmental stresses that threaten the Canadian socio-political and economic well-being because, put simply, environmental problems never stop or begin at state borders. The "environment" itself is difficult to locate and differentiate from social and political spaces, but Stoett's shift of focus from "traditional" security issues allows him to emphasize the arbitrary, socially constructed, and changing nature of both state territory and state sovereignty. In short, the four chapters of Part 3 demonstrate that by approaching Canadian security and identity and local-global connections from different analytical locations, Canadian security can be shown to take diverse meanings, to produce varied effects, and to generate new social and political spaces and practices.

Part 4 focuses on Canadian policy in Africa to explore the linkages between Canadian values, claims, and assumptions about global order and how and where the Canadian state conducts itself on the world scene. Challenging conventional accounts of global governance and Canadian foreign policy, in Chapter 10 Timothy Shaw shows how the Canadian multilateral tradition was not only eroded by an increasingly close relationship with the American government but also complicated by the heterogeneous coalitions of state and non-state actors engaged in matters of African development, rights, and security. The emergence of a multitude of actors and the increasing diversity of global coalitions indicate, Shaw argues, that global campaigns are often really networking for human development, rights, and security. As such, these connections and interactions can hardly be located and studied in a specific and delimited local or global setting. In Chapter 11, David Black and Malcolm Savage analyze the case of Canadian extractive industries in Africa. Their analysis suggests that conceptions of local and global overlap with conceptions of private and public, both working politically together to rationalize questionable practices. The examination of the close relationship between the Canadian state and Canadian mining companies in Africa highlights contradictions between discourse and practice of human security in Canadian foreign policy. Black and Savage's chapter suggests that when this relationship is the focus of analysis, Canadian security as promoted abroad takes a very different meaning and purpose. In Chapter 12, Jonathan Sears examines how Canadian security is translated and reworked in Mali and by Malians. Through his analysis of the Malian experience, Sears demonstrates how and where local knowledge and global knowledge are brought together, more specifically, how local knowledge was brought together with the expertise and humanitarianism developed in Canadian foreign policy. This production of knowledge in local-global connections suggests, Sears argues, that effective peace- and stability-building strategies can be formulated only in the space of local-global exchanges. In short, this last group of chapters underlines how conceptions of Canadian security are sustained, challenged, and rewritten in complex and various local-global connections.

All in all, taken together, the chapters in this collection highlight the inherently integrated and inseparable (except perhaps analytically) dynamics of local and global practices of political order.

Location, Politics, Knowledge

The focus on location, on locating global order, and on locating visible and invisible sites of political activity is a double research strategy that comes with significant ontological effects. First, the purposeful examination of location requires that we question and look beyond common abstractions and assumptions about where political activity occurs and where it ought to occur. Rampant state-centrism often reinforces these assumptions about the relationship between politics, authority, control, and their location. That is, conventional discourse and methodology often assume that the state is both the source and the solution to threats of security. However, when one considers the location of political and social action seriously, political activity, security, and authority are often not found where they are supposed to be. The close exploration of the relationship between location and politics challenges the ontological status of many if not all of the core concepts of IR scholarship. Second, revealing the ontological effects through an emphasis on location highlights the actual day-to-day strategies involved in using location, space, territory, and geography for political, social, and economic purposes. Here, state-centrism is shown to have at least two ideological effects. In modern political thought, power, authority, legitimacy, and politics have tended to be associated with and understood as delimited by the territoriality of the state. Intertwined with and inseparable from this first ideological effect, legitimate political, social, and economic practice is also largely understood as tied to the territoriality of the state. No matter one's own political persuasions, these assumptions have limited and restricted the domain of legitimate political activity within the territorial and legal domestic realm of the state. The politics of location, space, and geography are thus associated with territory (see especially Agnew 2009). Arguments that focus on how state authority is undermined, challenged, or transformed by global forces still assume the association of state authority with state territory. State-centric approaches have produced many insights, but they can also obscure or forget the contingencies associated with location, thus implicitly limiting the creation of and thinking about new political spaces. The historically and territorially complex locations of social practices are what articulate their political relevance.

Put another way, *Locating Global Order* is primarily about challenging the assumed certainties of where political activity occurs and ought to be occurring, and about emphasizing the increasing importance of uncertainties about the location of political activity. Historically, state authority has never been complete and has always had competition from other sources of authority. Today, this competition (of a sort) might be even more complex with the advent of international institutions and organizations, NGOs, global social movements, and influential international financial actors. But political activity has never occurred at, nor has political activity ever emanated from, a single location. The lines that draw up the boundaries of the legitimate sites of political activity are where social forces engage politically. The exercise of power involves the drawing of lines of political locations (see R.B.J. Walker 2010). Having said that, the various chapters in this book do not adhere to or promote a particular party line in terms of the legitimacy of the authority derived from claims of territory and sovereignty. What they do is provide case material with an aim to telling the stories of diverse practices in various locations, including those that are not generally deemed to be the purview of the state-as-actor model in the mainstream literature of IR and security studies. We argue that it is only through the telling of the stories, for example, of the experiences of Muslim women in Canada and of the implications of the new role in the war on terror of domestic police and security companies in Canada, or by highlighting how the Canadian traditional internationalist role can become significant in the resolution of conflict in Africa, that we can begin to see that the state and other ontological units have a local basis with local and global consequences. This book, we hope, will open up debate and will sustain discussion across many academic divides over the significance of the relationship between politics and location.

The contributions to this book identify a range of particular sites of dispute: local and global, state and society, public and private, inside and outside, and so on. These locations of dispute sometimes overlap, work together, or reinforce each other. The answers are not particularly obvious either. The point is to insist on the importance of these questions because they suggest that one can hardly make sense of political life by assuming the location of political life – by supposing where and how politics occurs according to state-centric conventions. Putting such questions front and centre challenges the standard clichés of state-centric approaches and disciplines, it opens up a variety of further questions, and it suggests a range of new research agendas. For instance, some chapters highlight issues and locations that are not always thought of in terms of a site of dispute: Sjolander and Trevenen, and Charbonneau and Parent suggest respectively that the representations in the media of Canadian women in combat and the mythology of Canada-as-peacekeeper convey ideas that are generally assumed not to be contested or controversial within mainstream Canadian politics. Both chapters, however, highlight the notions of militarism and of internationalism as part of the ideational fabric that keeps the process of Canadian foreign policy going, and how these notions can be and sometimes are disputed despite claims to the contrary. In short, taken together the chapters of this book suggest that the very subject matter for IR research on issues of global order and Canadian security is often not what and where one would expect it if one were to adhere to only a state-centric conception of politics. To be sure, some of the normative stances of some of these chapters view any form of practice that is dominant or supportive of the current global order as problematic, but this is not true of all the chapters. What they share, however, is a belief that approaching an understanding of global order through an examination of the politics and practices that occur within states, within societies, and within economies and marketplaces (to name but a few) is very much the subject matter of global politics.

A focus on social and political practices is thus very important, in fact crucial, to go beyond misleading abstractions. Abstractions not grounded in practice have often an ideological role, as they can depoliticize and dehumanize certain practices. Many examples can be found in the language of security and war: exceptions, rigorous peace missions, target acquisition, collateral damage, and so on are all conceptions that obscure specific human actions and their human consequences, that render invisible the sovereign power over life and death. The protection and promotion of the national interest, for instance, is almost meaningless to anyone other than state managers and certainly too vague to be of any explicative value for most people in their day-to-day lives. As a discursive practice, however, the reference to the national interest delocalizes, so to speak, the various practices and strategies of power embedded in terms such as "national interest." It is only when, for example, local practices impact on global or national considerations that the mainstream theories of IR attempt to appropriate these consequences into their understanding of world affairs and issues of security. So, for example, the "warlord," "tribal," and illiberal practices and the "civil war" in Afghanistan were relegated to the realm of Afghan domestic politics in the 1990s, that is, until the events of 9/11 made the Taliban regime an impediment to achieving the interests of Western powers that entered that country in 2001 in the name of creating stability and combating global terrorism – and therefore in the name of national and global security. The Taliban quickly became belligerents, thugs, or terrorists. Minority groups inside Canada and the United States have simply been a condition of modern globalized societies for the past one hundred years at least, but like the case of Japanese Canadians and Americans during the Second World War, Muslim and other allegedly radical ethnic communities became an increasing target of suspicion in the aftermath of 9/11. So since 9/11 and the NATO decision to enter Afghanistan and its consequent modifications to what is in the national interest and where the sources of insecurity lie in global politics, we can see that the state-centric discourse of security comes with real consequences not only for those foreign belligerents, thugs, or terrorists but also for anyone who can be associated with them. These associations tend to shatter the conventional logic of thinking of security and insecurity in territorial ways. Thus shattered, conventional thinking of security reveals its ontological commitments to questionable and polarizing ways of understanding race, nation, gender, culture, identity, and so on: if not all Muslims are terrorists, but most terrorists are understood to be Muslim, the logical conclusion of such polarizing conventional security thinking is that Canadian, American, or British citizens who identify themselves as Muslim are all potential terrorists. Moreover, it remains a key role of states to construct a unified national interest as best they can with whatever means they have. In the media, within public debate and discourse, or through representations, the discursive practice of (re)defining the national interest brings the global squarely into the lives of the local, both at home and abroad. Several of the chapters in this book bring this practice to light.

Our interrogations are not only research questions that demand empirical and theoretical explorations. They imply an engagement with questions about the role of academic communities and disciplines, about representations of the intellectual, and about the politics of knowledge production. They imply the self-examination of those (like us) who pretend to know or to be able to produce the answers. Our emphasis on location should not overlook the location of scholarly activity and the location of the production of knowledge: "In practice much knowledge about world politics ... involves the universalizing of what can be called 'doubtful particularisms.' These are interpretative projections from the knowledge experiences of specific places/times onto all places/times ... A great deal of interpretive projection is the result of the imposition of intellectual/political hegemonies from some places onto others" (Agnew 2007, 138). In a world where the production of knowledge comes from innumerable places (governments, universities, think tanks, media networks, private foundations, and so on); where the distinction between scholars, self-proclaimed experts, and popular public opinion figures is often dubious; where the abundance of information available to students of global politics is staggering; and where the connections and interactions between local and long-distance locations are increasing in importance, John Agnew is only one to underline the rising need for scholars to be self-conscious of their theoretical perspectives. The location of knowledge has significant effects on its constitution. According to Agnew, it is time to move beyond the opposition between positivism and relativism, beyond claims to universality or particulars, because all knowledge is located in particular locations and most "universals" are projected from local experiences onto the world at large. As he argues, "knowledge creation and dissemination are never innocent of at least weak ontological commitments, be they national, class, gender, or something else. This is precisely the point of referring to the geography of knowledge: the question of *where* brings together under the rubric of spatial difference a wide range of potential ontological effects" (Agnew 2007, 141-42).

So, in keeping with Agnew's call for scholarship to be reflective of the contexts from which knowledge emerges and how meaning is attached to it, the chapters in this book seek to either consider the consequences of only thinking in conventional theoretical ways or approach an understanding of global order through the lens of local experiences. From Dan O'Meara's revisiting of the origins of militarism in American culture and how this has permeated into the distinctly American view of the US role in global politics to Alex Macleod's overview of the advent of neoconservative state managers in the United States and how this fits into IR theory, through to discussions about the phases of Canadian foreign policy, the Canadian war in Afghanistan, media representations of Canadian women in combat, Canadian practices and self-perceptions of Canadian actions in Africa, and so on, this book could be considered a dog's breakfast from the perspective of traditional IR and Canadian foreign policy. This, we argue, is a very part of the problem that perpetuates global order and academic approaches that are, in many ways, hostile to local expression and local experiences. Global order is simply not suspended in space. It is constructed over time through human practices that are found in, and that produce new spaces of, global and local connections. Conceptually at least, it might be easier to think of global politics as a set of territorial containers, but once you settle on those containers, it proves very difficult to effectively know what is going on inside and among them. As Edward Said (1979, 50) reminds us, "Fields, of course, are made. They require coherence and integrity in time because scholars devote themselves in different ways to what seems to be a commonly agreed-upon subject matter." There seems to be no better example than the field of IR. For the most part, mainstream IR has been a state-centric field of study and, as such, it has not developed the concepts and intellectual tools to capture the interrelationship between the global and the local. To modify the concepts of John Agnew, our containers in IR all have lids, and not many observers have had the skill set necessary to open these lids and look inside. So, in keeping with more recent and critical scholarship (for example, Agnew 2009; Bigo and Tsoukala 2008; Grovogui 2006; Huysmans 2008; Shapiro 2004; R.B.J. Walker 2010), this book is an attempt to include both a reflective look at global order and Canadian politics from the traditional perspective and to step outside disciplinary boundaries so as to include the sort of analysis that one could expect to find in other fields of study. We, as editors at least, do not see this book as a dog's breakfast but, rather, as a starting point for an approach to understanding world politics that includes a diversity of subject matters and theoretical approaches that collectively chip away at the orthodoxy of a "common sense" to capture "the world as it is." From our perspective, a discipline of study in which the primary agents are selected at the exclusion of local and transnational identities, a field whose mainstream aspires to scientific objectivity and in doing so denies the possibility of its own normative preferences, and a field that claims to have a monopoly on truth and rationality is a field of study that denies that much of its scholarly contribution has been a part of that very hegemonic order. Rather than being a field of study that forecloses debate, diversity, and critical scholarship, our effort is a call to provide, through examples, alternatives to the conventional wisdom.

Indeed, while we locate this book within the tradition of IR, our contributors came with their own understanding of what IR is or should be, whether they identified themselves as IR scholars or not. As Didier Bigo and R.B.J. Walker through their project of international political sociology emphasize, academic disciplines, fields of knowledge, and practices of scholarship have participated historically, through the construction of distinctive and enclosed scholarly realms, in substantiating claims about boundaries such as the global-local one explored here. But such divisions are ever more flexible and contested because they express important historical dynamics: "The specific meanings we have learned to give to [the terms 'global' and 'local'] historically express the distinctions that have been made between them, and the distinctions that have been made between them have been crucial for the meanings we have learned to give them" (Bigo and Walker 2007, 2-3). Certainly, by bringing together scholars of various traditions and approaches (IR, development studies, women's studies, sociology, and criminology) to examine and debate global and local orders, this book adds to the fluidity and contestation of academic fields and thus confirms the complexity and importance of questions about the meanings we attach to something that we identify as global order, both as citizens and academics.

Where To? Concluding Thoughts on Relocating Global Order

If we have located global order (albeit rooted in a specific historical context), so what then? Where do we go from here? What does the future hold for global order, especially considering American, Canadian, and Western entanglements in Iraq and Afghanistan, and the 2008-09 global economic crisis? Can American hegemony and power be sustained in the face of military resistance and of (potentially) dramatic changes to American capitalism? What can or will – or should – Canadians do to prevent or encourage such reforms or transformations?

Disciplinary divisions are reflected in the symbolic character of politics and into the myths of Canadian peacekeeping, military history, multilateralism, multiculturalism, federalism, and so on. Such symbols and myths emphasize the unity of Canada and the universalizing character of Canadian principles and values, of being Canadian and living Canadian. At the same time, they obscure the fragmentation, inequalities, divisions, and disagreements over the very meaning of knowing what it is to be Canadian. This has particular significance for Canadian politics, notably for relations among provinces, regions, and Aboriginal, anglophone, francophone, and other communities.

Normative judgments and claims about the meaning of Canada; about being Canadian; about Canadian democracy, security, and liberty; about living with fellow human beings at home or abroad are difficult questions that are impossible to understand with abstractions alone. Such questions and matters of judgment raise serious challenges to established conceptions of human community and philosophical assumptions about political possibilities. It is far from clear on what grounds alternatives can be put forward or judged, but explorations for such alternatives seem clearly needed and even urgent. This book is merely one way to (re)present an understanding of global politics and the role and place of Canadian politics within it. To hope for fully formed alternatives is likely utopian or wishful thinking, but here lies the challenge in the exploration for such alternatives, in exploring, "to begin with, new understandings of where political life is supposed to occur, particularly in relation to the modern state" (R.B.J. Walker 1988, 82). Given the already well-trodden nature of the state-centric understandings of global politics, and what seems to us to be explicit normative links between that type of scholarship and state interests, we felt that an approach that gives primacy to neither state nor society, global nor local, would be a good place to start. As editors, we are not interested in altering the various understandings of global politics that comes with the individual chapters in this book, though the responsibility for how those chapters were selected and presented lies squarely with us. What we are interested in is opening up the debate and sustaining discussions that go beyond *and* engage with the established orthodox parameters of dominant or hegemonic scholarship.

In final conclusion, it must be said that although all of the chapters in this book are intended to be taken as subparts of a larger discourse on global order and the role that Canadian politics play within it, it should also be clear that there is no single party line here. Just as the interpretation of global order is a highly contestable thing, the ways in which various scholars participate, here and elsewhere, in the construction and in the legitimization of that order has depended on various factors, such as the overall role that a field of study plays, its ability to reflect on its origins and meanings, and how a scholar defines oneself and one's research. So although this book contains purposely selected chapters that address many key subject matters and themes, it also has chapters that further reflect the diversity of interpretations that too are a key part of our collective understanding of global order. In this sense, the intent is to produce a collection in which the overall volume is greater than the sum of its parts.

References

Abramovitz, J. 1996. Imperilled waters, impoverished future: The decline of freshwater ecosystems. Worldwatch Paper 128, Washington, DC.

Abu-Laban, Y. 2002. Liberalism, multiculturalism and the problem of essentialism. *Citizenship Studies* 6(4): 459-82.

Ackerly, B.A., M. Stern, and J. True, eds. 2006. *Feminist methodologies for international relations.* Cambridge: Cambridge University Press.

Adams, M.L. 1997. *The trouble with normal: Post war youth and the construction of heterosexuality.* Toronto: University of Toronto Press.

Adas, M. 2005. Improving on the civilizing mission? Assumptions of United States exceptionalism in the colonization of the Philippines. In Gardner and Young, 2005, 151-81.

Adger, W.N., J. Paavola, S. Huq, and M.J. Mace. 2006. *Fairness in adaptation to climate change.* Cambridge, MA: MIT Press.

Adriamirado, S., and V. Adriamirado. 2001. *Le Mali aujourd'hui.* Paris: Editions J.A.

Advisory Group Report. 2007. *National roundtables on corporate social responsibility (CSR) and the Canadian extractive industry in developing countries.* Ottawa: Department of Foreign Affairs and International Trade.

Afghanistan Compact. 2006. http://www.nato.int/isaf/docu/epub/pdf/Afghanistan_compact.pdf.

Agamben, Giorgio. 1998. *Homo sacer: Sovereign power and bare life.* Stanford, CA: Stanford University Press.

–. 2005. *State of exception.* Chicago: University of Chicago Press.

Agathangelou, A.M., and L.H.M. Ling. 2004. Power, borders, security, wealth: Lessons of violence and desire from September 11. *International Studies Quarterly* 48(3): 517-38.

Agnew, J. 2005. *Hegemony: The new shape of global power.* Philadelphia: Temple University Press.
—. 2007. Know-where: Geographies of knowledge in world politics. *International Political Sociology* 1(2): 138-48.
—. 2009. *Globalization and sovereignty.* Lanham, MD: Rowman and Littlefield.
Agnew, J., and S. Corbridge. 1995. *Mastering space: Hegemony, territory and international political economy.* London: Routledge.
Ahmed-Ghosh, H. 2006. Voices of Afghan women. *International Feminist Journal of Politics* 8(1): 110-28.
AIHRC [Afghanistan Independent Human Rights Commission]. 2007. *A call for justice: A national consultation on past human rights violations in Afghanistan.* http://www.aihrc.org.af/Rep_29_Eng/rep29_1_05call4justice.pdf.
—. 2008. *Evaluation report on general situation of women in Afghanistan.* http://www.aihrc.org.af/rep_eng_wom_situation_8_march.htm.
Alsultany, E. 2007. Selling American diversity and Muslim American identity through nonprofit advertising post-9/11. *American Quarterly* 59(3): 593-622.
Amevor, S. 2007. Ghana: Mining has not helped alleviate poverty. *Public Agenda (Accra),* 9 April.
Amnesty International. 2006. Canada: Security certificates – Time for reform. http://www.amnesty.ca/take_action/actions/canada_certificates.php.
—. 2007. *Amnesty International report 2007: The state of the world's human rights.* London, UK: Alden Press.
Amselle, J.-L. 1992. La corruption et le clientélisme au Mali et en Europe de l'est: Quelques points de comparaison. *Cahiers d'Études africaines* 32(4): 629-42.
Anderson, B. 1991. *Imagined communities: Reflections on the origin and spread of nationalism.* London: Verso.
Anderson, F., and A. Cayton. 2005. *The dominion of war: Empire and liberty in North America, 1500-2000.* New York: Penguin.
Andreas, P. 2000. *Border games: Policing the U.S.-Mexico divide.* Ithaca, NY: Cornell University Press.
Andreas, P., and E. Nadelmann. 2006. *Policing the globe: Criminalization and crime control in international relations.* New York: Oxford University Press.
Andreas, P., and R. Price. 2001. From war fighting to crime fighting: Transforming the American national security state. *International Studies Review* 3(3): 31-52.
Angus Reid Global Monitor. 2006. Canadians divided over Afghanistan mission. 17 April. http://www.angus-reid.com.
Angus Reid Strategies. 2007. Canada in Afghanistan: Canadians grow impatient. (National public opinion poll.) http://www.angusreidstrategies.com.
—. 2008. Canadians still oppose Afghan mission extension; Reject talks with Taliban. (National public opinion poll.) http://www.angus-reid.com.
Arar, M. 2006. A personal account. http://auto_sol.tao.ca/node.
Arrighi, G. 1993. The three hegemonies of historical capitalism. In *Gramsci, historical materialism and international relations,* ed. S. Gill, 148-85. Cambridge: Cambridge University Press.

Arrighi, G., and B.J. Silver. 1999. *Chaos and governance in the modern world system.* Minneapolis: University of Minnesota Press.

Ascher, W. 2005. The "resource curse." In Bastida, Walde, and Warden-Fernandez, 2005, 569-88.

Ashley, R. 1988. Untying the sovereign state: A double reading of the anarchy problematique. *Millennium* 17(2): 227-62.

Asia Foundation. 2006. *Afghanistan in 2006: A survey of the Afghan people.* Kabul: Asia Foundation. http://asiafoundation.org/pdf/AG-survey06.pdf.

Axworthy, L. 1992-93. Canadian foreign policy: A Liberal Party perspective. *Canadian Foreign Policy* 1(1): 7-15.

–. 1997. Canada and human security: The need for leadership. *International Journal* 52(2): 183-96.

–. 1999. Civilians in war: 100 years after the Hague Peace Conference. Department of Foreign Affairs and International Trade, *Statements and Speeches,* 99/48, New York, 24 September 1999.

–. 2003. *Navigating a new world: Canada's global future.* Toronto: Random House.

Azarbaijani-Moghaddam, S. 2007. On living with negative peace and a half-built state: Gender and human rights. *International Peacekeeping* 14(1): 127-42.

Bacevich, A.J. 2002. *American empire: The realities and consequences of US diplomacy.* Cambridge, MA: Harvard University Press.

–. 2005. *The new American militarism: How Americans are seduced by war.* New York: Oxford University Press.

Bagayogo, S. 1999. *Le cheminement du Mali vers un espace politique pluriel.* Bamako: Association Djoliba and Konrad Adenauer Foundation.

Bailleuil, C. 1996. *Dictionnaire Français-Bambara.* Bamako: Editions Donniya.

Baird, J. 2009. Corporate social responsibility and Canada's mineral exploration sector: Doing the right thing where we work. Speech to the Economic Club of Canada, 23 June.

Ball, N. 2005. Strengthening democratic governance of the security sector in conflict-affected countries. *Public Administration and Development* 25(1): 25-38.

Bannerji, H. 1995. *Thinking through: Essays on feminism, Marxism, and anti-racism.* Toronto: Women's Press.

–. 2000. *The dark side of the nation: Essays on multiculturalism, nationalism and gender.* Toronto: Canadian Scholar's Press.

Barakat, S., and G. Wardell. 2002. Exploited by whom? An alternative perspective on humanitarian assistance to Afghan women. *Third World Quarterly* 23(5): 909-30.

Baranyi, S. 2008. Introduction: What kind of peace is possible in the post-9/11 era? In *The paradoxes of peacebuilding post-9/11,* ed. S. Baranyi, 3-31. Vancouver: UBC Press.

Barkin, J.S. 2003. Realist constructivism. *International Studies Review* 5(3): 325-42.

Barnett, T.P.M. 2004. The Pentagon's new map: Interview with Brian Lamb. http://www.thomaspmbarnett.com.

Bastida, E., T. Walde, and J. Warden-Fernandez, eds. 2005. *International and comparative mineral law policy: Trends and prospects.* The Hague: Kluwer Law International.

BBC News Online. 2001. Cherie Blair attacks Taleban "cruelty." 19 November. http://news.bbc.co.uk.
–. 2006. "Tuareg rebels" leave Mali towns. 24 May. http://news.bbc.co.uk.
Beaupré, F. 2006. Eulogy for Nichola Goddard. Posted on eVeritas: The Newsletter of the RMC Club of Canada, no. 017 (2006). http://www.rmcclub.ca/eVeritas.
Beck, U. 1992. *The risk society: Towards a new modernity*. London: Sage.
Beisner, B.E., A.R. Ives, and S.R. Carpenter. 2003. The effects of an exotic fish invasion on the prey communities of two lakes. *Journal of Animal Ecology* 72(2): 331-41.
Bell, D. 1976. The end of American exceptionalism. In *The American commonwealth 1976*, ed. N. Glazer and I. Kristol, 193-224. New York: Basic Books.
Bell, S. 2007a. Internet plays role in "female jihadists": Report. *National Post*, 9 November.
–. 2007b. Somali drug may fund terrorism. *National Post*, 20 December.
Bellamy, A.J., and P.D. Williams. 2009. The West and contemporary peace operations. *Journal of Peace Research* 46(1): 39-57.
Bennetto, J. 2004. Scotland Yard chief reveals London link to Madrid bombing. *The Independent*, 19 March. http://www.independent.co.uk.
Benoist, J.-R. 1998. *Le Mali*. Paris: L'Harmattan.
Bercuson, D. 1996. *Significant incident: Canada's army, the airborne, and the murder in Somalia*. Toronto: McClelland and Stewart.
Berenyi, V. 2006. Capt. Nichola Goddard: A Remembrance Day tribute (Part 2 of 2); Series, Letters home. *Calgary Herald*, 11 November.
Bergen, P., and P. Cruickshank. 2007. The new face of terrorism: Women, no longer content with supporting roles, are increasingly joining the ranks of Islamic suicide bombers. *Montreal Gazette*, 19 August.
Berman, B. 2004. A "palimpsest of contradictions": Ethnicity, class and politics in Africa. *International Journal of African Historical Studies* 37(1): 13-31.
Berns-McGown, R. 2007-08. Redefining diaspora. *International Journal* 63(1): 3-20.
Betts, R.K. 2007. Not with *my* Thucydides, you don't. *American Interest* 87: 140-43.
BICC [Bonn International Center for Conversion]. 2006. *Who's minding the store? The business of private, public, and civil actors in zones of conflict*. BICC Brief 32.
Bigo, D., and A. Tsoukala. 2008. *Terror, insecurity and liberty: Illiberal practices of liberal regimes after 9/11*. London: Routledge.
Bigo, D., and R.B.J. Walker. 2007. International, political, sociology. *International Political Sociology* 1(1): 1-5.
Black, D. 2001. Human rights in foreign policy: Lessons for South Africa from Canadian experience? *International Journal of Human Rights* 5(1): 37-57.
–. 2006. Mapping the interplay of human security practice and debates: The Canadian experience. In MacLean, Black, and Shaw, 2006, 53-62.
–. 2007. Leader or laggard? Canada's enduring engagement with Africa. In *Readings in Canadian foreign policy*, ed. D. Bratt and C. Kukucha, 379-94. Don Mills, ON: Oxford University Press.
–. 2009. Out of Africa? The Harper government's new "tilt" in the developing world. *Canadian Foreign Policy* 15(2): 41-56.

Black, D., and C.T. Sjolander. 1996. Multilateralism reconstituted and the discourse of Canadian foreign policy. *Studies in Political Economy* 49 (Spring): 7-36.

Blackwood, E. 2006. Human security and corporate governance: A critical assessment of Canada's human security agenda. In MacLean, Black, and Shaw, 2006, 85-99.

Blanchfield, M. 2007a. PM shines light on "Canada at its best": Harper touts rebuilding of Afghanistan. *Calgary Herald,* 23 May.

–. 2007b. Top general calls Liberal rule "decade of darkness." *Calgary Herald,* 17 February.

Bland, D.L., ed. 2003. *Canada without armed forces?* Claxton Papers 4. Kingston, ON: School of Policy Studies, Queen's University.

Blatchford, C. 2006a. Daughter of Canada swaddled in the flag for her last journey. *Globe and Mail,* 27 May.

–. 2006b. Voice of pride and respect falls silent. *Globe and Mail,* 18 May.

–. 2007. *Fifteen days: Stories of bravery, friendship, life and death from inside the new Canadian army.* Toronto: Doubleday.

Boardman, R., and K. Beazely, eds. 2002. *Politics of the wild.* Oxford: Oxford University Press.

Böge, V., W.J. Fitzpatrick, and W.C. Paes. 2006. *Who's minding the store? The business of private, public and civil actors in zones of conflict.* Bonn: Bonn International Center for Conversion Brief no. 32.

Boggs, C. 2002. Globalization and the new militarism. *New Political Science* 24(1): 9-20.

–. 2005. *Imperial delusions: American militarism and endless war.* Lanham, MD: Rowland and Littlefield.

Bologh, R. 1979. *Dialectical phenomenology, Marx's method.* London: Routledge.

Bond, P. 2006. Resource extraction and African underdevelopment. *Capitalism Nature Socialism* 17(2): 5-25.

Bonnell, G. 2007. One in five people foreign-born stats reveal as Canada struggles with overt racism. *Canada Press NewsWire,* 4 December.

Boot, M. 2003. The new American way of war. *Foreign Affairs* 82(4): 41-58.

–. 2004. Think again: Neocons. *Foreign Policy* 140: 22-28.

Bose, A., and M.B. Johnson. 2005. *Report to the Special Senate Committee on the Anti-terrorism Act.* http://www.noivmwc.org.

Bosold, D., and W. von Bredow. 2006. Human security: A radical or rhetorical shift in Canada's foreign policy? *International Journal* 61(4): 829-44.

Bouchard, G., and C. Taylor. 2008. *Building the future: A time for reconciliation.* Report of the Consultation Commission on Accommodation Practices Related to Cultural Differences. Bibliothèque et Archives nationales du Québec, Gouvernement du Québec.

Boucher, J.-C. 2010. Evaluating the "Trenton effect": Canadian public opinion and military casualties in Afghanistan (2006-2009). *American Review of Canadian Studies* 40(2): 237-58.

Boucher, J-C., and S. Roussel. 2008. From Afghanistan to "Quebecistan": Quebec as the pharmakon of Canadian foreign and defence policy. In *Canada among nations 2008: What room for manoeuvre?* ed. J. Daudelin and D. Schwanen, 128-56. Montreal and Kingston, ON: McGill-Queen's University Press.

Bowman, G.W. 2007-08. Thinking outside the border: Homeland security and the forward deployment of the U.S. border. *Houston Law Review* 44(2): 189-251.

Brenner, W.J. 2006. In search of monsters: Realism and progress in international relations theory after September 11. *Security Studies* 15(3): 496-528.

Bretton Woods Project. 2003. *Poverty reduction strategy papers: A rough guide.* www.brettonwoodsproject.org.

Brewster, M. 2006. Canadian woman killed in combat. *Winnipeg Free Press,* 18 May.

–. 2008. Canadians still view troops as peacekeepers, leaked DND poll. *Maclean's,* 5 September.

Bright, C. 1998. *Life out of bounds: Bioinvasion in a borderless world.* New York: Norton.

Brison, S. 2006. Why I voted to support our Afghan mission. (Letter,) *National Post,* 20 May.

Brock, D., ed. 2003. *Making normal: Social regulation in Canada.* Toronto: Nelson.

Brooks, S.G., and W.C. Wohlforth. 2002. American primacy in perspective. *Foreign Affairs* 81(4): 20-33.

–. 2005. International relations theory and the case against unilateralism. *Perspectives on Politics* 3(3): 509-25.

–. 2008. *World out of balance: International relations and the challenge of American primacy.* Princeton and Oxford: Princeton University Press.

Brown, D. 2001. Finally, the media's noticed the feminist war against Western society. *Ottawa Citizen,* 6 October.

Brown, W. 2006. Africa and international relations: A comment on IR theory, anarchy and statehood. *Review of International Studies* 32(1): 119-43.

Burdon, R. 2003. *The suffering gene: Environmental threats to our health.* London: Zed Books.

Burgess, J.P., and T. Owen, eds. 2004. Special section: What is "human security"? *Security Dialogue* 35(3): 345-87.

Burns, W., ed. 2006. Special issue on the Precautionary Principle and its operationalisation in international environmental regimes and domestic policymaking. *International Journal of Global Environmental Issues* 5(1-2).

Buruma, I. 2008. After America: Is the West being overtaken by the rest? *New Yorker* 84(10): 126-30.

Bush, G.W. 2002a. *The national security strategy of the United States of America.* Washington, DC: White House.

–. 2002b. The president's remarks to the nation, 11 September 2002. News release. http://www.whitehouse.gov.

Buzan, B. 1991. *People, states, and fear: An agenda for international security studies in the post-Cold War era.* 2nd ed. Boulder, CO: Westview Press.

Buzan, B., O. Waever, and J. de Wilde. 1998. *Security: A new framework for analysis.* Boulder, CO: Lynne Rienner.

CACNP [Center for Arms Control and Non-Proliferation]. 2008. 2008-2009 U.S. Defense spending highest since WWII, tops Vietnam and Korea. 20 February. http://www.armscontrolcenter.org.

Calgary Herald. 2006. Our resolve honours soldier. 19 May.

Calleo, D.P. 1987. *Beyond American hegemony: The future of the Western Alliance*. New York: Basic Books.

Campbell, B. 1999. *Canadian mining interests and human rights in Africa in the context of globalization*. International Centre for Human Rights and Democratic Development. www.ichrdd.ca/english.

–. 2003. Factoring in governance is not enough: Mining codes in Africa, policy reform and corporate responsibility. *Minerals and Energy* 18(1): 2-13.

–. 2005. Memorandum presented to the Standing Senate Committee on Foreign Affairs. 19 April.

–. 2006. Good governance, security and mining in Africa. *Minerals and Energy* 21(1): 31-44.

Campbell, D. 1998. *Writing security: United States foreign policy and the politics of identity*. Rev. ed. Minneapolis: University of Minnesota Press.

Campbell, M., and F. Gregor. 2002. *Mapping social relations*. Toronto: Garamond.

Canada. 2008. *Canada's engagement in Afghanistan: Setting a course to 2011*. June report to Parliament, Ottawa.

Canada. Department of Justice. 1984. *Canadian Security Intelligence Service Act*. http://laws.justice.gc.ca/en.

–. 2008. *Criminal Code*. http://laws.justice.gc.ca/en/C-46.

Canada. Department of Public Safety. 2005. Implementation of the *Public Safety Act, 2002*. http://www.publicsafety.gc.ca/.

Canada. DFAIT [Department of Foreign Affairs and International Trade]. 1999. *Human security: Safety for people in a changing world*. http://www.summit-americas.org.

–. 2002. *Freedom from fear: Canada's foreign policy for human security*. http://geo.international.gc.ca.

–. 2003. *A dialogue on foreign policy*. 22 January. http://www.foreign-policy-dialogue.ca.

–. 2005. *A role of pride and influence in the world: Canada's International Policy Statement*. http://www.international.gc.ca/cip-pic/documents/IPS-EPI/overview-survol.aspx?lang=eng.

–. 2009. *Building the Canadian advantage: A corporate social responsibility (CSR) strategy for the Canadian international extractive sector*. http://www.international.gc.ca.

Canada. DND [Department of National Defence]. 2005. *International Policy Statement: Defence*. Ottawa: Department of National Defence.

Canada. House of Commons. 2007. *Edited Hansard*. 39th Parl., 1st sess., number 141. 26 April.

Canada. OPBO [Office of the Parliamentary Budget Officer, Library of Parliament]. 2008. *Fiscal impact of the Canadian mission in Afghanistan*. Ottawa: OPBO.

Canada. Privy Council Office. 2004. *Securing an open society: Canada's national security policy*. http://www.pco.gc.ca.

Canada. SCFAIT [Standing Committee on Foreign Affairs and International Trade]. 2005. *Fourteenth report: Mining in developing countries – Corporate social responsibility*, 38th Parl., 1st sess., Ottawa, June.

Canada. Senate. 2005. Proceedings of the Special Senate Committee on the Anti-terrorism Act. Issue 16. Special Senate Committee on Anti-terrorism. Ottawa: Parliament of Canada. http://www.parl.gc.ca.

–. 2008a. *How are we doing in Afghanistan? Canadians need to know.* Standing Senate Committee on National Security and Defence. 39th Parl., 2nd sess., Ottawa, June. http://www.parl.gc.ca.

–. 2008b. Proceedings of the Special Senate Committee on the Anti-terrorism Act. Issue 2. Special Senate Committee on Anti-terrorism. Ottawa: Parliament of Canada. http://www.parl.gc.ca.

Canadian Bar Association. 2001. *Submission on Bill C-36: Anti-Terrorism Act.* Ottawa: Canadian Bar Association.

Canadian Chamber of Commerce. 2007. *Response to the federal government on the advisory group report of the national roundtables on CSR and the Canadian extractive industry in developing countries.* 26 July.

Canadian Federation of Students. 2007. *Final report of the task force on the needs of Muslim students.* Toronto.

Canadian Peace Alliance. 2008. Peace groups in Canada. http://www.acp-cpa.ca.

Cardozo, B.L., O.O. Bilukha, C.A. Gotway, M.L. Wolfe, M.L. Gerber, and M. Anderson. 2005. Report from the CDC: Mental Health of Women in Postwar Afghanistan. *Journal of Women's Health* 14(4): 285-93.

Carpenter, C.R. 2005. Women, children and other vulnerable groups: Gender, strategic frames and the protection of civilians as a transnational issue. *International Studies Quarterly* 49(2): 295-334.

Carr, E.H. 1939/2001. *The twenty years' crisis 1919-1939: An introduction to the study of international relations.* New York: Palgrave.

Carroll, J. 2006. *House of war: The Pentagon and the disastrous rise of American power.* Boston: Houghton Mifflin.

Carter, A.B., and W.J. Perry. 1999. *Preventive defense: A new security strategy for America.* Washington, DC: Brookings Institution Press.

Cashore, B., G. Auld, and D. Newsom. 2004. *Governing through markets: The forest certification and the emergence of non-state authority.* New Haven, CT: Yale University Press.

CBC News. 2003. Agency uncovers $22 million of suspected terrorist funds. http://www.cbc.ca.

–. 2005a. Britain's MI5 decided London bomber posed no threat: Report. 17 July. http://www.cbc.ca.

–. 2005b. Tamil Tigers illegally fundraising in Toronto: Community member. 30 November. http://www.cbc.ca.

–. 2006a. Canadian woman 16th soldier killed in Afghanistan. 17 May. http://www.cbc.ca.

–. 2006b. Canadians tried to buy missiles for Tamil Tigers: US. 22 August. http://www.cbc.ca.

–. 2006c. Layton slams Harper as Bush's "cheerleader." 10 September. http://www.cbc.ca.

–. 2007. MPs defeat motion to pull troops from Afghanistan by 2009. 24 April. http://www.cbc.ca.

–. 2008. Canada's Afghan mission could cost up to $18.1B. 9 October. http://www.cbc.ca.

CCA [Canadian Council on Africa]. 2007. *Canada's commercial strategy for sub-saharan Africa: Consultation document.* Version 3.0, presented at Fredericton Roundtable, 16 March.

Ceasefire.ca. 2008. Video archived at http://www.ceasefire.ca/?cat=45&paged=3.

Cebrowski, Adm. A.K., and T.P.M. Barnett. 2003. The American way of war. *Transformation trends,* January, 42-43. http://www.oft.osd.mil.

Cerny, P. 1997. Paradoxes of the competition state: The dynamics of political globalization. *Government and Opposition* 32(2): 251-74.

Chabal, P., and J.-P. Daloz. 1999. *Africa works: Disorder as political instrument.* Oxford: James Currey.

Chandler, D. 2006. *Empire in denial: The politics of state-building.* Ann Arbor, MI: Pluto Press.

Chang, J. 2001. *Resist! A grassroots collection of stories, poetry, photos, and analyses from Quebec City FTAA protests and beyond.* Halifax: Fernwood.

Charbonneau, B. 2010. The security-development nexus: Reflections on international interventions and the purpose of force. Paper presented at International Studies Association's annual convention, New Orleans, USA, 17 February.

Charbonneau, B., and W.S. Cox. 2008. Global order, US hegemony and military integration: The Canadian-American defence relationship. *International Political Sociology* 2(4): 305-21.

Charlesworth, H., and C. Chinkin. 2002. Editorial comment: Sex, gender and September 11. *American Journal of International Law* 96(3): 600-5.

Checkel, J.T. 1998. The constructivist turn in international relations theory. *World Politics* 50(2): 324-48.

Cheung-Gertler, J.H. 2007. A model power for a troubled world? *International Journal* 62(3): 589-607.

Chomsky, N. 1999. *The new military humanism: Lessons from Kosovo.* Monroe, ME: Common Courage Press.

Christoff, S. 2007. Spies at work: CSIS questioning of Canadian Muslims threatens their jobs. *Montreal Mirror,* 16 April.

Chyba, C., and A. Greninger. 2004. Biotechnology and bioterrorism: An unprecedented world. *Survival* 46(2): 143-61.

CIDA [Canadian International Development Agency]. 2009a. A new effective approach to Canadian aid. Speaking notes for the Hon. Beverley J. Oda, Minister of International Cooperation, at the Munk Centre for International Studies. 20 May. http://www.acdi-cida.gc.ca/.

–. 2009b. Speaking notes for the Hon. Beverley J. Oda, Minister of International Cooperation, for a meeting with African ambassadors to Canada. 26 October. http://www.acdi-cida.gc.ca/.

Clark, R.P. 1997. Global life systems: Biological dimensions of globalisation. *Global Society* 11(3): 531-49.

Clarke, R.A. 2004. *Against all enemies: Inside America's war on terror*. Toronto: The Free Press.
Clarke, R.V., and G.R. Newman. 2007. Police and the prevention of terrorism. *Policing* 1(1): 9-20.
Cleaver, H. 2000. *Reading capital*. San Francisco: AK Press/AntiTheses.
CNCA [Canadian Network on Corporate Accountability]. 2007. *An important step forward: The final report of the national roundtables on corporate social responsibility and the Canadian industry in developing countries*. 30 March.
–. 2009. News release: Government squanders opportunity to hold extractive companies to account. 26 March.
Cohen, Andrew. 2003. *While Canada slept: How we lost our place in the world*. Toronto: McClelland and Stewart.
Colapinto, R. 2004. The clean-up ACT. *CA Magazine* 137(4): 20-27.
Colautti, R., and H. MacIsaac. 2004. A neutral terminology to define "invasive" species. *Diversity and Distributions* 10(2): 135-41.
Coll, S. 2008. Comment: Military conflict. *New Yorker* 84(9): 21-22.
Collier, R. 1974. *The plague of the Spanish lady*. New York: Allison and Busby.
Collings, H.T. 1924. The relation of the automobile industry to international problems of oil and rubber. *Annals of the American Academy of Political and Social Science* 116 (November): 254-58.
Collins, J., and R. Glover, eds. 2002. *Collateral language: A user's guide to America's new war*. New York: New York University Press.
Commission for Africa. 2005. *Our common interest: Report of the Commission for Africa*. London.
Commonwealth. 2003. *Making democracy work for pro-poor development: Report by a Commonwealth group of experts*. London: Singh Report.
–. 2007. Civil paths to peace: Report of the Commonwealth Commission on Respect and Understanding. London: Sen Report.
Conflict, Security and Development. 2004. *Special Issue on Security and Development* 4(3): 219-562.
Cooper, A.F. 2008. *Celebrity diplomacy*. Boulder, CO: Paradigm.
Cooper, A.F., and A. Antkiewicz, eds. 2008. *Emerging powers in global governance: Lessons from the Heiligendamm Process*. Waterloo, ON: WLU Press for CIGI.
Copeland, D. 2005. New rabbits, old hats: International policy and Canada's foreign service in an era of diminished resources. *International Journal* 60(3): 743-62.
Corrigan, P. 1981. On moral regulation. *Sociological Review* 29(2): 313-37.
–. 1990. *Social forms/human capacities*. London: Routledge.
Corrigan, P., and D. Sayer. 1985. *The great arch: English state formation as cultural revolution*. Oxford: Basil Blackwell.
Costigliola, F., and T.G. Paterson. 2004. Doing and defining the history of United States foreign relations: A primer. In *Explaining the history of American foreign relations*, 2nd ed., ed. M.J. Hogan and T.G. Paterson, 10-34. New York: Cambridge University Press.

Coulibaly, C., and M. Diarra. 2004. Démocratie et légitimation du marché: Rapport d'enquête Afrobaromètre au Mali – Décembre 2002. *Afrobarometer Working Paper* 35 (December). http://www.afrobarometer.org.

Cox, G. 1999. *Alien species in North America and Hawaii: Impacts on national ecosystems*. Washington, DC: Island Press.

Cox, R.W. 1981. Social forces, states and world orders: Beyond international relations theory. *Millennium* 10(2): 126-55.

–. 2005. A Canadian dilemma: The United States or the world. *International Journal* 60(3): 667-84.

Cox, W.S., and C.T. Sjolander. 1998. Damage control: The politics of national defence. In *How Ottawa spends, 1998-99,* ed. L. Pal, 217-42. Don Mills, ON: Oxford University Press.

CPCC [Canadian Peacebuilding Coordinating Committee]. 2003. *Peacebuilding challenges in the new millennium*. Ottawa, ON: CPCC Secretariat. www.peacebuild.ca.

CPHD [Center for Policy and Human Development with UNDP]. 2007. *Afghanistan human development report 2007*. Islamabad: Army Press. http://www.cphd.af/nhdr.

Crawford, S. 2001. *Salmonine introductions to the Laurentian Great Lakes: An historical review and evaluation of ecological effects*. Ottawa: NRC Press.

Crosby, A. 1986. *Ecological imperialism: The biological expansion of Europe*. Cambridge: Cambridge University Press.

Crosby, A.D. 2003. Myths of Canada's human security pursuits: Tales of tool boxes, toy chests, and tickle trunks. In Sjolander, Smith, and Stienstra, 2003, 90-107.

Crowson, P. 2005. Old wine in new bottles: Policy issues for the mining industry. In Bastida, Walde, and Warden-Fernandez, 2005, 607-20.

CTV News. 2007. GG presents first military valour declarations. 19 February. http://www.ctv.ca.

Dalby, S. 2006. Environmental security: Ecology or international relations? In Laferrière and Stoett, 2006, 17-33.

Daniels, R.J., P. Macklem, and K. Roach, eds. 2001. *The security of freedom: Essays on Canada's anti-terrorism bill*. Toronto: University of Toronto Press.

Darier, E., ed. 1999. *Discourses of the environment*. Malden, MA: Blackwell.

Darimani, A. 2005. Impacts of activities of Canadian mining companies in Africa. Background document prepared for Mining Watch Canada roundtable on "Regulating Canadian Mining Companies Operating Internationally," 20 October. http://www.miningwatch.ca/.

Dashwood, H. 2005. Canadian mining companies and the shaping of global norms of corporate social responsibility. *International Journal* 60(4): 977-98.

–. 2007. Canadian mining companies and corporate social responsibility: Weighing the impact of global norms. *Canadian Journal of Political Science* 40(1): 129-56.

Dauvergne, M., K. Scrim, and S. Brennan. 2008. Hate crime in Canada: 2006. Ottawa: Statistics Canada, Canadian Centre for Justice Statistics. http://www.statcan.ca.

David, C.-P., and J.-F. Gagné, eds. 2006-07. Natural resources and conflict. *International Journal* 62(1): 1-119.

Day, R. 2005. *Gramsci is dead: Anarchist currents in the newest social movements.* Toronto: Pluto Press/Between the Lines.

—. 2008. The Man with the hissing bomb: Anarchism and terrorism in the North American imagination. Paper presented at the Human Conditions Series Terror Conference, Georgian College, Laurentian University, Barrie, ON, 3 May.

D'Costa, B. 2006. Marginalized identity: New frontiers of research for IR? In Ackerly, Stern, and True, 2006, 129-52.

DDI [Diamond Development Initiative]. 2005. *Conference report: Report on the proceedings of the DDI conference.* Ottawa: Partnership Africa Canada for Diamond Development Initiative.

de Lint, W. 2006. Intelligence in policing and security: Reflections on scholarship. *Policing and Society* 16(1): 1-6.

Deflem, M. 2006. Europol and the policing of international terrorism: Counterterrorism in a global perspective. *Justice Quarterly* 23(3): 336-59.

Degnbol-Martinussen, J., and P. Engberg-Pedersen. 2003. *Aid: Understanding international development cooperation.* London: Zed Books.

Demante, M.-J. 2005. Crise, développement local et décentralisation dans la région de Gao (Mali). *Afrique contemporaine* 215(3): 195-217.

D'Emilio, J. 1983. Capitalism and gay identity. In *Powers of desire: The politics of sexuality,* ed. A. Snitow, C. Stansell, and S. Thompson, 100-13. New York: Routledge.

Devault, M. 1999. Institutional ethnography: A strategy for feminist inquiry. In *Liberating method, feminism and social research,* ed. M. Devault, 46-54. Philadelphia: Temple University Press.

Development Assistance Committee Network on Conflict, Peace and Development Co-operation. 2004. *A survey of security system reform and donor policy views from non-OECD countries.* Paris: Organisation for Economic Co-operation and Development Development Assistance Committee. http://unpan1.un.org/.

Di Boscio, N., and D. Humphreys. 2005. Mining and regional economic development. In Bastida, Walde, and Warden-Fernandez, 2005, 589-606.

Diène, D. 2003. Racism, racial discrimination, xenophobia and all forms of discrimination: Situation of Muslim and Arab peoples in various parts of the world in the aftermath of the events of 11 September 2001. Economic and Social Council, Commission on Human Rights. E/CN.4/2003/23. http://www.un.org/en/ecosoc/.

DiMento, J. 2003. *The global environment and international law.* Austin: University of Texas Press.

Dishman, C. 2005. The leaderless nexus: When crime and terror converge. *Studies in Conflict and Terrorism* 28(3): 237-52.

Dobson, A. 2003. *Citizenship and the environment.* Oxford: Oxford University Press.

Dolan, C.J. 2005. United States' narco-terrorism policy: A contingency approach to the convergence of the wars on drugs and against terrorism. *Review of Public Policy* 22(4): 451-71.

Donini, A. 2007. Local perceptions of assistance to Afghanistan. *International Peacekeeping* 14(1): 158-72.

Donnelly, T. 2000. *Rebuilding America's defenses: Strategies, forces, and resources for a new century*. Washington, DC: Project for the New American Century.

–. 2003. The underpinnings of the Bush doctrine. *National Security Outlook*. AEI Online, 1 February. http://www.aei.org/.

Drohan, M. 2003. *Making a killing: How and why corporations use armed force to do business*. Toronto: Random House Canada.

Duffield, M. 2001. *Global governance and the new wars: The merging of development and security*. London: Zed Books.

–. 2007a. *Development, security and unending war: Governing the world of peoples*. Cambridge, UK: Polity Press.

–. 2007b. Development, territories, and people: Consolidating the external sovereign frontier. *Alternatives: Global, Local, Political* 32(2): 225-46.

Dunbar-Ortiz, R. 2008. The opposite of truth is forgetting. *Upping the Anti: A Journal of Theory and Action* 6 (Spring): 47-58.

Dunn, K.C., and T.M. Shaw, eds. 2001. *Africa's challenge to international relations theory*. London: Palgrave.

Dunn, T. 1996. *The militarization of the U.S.-Mexico border 1978-1992: Low-intensity conflict doctrine comes home*. Austin: Center for Mexican American Studies.

Dyer-Witherford, N. 1999. *Cyber-Marx: Cycles and circuits of struggle in high technology capitalism*. Chicago: University of Illinois Press.

Earthworks/Oxfam. 2004. *Dirty metals: Mining, communities and the environment*. http://www.nodirtygold.org.

Ebrahim, S. 2008. *Muslim women in Canada*. http://www2.ohchr.org.

Echevarria, A.J. 2004a. *An American way of war or way of battle?* Carlisle, PA: Strategic Studies Institute, US Army War College. http://www.strategicstudiesinstitute.army.mil.

–. 2004b. *Towards an American way of war*. Carlisle, PA: Strategic Studies Institute, US Army War College. http://www.strategicstudiesinstitute.army.mil.

–. 2005. *Fourth generation warfare and other myths*. Carlisle, PA: Strategic Studies Institute, US Army War College. http://www.strategicstudiesinstitute.army.mil.

–. 2006. *Challenging transformation cliches*. Carlisle, PA: Strategic Studies Institute, US Army War College. http://www.strategicstudiesinstitute.army.mil.

Eckersley, R. 2004. *The green state: Rethinking democracy and sovereignty*. Cambridge, MA: MIT Press.

Edmonds, S. 2006. Captain's comrades pay solemn tribute. *Globe and Mail*, 1 June.

Edwards, K. 1998. A critique of the general approach to invasive plant species. In *Plant invasions: Ecological mechanisms and human responses*, ed. U. Starfinger, 85-94. Leiden: Backhuys.

Egan, R.D. 2002. Cowardice. In Collins and Glover, 2002, 53-63.

Ehrman, J. 1995. *The rise of neoconservatism: Intellectual and foreign affairs 1945-1955*. New Haven, CT: Yale University Press.

El Akkad, O., and G. McArthur. 2006. Hateful chatter behind the veil. *Globe and Mail*, 29 June.

El-Bushra, J. 2000. Transforming conflict: Some thoughts on a gendered understanding of conflict processes. In Jacobs, Jacobson, and Marchbank, 2000, 66-86.
Ellis, S. 1999. Elections in Africa in historical context. In *Election observation and democratization in Africa*, ed. J. Abbink and G. Hesseling, 37-49. London: Macmillan.
Emmot, B. 2008. *Rivals: How the power struggle between China, India and Japan will shape our next decade.* London: Penguin.
Englehardt, T. 1995. *The end of victory culture: Cold War America and the disillusioning of a generation.* Amherst: University of Massachusetts Press.
Enloe, C. 1990. *Bananas, beaches, and bases: Making feminist sense of international politics.* Berkeley: University of California Press.
—. 2006. Foreword. In Hunt and Rygiel, 2006, vii-ix.
Ericsson, M. 2005. Structural changes in the minerals industry. In Bastida, Walde, and Warden-Fernandez, 2005, 469-92.
Evans, M. 2007. New collaborations for international development. *International Journal* 62(2): 311-25.
Ewald, P. 1994. *Evolution of infectious disease.* Oxford: Oxford University Press.
Fantino, J. 2004. Countering hate crime: Toronto Police Service. http://www.torontopolice.on.ca.
Farhoumand-Sims, C. 2007. Unfulfilled promises. *International Journal* 62(3): 643-63.
Farrell, J. 2006. Calgary soldier dies in ambush: Commander describes fierce battle. *Calgary Herald*, 20 May.
Fatton, R. 1995. Africa in the age of democratization: The civic limitations of civil society. *African Studies Review* 38(2): 67-99.
Fay, C. 1995. La démocratie au Mali: Ou le pouvoir en. *Cahiers d'Etudes africaines* 35(1): 19-53.
Fenton, A. 2007. Canada in Iraq: Dedication to the war of terror. *New Socialist* 62 (Autumn): 26-27.
Ferguson, N. 2004. *Colossus: The rise and fall of the American empire.* London: Penguin.
FIDH [Fédération Internationale des Ligues des Droits de l'Homme]. 2007. *Mali: Mining and human rights; International fact-finding mission report.* Paris, FIDH, No. 477/2, September.
Fleming, D.F. 1961. *The Cold War and its origins.* New York: Doubleday.
Foot, R. 2008. Wanted. *Ottawa Citizen*, 29 January.
Forcese, C. 2001. "Militarized commerce" in Sudan's oilfields: Lessons for Canadian foreign policy. *Canadian Foreign Policy* 8(3): 37-56.
Fortney, V. 2006a. She was born with a taste for adventure (Part 1); Series, Letters home. *Calgary Herald*, 10 November.
—. 2006b. She was born with a taste for adventure (Part 2); Series, Letters home. *Calgary Herald*, 11 November.
Foucault, M. 1978. *The history of sexuality.* Vol. 1. New York: Vintage.
—. 1991. On governmentality. In *The Foucault effect: Studies in governmentality*, ed. G. Burchell, C. Gordon, and P. Miller, 87-104. Hemel Hempstead, UK: Harvester Wheatshaft.

Fousek, J. 2000. *To lead the free world: American nationalism and the cultural roots of the Cold War.* Chapel Hill: University of North Carolina Press.

Frampton, C., G. Kinsman, A.K. Thompson, and K. Tilleczek, eds. 2006. *Sociology for changing the world: Social movements/social research.* Halifax: Fernwood.

Francis, D. 2001. Yes, freedom of speech has limits. *Province,* 19 November.

François, P. 1982. Class struggles in Mali. *Review of African Political Economy* 9(24): 22-38.

Freedman, J. 2006-07. International remedies for resource-based conflict. *International Journal* 62(1): 108-19.

Freeman, L. 1985. The effect of the world crisis on Canada's involvement in Africa. *Studies in Political Economy* 17 (Summer): 107-39.

Freire, P. 2006. *Pedagogy of the oppressed.* New York: Continuum.

Friedman, M. 2005. *The neoconservative revolution: Jewish intellectuals and the shaping of public policy.* Cambridge: Cambridge University Press.

Friedman, T.L. 2003. *Longitudes and attitudes: The world in an age of terrorism.* New York: Anchor.

Fukuyama, F. 2006. *America at the crossroads: Democracy, power, and the neoconservative legacy.* New Haven, CT: Yale University Press.

Fulford, R. 2005. Multiculturalism's eloquent enemy. *National Post,* 15 August.

Furtado, F.J. 2008. Human security: Did it live? Has it died? Does it matter? *International Journal* 63(2): 405-21.

Gadd, J. 2001. Activist called terrorist. *Globe and Mail,* 30 June.

Gaddis, J.L. 2002. A grand strategy for transformation. *Foreign Policy* 133: 50-57.

Gandhi, U. 2007. McMaster professor was targeted before, she says. *Globe and Mail,* 14 April.

Gardner, L.C. 1993. *Spheres of influence: The great powers partition Europe, from Munich to Yalta.* Chicago: Ivan R. Dee.

Gardner, L.C., and M.B. Young, eds. 2005. *The new American empire: A 21st century teach-in on U.S. foreign policy.* London: The New Press.

Garrett, L. 2001. The nightmare of bioterrorism. *Foreign Affairs* January/February 80(1): 76-89.

Gee, M. 2001. World's feminists are divided on Afghan war. *Globe and Mail,* 20 November.

Giddens, A. 1993. *Contemporary critique of historical materialism.* In *The Giddens reader,* ed. P. Cassell. Basingstoke, UK: Macmillan.

Gill, S. 1990. *American hegemony and the Trilateral Commission.* Cambridge: Cambridge University Press.

Giorgetta, S. 2002. The right to a healthy environment, human rights and sustainable development. *International Environmental Agreements: Politics, Law and Economics* 2(2): 173-94.

Giroday, G. 2006. Sorrowful journey back. *Winnipeg Free Press,* 19 May.

Glasser, R. 2004. We are not immune: Influenza, SARS, and the collapse of public health. *Harper's Magazine,* July, 35-42.

Glenny, M. 2008. *McMafia: A journey through the global criminal underworld.* New York: Random House.

Global Issues. 2008. World military spending. http://www.globalissues.org.
Global Rights. 2008. *Living with violence: A national report on domestic abuse in Afghanistan*. Washington. http://www.globalrights.com.
Globe and Mail. 2006. Capt. Goddard's job. 19 May.
Gore, C., and P. Stoett, eds. 2009. *Environmental challenges and opportunities: Local-global perspectives on Canadian issues*. Toronto: Emond Montgomery.
Gorrie, P. 2004. Hydrilla plant alien in search of a predator. *Toronto Star*, 22 August.
Gotlieb, A. 2004a. Alan B. Plaunt Memorial Lecture. In *Visions of Canada: The Alan B. Plaunt Memorial Lectures 1958-1992*, ed. B. Ostry and J. Yalden, 526-40. Montreal and Kingston, ON: McGill-Queen's University Press.
–. 2004b. Romanticism and realism in Canada's foreign policy. Benefactors Lecture, Toronto, 3 November. http://www.cdhowe.org.
Gowan, P. 1999. *The global gamble: Washington's Faustian bid for world dominance*. New York: Verso Press.
Grace, E., and C. Leys. 1989. The concept of subversion and its implications. In *Dissent and the state*, ed. C.E.S. Franks, 62-85. Toronto: Oxford University Press.
Gramsci, A. 1971. *Selections from the prison notebooks of Antonio Gramsci*. London: Lawrence and Wishart.
Granatstein, J.L. 1986. Canada and peacekeeping: Image and reality. In *Canadian foreign policy: Historical readings*, ed. J.L. Granatstein, 232-37. Toronto: Copp Clark.
–. 1996. *Yankee go home? Canadians and anti-Americanism*. Toronto: HarperCollins.
–. 2003. The importance of being less earnest: Promoting Canada's national interests through tighter ties with the U.S. Benefactors Lecture, Toronto, 21 October. http://www.cdhowe.org.
–. 2004. *Who killed the Canadian military?* Toronto: HarperCollins.
–. 2007. *Whose war is it? How Canada can survive in the post-9/11 world*. Toronto: HarperCollins.
Gray, C.S. 2005. The American way of war: Critique and implications. In *Rethinking the principles of war*, ed. A.D. McIvor, 13-40. Annapolis, MD: Naval Institute Press.
–. 2006. *Irregular enemies and the essence of strategy: Can the American way of war adapt?* Carlisle, PA: Strategic Studies Institute, US Army War College. http://www.strategicstudiesinstitute.army.mil.
Grayson, K. 2004. Branding "transformation" in Canadian foreign policy: Human security. *Canadian Foreign Policy* 11(2): 41-68.
–. 2006. Promoting responsibility and accountability: Human security and Canadian corporate conduct. *International Journal* 61(1): 479-94.
–. 2008. *Chasing dragons: Security, identity, and illicit drugs in Canada*. Toronto: University of Toronto Press.
Greener, B.K. 2007. Liberalism and the use of force: Core themes and conceptual tensions. *Alternatives: Global, Local, Political* 32(3): 295-318.
Gregory, D. 2004. *The colonial present: Afghanistan, Palestine, Iraq*. Malden, MA: Blackwell.
Grémont, C., A. Marty, R. ag Mossa, and Y.H. Touré. 2004. *Les liens sociaux au Nord-Mali: Entre fleuve et dunes*. Paris: IRAM-Karthala.

Grigorovich, I., R. Colautti, E. Mills, K. Holeck, A. Ballert, and H. MacIsaac. 2003. Ballast-mediated animal introductions in the Laurentian Great Lakes: Retrospective and prospective analyses. *Canadian Journal of Fisheries and Aquatic Sciences* 60(6): 740-56.

Grondin, D. 2007. *La sécurisation de l'espace comme "champ de bataille" dans le discours astropolitique américain: La stratégie de construction identitaire des États-Unis comme puissance stratégique globale*. PhD diss., Université du Québec à Montréal.

Grovogui, S.N. 2006. *Beyond Eurocentrism and anarchy: Memories of international order and institutions*. New York: Palgrave Macmillan.

Gyulai, L. 2007. Muslim groups to file complaint against town. *Montreal Gazette*, 5 February.

Ha, T.T. 2007. Welcome to town, here are the rules. *Globe and Mail*, 5 February.

Haddad, L., and C. Knowles, eds. 2007. Reinventing development research. *IDS Bulletin* 38(2): xi-101.

Halifax Daily News. 2006a. A tragic milestone. 18 May.

–. 2006b. Friends remember Goddard's generosity. 19 May.

Halifax Initiative. 2006. Mining Map. http://halifaxinitiative.org/cotnent/mining-map-referenced.

Halliday, F., and J. Rosenberg. 1998. Interview with Kenneth Waltz. *Review of International Studies* 24(3): 371-86.

Halper, S., and J. Clarke. 2004. *America alone: The neo-conservatives and the global order*. Cambridge: Cambridge University Press.

Hamdani, D. 2005. Triple jeopardy: Muslim women's experience of discrimination. Canadian Council of Muslim Women. http://www.ccmw.com.

Hamilos, P. 2007. 21 guilty, 7 cleared over Madrid train bombings. *Manchester Guardian*, 31 October. http://www.guardian.co.uk.

Hamm, M.S. 2007. *Terrorism as crime: From Oklahoma City to al-Qaeda and beyond*. New York: New York University Press.

Harcourt, W., ed. 2007. The power of ideas. 50th anniversary special issue. *Development* 50: 1-161.

Hardt, M. 2004. Interviewed by T. Dunn. The theory and event interview. In *Empire's new clothes, reading Hardt and Negri*, ed. A. Passavant and J. Dean, 166-67. London: Routledge.

Harker, J.H. 2000. *Human security in Sudan: The report of a Canadian assessment mission*. Prepared for the Minister of Foreign Affairs, Ottawa, January. Department of Foreign Affairs and International Trade.

Harold. 1960-61. *A case history with observations*. In the holdings of the Canadian Lesbian and Gay Archives in Toronto.

Harper, S. 2006a. Address by the prime minister on new Canadian government assistance for the reconstruction of Afghanistan. Ottawa, 15 June. http://pm.gc.ca.

–. 2006b. Address by the prime minister to the Canadian Armed Forces in Afghanistan. Kandahar, 13 March. http://pm.gc.ca.

–. 2007. Prime Minister Stephen Harper speaks to Canadian troops during visit to Afghanistan. http://pm.gc.ca.

Harper's Index. 2008. *Harper's Magazine*, 317(1899) (August): 13.
Harsch, E. 1993. Accumulators and democrats: Challenging state corruption in Africa. *Journal of Modern African Studies* 31(1): 31-48.
Harvey, D. 2003. *The new imperialism*. Oxford: Oxford University Press.
–. 2007. *A brief history of neoliberalism*. Oxford: Oxford University Press.
Hataley, T.S., and K.R. Nossal. 2004. The limits of the human security agenda: The case of Canada's response to the Timor crisis. *Global Change, Peace and Security* 16(1): 5-17.
Hay, R.J. 1999. Present at the creation? Human security and Canadian foreign policy in the twenty-first century. In *Canada among nations 1999: A big league player?* ed. F.O. Hampson, M. Hart, and M. Rudner, 215-32. Toronto: Oxford University Press.
Heilbrunn, J. 2008. *They knew they were right: The rise of the neocons*. New York: Doubleday.
Hengeveld, R. 1989. *Dynamics of biological invasions*. London: Chapman and Hall.
Hennessy, R. 2000. *Profit and pleasure: Sexual identities in late capitalism*. London: Routledge.
Henry, B. 2006. Heartfelt thoughts for fallen soldier. (Letter,) *Calgary Herald*, 20 May.
Heymann, D. 2003. The evolving infectious disease threat: Implications for national and global security. *Journal of Human Development* 4(2): 191-207.
Hillmer, N. 1994. Peacekeeping: Canadian invention, Canadian myth. In *Welfare states in trouble: Historical perspectives on Canada and Sweden*, ed. J.L. Granatstein and S. Akerrnan, 159-70. Toronto: Swedish-Canadian Academic Foundation.
Hofstadter, R. 1965. *The paranoid style in American politics and other essays*. New York: Knopf.
Holloway, J. 2005. *Change the world without taking power: The meaning of revolution today*. Ann Arbor, MI: Pluto Press.
Holsti, K.J. 1990. L'État et l'état de la guerre. *Études internationales* 21(4): 705-17.
Homer-Dixon, T. 2002. The rise of complex terrorism. *Foreign Policy*, January/February, 52-63.
hooks, b. 1994. *Teaching to transgress: Education as the practice of freedom*. London: Routledge.
Hopf, T. 1998. The promise of constructivism in international relations theory. *International Security* 23(1): 171-200.
Hossein-Zadeh, I. 2006. *The political economy of U.S. militarism*. New York: Palgrave Macmillan.
Hubert, D. 2000. The landmine ban: A case study in humanitarian advocacy. Occasional Paper 42, Watson Institute, Brown University, Providence, RI.
Hughes, L. 2000. Biological consequences of global warming: Is the signal already apparent? *Trends in Ecology and Evolution* 15(7): 56-61.
Human Rights Watch. 2007. *The human cost: The consequences of insurgent attacks in Afghanistan*. http://www.hrw.org.
–. 2009. *We have the promises of the world: Women's rights in Afghanistan*. http://www.hrw.org.
Human Security Report Project. 2005. *Human security report 2005: War and peace in the 21st century*. Oxford: Oxford University Press.

Humphrey, J., and D. Messner. 2006. China and India as emerging governance actors: Challenges for developing and developed countries. *IDS Bulletin* 37(1): 107-14.

Humphreys, A. 2007. Radical believers: Imprisoned but unrepentant, killers of abortion doctors say they did God's work. *National Post*, 27 December.

Humphreys, D. 2005. Corporate strategies in the global mining industry. In Bastida, Walde, and Warden-Fernandez, 2005, 451-68.

Hunt, K. 2002. The strategic co-optation of women's rights. *International Feminist Journal of Politics* 4(1): 116-21.

–. 2006. "Embedded feminism" and the war on terror. In Hunt and Rygiel, 2006, 51-72.

Hunt, K., and K. Rygiel, eds. 2006. *(En)gendering the war on terror: War stories and camouflaged politics*. Hampshire, UK: Ashgate.

Hunter, D., J. Salzman, and D. Zaelke. 2006. *International environmental law and policy*. 3rd ed. New York: Foundation Press.

Hussain, S. 2002. Voices of Muslim women: A community research project. Mississauga, ON: Canadian Council of Muslim Women. http://www.ccmw.com.

Hutchful, E., and K. Fayemi. 2004. Security system reform in Africa. In Development Assistance Committee Network on Conflict, Peace and Development Cooperation, *A survey of security system reform and donor policy: Views from non-OECD countries*. Paris: Organisation for Economic Co-operation and Development Development Assistance Committee. http://unpan1.un.org/.

Hutchinson, S., and P. O'Malley. 2007. A crime-terror nexus? Thinking on some of the links between terrorism and criminality. *Studies in Conflict and Terrorism* 30(12): 1095-107.

Huysmans, J. 2008. The jargon of exception. *International Political Sociology* 2(2): 165-83.

ICISS [International Commission on Intervention and State Sovereignty]. 2001. *The responsibility to protect: Report of the International Commission on Intervention and State Sovereignty*. Ottawa: International Development Research Centre.

Ignatieff, M. 2003. *Empire lite: Nation-building in Bosnia, Kosovo and Afghanistan*. London: Vintage.

Ikenberry, G.J., ed. 2002. *America unrivalled: The future of the balance of power*. Ithaca, NY: Cornell University Press.

Illsley, B. 2002. Good neighbour agreements: The first step to environmental justice? *Local Environments* 7(1): 69-79.

Inayatullah, N., and D.L. Blaney. 2004. *International relations and the problem of difference*. New York: Routledge.

IRIN [Integrated Regional Information Networks]. 2006. Mali: Government strikes new peace deal with Tuareg rebels. Nairobi: UN Office for the Coordination of Humanitarian Affairs. 5 July. http://www.irinnews.org.

–. 2007. Mali: Indignation dominates reaction as attacks in north escalate. Nairobi: UN Office for the Coordination of Humanitarian Affairs. 31 August. http://www.irinnews.org.

Irwin, R., ed. 2001. *Ethics and security in Canadian foreign policy*. Vancouver: UBC Press.

Isaak, G. 2006. Heartfelt thoughts for fallen soldier. *Calgary Herald,* 20 May.
Ish-Shalom, P. 2006. "The civilization of clashes": Neoconservative reading of the theory of democratic peace. Paper presented at the ISA annual conference, San Diego.
Iverson, L., M. Schwartz, and A. Prasad, eds. 2004. How fast and far might tree species migrate in the eastern U.S. due to climate change? *Global Ecology and Biogeography* 13(3): 209-19.
Jackson, M.F., and G. González. 2006. *What have they built you to do? The Manchurian candidate and Cold War America.* Minneapolis: University of Minnesota Press.
Jacobs, L.A. 2003. Securer freedom for whom: Risk profiling and the new Anti-Terrorism Act. *UBC Law Review* 36(2): 375-84.
Jacobs, S., R. Jacobson, and J. Marchbank, eds. 2000. *States of conflict: Gender, violence and resistance.* London: Zed Books.
Jacobson, R. 2000. Women and peace in Northern Ireland: A complicated relationship. In Jacobs, Jacobson, and Marchbank, 2002, 179-98.
Jager, S.M. 2007. *On the uses of cultural knowledge.* Strategic Studies Institute, US Army War College, Carlisle, PA. http://www.strategicstudiesinstitute.army.mil.
Jagose, A. 1996. *Queer theory: An introduction.* New York: New York University Press.
Jaimet, K., with files from Chris Wattie. 2006. Reaction reflects how female soldiers are perceived: "Accept and grieve." *National Post,* 18 May.
Jervis, R. 2002. An interim assessment of September 11: What has changed and what has not. *Political Science Quarterly* 117(1): 37-54.
–. 2003. The compulsive empire. *Foreign Policy* 137: 82-87.
Jimenez, M., C. Freeze, and V. Burnett. 2003. Case of 19 terrorists starts to unravel. *Globe and Mail,* 30 August.
Johnson, C. 2000. *Blowback: The costs and consequences of American empire.* New York: Henry Holt.
–. 2004. *The sorrows of empire: Militarism, secrecy and the end of the republic.* New York: Metropolitan Books.
–. 2006. *Nemesis: The last days of the American republic.* New York: Metropolitan Books.
Jolly, R., L. Emmerij, and T.G. Weiss. 2005. *The power of ideas: Lessons from the first 60 years.* New York: United Nations Intellectual History Project.
Judis, J.B. 1995. Trotskyism to anachronism: The neoconservative revolution. *Foreign Affairs* 74(4): 123-29.
Kagan, R. 2004. *Of paradise and power: America and Europe in the new world order.* New York: Vintage.
–. 2006. Our "messianic impulse." *Washington Post,* 10 December.
–. 2008. *The return of history and the end of dreams.* New York: Knopf.
Kane, S., and P. Greenhill. 2007. A feminist perspective on bioterror: From anthrax to critical art ensemble. *Journal of Women in Culture and Society* 33(1): 53-80.
Kaplan, R.D. 2007. On forgetting the obvious. *American Interest* 2(6): 6-15.
Kashmeri, Z. 1991. *The gulf within: Canadian Arabs, racism and the Gulf War.* Toronto: James Lorimer.

Katzenstein, P.J., ed. 1996. *The culture of national security: Norms and identity in world politics.* New York: Columbia University Press.

Kay, B. 2006. An exceptional woman. *National Post,* 25 May.

Kearns, R.L. 1992. *Zaibatsu America: How Japanese firms are colonizing vital U.S. industries.* New York: The Free Press.

Keating, T. 2002. *Canada and world order: The multilateralist tradition in Canadian foreign policy.* 2nd ed. Toronto: Oxford University Press.

Keating, T., and W.A. Knight, eds. 2004. *Building sustainable peace.* Edmonton: University of Alberta Press.

Keeble, E., and H. Smith. 2001. Institutions, ideas, women and gender: New directions in Canadian foreign policy. *Journal of Canadian Studies* 35(4): 130-41.

Kelle, A. 2007. The securitization of international public health: Implications for global health governance and the biological weapons prohibition regime. *Global Governance* 13(2): 217-35.

Kennedy, P. 1988. *The rise and fall of the great power: Economic change and military conflict from 1500 to 2000.* New York: Random House.

Keohane, R.O. 1984. *After hegemony.* Princeton, NJ: Princeton University Press.

Khanna, P. 2008. *The second world: Empires and influence in the new global order.* New York: Random House.

Khattak, S.G. 2004. Adversarial discourses, analogous objectives. *Cultural Dynamics* 16(2-3): 216-36.

Kim, S.S. 1984. *The quest for a just world order.* Boulder, CO: Westview Press.

Kinsman, G. 1996. *The regulation of desire: Homo and hetero sexualities.* Montreal: Black Rose.

–. 2005a. The politics of revolution: Learning from autonomist Marxism. In *Upping the Anti: A Journal of Theory and Action* 1 (Spring): 43-52.

–. 2005b. Vectors of hope and possibility. *Sexuality, Research and Social Policy* 2(2): 99-105.

Kinsman, G., D. Buse, and M. Steedman, eds. 2000. *Whose national security? Canadian state surveillance and the creation of enemies.* Toronto: Between the Lines.

Kinsman, G., and P. Gentile. 2010. *The Canadian war on queers: National security as sexual regulation.* Vancouver: UBC Press.

Kitch, S.L., and M.A. Mills. 2004. Appropriating women's agendas. *Peace Review* 16(1): 65-73.

Klare, M.T. 2002. *Resource wars: The new landscape of global conflict.* New York: Owl.

–. 2005. Imperial reach: The Pentagon's new basing strategy. *The Nation.* 25 April. http://www.thenation.com.

Klein, N. 2001. *No logo.* London: Flamingo.

Klute, G., and T. von Trotha. 2002. *Décentralisation et para-étatisme.* Bamako: Point Sud Research Centre conference paper. February.

Kolar, C., and D. Lodge. 2000. Freshwater nonindigenous species: Interactions with other global changes. In Mooney and Hobbs, 2000, 3-30.

Konaré, A.B. 2000. Perspectives on history and culture: The case of Mali. In *Democracy and development in Mali,* ed. R.D. Bingen, D. Robinson, and J.M. Staatz, 15-22. East Lansing: Michigan State University Press.

Konaté, M., P. Simard, C. Giles, and L. Caron. 1999. *Sur les petites routes de la démocratie: l'expérience d'un village malien.* Montreal: Ecosociété.

Kramer, P. 2008. The water cure: Debating torture and counterinsurgency – A century ago. *New Yorker* 84(2): 38-43.

Krause, K., and M.C. Williams, eds. 1997. *Critical security studies.* Minneapolis: University of Minnesota Press.

Krauthammer, C. 2004. *Democratic realism: An American foreign policy for a unipolar world.* Washington, DC: American Enterprise Institute.

Kreisler, H. 2003. Theory and international politics: Conversation with Kenneth N. Waltz. http://globetrotter.berkeley.edu.

Kristol, I. 2003. The neoconservative persuasion: What it was, and what it is. *Weekly Standard* 8(47), 25 August.

Kristol, W. 2004. Postscript – June 2004: Neoconservatism remains the bedrock of U.S. foreign policy. In Stelzer, 2004b, 75-77.

Kristol, W., and R. Kagan. 1996. Toward a neo-Reaganite foreign policy. *Foreign Affairs* 75(4): 18-32.

–. 2000. Introduction: National interest and global responsibility. In *Present danger: Crisis and opportunity in American foreign and defense policy,* ed. R. Kagan and W. Kristol, 3-24. San Francisco: Encounter Books.

Kronsell, A. 2006. Methods for studying silences: Gender analysis in institutions of hegemonic masculinity. In Ackerly, Stern, and True, 2006, 108-28.

Laferrière, E., and P. Stoett. 1999. *International relations theory and ecological thought: Towards a synthesis.* London: Routledge.

–, eds. 2006. *International ecopolitical theory: Critical reflections.* Vancouver: UBC Press.

Lambert, B. 2009. Canada risks being "colonial exploiters." *National Newspaper,* 23 June. http://www.thenational.ae.

Layne, C. 1993. The unipolar illusion: Why new great powers will rise. *International Security* 17(4): 5-51.

–. 1994. Kant or cant: The myth of the democratic peace. *International Security* 19(2): 5-49.

–. 2004. The war on terrorism and the balance of power: The paradox of American hegemony. In Paul, Wirtz, and Fortmann, 2004, 103-26.

–. 2006a. *The peace of illusions: American grand strategy from 1940 to the present.* Ithaca, NY: Cornell University Press.

–. 2006b. The unipolar illusion revisted: The coming end of the United States's unipolar moment. *International Security* 31(2): 7-41.

Le Billon, P. 2006-07. Securing transparency: Armed conflicts and the management of natural resource revenues. *International Journal* 62(1): 93-107.

Leblanc, D. 2001. 80 per cent would back national ID cards. *Globe and Mail,* 6 October.

Le Droit. 2006. La courtoisie libérale s'effrite. 12 June.

Leffler, M.P. 1992. *A preponderance of power: National security, the Truman administration and the Cold War.* Stanford, CA: Stanford University Press.

Leiss, W. 2001. *In the chamber of risks: Understanding risk controversies.* Montreal and Kingston, ON: McGill-Queen's University Press.

Leiss, W., and M. Tyshenko. 2002. Some aspects of the "new biotechnology" and its regulation in Canada. In *Canadian environmental policy: Context and cases*, ed. D. Vannijnatte and R. Boardman, 321-43. Oxford: Oxford University Press.

Lemieux, A. 2005. Canada's global mining presence. In *Canadian mineral yearbook, 2005*, 7.1-7.21. Ottawa: Natural Resources Canada. http://www.nrcan.gc.ca/.

Lemke, D. 2003. African lessons for international relations research. *World Politics* 56(1): 114-38.

Leonard, M. 2008. *What does China think?* New York: HarperCollins.

Lepore, J. 2008. The divider. *New Yorker* 84(5): 90-91.

Levant, V. 1986. *Quiet complicity: Canadian involvement in the Vietnam War*. Toronto: Between the Lines.

Liberal Party of Canada. 1993. *Creating opportunity: The Liberal plan for Canada*. Ottawa: Liberal Party of Canada.

Lieber, R.J. 2003. The folly of containment. *Commentary*, April: 15-21.

Liotta, P.H. 2002. Boomerang effect: The convergence of national and human security. *Security Dialogue* 33(4): 473-88.

Litfin, K. 1998. *The greening of sovereignty in world politics*. Cambridge, MA: MIT Press.

Litwak, R.S. 2002-03. The new calculus of pre-emption. *Survival* 44(4): 53-80.

Lock-Pullan, R. 2006. The US way of war and the "war on terror." *Politics and Policy* 34(2): 374-99.

Lovell, G. 1992. The real country and the legal country: Spanish ideals and Mayan realities in colonial Guatemala. *Geojournal* 26(2): 181-85.

Lubold, G. 2008. Military revisits Afghanistan plan. *Christian Science Monitor*, 24 July.

Macamo, E., and D. Neubert. 2002. *Lorsque l'Etat post-révolutionnaire décentralise*. Bamako: Point Sud Research Centre conference paper. February.

MacArthur, J. 2008. A responsibility to rethink? Challenging paradigms in human security. *International Journal* 63(2): 422-43.

MacEachern, L. 2006. She could have done anything. *Halifax Daily News*, 19 May.

MacFarlane, S.N., and Y.F. Khong. 2006. *Human security and the UN: A critical history*. Bloomington: Indiana University Press.

MacKay, P. 2006. Canadian foreign policy and our leadership role in Afghanistan. Ottawa, 30 October. http://w01.international.gc.ca.

MacKinnon, M., and B. McKenna. 2001. Use of lethal force, officers authorized to use extreme tactics on protestors in guidelines issued for summit. *Globe and Mail*, 25 April.

MacLean, G. 2000. Instituting and projecting human security: A Canadian perspective. *Australian Journal of International Affairs* 54(3): 269-76.

MacLean, S.J., D.R. Black, and T.M. Shaw, eds. 2006. *A decade of human security: What prospects for global governance and new multilateralisms?* Aldershot, UK: Ashgate.

MacMillan, M. 2001. *Paris 1919: Six months that changed the world*. New York: Random House.

Madison, J. 1795/1865. Political observations, 20 April 1795. In *Letters and other writings of James Madison*. Vol. 5. Philadelphia: J.B. Lipincott.

Mahan, Capt. A.T. 1890/1957. *The influence of sea power on history, 1660-1783*. New York: Hill and Wang.

Mahnken, T.G. 2003. The American way of war in the twenty-first century. In *Democracies and small wars*, ed. E. Inbar, 73-84. Portland: Frank Cass.

Makarenko, T. 2004. The crime-terror continuum: Tracing the interplay between transnational crime and terrorism. *Global Crime* 6(1): 129-45.

Maloney, S.M. 2002. *Canada and UN peacekeeping: Cold War by other means, 1945-1970*. St. Catharines, ON: Vanwell.

–. 2006-07. Canada, Afghanistan and the blame game. *Policy Options*, December/January: 21-27.

Manley, J., D.H. Burney, J. Epp, P. Tellier, and P. Wallin. 2008. *Independent panel on Canada's future role in Afghanistan*. Ottawa: Minister of Public Works and Government Services.

Manning, P. 1998. *Francophone sub-Saharan Africa, 1880-1995*. New York: Cambridge University Press.

Marsella, A.J. 2005. Reflections on international terrorism: Issues, concepts and directions. In *Understanding terrorism: Psychosocial roots, consequences and interventions*, ed. F.M. Moghaddam and A.J. Marsella, 11-47. Washington, DC: American Psychological Association.

Martin, P. 2003a. Canada's role in a complex world. Paper presented at the Canadian Newspaper Association, Toronto, 30 April.

–. 2003b. Speech to the Liberal Party leadership convention, Toronto, 14 November. http://www.cbc.ca/news.

–. 2004. Speech by the prime minister, Montreal, 10 May. National Library of Canada Electronic Collection.

Martineau, M. 2004. Rebirth of gold mining in sub-Saharan Africa. *Mining Journal* 4 (February): 3-5.

Marty, A. 2007. De la rébellion à la paix au Nord-Mali: L'indispensable complémentarité de L'Etat et de la société civile. In *Etats et sociétés fragiles: Entre conflit, reconstruction et développement*, ed. J.-M. Châtaigner and H. Magro, 291-306. Paris: Karthala.

Mastanduno, M. 1999. Preserving the unipolar moment: Realist theories and U.S. grand strategy after the Cold War. In *Unipolar politics: Realism and state strategies after the Cold War*, ed. E.B. Kapstein and M. Mastanduno, 138-81. New York: Columbia University Press.

Mathews, J.T. 1989. Redefining security. *Foreign Affairs* 68(2): 162-77.

Matthews, R. 2005. Sudan's humanitarian disaster: Will Canada live up to its responsibility to protect? *International Journal* 60(4): 1049-64.

McCarthy, E. 2002. Justice. In Collins and Glover, 2002, 123-37.

McCormick, T.J. 1989. *America's half-century: United States foreign policy in the Cold War*. Baltimore: Johns Hopkins University Press.

–. 2005. American hegemony and European autonomy, 1989-2003: One framework for understanding the war in Iraq. In Gardner and Young, 2005, 75-112.

McDonough, D.S. 2007. The paradox of Afghanistan: Stability operations and the renewal of Canada's international security policy? *International Journal* 62(3): 620-41.

McGarrell, E., J.D. Freilich, and S. Chermak. 2007. Intelligence-led policing as a framework for responding to terrorism. *Journal of Contemporary Criminal Justice* 23(2): 142-58.

McGinnis, S. 2006. "Huge smile ... bigger heart": Family grieves for fallen soldier. *Calgary Herald*, 19 May.

–, with files from Brad Linn. 2006. Fallen soldier's body returned to Calgary. *Calgary Herald*, 25 May.

McGrew, A. 2005. Globalization and global politics. In *The globalization of world politics: An introduction to international relations*, ed. J. Baylis and S. Smith, 19-40. Oxford: Oxford University Press.

McKeon, C. 2003. From the ground up: Exploring dichotomies in grassroots peacebuilding. Conciliation Resources. http://www.c-r.org.

McMichael, A., and M. Bouma. 2000. Global changes, invasive species, and human health. In Mooney and Hobbs, 2000, 191-210.

McNally, D. 2001. *Bodies of meaning, studies on language, labour, and liberation.* Albany: State University of New York Press.

–. 2002. *Another world is possible.* Winnipeg: Arbeiter Ring.

McNeely, J., H. Mooney, L. Neville, P. Schei, and J. Wagge, eds. 2001. *Global strategy on invasive species.* Gland, Switzerland: International Union for Conservation of Nature.

McRae, R., and D. Hubert, eds. 2001. *Human security and the new diplomacy: Protecting people, promoting peace.* Montreal and Kingston, ON: McGill-Queen's University Press.

Mearsheimer, J. 1990. Back to the future: Instability in Europe after the Cold War. *International Security* 15(1): 5-56.

–. 2001. *The tragedy of great power politics.* New York: W.W. Norton.

–. 2005. Hans Morgenthau and the Iraq War: Realism versus neo-conservatism. *Open Democracy*, 18 May. http://www.opendemocracy.net.

Mearsheimer, J., and S.M. Walt. 2003. An unnecessary war. *Foreign Policy* 134: 50-59.

Miller, J., and C. Gall. 2002. Women suffer most in Afghan health crisis, experts say. *New York Times*, 27 October.

Mills, C.W. 1956. *The power elite.* New York: Oxford University Press,

–. 1959. *The sociological imagination.* New York: Oxford University Press.

Mitchell, T. 1991. The limits of the state: Beyond statist approaches and their critics. *American Political Science Review* 85(1): 77-95.

Modelski, G. 1978. The long cycle of global politics and the nation-state. *Comparative Studies in Society and History* 20(2): 214-35.

Moody, C. 2006. Grateful. (Letter,) *Calgary Herald*, 31 May.

Mooney and R. Hobbs, H., eds. 2000. *Invasive species in a changing world.* Washington, DC: Island Press.

Moore, M. 1998. Toward a useful consensus. *IDS Bulletin* 29(2): 39-48.

Moore, O. 2006. Captain "loved her job," grieving husband says. *Globe and Mail*, 18 May.
Moreau, K. 2006. *Criminals, hooligans, violence: A case study and discursive analysis of the criminalization of political dissent*. MA diss., Laurentian University.
Morgenthau, H.J. 1967. *Politics among nations: The struggle for power and peace*. 4th ed. New York: Knopf.
–. 1973. *Politics among nations: The struggle for power and peace*. 5th ed. New York: Knopf.
Muggah, R., ed. 2009. *Security and post-conflict reconstruction: Dealing with fighters in the aftermath of war*. Abingdon, UK: Routledge.
Mulligan, S. 2000. Biosafety, risk, and the global knowledge structure. *Peace Review* 14(4): 571-77.
Munton, D. 2002-03. Whither internationalism? *International Journal* 58(1): 155-80.
Muravchik, J. 2004. The neoconservative cabal. In Stelzer, 2004b, 241-57.
–. 2006. The neocons will ride again. *Sydney Morning Herald*, 28 November.
–. 2007. The past, present, and future of neoconservatism. *Commentary*, October: 19-23.
Murphy, C.N., and J. Yates. 2009. *The International Organization for Standardization (ISO): Global governance through voluntary consensus*. New York: Routledge.
Mychajlyszyn, N., and T.M. Shaw, eds. 2005. *Twisting arms and flexing muscles: Humanitarian intervention and peacebuilding in perspective*. Aldershot, UK: Ashgate.
Naghibi, N. 2007. *Rethinking global sisterhood: Western feminism and Iran*. Minneapolis: University of Minnesota Press.
Naím, M. 2003. Five wars of globalization. *Foreign Policy*, January-February: 29-37.
National Post. 2001. "The war will be won," Chretien promises: Military aid will be provided, PM tells Bush. 8 October.
–. 2006. Soldier "died doing something she believed was important": Killed by Taliban. 19 May.
–. 2008. He died for a good cause. 22 July.
Nau, H.R. 1990. *The myth of America's decline: Leading the world economy into the 1990s*. New York: Oxford University Press.
Naylor, R.T. 2006. Ghosts of terror wars past? Crime, terror and America's first clash with the Saracen hordes. *Crime, Law and Social Change* 45(2): 93-109.
Nehring, H. 2010. The forgotten impact of a war that didn't happen. *openDemocracy*, 30 March. http://www.opendemocracy.net.
Neigh, S. 2008. National security certificates: Organizing against secret trials in Canada. Paper presented at Canadian Security into the 21st Century: (Re)Articulations in the Post-9/11 World, Laurentian University, Sudbury, ON, 5 March.
Neufeld, M. 1995. Hegemony and foreign policy analysis: The case of Canada as a middle power. *Studies in Political Economy* 48 (Autumn): 7-29.
Neufeld, M., and S. Whitworth. 1997. Imag(in)ing Canadian foreign policy. In *Understanding Canada: Building on the new Canadian political economy*, ed. W. Clement, 197-214. Montreal and Kingston, ON: McGill-Queen's University Press.

Newman, E. 2007. Weak states, failed states and terrorism. *Terrorism and Political Violence* 19(4): 463-88.
NGRC [National Gay Rights Coalition]. 1976. RG 146, vol. 3115, "Community Homophile Association of Toronto, Ont."
No One Is Illegal Vancouver. 2008. *Anti-Olympics.* http://noii-van.resist.ca.
Norgaard, R. 1988. The rise of the global exchange economy and the loss of biological diversity. In *Biodiversity,* ed. E. Wilson, 206-10. Washington, DC: National Academy Press.
Nossal, K.R. 1994. Quantum leaping: The Gulf debate in Australia and Canada. In *The Gulf War: Critical perspectives,* ed. Michael McKinley, 48-71. Sydney: Allen and Unwin.
–. 1995. Seeing things? The adornment of "security" in Australia and Canada. *Australian Journal of International Affairs* 49(1): 33-47.
–. 1997. "Without regard for the interests of others": Canada and American unilateralism in the post-Cold War era. *American Review of Canadian Studies* 27 (Summer): 179-97.
–. 1998-99. Pinchpenny diplomacy: The decline of "good international citizenship" in Canadian foreign policy. *International Journal* 54(1): 88-105.
–. 2003. "The world we want"? The purposeful confusion of values, goals and interests in Canadian foreign policy. Calgary: Canadian Defence and Foreign Affairs Institute. http://www.cdfai.org.
–. 2004. Defending the "realm": Canadian strategic culture revisited. *International Journal* 59(3): 503-20.
–. 2005. Ear candy: Canadian policy toward humanitarian intervention and atrocity crimes in Darfur. *International Journal* 60(4): 1017-32.
–. 2007a. Anti-Americanism in Canada. In *Anti-Americanism: History, causes, and themes.* Vol. 3 of *Comparative perspectives,* ed. B. O'Connor, 59-76. Oxford: Greenwood World.
–. 2007b. Defense policy and the atmospherics of Canada-U.S. relations: The case of the Harper Conservatives. *American Review of Canadian Studies* 37(1): 23-34.
–. 2008. A thermostatic dynamic? Electoral outcomes and anti-Americanism in Canada. In *The political consequences of anti-Americanism,* ed. R.A. Higgott and I. Malbasic, 129-41. London: Routledge.
–. 2009. No exit: Canada and the "war without end" in Afghanistan. In *NATO and the international engagement in Afghanistan,* ed. Hans-Georg Ehrhart and Charles C. Pentland, 157-73. Montreal and Kingston: McGill-Queen's University Press.
Nossal, K.R., and S. Roussel. 2000. Canada and the Kosovo war: The happy follower. In *Alliance politics, Kosovo, and NATO's war: Allied force or forced allies?* ed. P. Martin and M.R. Brawley, 181-99. New York: Palgrave.
Nye, J.S. Jr. 1991. *Bound to lead: The changing nature of American power.* New York: Basic Books.
O'Brien, R., A.M. Goetz, S.A. Scholte, and M. Williams. 2000. *Contesting global governance: Multilateral economic institutions and global social movements.* Cambridge: Cambridge University Press.

O'Connor, D. 2006. *A new review mechanism for the RCMP's national security activities: Commission of inquiry into the actions of Canadian officials in relation to Maher Arar*. Ottawa: Public Works and Government Services Canada.

O'Connor, G. 2006. Speaking notes for the Honourable Gordon J. O'Connor, PC, MP, minister of national defence for the NATO Parliamentary Association Meeting. Quebec City, 17 November. http://www.forces.gc.ca.

—. 2007. Speaking notes for the Honourable Gordon J. O'Connor, minister of national defence, for the January cross-country tour. Edmonton, 20 January. http://www.dnd.ca/site.

O'Dwyer, D. 2006. First landmines, now small arms? *Irish Studies in International Affairs* 17(48): 77-97.

O'Meara, D. 2006. "American empire" and "US imperialism" after the war in Iraq? The American state in the contemporary global order. *Labour, Capital and Society* 39(1): 4-33.

Offman, C. 2007. Canadians with faces veiled can vote: Masks are a no go; Elections Canada ruling senseless, politicians say. *National Post*, 8 September.

Okafor, O. 2000. The 1997 APEC Summit and the security of internationally protected persons: Did someone say "Suharto"? In *Pepper in our eyes: The APEC affair*, ed. W. Pue, 185-96. Vancouver: UBC Press.

Olson, W.J. 2007. War without a center of gravity: Reflections on terrorism and post-modern war. *Small Wars and Insurgencies* 18(4): 559-83.

Olsson, C. 2007. Guerre totale et/ou force minimale? Histoire et paradoxes des "coeurs et des esprits." *Cultures & Conflits* 67(3): 35-62. http://www.conflits.org.

Olympic Resistance Network. 2008. No 2010 Olympics on stolen Native land: Resist the 2010 corporate circus. http://www.no2010.com.

Owens, H., and B. Arneil. 1999. The human security paradigm shift: A new lens on Canadian foreign policy? *Canadian Foreign Policy* 7(1): 1-12.

Owens, M.T. 2006. Realism, Iraq and the Bush doctrine: Some clarification is desperately needed. *National Review Online*, 12 December.

Oxfam America. 2006. *Tarnished gold: Mining and the unmet promise of development*. http://www.oxfamamerica.org.

PAC [Partnership Africa Canada]. 2008. Year in review 2007. Ottawa: PAC.

Paine, T. 1775/1989. An occasional letter on the female sex. Repr. *The Truth Seeker* (May/June): 8-9.

Pankhurst, D. 2003. The "sex war" and other wars: Towards a feminist approach to peace building. *Development in Practice* 13(2-3): 154-77.

Pape, R.A. 2005. Soft balancing against the United States. *International Security* 30(1): 7-45.

Paris, R. 2001. Human security: Paradigm shift or hot air? *International Security* 26(2): 87-102.

Paterson, M., and S. Dalby. 2006. Empire's ecological tyreprints. *Environmental Politics* 15(1): 1-22.

Paul, T.V., J. Wirtz, and M. Fortmann, eds. 2004. *Balance of power: Theory and practice in the 21st century*. Stanford, CA: Stanford University Press.

Payan, T. 2006. *The three U.S.-Mexico border wars: Drugs, immigration and homeland security*. Westport, CT: Praeger Security International.

Payton, L. 2006. Goddard laid to rest in Ottawa: Soldier interred at military cemetery. *Calgary Herald*, 8 June.

Pearlston, K. 2000. APEC days at UBC: Student protests and national security in an era of trade liberalization. In Kinsman, Buse, and Steedman, 2000, 267-77.

Pedro, A. 2006. Mainstreaming mineral wealth in growth and poverty reduction strategies. *Minerals and Energy* 21(1): 2-16.

People's Commission on Immigration Security Measures. 2007. *Final Report*. http://www.peoplescommission.org/.

Perret, G. 1989. *A country made by war: From the revolution to Vietnam – the story of America's rise to power*. New York: Random House.

Peterson, V.S. 1992. Security and sovereign states: What is at stake in taking feminism seriously? In *Gendered states: Feminist (Re)visions of international relations theory*, ed. V.S. Peterson, 31-64. Boulder, CO: Lynne Rienner.

Petit, R. 2004. Biological invasions at the gene level. *Diversity and Distributions* 10(3): 159-65.

Pettman, J.J. 2004. Feminist international relations after 9/11. *Brown Journal of World Affairs* 10(2): 85-96.

–. 2007. Reflections on the gendering of states, sovereignty and security in the study of international relations. *Intersections: Gender, history and culture in the Asian context*. Perth: Murdoch University.

Picarelli, J.T. 2006. The turbulent nexus of transnational organized crime and terrorism: A theory of malevolent international relations. *Global Crime* 7(1): 1-24.

Pigott, P. 2007. *Canada in Afghanistan: The war so far*. Toronto: Dundurn.

Podhoretz, N. 1996. Neoconservatism: A eulogy. AEI Bradley Lecture Series, American Enterprise Institute.

Pollard, R.A. 1985. *Economic security and the origins of the Cold War*. New York: Columbia University Press.

Post, J.M. 2007. *The mind of the terrorist: The psychology of terrorism from the IRA to al-Qaeda*. New York: Palgrave.

Potter, E.H. 2002. Canada and the new public diplomacy. Discussion Paper in Diplomacy, Netherlands Institute of International Relations Clingendael.

Poulton, R.-E., and I. ag Youssouf. 1998. *A peace of Timbuktu: Democratic governance, development and African peacekeeping*. UNIDIR/98/2. New York: UN Institute for Disarmament Research.

Poulton, R.-E., I. ag Youssouf, and J. Seck. 1999. *Collaboration internationale et construction de la paix en Afrique de l'Ouest: L'exemple du Mali*. Geneva: UN Institute for Disarmament Research.

PPC [Pearson Peacekeeping Centre]. 2006. *Annual report 2005-2006*. Ottawa, ON. http://www.peaceoperations.org.

Pratt, C. 1983-84. Dominant class theory and Canadian foreign policy: The case of the counter-consensus. *International Journal* 39(1): 99-135.

Preston, R. 1994. *The hot zone*. New York: Random House.

Prestowitz, C. Jr. 1988. *Trading places: How we allowed Japan to take the lead.* New York: Basic Books.
Price-Smith, A. 2002. *The health of nations: Infectious disease, environmental change, and their effects on national security and development.* Cambridge, MA: MIT Press.
Pring, G., and L. Siegle. 2005. International law and mineral resource development. In Bastida, Walde, and Warden-Fernandez, 2005, 127-48.
Radstone, S., and K. Hodgkin, eds. 2003a. *Contested pasts: The politics of memory.* London: Routledge.
–. 2003b. *Regimes of memory.* London: Routledge.
Rajamani, L. 2006. *Differential treatment in international environmental law.* Oxford: Oxford Monographs in International Law.
Ral, N. 2008. *La stratégie sécuritaire des États-Unis dans la Corne de l'Afrique depuis le 11 septembre 2001.* MA diss., Université du Québec à Montréal.
Ramsbottom, A., A.M.S. Bah, and F. Calder. 2005. Enhancing African peace and security capacity: A useful role for the UK and G8? *International Affairs* 81(2): 325-39.
Razack, S. 2004. *Dark threats and white knights: The Somalia Affair, peacekeeping and the new imperialism.* Toronto: University of Toronto Press.
–. 2008. *Casting out: The eviction of Muslims from Western law and politics.* Toronto: University of Toronto Press.
Read, N. 2004. Gigantic killer frogs overrun B.C. *National Post,* 8 July.
REAP [Research-Education-Advocacy-People of the United Food and Commercial Workers]. n.d. Selected historical dates in the U.S. trade union movement. http://www.reapinc.org.
Record, J. 2006. The American way of war: Cultural barriers to successful counterinsurgency. Policy Analysis Series, no. 577, Cato Institute.
Rediehs, L.J. 2002. Evil. In Collins and Glover, 2002, 65-77.
Remington, R. 2006a. Goddard "humbled" by mission. *Calgary Herald,* 27 May.
–. 2006b. Goddard's sacrifice touches us all. *Calgary Herald,* 25 May.
Rengger, N.J. 2000. *International relations, political theory and the problem of order: Beyond international relations theory?* London: Routledge.
Reno, W. 1999. *Warlord politics and African states.* Boulder, CO: Lynne Rienner.
Rice, C. 2004. The president's national security strategy. In Stelzer, 2004b, 81-87.
Richmond, O.P. 2007. Critical research agendas for peace: The missing link in the study of international relations. *Alternatives: Global, Local, Political* 32(2): 247-74.
Roach, K. 2006. National security, multiculturalism and Muslim minorities. *Singapore Journal of Legal Studies* 2 (Winter): 405-38.
Roberts, J.T., and B. Parks. 2006. *A climate of injustice: Global inequality, north-south politics, and climate policy.* Cambridge, MA: MIT Press.
Robin, R. 2001. *The making of the Cold War enemy: Culture and politics in the military-intellectual complex.* Princeton, NJ: Princeton University Press.
Robinson, W.I. 1996. *Promoting polyarchy: Globalization, US intervention, and hegemony.* Cambridge: Cambridge University Press.

Rogin, M. 1988. *Ronald Reagan the movie: And other episodes in political demonology*. Berkeley: University of California Press.

Roosevelt, T. 1882. *The naval war of 1812: Or the history of the United States during the last war with Great Britain*. New York: Putnam.

–. 1889-1896/2004. *The winning of the West*. 4 vols. Whitefish, MT: Kessinger.

–. 1923. *The Americanism of Theodore Roosevelt: Selections from his writings and speeches*. Compiled by H. Hagedorn. Boston: Houghton Mifflin.

Rose, T. 1996. *Post-conflict peacebuilding at work: The case of Mali*. Presentation of the high-level consultation on the consolidation of peace in West Africa, United Nations, New York and United Nations Development Programme (UNDP), Mali.

Rosencrance, R., ed. 1976. *America as an ordinary country: U.S. foreign policy and the future*. Ithaca, NY: Cornell University Press.

Ross, K. 2002. *May '68 and its afterlives*. Chicago: University of Chicago Press.

Rostami-Povey, E. 2003. Women in Afghanistan: Passive victims of the *borga* or active social participants? *Development in Practice* 13(2-3): 266-77.

Rothkopf, D. 2005. *Running the world: The inside story of the National Security Council and the architects of American power*. New York: Public Affairs.

Ruggie, J.G. 1998a. *Constructing the world polity: Essays on international organization*. London: Routledge.

–. 1998b. What makes the world hang together? Neo-utilitarianism and the social constructivist challenge. *International Organization* 52(4): 855-85.

–. 2004. Reconstituting the global public domain – issues, actors, and practices. *European Journal of International Relations* 10(4): 499-531.

Ruiz, G., and J. Carleton, eds. 2003. *Invasive species and management strategies*. Washington, DC: Island Press.

Russo, A. 2008. The Feminist Majority Foundation's campaign to stop gender apartheid. *International Feminist Journal of Politics* 8(4): 557-80.

Sachs, W. 1999. *Planet dialectics: Explorations in environment and development*. London: Zed Books.

Said, E.W. 1979. *Orientalism*. New York: Vintage.

Sanders, J., and P. Stoett. 2006. Fighting extinction and invasion: Transborder conservation efforts. In *Continental ecopolitics: Canadian-American relations and environmental policy*, ed. P. LePrestre and P. Stoett, 157-78. London: Ashgate.

Saul, B. 2003. International terrorism as a European crime: The policy rationale for criminalization. *European Journal of Crime, Criminal Law and Criminal Justice* 11(4): 323-49.

Sayre, N. 1978. *Running time: Films of the Cold War*. New York: Dial Press.

Schmid, A.P. 2004. Frameworks for conceptualizing terrorism. *Terrorism and Political Violence* 16(2): 197-221.

Schmidt, B.C., and M.C. Williams. 2007. The Bush doctrine and the Iraq War: Neoconservatives vs. realists. Paper presented at the annual conference of the British International Studies Association, Cambridge, UK, 17-19 December.

Schrijver, N., and F. Weiss, eds. 2004. *International law and sustainable development: Principles and practice*. Leiden: Martinus Nijhoff.

Schumann, R.E. 2003. Compensation from World War II through to the Great Society. Reproduced in U.S. Department of Labor, Bureau of Labor Statistics, *Compensation and working conditions outline*. http://www.bls.gov.

Schwartz, B., and C. Layne. 2002. A grand new strategy. *Atlantic Monthly*, January: 36-40.

Sears, J. 2007. *Deepening democracy and cultural context in the Republic of Mali*. PhD diss., Queen's University.

Sedgwick, E. 1991. *Epistemology of the closet*. Berkeley: University of California Press.

Sending, O., and I. Neumann. 2006. Governance to governmentality: Analyzing NGOs, states, and power. *International Studies Quarterly* 50(3): 651-72.

Senlis Council. 2006. *Losing hearts and minds in Afghanistan: Canada's leadership to break the cycle of violence in southern Afghanistan*. Ottawa: Senlis Council Security and Development Policy Group.

–. 2007a. *Canada in Afghanistan: Charting a new course to complete the mission*. Ottawa: Senlis Council Security and Development Policy Group.

–. 2007b. *The Canadian International Development Agency in Kandahar: Unanswered questions*. Ottawa: Senlis Council Security and Development Policy Group.

–. 2008. *Afghanistan: A decision point*. Ottawa: Senlis Council Security and Development Policy Group.

Shantz, J. 2003. Fighting to win: The Ontario Coalition against Poverty. In *We are everywhere: The irresistible rise of global anticapitalism*, ed. Notes from Nowhere, 464-71. New York: Verso Press.

Shapiro, M.J. 2004. *Methods and nations: Cultural governance and the indigenous subject*. New York: Routledge.

Sharma, N. 2006. *Home economics: Nationalism and the making of "migrant workers" in Canada*. Toronto: University of Toronto Press.

Shaw, T.M. 2006. Two Africas? Two Ugandas? An "African democratic developmental state"? Or another "failed state"? In MacLean, Black, and Shaw, 2006, 101-12.

–. 2008. *Commonwealth: Inter- and non-state contributions to global governance*. London: Routledge.

Shelley, L.I., and J.T. Picarelli. 2002. Methods not motives: Implications of the convergence of international organized crime and terrorism. *Police Practice and Research* 3(4): 305-18.

Shephard, M. 2007. Gitmo north's last prisoner in limbo after 6 years. http://www.thestar.com.

Shepherd, L. 2006. Veiled references: Constructions of gender in the Bush administration discourse on the attacks on Afghanistan post-9/11. *International Feminist Journal of Politics* 8(1): 19-41.

Shiva, V. 1993. *Monocultures of the mind*. New Jersey: Zed Books.

Shoup, L., and W. Minter. 1977. *Imperial brain trust: The Council on Foreign Relations and the United States foreign policy*. New York: Monthly Review Press.

Simpson, J. 2008. Are Canadians getting the truth about Afghanistan? *Globe and Mail*, 15 July.

Singer, P.W. 2005. Outsourcing war. *Foreign Affairs* 84(2): 119-33.

Sjolander, C.T., H.A. Smith, and D. Stienstra, eds. 2003. *Feminist perspectives on Canadian foreign policy.* Don Mills, ON: Oxford University Press.
Slotkin, R. 1973. *Regeneration through violence: The mythology of the American frontier, 1600-1860.* Middletown, CT: Wesleyan University Press.
–. 1992. *Gunfighter nation: The myth of the frontier in twentieth-century America.* New York: Atheneum.
Smaldone, J.P. 1999. Mali and the West African Light Weapons Moratorium. In *Light weapons and civil conflict: Controlling the tools of violence,* ed. J. Boutwell and M.T. Klare, 129-46. Lanham, MD: Rowman and Littlefield.
Smith, A. 2005. *Conquest: Sexual violence and American Indian genocide.* Cambridge, MA: South End Press.
Smith, B.L., K.R. Damphousse, and P. Roberts. 2006. *Pre-incident indicators of terrorist incidents: The identification of behavioural, geographic and temporal patterns of preparatory conduct.* Washington, DC: US Department of Justice.
Smith, D.E. 1987. *The everyday world as problematic: A feminist sociology.* Toronto: University of Toronto Press.
–. 1990a. *The conceptual practices of power: A feminist sociology of knowledge.* Toronto: University of Toronto Press.
–. 1990b. *Texts, facts, and femininity: Exploring the relations of ruling.* London: Routledge.
–. 1999. *Writing the social.* Toronto: University of Toronto Press.
–. 2005. *Institutional ethnography: A sociology for people.* Oxford: Alta Mira Press.
Smith, G. 2007. *Canada in Afghanistan: Is it working?* Calgary: Canadian Defence and Foreign Affairs Institute.
–. 2008. Growing violence in Kandahar "insignificant," top soldier says. *Globe and Mail,* 13 July.
Smith, G.O. 1926. Theory and practice of national self-sufficiency in raw materials. *Proceedings of the Academy of Political Science in the City of New York* 12(1): 116-22.
Smith, S. 2001. Kelp rafts in the southern ocean. *Global Ecology and Biogeography* 11(1): 67-69.
Smith, T. 2007. *A pact with the Devil: Washington's bid for world supremacy and the betrayal of the American promise.* New York: Routledge.
Smith, Z.K. 1997. From demons to democrats: Mali's student movement 1991-1996. *Review of African Political Economy* 24(72): 249-63.
Snyder, J. 2004. One world, rival theories. *Foreign Policy* 145: 52-62.
Sokolsky, J. 2002. Exporting the "Gap"? The American influence. In *The soldier and the state in the post-Cold War era,* ed. A. Legault and J. Sokolsky, 211-36. Kingston, ON: Royal Military College.
Sorger, C., and E. Hoskins. 2001. Protecting the most vulnerable: War-affected children. In McRae and Hubert, 2001, 134-51.
Spears, T. 2004. Evolving superbugs threaten humans. *St. John's Telegram,* 3 October.
Spirit of Warrior Harriet Nahanee. 2008. http://harrietspirit.blogspot.com.
Spivak, G.C. 1988. Can the subaltern speak? In *Marxism and the interpretation of culture,* ed. C. Nelson and L. Grossberg, 271-313. Chicago: University of Illinois Press.

St. Hilaire, C., C. Ribble, E. Stephen, G. Anderson, G. Kurath, and M. Kent. 2002. Epidemiological investigation of infectious hematopoietic necrosis virus in salt water net-pen reared Atlantic salmon in B.C., Canada. *Aquaculture* 212(1-4): 49-68.

Stairs, D. 2001. Canada in the 1990s: Speak loudly and carry a bent twig. *Policy Options* (January/February): 43-49.

–. 2003a. Challenges and opportunities for Canadian foreign policy in the Paul Martin era. *International Journal* 58(4): 481-506.

–. 2003b. Myths, morals and reality in Canadian foreign policy. *International Journal* 58(2): 240-56.

Staples, W.G. 1997. *The culture of surveillance: Discipline and social control in the United States.* New York: St. Martin's Press.

Statistics Canada. 2006. Immigration in Canada: A portrait of the foreign-born population. http://www12.statcan.ca.

Stein, J.G., and E. Lang. 2007. *The unexpected war: Canada in Kandahar.* Toronto: Viking.

Stelzer, I. 2004a. Neoconservatives and their critics: An introduction. In Stelzer, 2004b, 3-28.

–, ed. 2004b. *The neocon reader.* New York: Grove Press.

Stephanson, A. 1996. *Manifest destiny: American expansion and the empire of right.* New York: Hill and Wang.

Sterling-Folker, J. 2002. Realism and the constructivist challenge: Rejecting, reconstructing or rereading. *International Studies Review* 4(1): 73-97.

–. 2004. Realist constructivism and morality. *International Studies Review* 6(2): 341-43.

Stoett, P. 1999. *Human and global security: An exploration of terms.* Toronto: University of Toronto Press.

–. 2006. Biosecurity: The next public policy imperative for Canada and the world. *Policy Options Politiques* 26(2): 24-30.

–. 2007. Counter-bioinvasion: Conceptual and governance challenges. *Environmental Politics* 16(3): 433-52.

Stone, G.R. 2004. *Perilous times: Free speech in wartime from the Sedition Act of 1798 to the war on terrorism.* New York: W.W. Norton.

Stopford, J., and S. Strange. 1991. *Rival states, rival firms.* Cambridge: Cambridge University Press.

Strategic Counsel. 2008. *A report to the Globe and Mail and CTV: Economy, leader positives/negatives, Afghanistan, carbon tax.* 14 January. http://www.thestrategiccounsel.com.

Suhrke, A. 2008. Reconstruction as modernisation: The post-conflict project in Afghanistan. *Third World Quarterly* 28(7): 1291-308.

Sunday Times. 2005. Designer fakes are funding Al-Qaeda. 20 March. www.timesonline.co.uk.

Sunshine Project. 2002. *An introduction to biological weapons, their prohibition, and the relation to biosafety.* Penang: Jutaprint.

Sutherst, R. 2000. Climate change and invasive species: A conceptual framework. In Mooney and Hobbs, 2000, 211-40.

Swanstrom, N. 2007. The narcotics trade: A threat to security? National and transnational implications. *Global Crime* 8(1): 1-25.
Swift, R. 2002. *No-nonsense guide to democracy*. Toronto: Between the Lines.
Sylvester, C. 2007. Whither the international at the end of IR. *Millennium* 35(3): 551-73.
Taillefer, G. 2008. Dire et se dédire. *Le Devoir*, 24 July. http://www.ledevoir.com.
Tassava, C.J. n.d. The American economy in World War II. Economic History Services, EH Net. http://eh.net/encyclopedia.
Thachuk, K.L., ed. 2007. *Transnational threats: Smuggling and trafficking in arms, drugs and human life*. Westport, CT: Praeger Security International.
Thakur, R.C., A.F. Cooper, and J. English, eds. 2005. *International commissions and the power of ideas*. Tokyo: United Nations University Press.
Theodoropoulas, D. 2003. *Invasion biology: Critique of a pseudoscience*. Blythe, CA: Avvar Books.
Thérien, J.-P. 1999. Beyond the north-south divide: The two tales of world poverty. *Third World Quarterly* 20(4): 723-42.
Thérien, J.-P., and V. Pouliot. 2006. The global compact: Shifting the politics of international development? *Global Governance* 12(1): 55-75.
Thobani, S. 2001. It's Bloodthirsty Vengeance. Speech delivered at Women's Resistance: From Victimization to Criminalization conference, Ottawa, 1 October. http://www.casac.ca/content/sunera-thobanis-speech.
–. 2003. War and the politics of truth-making in Canada. *International Journal of Qualitative Studies in Education* 16(3): 399-414.
–. 2007. *Exalted subjects, studies in the making of race and nation in Canada*. Toronto: University of Toronto Press.
Thomas, C., and M. Weber. 2004. The politics of global health governance: Whatever happened to "Health for all by the year 2000"? *Global Governance* 10(2): 187-205.
Thompson, E.P. 1968. *The making of the English working class*. Harmondsworth, UK: Penguin.
Tibbetts, Janice. 2009. Federal Court quashes security certificate against Hassan Almrei. Canwest News Services, 14 December. http://www.canada.com/news/.
Tickner, J.A. 2006. Feminism meets international relations: Some methodological issues. In Ackerly, Stern, and True, 2006, 19-41.
Tienhaara, K. 2006. Mineral investments and the regulation of the environment in developing countries: Lessons from Ghana. *International Environmental Agreements* 6(4): 371-94.
Tolchin, M., and S.J. Tolchin. 1992. *Selling our security: The erosion of America's assets*. New York: Knopf.
Tomlin, B.W. 1998. On a fast-track to a ban: The Canadian policy process. *Canadian Foreign Policy* 5(3): 3-24.
Toronto Star. 2008. Our goals in Afghanistan. 13 April. http://www.thestar.com.
Trachtenberg, M. 2007. Preventive war and U.S. foreign policy. *Security Studies* 16(1): 1-31.
Treasury Board of Canada Secretariat. 2007. Contribution program for the promotion of the defence diplomacy objectives implemented by the Military Assistance Training Programme. http://www.tbs-sct.gc.ca.

Turner, F.J. 1893/2003. *The significance of the frontier in American history.* History Department at the University of San Diego. http://history.sandiego.edu.
Ullman, R.H. 1983. Redefining security. *International Security* 8(1): 129-53.
UN [United Nations]. 2003. *Human security – now.* Report of the Commission on Human Security. New York: United Nations.
–. 2004. *A more secure world: Our shared responsibility.* Report of the High-level Panel on Threats, Challenges and Change. New York: United Nations.
–. 2005. *In larger freedom: Towards development, security and human rights for all.* Report of the secretary-general for the Millennium Summit. New York: United Nations.
UN News Centre. 2008a. Demand for peace by violence-plagued Afghans "overwhelming" – UN. 15 September.
–. 2008b. UN rights chief urges protection amid sharp rise in Afghan civilian death. 16 September.
UNAC [United Nations Association in Canada]. 2007. *Peacekeeping to peacebuilding: Lessons from the past, building for the future.* Report on the UNA-Canada 50th anniversary of United Nations peacekeeping. International Panel Series 2006-07. http://www.unac.org/.
UNAIDS/WHO [Joint United Nations Programme on HIV/AIDS / World Health Organization]. 2003. Aids epidemic update. Geneva.
UNCTAD [United Nations Conference on Trade and Development]. 2005. Economic Development in Africa: Rethinking the role of foreign direct investment. UNCTAD/GDS/AFRICA/2005/1. Geneva: United Nations.
UNDP [United Nations Development Programme]. 1994. *Human development report 1994.* New York: Oxford University Press.
–. 2002. *Democratizing security to prevent conflict and build peace.* Human Development Report 2002. New York: Oxford University Press.
UNEP [United Nations Environment Programme]. 2002. *GEO 3.* London: Earthscan.
UNHCR [United Nations High Commissioner for Refugees] Global Appeal. 1999. Mali. http://www.unhcr.org.
UNIFEM [United Nations Development Fund for Women]. 2008. *Fact sheet 2008: Progress for women is progress for all.* http://afghanistan.unifem.org.
United Kingdom. DFID [Department for International Development]. 2005a. *Fighting poverty to build a safer world: A strategy for security and development.* London: Department for International Development.
–. 2005b. *Why we need to work more effectively in fragile states.* London: Department for International Development.
United States. Congressional Research Service. 2007. *Terrorist precursor crimes: Issues and options for Congress.* RL34014. Washington, DC.
United States. DOD [Department of Defense]. 2002a. *Base structure report (a summary of DOD's real property inventory): Fiscal year 2002 baseline.* Washington, DC: Office of the Deputy Under Secretary of Defense (Installations and Environment). http://www.theblackvault.com.
–. 2002b. *July 2002 status of forces survey of active duty members.* DMDC report no. 2002-21. Washington, DC: Defense Manpower Data Center. http://www.dmdc.osd.mil.

–. 2007a. *Base structure report: Fiscal year 2007 baseline (a summary of DOD's real property inventory)*. Washington, DC: Office of the Deputy Under Secretary of Defense (Installations and Environment). http://www.defenselink.mil.

–. 2007b. *Personnel and procurement statistics: Military personnel statistics – active duty military personnel by service, by country/region; Total DOD 30 September 2007 (309A)*. Washington, DC: Statistical Information Analysis Division. http://siadapp.dmdc.osd.mil.

United States. DOT [United States Department of the Treasury]. 2007. Major foreign holders of treasury securities. http://www.treas.gov.

–. 2008. Treasury international capital system: U.S. gross external debt. Washington, DC. http://www.ustreas.gov.

United States. OMB [Office of Management and Budget]. 2008. *Budget of the U.S. government: Fiscal year 2009*. http://www.whitehouse.gov/omb.

United States Army. 2008. *2008 U.S. Army Posture Statement: Addendum F: Reset*. http://www.army.mil.

Upton, E. 1905/1917. *The military policy of the United States*. Washington, DC: Government Printing Office.

USAF [United States Air Force]. n.d. *United States Air Force: Our history*. http://www.airforce.com.

Van Driesche, J., and R. van Driesche. 2000. *Nature out of place: Biological invasions in the global age*. Washington, DC: Island Press.

van Ham, P. 2001. The rise of the brand state: The postmodern politics of image and reputation. *Foreign Affairs* 80 (September/October): 2-6.

Van Natta, D., and E. Sciolino. 2005. Timers used in blast, police say, parallels to Madrid are found. *New York Times*, 8 July. http://www.nytimes.com.

Vasquez, J.A., and C. Elman, eds. 2003. *Realism and the balancing of power: A new debate*. Princeton, NJ: Prentice Hall.

Verner, J. 2006. Canada's contribution to the reconstruction process in Afghanistan. 15 November. http://www.acdi-cida.gc.ca.

Viles, T. 2008. Hawala, hysteria and hegemony. *Journal of Money Laundering Control* 11(1): 25-33.

Volman, D. 2006. U.S. military programs in sub-Saharan Africa, 2005-2007. Association of Concerned African Scholars. http://www.prairienet.org.

Waever, O. 1995. Securitization and desecuritization. In *On security*, ed. R. Lipschutz, 46-86. New York: Columbia University Press.

Wagner, E. 2006-07. The peaceable kingdom? The national myth of Canadian peacekeeping and the Cold War. *Canadian Military Journal* 7(4): 45-54.

Walker, P. 2008. *Getting humanitarian aid right*. Paper presented at University of Manitoba, Winnipeg, 18 April.

Walker, R.B.J. 1988. *One world, many worlds: Struggles for a just world peace*. Boulder, CO: Lynne Rienner.

–. 1993. *Inside/outside: International relations as political theory*. Cambridge: Cambridge University Press.

–. 2006. Lines of insecurity: International, imperial, exceptional. *Security Dialogue* 37(1): 65-82.

—. 2010. *After the globe, before the world*. New York: Routledge.
Wallerstein, I. 1984. Three instances of hegemony in the history of the capitalist world-economy. *International Journal of Comparative Sociology* 24(12): 100-8.
Walt, S.M. 2005. *Taming American power: The global response to U.S. primacy*. New York: W.W. Norton.
Waltz, K.N. 1979. *Theory of international politics*. New York: McGraw-Hill.
—. 1993. The emerging structure of international politics. *International Security* 18(2): 44-79.
—. 2002. Structural realism after the Cold War. In Ikenberry, 2002, 29-67.
Wälzholz, G. 1997. *La problématique Touarègue au Mali: Le double enjeu de l'autodétermination et de l'intégration nationale*. Diploma theses, Institut d'Etudes de Sciences Politiques de Paris.
Warner, C.M. 2001. The rise of the state system in Africa. *Review of International Studies* 27 (December): 65-89.
Warner, M. 1993. *Fear of a queer planet: Queer politics and social theory*. Minneapolis: University of Minnesota Press.
Warner, T. 2002. *Never going back: A history of queer activism in Canada*. Toronto: University of Toronto Press.
Webb, M. 2007. *Illusions of security, global surveillance and democracy in the post-9/11 world*. San Francisco: City Lights.
Weber, M. 2006. IR theory, green political theory, and critical approaches: What prospects? In Laferrière and Stoett, 2006, 104-21.
Weigley, R.F. 1973. *The American way of war: A history of U.S. military strategy and policy*. London: Macmillan.
Weiss, T.G. 2000. Good governance and global governance: Conceptual and actual challenges. *Third World Quarterly* 21(5): 795-814.
Weldes, J. 1999. *Constructing national interests: The United States and the Cuban Missile Crisis*. Minneapolis: University of Minnesota Press.
Welsh, J.M. 2002. From right to responsibility: Humanitarian intervention and international society. *Global Governance* 8(4): 503-21.
—. 2004. *At home in the world: Canada's global vision for the 21st century*. Toronto: HarperCollins.
—. 2006. The 2005 International Policy Statement: Leading with identity? *International Journal* 61(4): 909-28.
Welsh, J.M., C.J. Thielking, and S.N. Macfarlane. 2005. The responsibility to protect: Assessing the report of the ICISS. In Thakur, Cooper, and English, 2005, 198-220.
Wendt, A. 1992. Anarchy is what states make of it: The social construction of power politics. *International Organization* 46(2): 391-425.
—. 1999. *Social theory of international politics*. Cambridge: Cambridge University Press.
White, D. 1993. *Invasive plants of natural habitats in Canada*. Ottawa: Canadian Wildlife Service.
White House. 2002. President Bush delivers graduation speech at West Point, 1 June. http://www.whitehouse.gov.
Whiteside, K. 2006. *Precautionary politics: Principle and practice in confronting environmental risk*. Cambridge, MA: MIT Press.

Whitworth, S. 2002. 11 September and the aftermath. *Studies in Political Economy* 67 (Spring): 33-38.

–. 2003. Militarized masculinities and the politics of peacekeeping: The Canadian case. In Sjolander, Smith, and Stienstra, 2003, 76-89.

–. 2004. *Men, militarism, and UN peacekeeping: A gendered analysis.* Boulder, CO: Lynne Rienner.

WHO [World Health Organization]. 2002. *World health report 2002: Reducing risks, promoting healthy life.* Geneva: WHO.

Williams, M.C. 2005. What is the national interest? The neoconservative challenge in IR theory. *European Journal of International Relations* 11(3): 307-37.

–. 2007a. *Culture and security: Symbolic power and the politics of international security.* London: Routledge.

–. 2007b. Morgenthau now: Neoconservatism, national greatness, and realism. In *Realism reconsidered: The legacy of Hans Morgenthau in international relations,* ed. M.C. Williams, 216-40. Oxford: Oxford University Press.

Williams, W.A. 1959/1984. *The tragedy of American diplomacy.* New York: W.W. Norton.

–. 1961/1973. *Contours of American history.* New York: New Viewpoints.

Williamson, K. 2006a. Captain's father assails media ban: Nichola Goddard funeral. *National Post,* 27 May.

–. 2006b. Charismatic captain honoured. *Calgary Herald,* 26 May.

Wilson Center. n.d. Famous quotations from Woodrow Wilson. *About Woodrow Wilson.* Woodrow Wilson International Center for Scholars. http://www.wilsoncenter.org.

Windsor Peace Committee. 2001. *Windsor OAS days of action: The criminalization of dissent.* Windsor, ON: Windsor Peace Committee.

Winnipeg Free Press. 2006a. Canada is with her. 19 May.

–. 2006b. Letter #7 from Capt. Nichola Goddard at the front. 19 May (online extra).

Winslow, D., and J. Dunn. 2002. Women in the Canadian forces: Between legal and social integration. *Current Sociology* 50(5): 641-67.

Wohlforth, W.C. 1999. The stability of a unipolar world. *International Security* 24(1): 5-41.

Wolfson, A. 2004. Conservatives and neoconservatives. In Stelzer, 2004b, 215-31.

Womankind Worldwide. 2008. Taking stock update: Afghan women and girls seven years on. http://www.womankind.org.uk.

Wood, E. 1995. *Democracy against capitalism: Renewing historical materialism.* Cambridge: Cambridge University Press.

Wood, P. 2000. *Biodiversity and democracy: Rethinking society and nature.* Vancouver: UBC Press.

World Bank. 2002. *World Bank group work in low-income countries under stress: A task force report.* Washington, DC, September.

Yergin, D. 1977. *The shattered peace: The origins of the Cold War and the national security state.* Boston: Houghton Mifflin.

–. 1992. *The prize: The epic quest for oil, money and power.* New York: Simon and Schuster.

York, G. 2006. Death clouds Afghanistan debate. *Globe and Mail*, 18 May.
Young, C. 1994. *The African colonial state*. New Haven, CT: Yale University Press.
Zacher, M., and T. Keefe. 2008. *The politics of global health governance: United by contagion*. London: Palgrave.
Zakaria, F. 2008. *The post-American world*. New York: W.W. Norton.
Zerrougui, L., S.V. de Biedermann, and M. Hashemi. 2005. Press release: Press conference by the Working Group on Arbitrary Detention of the United Nations Commission on Human Rights. Ottawa: UNHCR. http://www.unhchr.ch.
Zulfacar, M. 2006. The pendulum of gender politics in Afghanistan. *Central Asian Survey* 25(1-2): 27-59.

Contributors

David Black is Director of the Centre for Foreign Policy Studies and Professor of Political Science and International Development Studies at Dalhousie University. His current research interests focus on Canada and sub-Saharan Africa, with emphases on human security, development assistance, multilateral diplomacy, and extractive industry investment. His recent publications include *The International Politics of Mass Atrocities: the Case of Darfur*, co-edited with Paul Williams (2010), an edited section of the *Canadian Journal of Development Studies* (2007) on "Canadian aid policy in the new millennium," and *A decade of human security*, co-edited with Sandra MacLean and Timothy Shaw (2006). He has been President of the International Studies Association's Canadian region, a member of the executive committee of the Canadian Association for the Study of International Development, and a member of the executive council of the Canadian Consortium on Human Security.

Siobhan Byrne is Assistant Professor of Political Science at the University of Alberta. Before joining the department in July 2009, she held a postdoctoral fellowship at the John Hume Institute for Global Irish Studies and the School of Politics and International Relations, University College Dublin, Ireland. She completed an MA and PhD in Political Studies at Queen's University, Kingston, and received an undergraduate degree in Journalism and Political Science from Carleton University. Her primary areas of research include feminist anti-war activism and peace-building in societies in transition from conflict, with a particular focus on Northern Ireland and Israel/Palestine.

Bruno Charbonneau is Associate Professor of Political Science at Laurentian University. He obtained his PhD from Queen's University in Kingston in 2006. His research interests include humanitarian interventions, peacebuilding, Francophone Africa, and Africa-France-Europe security relations. He is the author of *France and the new imperialism: Security policy in sub-Saharan Africa* (2008). Other publications on security relations in Africa have appeared in *Alternatives, International Peacekeeping, Modern and Contemporary France,* and the *Journal of Military and Strategic Studies.* He also contributed to the book by David Black and Paul Williams, *The international politics of mass atrocities: The case of Darfur,* writing the chapter on France's approach to the crisis (2010). His work on Canadian foreign policy has been published in *International Political Sociology* (2008) and the *Canadian Foreign Policy Journal* (2010).

Wayne S. Cox has been with the Department of Political Studies at Queen's University in Kingston since 2001 and also taught at the Royal Military College of Canada in the mid-late 1990s. His primary research and teaching are in the areas of Middle Eastern politics, international relations, and the international political economy. Professor Cox has published on contemporary debates in international relations theory, identity and war in the Middle East, identity and globalization, Canadian defence policy, and Turkish/Kurdish issues. He has been a frequent media expert for a wide variety of Canadian and international media sources in print, television, and radio.

T.S. (Todd) Hataley is employed in the Canadian security sector. He also holds appointments as adjunct professor at the Royal Military College of Canada and Queen's University. His current research interests include radicalization, regional security, and transnational crime. Among his publications are: *Narratives and counter-narratives for global Jihad: Opinion versus action* (2010); *Winning the battle but losing the war: Narrative and counter-narrative strategy* (2010); *The "Idea" of borders: The bordering process and the weight of history* (2009); *Towards a new trilateral security relationship: United States, Canada and Mexico 2012* (2009); *Catastrophic terrorism at the Canada-United States border* (2007); and *Drug trade and the war on drugs* (2007).

Gary Kinsman teaches sociology at Laurentian University in Sudbury. He is the author of *The regulation of desire: Homo and hetero sexualities* (1996); an editor of *Whose national security? Canadian state surveillance and the creation of enemies* (2000); an editor of *Mine mill fights back* (2005); an editor of *Sociology for changing the world: Social movements/social research* (2006); and co-author with Patrizia Gentile of *The Canadian war on queers: National security as sexual regulation* (2010). He has been active in gay/queer liberation, AIDS, anti-poverty, global justice, anti-war, and anti-capitalist movements.

Alex Macleod is Professor of Political Science at the Université du Québec à Montréal (UQAM), director of the Centre for Foreign Policy and Security Studies at UQAM and Concordia University, and the international political sociology section editor for the *International Studies Compendium*. His recent publications include three edited volumes: *Diplomaties en guerre: Sept États face à la crise iraquienne,* with David Morin (2005); *La lutte antiterroriste et les relations internationales* (2006); and *Théories des relations internationales: Contestations et résistances,* with Dan O'Meara (2007). He is currently working on popular culture and international relations, particularly American cinema and the Cold War.

Kim Richard Nossal is Sir Edward Peacock Professor of International Relations with the Department of Political Studies at Queen's University (Kingston), where he was head of the Department between 2001 and 2008. He has served as president of the Australian and New Zealand Studies Association of North America (1999-2001) and as president of the Canadian Political Science Association (2005-06). Among his books are *Relocating middle powers: Australia and Canada in a changing world order* (with Andrew F. Cooper and Richard A. Higgott, 1993); *Rain dancing: Sanctions in Canadian and Australian foreign policy* (1994); *The politics of Canadian foreign policy* (1997); *The patterns of world politics* (1998); *Diplomatic Departures: The Conservative era in Canadian foreign policy* (ed. with Nelson Michaud, 2001); *Politique internationale et défense au Canada et au Québec* (with Stéphane Roussel and Stéphane Paquin, 2007); *Architects and innovators: Building the Department of Foreign Affairs and International Trade, 1909-2009* (ed. with Greg Donaghy, 2009). His forthcoming book is *International policy and politics in Canada* (with Stéphane Roussel and Stéphane Paquin).

Dan O'Meara is a graduate of Witwatersrand University (South Africa) and of Sussex University (England). He is Professor in the Department of Political Science at Université du Québec à Montréal and Research Director at the Centre for Foreign Policy and Security Studies. He is author or co-author of six books on political conflicts in southern Africa, and of over sixty articles on southern Africa, Great Britain, and the United States. His latest book (co-edited with Alex Macleod) is *Théories des relations internationales: Contestations et résistances* (2007).

Geneviève Parent is Assistant Professor of Conflict Studies at Saint-Paul University in Ottawa. She specializes in victimology, victims of violence, and research methods. Specifically, her research interests include phenomenology, victims' rights, victims of war, the effects of mass violence on individuals and communities, and questions of healing, transitional justice, and reconciliation in peace-building practices. Her most recent publication, "Reconciliation and Justice after Genocide: A Theoretical Exploration," was published in *Genocide Studies and Prevention* (2010). She is presently working on a book on peace-building and psychologies of peace based upon the comparative analyses of African conflict victims.

Malcolm Savage is currently a student at Queen's University Faculty of Law in Kingston. His current areas of interest are Canadian criminal and constitutional law. Before entering law school, Malcolm completed a master of arts degree in political science at Dalhousie University. His area of study was international development, with a focus on Africa; he wrote his thesis on small-scale industries in Ghana. Malcolm had an opportunity to visit Ghana during a field school organized through the University of Calgary, where he completed a bachelor's degree. Upon completing law school, Malcolm plans to practice criminal law in the Ottawa area.

Jonathan Sears received his PhD from Queen's University in Kingston. He is Assistant Professor in International Development Studies at Menno Simons College, Canadian Mennonite University/University of Winnipeg. Jon approaches international development studies from a multidisciplinary academic background – philosophy, comparative politics of development, and political theory. His PhD dissertation on democratic deepening in the Republic of Mali addresses, from political culture and political economy perspectives, how citizen identity is rooted in indigenous, Islamic, and Western norms and practices. His broader research interests include politics in Africa, development policy (especially governance), political culture, and political economy.

Timothy M. Shaw is Director and Professor at the Institute of International Relations, the University of the West Indies, St. Augustine; Visiting Professor, Makerere University Business School and Mbarara University of Science and Technology in Uganda; Visiting Professor, the University of Stellenbosch, South Africa; and Professor Emeritus at University of London. Dr. Shaw has published extensively on conflict in Africa, Caribbean and Pacific Islands, international development, and global governance. He served as a member of the Civil Society Advisory Committee to the Commonwealth Foundation and was a member of the Special Advisory Group to the Summit Secretariat in Trinidad for the 2009 Commonwealth heads of government meeting. Dr. Shaw continues to edit two book series: International Political Economy for Palgrave Macmillan and IPE of New Regionalisms for Ashgate Publishing.

Claire Turenne Sjolander is Professor of Political Science at the School of Political Studies and Director of the Institute of Women's Studies, University of Ottawa. From 2000 to 2006, she held a number of administrative positions in the Faculty of Social Sciences, including Director of the School and Associate Dean of the Faculty. She was the recipient of the University of Ottawa's Excellence in Education Award (2009) and was 2007-08 Distinguished Scholar in Residence at the State University of New York's Centre for the Study of Canada. Her teaching and research have focused on international relations theory and Canadian Foreign Policy, specially focused on gender and foreign policy. Author of numerous articles, her most recent volumes include *Feminist perspectives on Canadian foreign policy* (2003; edited with Heather Smith and Deborah Stienstra), and *Gender and Canadian foreign policy* (2005; a special issue of the journal *Canadian Foreign Policy*, edited with Heather Smith).

Peter J. Stoett is Professor of Global Politics and Chair of the Department of Political Science at Concordia University in Montreal. He obtained his PhD in Political Studies from Queen's University in Kingston in 1994. His main areas of expertise include international relations and law, human rights and environmental issues, and Canadian foreign policy. Recent books (authored, co-authored, and co-edited) include *Environmental challenges and opportunities: Local-global perspectives on environmental issues* (2009); *Bilateral ecopolitics: Canadian-American environmental relations* (2006); *International ecopolitical theory: Critical reflections* (2006); and *Global politics: Origins, currents, directions*, 3d ed. (2005). Dr. Stoett also teaches at the United Nations' University for Peace in San Jose, Costa Rica. He is currently working on a forthcoming book, *Global biosecurity: The international politics of denial, fear, and injustice,* to be published by UTP/Broadview Press.

Kathryn Trevenen is currently Assistant Professor at the Institute of Women's Studies and the School of Political Studies at the University of Ottawa. Her teaching and research focus on gendered media representations of war, gendered aspects of political and cultural ideologies, transnational women's issues and rights, the impact of the HIV/AIDS pandemic on women, and on LGBT human rights and citizenship. Her work has been presented and published in a variety of venues, including several edited volumes, *Political Theory, Urban Affairs Review,* and *Theory and Event.*

Index

Note: CSR stands for "corporate social responsibility"; IR, for international relations.

Aarhus Convention, 210
Abu-Laban, Yasmeen, 169-70
Adams, Mary Louise, 155
Afghan women: deteriorating conditions (after 2001), 100-2; as justification for Canadian mission, 88, 97-100, 173-74; portrayal as innocent victims, 88, 97-100, 173
Afghanistan, Canadian mission in: Afghan women and children as justification for, 88, 97-100, 173-74; aim of mission, 96-97; Canada's priorities (2008-11), 103-4; CIDA's lack of results, 103; cost of humanitarian projects vs cost of war, 104; deteriorating conditions for Afghan women since 2001, 100-2; development in Afghanistan, 94-96, 97, 100-5; extension after Goddard's death, 142-44; gendered representation (*see* Goddard, Nichola); gendered representations and reinforcement of peace-keeping myths re Canada, 127-28, 136-37; government efforts to increase public support for, 120-24; "hearts and minds" military campaigns, 104-5; humanitarian aspects promoted by government, 19, 87, 89-92, 96, 116; humanitarian management of Afghan life, 96-97; ideal characteristics for Canada's global engagement, 115-16; level of public support, 19, 116-20, 122-24, 280; level of support by political parties, 119; multilateral nature, 115-16; national interest/security as justification for mission, 88, 121, 123-24, 286-87; offensive operation rather than peace-keeping, 22-23; post-colonial effort to impose global order, 88, 94; promotion of peace through war, 92, 105; signature projects, 104-5; war of security for development, 94-96, 105
Afghanistan Compact, 115-16

Afghanistan human development report (CPHD), 101
Africa and Canadian foreign policy: advocacy for liberalized mining sector, 242; Canadian military security missions along with US, 26; Diamond Development Initiative (DDI), 230-31; erosion of Canada's multilateral tradition, 26-27, 229, 283; Extractive Industries Transparency Initiative (EITI), 230, 231-33, 253, 258n4; government disregard for CSR, 237, 246, 248-49, 252-56; humanitarian goals vs support for extractive industries, 27, 235-36, 246, 247-48, 250-51, 256, 257-58, 283; Kimberley Process re conflict diamonds, 220, 221, 222, 230-31, 254; Partnership Africa Canada (PAC), 230-31; perception vs reality in Canadian policies, 239-41; Publish What You Pay coalition, 230, 231. *See also* corporate social responsibility (CSR); extractive industries (Canadian) in Africa
Agamben, Giorgio, 163-64
Agathangelou, Anna M., 170
Agnew, John, 6-7, 288
al-Qaeda: alleged link with Iraq, 63; invasion of Afghanistan to remove Taliban support, 115, 121; involvement in drug trade, 189; as non-state actor in realist theory, 70
Almalki, Abdullah, 161
Almrei, Hassan, 162-63
Americanism: belief in primacy of the American way, 42-43; definition, 38; "elastic geography" or expansion of US, 46-48; how United States is imagined, 45-46; militarism and, 38-39, 42-45, 64; "open door" policy to extend US economic interests, 48; public culture and, 38, 65n5; tropes underlying the American war story, 43-45

Amnesty International, 172
Andreas, Peter, 183-84
Anti-Terrorism, Crime and Security Act (United States), 167
Anti-Terrorism Act (Canada), 167, 170, 171
antibiotics, impact on environment, 209
APEC (Asia-Pacific Economic Cooperation), 158-59
Arar, Maher, 25, 161, 172, 181
Ashley, Richard, 9
Asian carp, 200, 202-3
avian flu H7N3, 206-7
Axworthy, Lloyd: on alternatives to the hegemon (US), 110, 112; anti-hegemonic attitude toward US, 109-10; anti-landmine treaty, 227; Canada as global citizen, not motivated by national interest, 108-9; on human and state security, 90-91; investigation of Talisman Energy controversy, 247-48; multilateral efforts as foreign minister, 221; multilateralism as core principle of Canadian foreign policy, 110; notion of human security, 110-11; Ottawa and Kimberley processes, 220, 222, 227; support for human security agenda, 240
Azarbaijani-Moghaddam, S., 99

Bailey, Morgan, 131
Bannerji, Himani, 154, 176
Barrick Gold Corporation, 250
Baudouin, D., 273
Beam, Jason, 130, 141
Benatta, Benamar, 161
Benjamin, Walter, 151
Bergen, Peter, 176
Betts, Richard, 81
Bigo, Didier, 289-90
bioimperialism (spread of biota), 210-12
biosecurity: bioimperialism (spread of biota), 210-12; definition, 201, 214n2; genetically modified organisms,

204, 214n3; global reduction in biodiversity and, 209; human-induced environmental change, 208-10; infectious diseases, 205-8, 212-13; invasive (alien) species, 200, 202-5; levels of action to counteract, 213-14; possible terrorist targets, 212; securitizationist responses, 201-2, 206, 211-12; shift in balance of power in human-nature relationship, 208-10; sovereignty of biosecurity, 210-12; threats to Canadian economic and political well-being, 26, 282-83
Black, David, 27, 235-59, 283
Blair, Cherie, 173
Bloc Québécois and Afghanistan mission, 119
Bonn International Center for Conversion (BICC), 222, 232
Bonte Gold Mines controversy, 249-50
Boot, Max, 78
Boucher, J-C., 119
Brand Canada Program, 245
Brenner, William, 69, 70
Bretton Woods and global governance, 225
Brison, Scott, 142-44
Brown, Dave, 174
Building the Canadian advantage (DFAIT), 255-56, 257
Bulyanhulu Gold Mine (Tanzania) controversy, 250
Bush, George H.W., 82-83
Bush, George W.: belief in American exceptionalism, 41; belief in American universalism, 42-43; delineation of those "with us" or "against us," 12; legacy left for country, 33; national security coalition post-9/11, 63; neoconservative doctrine, 67, 77-79; neoconservative doctrine, realist responses to, 79-81; planned response to outbreak of infectious disease, 206; those who resist American beliefs labelled as "enemies of freedom," 41
Bush, Laura, 173
Bush doctrine, 67, 76-79, 79-81. *See also* neoconservatism
Buzan, B., 186
Byrne, Siobhan, 24-25, 167-82, 260, 281-82

Calgary Herald, 130-31, 142-44
Campbell, Bonnie, 239, 243
Canada: component of American and Western forms of power and order, 4; economic relationship with US, 15-16; multiculturalism, 15. *See also* Afghanistan, Canadian mission in; Canada–US relations; extractive industries (Canadian) in Africa; foreign policy, Canadian; military practices of Canada; national security (Canada); peace-keeping (Canadian)
Canada Border Services Agency, 194-95
Canada Evidence Act (Canada), 170
Canada Fund for Africa, 239-40, 245
Canada Investment Fund for Africa, 245
Canada Out of Afghanistan campaign, 120
Canada Pension Plan, 245, 250
Canada–US relations: Canada's role in and its relationship with US, 13-14; Canadian foreign policy at odds with US conceptualization of Canada's role, 23, 112; defence integration with Canada, 16, 17-20, 113; population's rethinking of Canada's role in world and with US (1993-2006), 23, 107-8, 124, 281; US hegemony and location of countries, 278
Canadian Bar Association, 171
Canadian Consortium on Human Security, 228
Canadian Council of Muslim Women, 179

Canadian Network on Corporate Accountability, 248, 252, 253, 256
Canadian Peace Alliance, 120
Canadian Research Institute for the Advancement of Women, 180
Canadian Security Intelligence Service (CSIS), 160-61, 177
Canadian Security Intelligence Service Act, 170, 187
Canadian war on queers: National security as sexual regulation (Kinsman and Gentile), 150-51
Centre canadien d'étude et de coopération internationale (CECI), 267
Charbonneau, Bruno, 1-29, 87-106, 260, 276-91
Charchuk, Andrew, 139
Charities Registration (Security Information) Act (Canada), 170
Charkaoui, Adil, 162
Charlesworth, Hilary, 169
Chen, Marie, 180
Chermak, S., 188, 196
China, 233, 244
Chinkin, Christine, 169
Chrétien, Jean: anti-hegemonic stance and decision not to join US invasion of Iraq, 110, 112, 123, 124; attitude toward Canadian Armed Forces, 113; Chrétien doctrine, 110; policy of defying the US, 114; population encouraged to rethink Canada's role in world and with US (1993-2006), 23, 107; support for Africa, 239-40
CIA (Central Intelligence Agency), 61
CIDA (Canadian International Development Agency), 103, 241, 245-46, 262
Clark, Robert, 212-13
Clarke, John, 159
Clarke, R.V., 192-93
climate change and biosecurity, 205, 208-10
Coalition for the ICC, 233
Commission for Africa (United Kingdom), 232-33

Commission of Inquiry into the Actions of Canadian Officials in Relation to Maher Arar, 172
Commonwealth commissions on security, 228-29
Conservative Party of Canada: erosion of multilateralism, 221-22, 223; position on Afghanistan mission, 119, 173-74; position on human security, 112-13, 121, 221-22; security certificate program, 163. *See also* Harper, Stephen
Consultation Commission on Accommodation Practices Related to Cultural Differences in Québec, 178
continental defence, post-WWII and post-9/11, 17-19
corporate social responsibility (CSR): accountability demanded by civil society, 246-47, 248, 253-56, 257; Canadian government's disregard for, 237, 246, 248-49, 252-56; Canadian parliamentary committee report on, 251-52; Canadian roundtables on, 252-55, 256-58; impact of Talisman controversy, 247-48; non-governmental advisory group, 252, 255-56, 257-58; OECD guidelines and their observance, 248-49
Council of Canadians, 120
Cox, Robert, 11
Cox, Wayne S., 1-29, 276-91
Crawford, Harry, 131, 139
criminality: convergence of terrorist and criminal activities, 183, 185-86, 188-92, 197, 198n10; definitions of crime, 185; Egmont Group tracking money laundering, 190-91; impact of globalization, 191; impact of internet, 191; intelligence-led policing to detect, 192-95, 198n11; international drug trade and terrorism, 189; motivation vs motivation for terrorism, 185-86; organized crime, 186; precursor criminal activity (to

terrorism), 188-89, 193, 195; transnational crime, 186
Crosby, Ann Denholm, 28n2, 92
Crowson, Philip, 257
Cruickshank, Paul, 176

Dahla Dam restoration (Afghanistan), 104
Daily News (Halifax), 129
Darier, E., 212
Darimani, Adbulai, 251
Dashwood, H., 253-54
Davinic, Prvoslav, 273
de Wilde, J., 186
defence policy, Canadian. *See* national security (Canada)
Defense Intelligence Agency, 61
Department of National Defence (Canada), 113, 114-15, 262, 266
Department of Public Safety and Emergency Preparedness (Canada), 171
Desbiens, Patrick, 135
development in Afghanistan: CIDA's lack of results, 103; as counterinsurgency effort, 97, 100-5; criticism of aid efforts, 102; "hearts and minds" military campaigns, 104-5; misleading claims of progress, 102-3; signature projects, 104-5; war of security for development, 94-96
Le Devoir, 128
Diagouraga, Mahamadou, 273
Diamond Development Initiative (DDI), 230-31
Dion, Stéphane, 119, 179
Dishman, Chris, 186
Donini, Antonio, 103
Donnelly, Thomas, 78
Duffield, Mark, 91, 94, 95, 226

Ebrahim, Salima, 179
Eckersley, R., 211
École de Maintien de la Paix (Mali), 268
École militaire d'administration (Mali), 268
École militaire inter-arme (Mali), 268
Economic Community of West African States (ECOWAS), 266
Eisenhower, Dwight, 58
El Maati, Ahmad, 161
elites: in early US history, 38, 46; enrichment of elites in Africa, 257, 264; ideology re military force to obtain objectives, 39, 49-50; lack of concern re biosecurity, 204; US elites' abandonment of peace (1950s), 61; US elites' decision re global leadership post-WWII, 35-38; Western values adopted by urban African elites, 263
Englehardt, T., 43-45
Enloe, Cynthia, 169, 174
environmental security, 201. *See also* biosecurity
Ericsson, Magnus, 237, 241, 242
exceptionalism, American, 40-41, 71-72, 83
Export Development Canada (EDC), 245-46, 250
extractive industries (Canadian) in Africa: accountability demands from civil society, 246-47, 248, 253-56, 257; Bonte Gold Mines (Ghana) controversy, 249-50; Bulyanhulu Gold Mine (Tanzania) controversy, 250; Canadian government assistance to, 244-46; Canadian government disregard for CSR, 237, 246, 248-49, 252-56; competition from India and China, 244; consolidation through mergers/acquisitions, 242-43; Diamond Development Initiative (DDI), 230-31; environmental and social impact of mining, 236, 238-39; exploration and mining companies, 241, 243-44; Extractive Industries Transparency Initiative (EITI), 230, 231-33, 253, 258n4; human rights abuses, 236; humanitarian goals vs support for extractive

industries, 27, 235-36, 246, 247-48, 250-51, 256, 257-58, 283; impact of roundtables on CSR, 252-56; implications of activities, 27, 249-51; importance to African countries, 238, 258n3; Kimberley Process re conflict diamonds, 220, 221, 222, 230-31, 254; liberalized mining sector required by investor countries, 239, 242, 258n5; Sadiola Gold Mine (Mali) controversy, 250-51; Talisman Energy controversy, 247-48

Extractive Industries Transparency Initiative (EITI), 230, 231-33, 253, 258n4

Fantino, Julian, 178
federal policing. *See* policing
Fédération Internationale des Ligues des Droits de l'Homme, 250-51
Federation of Law Societies, 172
FINTRAC (Financial Transactions and Reports Analysis Centre of Canada), 190
Food Biosecurity Action Team (United States), 208
foot-and-mouth disease, 206
Forcese, Craig, 248
Foreign Affairs and International Trade Canada, 111, 112, 245, 252, 266
foreign policy, Canadian: Afghanistan (*see* Afghanistan, Canadian mission in); Africa and (*see* Africa and Canadian foreign policy; extractive industries [Canadian] in Africa); anti-hegemonic attitude of Canada toward US, 109, 114; Canada as an alternative to the hegemon, 110; driven by domestic politics, 113; human security the proper focus of security, 110-11; multilateralism as core principle, 110; Nichola Goddard's death and (*see* Goddard, Nichola); at odds with US conceptualization of Canada's role in world politics, 23, 112; population's rethinking of Canada's role in world and with US (1993-2006), 23, 107-8, 124, 281; self-congratulatory view of Canada as global citizen, not motivated by national interest, 108-9, 124; state as masculine "protector" and gender neutral soldiers, 126-27, 129-30, 136; support for humanitarian intervention, 111-12, 121-22

Foucault, M., 201, 211
Francis, Diane, 174
Fraser, David, 129
Free Trade Area of the Americas, 159
Freilich, J.D., 188, 196
Fukuyama, Francis, 76
Fulford, Robert, 175
Fung, R.I., 272-73
Furtado, F.J., 111

Gaddis, John Lewis, 78
Gee, Marcus, 174
G8 meeting (Kananaskis 2002), 239-40
gender: gender-neutral soldiers and state as male "protector," 126-27, 129-30, 136, 142; gendered representations of war and peacekeeping myths re Canada, 127-28, 136-37; Goddard's gender denied in media as relevant but focused on, 134-36, 281; media coverage of Goddard as gender-neutral soldier, 23, 127, 129-36, 144. *See also* Afghan women; Muslim women
Gentile, Patrizia, 150-51
geographies of security, 7-8, 47
Giroday, Gabrielle, 135
Glasser, Ronald, 207
Global Ballast Water Management Programme, 204
Global Center for R2P, 227
global governance, 223-25, 233
Global Invasive Species Programme, 204
global-local nexus: authorization of authority, 10-11; interdependency and

linking of, 4, 10-12; relationship contingent and contested, 4, 10, 276-78

global order: Canada's role in world and its relationship with US, 13-14; complex nature of, 2-3, 4, 11-12, 279-80; construction of, 288-89; defined as in need of transformation, 10; defined as international stability and maintenance of status quo, 8-9; defined as reformed governance, 9-10; evolution of US power from bilateral to unilateral, 223; externalization and demonization of challenges to status quo, 12-13; location in diversity of spaces, 2-3, 5, 284-86; perception as centralized and hierarchical, 2-3; political order and, 2, 3-4, 5-6; relationships with local order, 3-4, 276-78; US as global power, 35-38. *See also* hegemony (American); militarism (American); peace-keeping (Canadian)

globalization: of security after 9/11, 8; and state sovereignty, 6-7

Globe and Mail, 135, 174, 176

glocal condition, 201

Glyn Berry Program for Peach and Security, 266

Goddard, Nichola: background and motive for joining military, 137-39; circumstances of death, 129; death and its influence on government's extension of mission, 142-44; gender as reinforcement of Canadian peacekeeping myths, 127-28, 136-37; gender concerns in camp and management of, 133; gender denied in media as relevant but focused on, 134-36, 281; gender neutral soldiers and state as male "protector," 126-27, 129-30, 136, 142; justification for the Afghan mission, 23-24, 137, 141-43, 281; leadership abilities and competence, 138-39; media coverage as gender-neutral soldier, 23, 127, 129-36, 144, 286; media coverage as peace-keeping and compassionate soldier, 23, 127, 139-43, 144; media portrayal reinforces Canadian foreign policy goals, 128, 144

Goddard, Tim, 130, 138

Gorelick, Jamie, 183

Gotlieb, Allan, 110, 111

Grace, E., 158

Graham, Bill, 109, 123

Granatstein, J.L., 90

Gray, Colin, 45-46

Gray, John, 93

Grayson, Kyle, 240

Great Lakes Fishery Commission, 203

Greater Nile Petroleum Operating Company, 247-48

Greener, B.K., 93

Hamm, Mark, 188-89, 195

Hardt, Michael, 164

Harkat, Mohamed, 162

Harker Commission, 247

Harper, Stephen: on Afghan mission as in Canada's national interest, 121; on Afghan mission as rescue for Afghan women, 173-74; erosion of multilateralism under this government, 221-22, 223; panel on Afghanistan, 103, 117; position on human security, 112-13, 121, 221-22; on wearing of veils while voting in elections, 179. *See also* Conservative Party of Canada

Hataley, T.S. (Todd), 25, 183-99, 282

Hay, John, 48

hegemony: aspects, 35; local and national struggles in Mali, 263-65, 268-69

hegemony (American): assumption of global power, 35-38, 223; "blowback" (local armed resistance to US dominance), 63; Canadian anti-

hegemonic attitude toward US, 109-10, 112, 114, 123, 124; declinism regarding US hegemony, 33-34, 62-63; elites' abandonment of peace (1950s), 61; elites' decision re global leadership post WWII, 35-38; growth of, 35-38, 278; location's effect on relationship with politics, 278; militarism integral part of US hegemony, 38, 62; national security as ideological practice, 149-50. *See also* militarism (American)
Heiligen-damm Process, 222
Heinbecker, Paul, 108
Hérouxville (QC), 178-79
Hezbollah, 189
Hillier, Rick, 88, 104, 113
Hirsi Ali, Ayaan, 175
HIV/AIDS treatment, 207
homosexuals. *See* queers
Hope, Ian, 129
Hubert, D., 229-30
Hughes, Robert, 41
human security: aim of Canadian mission in Afghanistan, 95-96, 115-16, 124; Canadian roundtables on, 252-55; definition of, 90-91; development/economic growth and, 95-96, 226-29, 236; as focus in Canadian foreign policy, 92-93, 95-96, 110-12, 121, 240; human security agenda of Canada, 92-93, 115, 121, 223, 240, 246; humanitarian goals vs support for extractive industries in Africa, 27, 235-36, 246, 247-48, 250-51, 256, 257-58, 283; majority-based conception of in Canada, 170; national interest and, 91; prevention of, rather than reaction to, conflict, 274; "responsibility to protect" (R2P) or humanitarian intervention, 227-28. *See also* corporate social responsibility (CSR)
Human security report (Canada), 228
Humphrey, J., 233

Humphreys, Adrian, 177
Humphreys, David, 243
Hunt, Krista, 173
Huntington, Samuel, 70
Hutchinson, S., 189

ICBL (International Campaign to Ban Landmines), 230, 231
Ignatieff, Michael, 91, 119, 142-44
Independent Panel on Canada's Future Role in Afghanistan, 96, 103, 117, 120
India, 233, 244
infectious diseases and biosecurity, 205-7, 212-13
Influence of sea power on history (Mahan), 57-58
influenza, 206-7
Integrated Threat Assessment Centre (Canada), 171, 176, 190
International Commission on Intervention and State Sovereignty (ICISS), 111, 227
International Criminal Court, 220, 233
international relations theory: adaptation to neoconservatism, 21-22; Bush doctrine as response to 9/11, 76-79; critical theory, 214; differing understandings of field of study, 289-90; feminist IR approaches, 168-70; integral part of military-intellectual complex, 61; neoconservative movement and, 21-22; political consequences, 82-83; state-centric field of study, 289. *See also* neoconservatism; realist theory
internationalism: Canadian internationalism, 262; Canadian support for decentralization and local empowerment, 266; "local knowledge internationalism," 261, 274; localism model of peace-building, 265-66, 274; mythologizing Canada's selfless, liberal internationalism, 265
invasive (alien) species, 202-5

investment in Africa. *See* extractive industries (Canadian) in Africa
Islamic Movement of Uzbekistan, 189
Islamophobia, 167-68, 177-80
ISO (International Organization for Standardization), 232

Jaballah, Mahmoud, 162
Jacobs, Lesley, 171
Jervis, Robert, 69-70, 80
Johnson, Chalmers, 49

Kagan, Robert, 73-74
Kay, Barbara, 133-34
Kelle, A., 201
Kimberley Process re conflict diamonds, 220, 221, 222, 230-31, 254
Kinsman, Gary, 24, 149-66, 260, 281-82
Kofi Annan International Peacekeeping Training Centre (Ghana), 268
Konaré, Alpha Oumar, 270, 273
Krauthammer, Charles, 76
Kristol, William, 73-75

Laferrière, Eric, 214
Lannigan, John, 131, 140
Layne, Christopher, 68
Lemieux, A., 241
Leys, C., 158
liberal imperialism, 72
liberal internationalism, 72
Liberal Party of Canada, 23, 108-14, 119, 281
Liberation Tigers of Tamil Eelam, 189-90
Ling, L.H.M., 170
Litfin, K., 211
Litwak, R.S., 76, 78
Liu Institute for Global Issues, 228
local order: local security of secondary importance after 9/11, 8; location in sovereign state, 5; relationships with global order, 3-4, 276-78. *See also* state-centrism
location of global order, 2-3, 5, 284-86

location of knowledge, 287-88
location of politics, 3-4, 6-7
Lodge, Henry Cabot, 41
London bombing (2005), 192, 195-96

MacArthur, Julie, 111
MacKay, Peter, 121
Macleod, Alex, 21-22, 67-83, 278-79, 288
MacMillan, Margaret, 71
MacNeil, Brian, 138
mad cow disease (BSE), 206
Madison, James, 39-40
Madrid bombing (2004), 189, 195-96
Mahan, Alfred Thayer, 57-58
Mahjoub, Mohammad, 162
Mali: Sadiola Gold Mine (Mali) controversy, 250-51; UN agency operations in, 266-67. *See also* peace-building in Mali
manifest destiny (US), 41
Manji, Irshad, 175
Manley, John, 117
Manley commission, 96, 103, 117, 120
marginalization of societal elements, 24
Marsella, Anthony, 185
Martin, Paul: anti-hegemonic stance and decision not to join US Ballistic Missile Defense scheme, 110, 112, 123, 124; on deployment of troops to Afghanistan, 123; encouragement of anti-Americanism, 114; population encouraged to rethink Canada's role in world and with US (1993-2006), 23, 107; self-congratulatory view of Canada as global citizen, not motivated by national interest, 109; support for Africa, 240; support for human security, 111; support for humanitarian intervention, 111-12; support for military, 113
McDonell, Mike, 177
McGarrell, E., 188, 196
McGarry, Liam, 139
McGrew, Anthony, 224

McNally, David, 151
McVeigh, Timothy, 192
Mearsheimer, John, 68, 79, 80
media: controversy over hijab, 174; coverage of Goddard as gender-neutral soldier, 23, 127, 129-36, 144, 281; coverage of Goddard as peace-keeping and compassionate soldier, 23, 127, 139-43, 144, 281; gendered representations of war and peace-keeping myths re Canada, 127-28, 136-37; Goddard's gender denied as relevant but focused on, 134-36, 281; Muslim women portrayed as victims of oppression, 25; portrayal of Goddard and Canadian foreign policy goals, 128, 144; racialized/gendered representation of Muslims, 170; representation of Canadian women in combat, 23-24, 286
Messner, D., 233
militarism (American): American way of war, 34, 45-46, 64; Americanism and, 38-39, 42-45, 64; Americans' reaction to Pearl Harbor and 9/11, 47-48; anti-militarism of many Americans, 40; "blowback" (local armed resistance to US dominance), 63; civil-military relations, evolution of, 56-57, 59; definition, 39; distancing of war and belief in inviolability of American space, 47-48; "elastic" geography (expansion of US), 46-51; expanded network of military bases, 49-51, 52(t)-56(t), 65n10; force design, evolution of, 56-59; foundation myths, 40-41; impact on US view of its role in global politics, 278, 288; industries' interest in continued military spending, 58-59; integral part of US hegemony, 38, 62; militarized notion of security, 21; military-industrial complex, 58-62; national identity and, 40-46, 62; origins in American culture, 21; "regeneration through violence" view of the past, 45; reliance on military to impose "rules" globally, 62-63; role of warfare in US history, 39-40; strategic culture, evolution of, 56-57, 64; threat discourse, evolution of, 56-57; tropes in the American war story, 43-45; warfare main instrument of expansion of US, 46-47, 62
military practices of Canada: defence integration with US, 17-20, 113; military and security arrangements with US, 16, 113; policies on Iraq and Ballistic Missile Defense, 110, 112, 113, 123. *See also* Afghanistan, Canadian mission in; peace-keeping (Canadian)
military practices of United States: changes in recruitment and deployment practices, 63-64; military and security arrangements with Canada, 16, 113. *See also* militarism (American)
Mills, C. Wright, 151
Mining in developing countries – Corporate social responsibility (Standing Committee on Foreign Affairs and International Trade), 251-52
Mitchell, Timothy, 7
Montreal campaign against gays, 157
Montreal Gazette, 176
Moreau, Katherine, 160
Morgenthau, Hans, 81
multiculturalism in Canada, 15. *See also* myths about Canada
multilateralism: Afghanistan the preoccupation of Harper regime, not multilateral policy initiatives, 221-22, 223; Canada's preference for, 265-66; Coalition for the ICC, 233; coalitions to ameliorate contemporary global issues, 221, 226-29, 233; collective security, 228; "complex"

vs "old" multilateralism, 225; conflict/security and development, 226-33, 273-74; core principle of Canadian foreign policy, 110, 220; Diamond Development Initiative (DDI), 230-31; erosion of Canada's multilateralism tradition with closer relationship with US, 26-27, 220, 283; evolution of American power from bilateral to unilateral, 223; Extractive Industries Transparency Initiative (EITI), 230, 231-33, 253, 258n4; and global governance, 224-25; global issues, why some receive attention and others not, 222-23, 229-30; ICBL (International Campaign to Ban Landmines), 230, 231; International Commission on Intervention and State Sovereignty (ICISS), 111, 227; International Criminal Court, 220, 233; Kimberley Process re conflict diamonds, 220, 221, 222, 230-31, 254; Ottawa Process re landmines, 220, 221, 222, 229-30, 231-32; Partnership Africa Canada (PAC), 230-31; Publish What You Pay coalition, 230, 231; "responsibility to protect" (R2P) or humanitarian intervention, 227-28; SIDS (small island developing states), 220, 230. *See also* Afghanistan, Canadian mission in; Africa and Canadian foreign policy; Mali

Muravchik, Joshua, 74-75

Muslim communities: construction of Muslim men as terrorists, 25, 168, 170, 176-77, 181; cultural accommodation controversies, 178-79; increased insecurity as result of security policies, 24-25, 167-68, 180-81, 282; Islamophobia, 167-68, 177-80; national security certificate program, 161-63, 171-72; Othering of Arab- and Islamic-identified people after 9/11, 160-63, 167-68, 169, 171-72, 181; Project Thread, 25, 168, 172; rendition, 161, 172; risk profiling and radicalization of young Muslim men, 176-77, 181; source of suspicion post-9/11, 14, 287. *See also* Arar, Maher; Muslim women

Muslim women: construction as oppressed, 25, 168, 173-76, 181; construction as threats to security, 176; harassment and discrimination, 167-68; hijab controversy in media, 174; veil controversy regarding elections, 179; vulnerable position in Canada, 179-80, 282

myths about Canada: as benevolent internationalist power, 15, 17, 144, 281; as good international citizen, 15, 17, 281; obscuring inequalities and divisions within Canada, 290; as peacekeeper, 15, 19, 89-92, 105, 127-28, 136-37, 281

myths about United States: American exceptionalism, 40-41, 71-72, 83; American universalism, 41-43; America's manifest destiny, 41; foundations for Othering those who are different, 41-43

Naím, Moisés, 219

National Defence Act (Canada), 170

national interest: argument for Canadian involvement in Afghanistan, 88, 121, 123-24, 286-87; defined as social, political, and economic stability, 152; human security policies and, 91; militarism and, 39; neoconservatist view of moral purpose in harmony with national interest, 74; neoconservatist view of need for extraterritorial action, 74; realist conception of, 76, 80-81; rejected as driver of Canada's foreign policy, 108, 112; terrorism as threat to Canada's national interest, 95

National Organization of Immigrant and Visible Minority Women of Canada (NOIVMWC), 180
National Post, 126, 128, 133-34, 140, 144, 175, 177
national security: based on territorialized sovereignty and national identity, 14-15; definitions, 186-88; as hegemonic ideological practice, 149-50; inclusion/exclusion of particular groups, 150-51, 155-56; Othering of those defined as national security risks, 150. *See also* biosecurity
national security (Canada): Afghanistan mission in name of security, 88; anti-terrorism legislation and institutional changes, 161, 167, 170-71; based on territorialized sovereignty and national identity, 14-15; campaigns against queers as national security problems (1950s to 1970s), 149-51, 155-57, 158, 165n5, 282; campaigns against "subversives," 158-60; continuities between earlier and current national security campaigns, 153; defence integration with US, 17-20, 113; definitions, 186-88; differences defined as problems of national security, 152, 282; inclusion/exclusion of particular groups and "social organization of forgetting," 150-51, 155-56; Liberals' attitude toward Canadian Armed Forces (1993-2003), 112-13; link with US, 13-14, 17-19, 279; member of Egmont Group, 190-91; nation-state portrayed as unitary entity, 151-52; National Security Policy, 186-88; Othering of Arab- and Islamic-identified people after 9/11, 160-63, 167-68, 169, 171-72, 181; part of global and American projects, 4; policies at odds with US conceptualization of Canada's role in world politics, 23, 112; rendition, 161; resistance by Canadians to "war against subversives," 164-65; security certificate program, 161-63, 171-72; state as legitimate location of policy making, 7-8; war on terror and state of exception to rule of law, 163-64. *See also* military practices of Canada; Muslim communities; policing; terrorism
national security (US): anti-terrorism legislation, 167; Bush doctrine, 77-79; defence integration with Canada, 16, 17-20, 113; intelligence services post-WWII, 61; interrelatedness of events outside country, 60; militarized notion of security, 21; military and security arrangements with Canada, 16, 113; military-industrial complex, 58-62; national security coalition post-9/11 through manipulation, 63; post-WWII, 60-62; security imaginary of US, 37, 61; US evolution into surveillance state, 61-62. *See also* militarism (American); military practices of United States; neoconservatism
National Security Act (US, 1947), 61
National Security Agency, 61
national security certificate program, 161-63, 171-72
National security strategy of the United States of America (NSS), 77-79
NATO and integration with Canadian national defence, 17-18
Natural Resources Canada, 245
neoconservatism: basic tenets, 74-75; Bush doctrine, 67, 76-79; Bush doctrine, realist responses to, 79-81; consequences in post-9/11 world, 82-83, 279; description, 70-71, 72; "ethics of conviction," 81; revival in early 1990s, 73-75; roots of, 71-75; vs realism, 72, 75-76, 82-83; vs traditional conservatism, 72-73

New Democratic Party, 119
Newman, G.R., 192-93
Niang, Abdourahmane, 273
Nichols, Terry, 192
Nile perch, 202
9/11: impact on perception of world order, 1-2; modification to American basing strategy post-9/11, 50-51
Nixon, Richard, 82-83
NORAD, integration of Canadian national defence with US, 17
North American Plan for Avian and Pandemic Influenza, 206-7
Nossal, Kim Richard, 23, 107-25, 223, 281
Nureddin, Muayyed, 161

O'Brien, Robert, 225
O'Connor, Dennis, 172, 177-78
O'Connor, Gordon, 121-22
OECD guidelines for Multinational Enterprises, 249
OECD guidelines on corporate social responsibility, 248-49
Official Secrets Act (Canada), 170
Olsson, Christian, 105
O'Malley, P., 189
O'Meara, Dan, 21, 33-66, 278, 288
Ontario Coalition against Poverty, 159
Organization of American States, 159
Othering: of Afghan women and children and of Taliban, 98; of Americans challenging American worldview, 61; of Arab- and Islamic-identified people after 9/11, 160-63, 167-68, 169, 171-72, 181; inhumanity of in the American war story, 44-45; of Native Americans during expansion of US, 46-47; relational process, 154; of societal elements deemed "different," 24, 41-43; of Thobani who challenged portrayal of Muslim women as oppressed, 174-75; of those defined as national security risks, 150; of those who oppose American values, 41-43; using American foundation myths, 41-43
Ottawa Process re landmines, 220, 221, 222, 229-30, 231-32

Paine, Thomas, 136-37
Panel of Experts on the Illegal Exploitation of Natural Resources and Other Forms of Wealth (UN), 248-49
Parent, Geneviève, 87-106, 260, 281, 286
Partnership Africa Canada (PAC), 230-31
Patriot Act (United States), 167
peace: association with international stability, 95-96; as synonymous with national defence and security, 16-17, 89
Peace of Timbuktu (UN), 260
peace-building: Canadian expertise and actors with non-state actors, 263; complexity of interventions, 262-63; extending values of donor-interveners, 261-62; link with reconstruction of identities, 260-62; mythologizing Canada's selfless, liberal internationalism, 265; in neoliberal world order, 262; valorizing local knowledge, 261-62; vs peace enforcing, 266. *See also* peace-building in Mali
peace-building in Mali: administrative decentralization and local involvement, 270-73; background of conflict in north, 260-61, 269-71; capacity-building and security sector reform, 266-67; emphasis on local culture in education, 268; local and national hegemonic struggles, 263-65, 268-69; localism model of peace-building, 265-66, 283-84; partnerships among "insiders," "insiders partial," and "outsiders," 272-73; peace education and, 267-68; reasons for success, 272-73; reconciling Canadian/

universal and Malian values, 27-28, 263-66; role of Canada, 27-28, 265-66, 266-69, 273, 275n1; training, 267-68
peace-keeping (Canadian): Canadians' view of Canada as peacekeeper, 15, 16-17, 19, 144; gendered representations of Goddard and reinforcement of peace-keeping myths re Canada, 127-28, 136-37; media coverage of Goddard as peace-keeping and compassionate soldier, 23, 127, 139-43, 144, 281; myths about, 15, 19, 89-92, 105, 127-28, 136-37, 281; peacekeeper that wages war, 88; portrayal of Canadian soldiers and the Somalia Affair, 92-93; portrayal of Canadian soldiers in Afghanistan, 100; targeting ineffective states, 91; views of Canada in Afghanistan, 89-91. *See also* military practices of Canada
Peacekeeping and Security Capacity-Building Project for Francophone Africa, 268
Pearson Peacekeeping Centre, 262
People's Commission on Immigration Security Measures, 162
Pettman, Jan Jindy, 169, 173
Picarelli, J.T., 186
Podhoretz, Norman, 73
policing: domestic policing function, 184, 280-81; intelligence-led policing, 192-93, 197, 198n11; intelligence-led policing, limitations, 193-95, 199n13; international focus needed to combat terrorism, 195-97, 282; poor coordination of policing levels, 25; role in combating terrorism, 183-84, 197
Posse Comitatus Act of 1878 (United States), 206
Post, Jerrold, 184-85
precursor criminal activity, 188-89, 193, 195

Price, Richard, 183-84
Price-Smith, A., 209
Pring, G., 244
Proceeds of Crime (Money Laundering) and Terrorist Financing Act (Canada), 170
Project Thread, 25, 168, 172
Public Safety Act (Canada), 170
Public Safety Canada, 171
Publish What You Pay coalition, 230, 231
purple loosestrife, 204

Quebec and "reasonable accommodation," 178-79
Quebec City, Summit of the Americas riot (2001), 159-60
queer theory, 152-53, 165n8
queers: campaigns against, in name of national security, 149-51, 155-57, 158, 165n5, 282; queering national security, 153; queering of historical materialism, 154; RCMP surveillance of homosexuals in 1950s and 1960s, 149, 156-57; resistance against security police, 156-57, 164

Rae, Bob, 119
Razack, Sherene, 137, 154
RCMP (Royal Canadian Mounted Police): control of activists at APEC meeting, 158-59; investigation of Sunera Thobani, 174-75; risk profiling and radicalization of young Muslim men, 177; role in Maher Arar rendition, 172; surveillance of homosexuals in 1950s and 1960s, 149, 156-57
realist theory: adaptation at end of Cold War, 68-69; classical vs neoclassical realism, 69; constructivist challenge and, 68-69; description, 61; dominant school of foreign policy during Cold War, 68, 82-83; "ethics of responsibility," 81; neoconservative

challenge and, 21-22; in post-9/11 era, 69-70, 82; responses to Bush doctrine, 79-81; vs neoconservatism, 72, 75-76, 82-83
Reiffenstein, Mary, 131, 139
Reno, Will, 226
"responsibility to protect" (R2P), 227-28
Ressam, Ahmed, 190, 193
Rice, Condoleezza, 78-79
Richmond, Oliver, 89, 91-92
Rideau Institute on International Affairs, 120, 122
Roach, Kent, 171, 177
Roosevelt, Theodore, 42, 48
Rose, Tore, 273
Roussel, S., 119
Ruggie, John, 236, 254, 278

Sadiola Gold Mine (Mali) controversy, 250-51
Said, Edward, 154, 289
Saul, B., 188
Savage, Malcolm, 27, 235-59, 283
Schmidt, Brian, 83
Schmitt, Carl, 163
sea lamprey, 200, 202, 203
Sears, Jonathan, 27-28, 260-75, 283-84
Securing an open society: Canada's national security policy (Privy Council Office), 187
securitization, 201-2, 206, 211-12
security: collective security, 228; conflict/security and development, 226-29; continental defence, 17-19; externalization and demonization of challenges to status quo, 12-13; geographies of security, 7-8, 47; globalization after 9/11, 8; state as legitimate location of policy making, 7-8; relationship with development. *See also* military practices of Canada; military practices of United States; national security
security (United States). *See* national security (US)
security certificate program, 161-63, 171-72
security imaginary: Afghan mission's ideal characteristics for Canada's global engagement, 115-16; anti-hegemonic attitude of Canada toward US, 109, 114; Canadian security imaginary at odds with US conceptualization of Canada's role in world politics, 23, 112; Canadians' rethinking of Canada's role in world and with US (1993-2006), 23, 107-8, 124, 281; Canadians' view that armed forces to be used for peaceful ends, 114-15; definition, 64n4; human security the proper focus of security in Canada, 110-11; multilateralism as core principle of Canada, 110; self-congratulatory view of Canada as global citizen, not motivated by national interest, 108-9; socialization of allies and rivals, 37, 107; support for humanitarian intervention in Canada, 111-12; of United States, 37, 61
Sen, Amartya, 229
Senlis Council, 103, 120
September 11, 2001. *See* 9/11 (alphabetized as "nine")
Sharma, Nandita, 154
Shaw, Timothy M., 26-27, 219-34, 283
Shelley, L.I., 186
SIDS (small island developing states), 220, 230
Siegle, L., 244
Sjolander, Claire Turenne, 23-24, 126-45, 281, 286
Smith, Andrea, 154
Smith, Dorothy E., 153
Smith, Gordon, 117
Smith, Tony, 72
Snyder, Jack, 69
"social organization of forgetting," 151
society, 7, 20
Somalia Affair, 92-93, 113

sovereignty, state, 6-7
Spanish flu, 206
St. John's Campaign against the War, 120
Stairs, Denis, 113-14, 127
Standing Committee on Foreign Affairs and International Trade (SCFAIT) (Canada), 251-52
Standing Senate Committee on National Security and Defence (Canada), 117, 119
Staples, Steve, 122
state: as legitimate location of security policy making, 7-8; separate from society, 7
state sovereignty, 6-7
state-centrism: in international relations field, 289; maintenance of status quo, 280; traditional understanding of, 6-7, 284-85; Westphalian model, 6
Stoett, Peter, 25-26, 200-15, 282-83
Summit of the Americas, riot, 159-60
Supreme Court of Canada and security certificate program, 162, 172
Sutton Resources, 250
Swanstrom, N., 188
Symington, W. Stuart, 59

Taliban: invasion of Afghanistan to remove al-Qaeda, 115, 121; Othering of, 98; treatment of women as justification for invasion, 173. *See also* Afghanistan, Canadian mission in
Taliban's War against Women (US State Department), 173
Talisman Energy controversy, 247-48
Tamil community (Toronto), 189-90
Task Force on the Needs of Muslim Students, 179-80
Team Canada Inc, 245
terrorism: Bush doctrine, 77-79; construction of Muslim men as terrorists, 25, 168, 170, 176-77, 181; convergence of terrorist and criminal activities, 183, 185-86, 188-92, 197, 198n10; decentralization of terrorist cells, 192; decline in state support for terrorist organizations, 191; definitions, 184-85; domestic terrorism, 185; Egmont Group tracking money laundering, 190-91; and globalization of security post-9/11, 8; impact of internet, 191, 196, 197; intelligence-led policing against, 192-95, 198n11; international terrorism, 183, 185; London bombing (2005), 192, 195-96; Madrid bombing (2004), 189, 195-96; main threat to US and international system, 77; motivation vs motivation for criminality, 185-86; "narco-terrorism," 189; need for international policing focus to combat, 195-97; possible terrorist targets, 212; possible threats to biosecurity, 212; precursor criminal activity, 188-89, 193, 195; threat to Canada's national interest, 95; transnational terrorism, 185. *See also* war on terror
Thachuk, K.L., 188
Thérien, Jean-Philippe, 225
Third World Network – Africa Secretariat, 249-50, 251
Thobani, Sunera, 154, 174-75
Thomas, C., 213
Thompson, E.P., 153
Touré, Amadou Toumani, 270, 275n2
Trachtenberg, M., 78
Trevenen, Kathryn, 23-24, 126-45, 281, 286
Trouble with Islam Today (Manji), 175
Truman, Harry, 50, 59, 60
Turner, Frederick Jackson, 48

Ullman, Richard, 187
UN Environmental Programme, 209
UN Regional Centre for Disarmament in Africa, 272-73
UNCTAD (United Nations Conference on Trade and Development), 237

United Nations: authorization for invasion of Afghanistan, 115; Canada as peacekeeper in UN-sponsored missions, 108-9; global governance and, 225; *A peace of Timbuktu,* 260; support for UN a core Canadian principle, 110; UN agency operations in Mali, 266-67

United States: Americanism (*see* Americanism); central to global order, 4; challenges to American power, 13-14; character of American power, 13-14; declinism regarding US, 33-34; economic relationship with Canada, 15-16. *See also* Bush, George W.; hegemony (American); militarism (American); military practices of United States; national security (US); war on terror

University of British Columbia, 174-75

Upton, Emery, 57, 59

US Air Force, 59-60

US Army, 58, 63-64

US Army Air Forces, 58

US Department of Agriculture (USDA), 208

US Navy, 57-58

US State Department, 173

van Driesche, J., 203

van Driesche, R., 203

van Ham, Peter, 240

Vandenberg, Arthur, 60

Verner, Josée, 121

Voice of Women, 28n2

Voices of Muslim women (Canadian Council of Muslim Women), 179

Waever, O., 186

Walker, Muriel, 180

Walker, R.B.J., 4-6, 289-90

Walt, S.M., 79, 81

Waltz, Kenneth, 68, 79

war on terror: acts of contestation, effects of, 12; anti-terrorism legislation and institutional changes, 161, 167, 170-71; criticism of war not allowed, 168; globalization of security after 9/11, 8; state of exception to rule of law, 163-64. *See also* terrorism

Weber, Martin, 211-12, 213

Weber, Max, 81

Weigley, Russell, 34

Weiss, Tom, 224

Welsh, Jennifer, 109

Wendt, Alexander, 186-87

Westphalian model of state sovereignty, 6

Whitworth, Sandra, 92-93, 144

Williams, M.C., 75

Williams, Michael, 83

Wilson, Woodrow, 41

Wilsonianism, 72

Winnipeg Free Press, 131, 135, 142-44

women. *See* Afghan women; gender; Muslim women

zebra mussels, 203-4, 205